Edinburgh

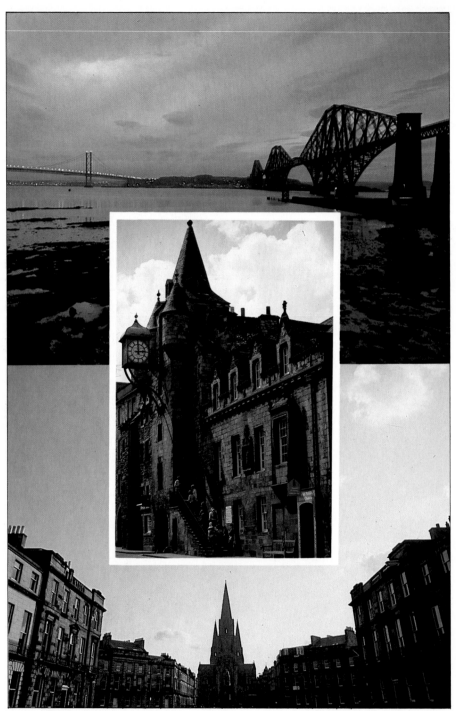

Top The Forth rail and road bridges, **centre** Canongate Tolbooth, **below** St Mary's Cathedral.

Edinburgh

The complete guide to Scotland's capital city

HARPERS
Handbook

First published 1981 by Noel Collins Ltd. 2 Dundonald Street, Edinburgh
ISBN 0 907686 00 1 (case) 0 907686 01 X (limp)

Publisher Noel Collins
Marketing Director Bob Saunders
Project Editor Catherine Carpenter
Art Editor Graham Davis
Project Designer Steven Duwensee
Art Director Bob Morley
Editorial Director Jeremy Harwood
Designed and Production
Quarto Publishing
32 Kingly Court
London W1

Editorial and Marketing
Harpers Handbooks
2 Dundonald Street
Edinburgh

Harpers Handbooks
Marketing/Advertising/Sales
Bob Saunders
Editorial Noel Collins
Administration Aileen Robertson
Carina Haddow

Acknowledgements

Authors
Myrtle Ashmole
Francis Bamford
Geoffrey Baskerville
Alice Beberman
Robin Bell
Joana Blythman
Patricia Brindle
Andrew Brown
Ann Charlish
Jane Collins
Patrick Conyngham
Ank Crees
George Dalgleish
Andrew Dalmayer
Danuta Doroszenko
Allan Edwards
Richard Emerson
Dr. R. A. Fawcett
Gilly Gaskell
John Gifford
Gilly Glass
Veronica Gordon-Smith
Rory Knight-Bruce
Gordon Knott
Carolyn McAdam

Brian McAbe
Sheena McDonald
Janet McEwan
Ann McKim
Bill McLean
Julia Merrick
Glen Murray
Norman Orr
Alice Rugheimer
Ann Simpson
Anne Simpson
Betty Smith
Gill Summers
Kim Tweedie
Hilary Whyte
Andrew Williams
Conrad Wilson
Editors
Liv O'Hanlon
Hope Cohen
Ronald Thompson
Marilyn Bowering
Cartography
Cartografics (Edin) Ltd.
Illustrators
Richard Blakely

Marilyn Bruce
Terry Burton
Bob Chapman
Chris Forsey
Sheila Hadley
Elaine Keenan
Edwina Keene
Sally Launder
Brian Sayers
Rosalind Taylor
Lorna Turpin
David Weeks
Photographers
Trevor Wood
John Wyand
Picture Research
Judy Garlick
Liz Ogilvy
Design Assistants
Andrew Fenton
Simon Borrough
Paul O'Connor
The Directory was edited
by The Paul Press,
Nigel Perryman, Jean Train,
Richard Williams

The publishers would like to express sincere thanks to the following for their help with the compilation of this book:

British Tourist Authority, Dawson International, Edinburgh City Libraries (the Edinburgh Room), Herbert Coutts, Edinburgh City Museums, Edinburgh District Council, Edinburgh Zoological Park, Faculty of Advocates, The Glenlivet Distillers Ltd., The Marquis and Marchioness of Linlithgow, Lothian Regional Council, Department of Recreation and Leisure, Mrs Patricia and Miss Jean Maxwell-Scott, Mr and Mrs Peter Maxwell-Stuart, The National Museum of Antiquities, Trustees of the National Gallery of Scotland, National Library of Scotland, National Trust of Scotland, The Earl and Countess of Rosebery, Douglas Henderson, Regius Keeper the Royal Botanic Garden, Royal College of Surgeons, Royal Scottish Museum, Scottish Development Department for Ancient Monuments, Scottish Tourist Board.

Contents

Edinburgh has been fortunate in many ways. It has a rich and varied history as Scotland's capital and many of the landmarks of that history have been preserved in its buildings, streets and museums. While it never achieved the industrial and commercial wealth that came to Glasgow in the 18th and 19th Centuries, neither did it have to suffer the full impact of the rapid development and population growth that has caused so many problems for Glasgow ever since.

Edinburgh's cultural heritage is consequently more visible and more accessible and after 30 years of enlightened improvement, restoration and conservation there is a very wide choice for the interested visitor, and probably a lot to be learned by the interested inhabitant. This book should serve both their needs and in years to come it will provide an invaluable record of Edinburgh in the 1980's.

1981

Introduction

*S*cotland's capital is one of the most
rewarding cities in the world. This guide book is purpose-
planned to enable every reader
to get the most out of everything Edinburgh has to offer.
Not only is Edinburgh
one of the most historic cities of Europe;
it is also one of the most attractive, with architectural
glories, such as the New Town
and Hollyroodhouse, vying with treasures of the national
heritage, such as the vast art collections
of the Scottish National Gallery and the other great
museums of the city.
Edinburgh, however, is much more than even this.
Its Festival is world-famous. In addition, there is no city sprawl.
Within a few minutes' walk of the city centre
can be found the small village communities, oases
of quiet calm that have
existed in Edinburgh for many centuries.
Harper's *Edinburgh* is *the* ultimate handbook to all this and to
much more. Not only does it include
an authoritative guide to all the city's major places
of interest, lavishly illustrated with hundreds
of specially commissioned colour photographs and drawings;
it also covers such important areas as
shopping, history, literature, folklore, statues and
monuments and stately homes.
And the book has an added bonus. The Directory of Essential
Information makes it literally two books for the price of one.
This lists and, where appropriate, selects
and reviews the city's major consumer services from
hotels, pubs and restaurants to car hire, sports
facilities and travel information. All of this is keyed to an
18-page street-finder section.
Harper's *Edinburgh* is an essential reference whether you are
a visitor to Edinburgh or live in the city.

The Story of Edinburgh

A town born in trouble and beset by rebellion that has blossomed in
maturity to become one of the most distinguished cities in the world

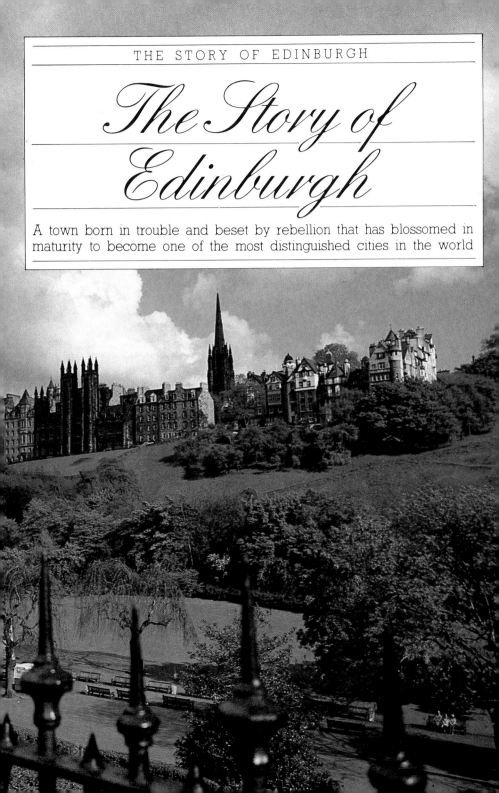

*E*dinburgh, like Rome, is built on seven hills. But, in the words of Robert Louis Stevenson, 'Edinburgh pays cruelly for her high seat in one of the vilest climates under heaven. She is liable to be beaten upon by all the winds that blow, to be drenched with rain, to be buried in cold sea fogs out of the east, and powdered with the snow as it comes flying southward from the Highland hills. The weather is raw and boisterous in winter, shifty and ungenial in summer, and a downright meteorological purgatory in the spring.'

In this turbulent climate the city's history, too, has been tumultuous. It has been the site of endless warring and argument, fighting and rebellion. But now, after centuries of history – and prehistory – the city stands as one of the most ordered and classically beautiful in Europe.

The fighting began thousands of years ago. The first people to arrive were the stone-using hunters, about 5000 years ago. They were followed by primitive farmers 2000 years later and immigrant Beaker people who brought pottery and metal-working skills from the continent.

The Celts started arriving, too, driven north by successive invasions of England by tribes from lowland Europe, and they caused more warring and battling with the natives. The long brawl of Scottish history had begun.

The Romans came north in AD 78 and defeated Calgacus 'the Swordsman', who, according to Tacitus, said, 'They made a desert, and they called it peace.' When the Romans left, in the second century, the people were faced with ceaseless invasions. There came Angles, Britons, Vikings and eventually the Scots from Western Ireland – after whom the country takes its name.

The Scots finally took possession of the Castle Rock in Edinburgh when the Northumbrians abandoned their northern border town. In 1018 Malcolm II managed to push the boundary further south and Edinburgh ceased to be a frontier stronghold.

Ironically the Southerners – or a few of them anyway – were welcomed back 50 years later after the Norman invasion of England in 1066. Among the refugees who went to the court of Malcolm III (Canmore) was Margaret, sister of Edgar Atheling, King-elect of England after Harold's death at Hastings.

Margaret and Malcolm married and produced six sons, four of whom in time were kings.

In the meantime Margaret spread her sophisticated Saxon culture and her profound religious thinking among her new people. She lived periodically at Castle Rock and died there. On the rock was built the small Norman chapel in her memory that is Edinburgh's oldest chapel and the oldest ecclesiastical building in use in Scotland.

David I founded the Abbey of Holyrood in 1128. Legend has it that after a miracle prevented his being killed by a stag, the wounded David heard voices telling him to found a house of canons devoted to the Cross. So the abbey was built – by 20 skilled men summoned from France.

In the foundation charter for the abbey, King David refers to 'my town' which suggests that Edwinesburgh was at least from that time regarded as a royal burgh. But, at least 600 years before, the town had been known as Dun Edin, hillfort of Edin.

Along with the abbey the Augustinian canons were given the right to build a burgh (later the Canongate) between the abbey and the royal burgh. Thus the future city began to grow. The burghers or 'burgesses' of this new village were given privileges to sell their wares and buy freely in the Edinburgh market.

David began establishing Anglo-Norman families in Scotland and over the next century they married into the Scottish nobility. Some, like Robert the Bruce (the elder), acquired, along with the earldoms, claims to the throne in these unions of families. The upshot was that by 1286 Scotland was under the rule of a succession of regents as there was total confusion about who was the rightful heir to the Scottish throne.

Edward I was asked to arbitrate for the regents who could come to no decision. It was a chance that the land-hungry Edward had been waiting for. He chose a puppet monarch, John Balliol, whose claim to the throne was through his mother Devorguilla, the foundress of Balliol College, Oxford, in 1250.

Balliol was summoned to Edward's court where he was told to supply money and men for the King's French war but the Scots would have none of it. Four Scottish bishops, four earls and four barons formed a council and in October 1295 concluded the first formal treaty with the French. The alliance was a constant feature of Scottish history over the next 500 years – so much so that it became known as the 'Auld Alliance'.

Edward was furious and in 1296 sent north an invading army who put the leaderless Scots to the sword, deposed Balliol and looted the Castle. The Stone of Destiny on which Scottish monarchs were traditionally crowned was removed to London from Scone. It forms part of the coronation chair in Westminster Abbey, on which monarchs are crowned today. For his ferocity, Edward earned the title 'the Hammer of the Scots'.

The fighting of these continuing wars of independence with the English came to a pause in 1314 when Robert the Bruce succeeded in defeating the English at Bannockburn. But the English returned to Scotland in 1322, under Edward II, and sacked Holyrood Abbey. Bruce prevailed and in 1329 gave his principal city its first recorded charter.

The charter gave the burgh and the Port of Leith (for 52 marks, about £34, a year) to the burgesses and recognition to the huddle of rough buildings sheltering by the castle.

After the death of Bruce, Edinburgh was once again in trouble. Edward III plundered the town and King Edward Balliol (who had no real claim to the throne) was forced to surrender his crown and in 1334 gave land in the southern counties to the English Crown.

The Scots were in despair and sent their boy king, David II, to France where he stayed until 1341. He was able to return only when Edward's attention was centred on the French throne and the Hundred Years' War between England and France.

Scotland, impoverished by war and disorder, needed peace and good government. David II gave neither. In fact he brought more war with the English and ended up lodged in the Tower of London. He was liberated by the promise to pay a 100,000 marks ransom to the English.

He returned to Scotland in 1357 and found the country wasted by constant war and the Black Death. There followed an uneasy truce with England and experiments in taxation which gave the burghs of Scotland more power. Edinburgh's port at Leith developed and the burgesses shook off the direct control of the financial officers of the Crown. The town, at last, began to prosper.

$\mathscr{R}$ecords show that in 1376 the population of Edinburgh was about 2000 with 400 houses. The inhabitants must have been a hardy bunch, well used to adversity Richard II wrought more havoc in the city in 1385, and Henry IV laid siege in 1400.

In 1424, James I landed at Leith with his Queen and succeeded to the Scottish throne after 19 years as captive of the English.

The couple received a welcome and as they rode through the town James must have noted the tremendous changes. The houses of the Royal Mile were rising higher. Timber was giving way to stone and thatch was being replaced by sturdier roofing. But thatch had had its advantages. During the endless firings of the town by the English, the Edinburgh townsfolk would load all their goods and chattels on wagons and 'take to the heather' – and they took their highly inflammable roofing with them.

James I made Scotland a place fit to live in again. His legislation was aimed at keeping 'firm and sure peace' throughout the country and building a firm foundation for the economy. He also instituted a system for 'a poor man's advocate

whose services went to 'any poor creature who could not pay for his own defence'.

But James was not without enemies and in 1437 two of his lords, eager to put the Earl of Atholl on the throne, had him stabbed to death at Perth, where he was spending Christmas.

James II became King of the Scots at the age of six. He had been smuggled from the Castle in 1438 in his mother's trunk and it was he who, some years later, gave a charter for a city wall starting below the northeastern rock of the Castle. The King also ordered that his pleasure garden should be swept away to create the Nor' Loch directly below the Castle as a defence.

But he too was killed – by one of his own cannon bursting at a siege of Roxburgh Castle near Kelso in 1460. He was followed by James III who fell foul of his power-grasping lords and was murdered in 1488.

James III had, though, in 1482, rewarded the loyalty of the Edinburgh burgesses by granting the provost and bailies (magistrates) important privileges including the almost complete control over the dispensing of justice – an independence they maintained until the Union of Parliaments in 1707.

At the beginning of the fifteenth century the King, his court, Parliament and courts of justice were itinerant. But by 1483 Edinburgh was the undisputed capital of Scotland: it was the permanent seat of government, and had the principal Royal residence – Holyrood – the central administration and the law courts.

Peace, prosperity and a new enlightenment reigned with James IV. 'There is as great a difference between the Scotland of the old time and the Scotland of today as there is between good and bad,' wrote a Spanish diplomat in 1498.

The King had an intelligent and questing mind. He was a patron of the arts and a great promoter of learning: he granted in 1506 a royal charter to the college of surgeons in Edinburgh and founded, among other institutions, the nation's third university at Aberdeen. He also granted a charter to two burgesses of Edinburgh, Andrew Myllar and Walter Chapman, to set up the first Scottish printing press for the purpose of producing books of laws, Acts of Parliament, chronicles, and Mass books 'after our Scottish use'.

This era of renaissance and chivalry – when jousting tourneys were held at the King's Stables area, west of the Grassmarket – came to an end with the tragedy of Flodden.

James had left his Queen and baby to lead his army against the English at Flodden Field in September 1513. The Scottish army was annihilated on the nation's blackest day and many Edinburgh men, including all the bailies, died with their King. When news reached the town lamentation was mingled with fear of immediate invasion by the English.

A town guard was formed and a new wall speedily thrown up, within which plague soon spread through the streets. Not for the next 250 years did the citizens dare build outside this Flodden Wall in case of invasion. Instead they built upwards, as the population increased, storey upon storey to a height of eight or ten floors – unmatched elsewhere in Europe.

James's body was found on the field at Flodden and taken to London where Henry VIII designed a splendid funeral. It did not take place. The royal corpse lay in its lead at Sheen until the house was ruined after the Reformation. Eventually the embalmed head was hacked off by Queen Elizabeth I's master-glazier who used it as a sort of pot until he tired of it!

James's infant son of 13 months became King James V and yet another bloody power struggle between the leading nobles ensued for control of the kingdom. The fight between English and French interests ended with a coup d'état, led by the Earl of Angus, which put James in nominal control at the age of 14.

The King grew to be greedy and brutal and succeeded in making himself the most disliked of the Stuart kings of Scotland.

It was during his reign that the first voices spoke out against Roman Catholicism.

The Roman Church had reigned supreme from the time of Malcolm II until 1559 when, a little behind the rest of Europe, Scotland was overturned by the Reformation. And as in the Reformations elsewhere it was more than a change in the Church system – it was also a political and economic revolt.

The Church in Scotland during the fifteenth and early sixteenth centuries had enormous political influence. It was far richer than the state – the revenue was 15 times that of the Crown – and the taxes it demanded of each commoner nurtured bitterness among the people.

Bishoprics were allocated by favouritism; bastardy, in a church that supposedly practised celibacy, was common among all ranks of the

---

*T*he speech of Edinburgh reflects the city's history as vividly as does its architecture. The stylized Morningside accent can be traced back precisely to 1761, when a group of citizens eager to ditch their Scottish accents engaged as their elocution teacher Thomas Sheridan, father of the playwright-actor and Irishman.

This would not have happened in Glasgow which never shared Edinburgh's Anglophilia or literary aspirations. The everyday speech of the rival cities, only a 45-minute train ride apart, differs widely. A naked child in Edinburgh is 'a bairn in his bare buff' and in Glasgow 'a wean in his bare scuddie'. Truant children in Edinburgh 'plunk or kip school' and in Glasgow they 'dog the school'.

The Scottish language, still in use, is mainly based on an Anglo-Saxon dialect and supplanted the historic language of Gaelic, still spoken in the highlands and islands. Scots was the national language until the Union of the Parliaments in 1707 and has been revived in literature over the past 60 years.

Naturally many common words were carried over from Gaelic, including *loch, glen, bog, cairn and caber,* as in 'tossing the caber'. But other words as distinctively Scottish as these are corruptions of continental languages introduced by settlers or traders. The famous Edinburgh cry to warn passers-by that rubbish and slops are about to fall on them from tenement windows above is 'gardyloo' from the eighteenth-century French, 'gare de l'eau', look out for water. The Auld Alliance between Scotland and France, lasting from 1295 until the Reformation, and the presence of numerous Norman settlers accounts for many Scots words of French origin – tartan from *tiretaine,* petticoat tails from *petit gateau* and Hogmanay from *aguillaneuf.*

Viking settlers bequeathed Norse words: *flit,* (move), as in 'moonlicht flit'; *lug,* (ear), as in 'lug-hole'; and the various 'k'-ending words, *kirk* for church, and *dike* for ditch.

In its turn the Scots language has given many words to the English-speaking world, including blackmail, canny, uncanny, cosy, eerie, flunkey, fogie, heckle, pony, and spate.

Scottish languages and dialects have survived four centuries of erosion by the English – erosion which can be traced back to the introduction of the English bible in the 1500s. In Edinburgh literary figures faced a particular dilemma: how to preserve their heritage and excel as Britons. The philosopher David Hume and novelist Robert Louis Stevenson solved it by speaking Scots but writing English and Walter Scott combined dialect and Standard English.

Today, when English with very rolled r's and a generous sprinkling of Scotticisms is the norm, visitors to Edinburgh often still find that written communication with the Scots is easier than the verbal variety.

priesthood; and priests failed in their pastoral duties.

The records of the Edinburgh Town Council in 1501 show that the civil bailies had to take legal action against the prebendaries of St. Giles to force them to say masses.

Pockets of reform, however, were emerging and found support among the less corrupt clergy and the nobility and merchant classes who controlled the council. The time was ripe for revolution.

Had the next monarch, Mary, been more far-sighted perhaps some of the ferocity of the coming years would have been avoided.

Mary, Queen of Scots, was proclaimed Queen as a seven-day-old child on the death of her father James V in 1542. Two years later Edinburgh was laid waste by Henry VIII's army, the houses put to fire and the countryside for seven miles around was ravaged – Holyrood Palace, the castles of Craigmillar and Rosslyn, the town of Leith and its pier, all were destroyed – simply because the Scots revoked an earlier agreement that Henry's son should be married to the young Queen. It was the beginning of Henry's 'rough wooing'.

The Queen's mother, Mary of Guise-Lorraine, appealed to her native France for help which came. But in return the Scots had to send their little Queen to Paris where she was bethrothed, and later married, to the Dauphin. The English, knowing they were outmanoeuvred, left Scotland.

With the English gone, the French stayed on to protect Catholic interests, but all that they achieved was the antagonism of the many Scots who already supported the new doctrines of Calvin and the reformed Church.

The new religious movement was also allowed its leader back – a tactical mistake on the part of Mary of Guise who had been made Regent in 1554. He was John Knox who had fled Scotland in 1547. The teachings of George Wishart had formed the basis for Knox's views on religion and politics. Wishart had set out the first principles of the reformed faith in his writings, stating that the only sources of truth were the Holy Scriptures; that the Pope's role was invalid; and that there were only two sacraments – Baptism and Holy Communion. He was burnt at the stake for heresy.

Knox spent most of his exile in Geneva at the church of John Calvin which Knox described as 'the most perfect school of Christ that ever was on earth since the days of the Apostles'.

The news of his return to Edinburgh on May 2, 1559, spread like wild fire through the streets: 'John Knox is come, John Knox is come' was the message and soon, by way of merchants, travellers, fishermen and shepherds, much of the country knew it too.

John Knox

Knox's powers of oratory stirred first of all the crowds in Perth to violent action – they sacked the town's monasteries, pillaged, burned and looted every friary in the city. Mary of Guise sent her troops into action but underestimated the support the new Church had. She was forced to retire.

Knox and his followers moved on to St. Andrews where Knox preached – lambasting the Church of Rome as the 'synagogue of Satan'; the Pope as that 'man of sin of whom the Apostle speaks'; the Virgin Mary as 'that Roman harlot'; and said the Roman Church was 'polluted with all kinds of spiritual fornication'. Once more the incited crowds ransacked all the religious establishments, burning 'idols' and sharing out the spoils of the friaries.

At the end of June they marched to Edinburgh and the Queen Regent retired to Dunbar. On July I, 1559, Knox preached his first sermon from the pulpit of St. Giles. It seemed as if, in the space of two months, the Reformation had been achieved, but it was in fact only the start of a battle that continued for 130 years from the establishment of the reformed Church. Knox never witnessed a secure Kirk.

In 1559 a Protestant league known as the Lords of the Congregation turned to the new Queen in England, Elizabeth I, for help in their armed struggle against Mary of Guise. The French, who had heavily fortified Leith, were besieged. Mary, who had left Holyrood and had a sumptuous mansion at Leith, tried to arrange a truce but died of dropsy in June 1560 before it was achieved. The following month, in the Treaty of Edinburgh, it was agreed that all French troops should leave Scotland.

Shortly afterwards the city's council ordered that the Leith fortifications which faced Edinburgh should be demolished 'in caiss strangearis sall at ony time hereafter intruse thameselfs thairin'.

At a meeting in August , Parliament rejected the supremacy of the Pope, / Continued on page 18

Folklore

Headless phantoms, body snatchers, witches…and a faithful terrier

Edinburgh is a city of ghosts and goblins, horrors and hauntings, with a blood-steeped folklore handed down through the centuries and undoubtedly often embellished in the taverns of the town. There are tales of phantom squadrons of soldiers, a sword-wielding White Lady, a death coach drawn by headless horses, an evil major who rises from the grave, and a 'Street of Sorrow' where the spirits of plague victims roam in anguish.

In a chronicle laden with terror, witchcraft and bloodlust, one of the few folk characters remembered with fondness is Greyfriars Bobby, a Skye terrier who kept a 14-year vigil by his master's grave. He belonged to a shepherd named Jock Gray who died in 1858, and from then until his own death in 1872 Bobby maintained night-and-day watch over the grave in Greyfriars Churchyard. The faithful terrier became a legend in his own lifetime when he was granted virtual freedom of the city in 1867. As recently as 1981 a new memorial was erected to Greyfriars Bobby and a pop song was written about him.

But villainy and nightmarish events predominate in Edinburgh folklore, none less than the story of Major Thomas Weir, Captain of the Town Guard and among the most respected of preachers. In a city-shaking scandal, the major suddenly confessed publicly in 1670 that he had dedicated much of his life to fornication, bestiality and incest with his sister. Outrage succeeded disbelief among his followers, and Weir and his sister were burned at the stake for making a compact with the devil. Long after his death the major was said to ride furiously

Right Body-snatchers Hare and Burke.
Below right William Burke's execution.
Below Deacon Brodie – the original Jekyll and Hyde.

through Leith – the district of his death – on a black horse and then vanish in a burst of flames while lights blazed miraculously in his empty house. Another character with two lives was Deacon Brodie, a city councillor and thriving businessman thought to be the inspiration of Robert Louis Stevenson's famous novel *Dr. Jekyll and Mr. Hyde.* His fortune dissipated by gambling, the Deacon went in for a night-time career of burglary and mayhem which led him to the hangman at the Tolbooth on October 1, 1788, watched by 40,000 people. His moaning apparition is said to linger at the site of the gallows, which he mounted three times before the gibbet worked.

The visitor who might happen to hear midnight drums and the tramping of feet on the Castle Esplanade can take some comfort from the fact that a ghostly squadron of troops has been on the move there since the days of Oliver Cromwell.

The mystery column was first seen in 1650, according to legend, by sentries guarding the Castle against a threatened attack by Cromwell's army. Ancient documents also record that in the same area a 'death coach' pulled by fire-flashing steeds races headlong from Holyrood to the Castle to warn of impending disaster.

The White Lady of Corstophine was Christian Nimmo, the wife of a prosperous merchant, who used to meet her lover under a sycamore tree and finally killed him with a sword for being drunk. She was beheaded in 1679, but the story goes that she still appears near the sycamore, wearing a stark white robe and carrying a bloody sword. The Street of Sorrow is Mary King's Close, whose residents were totally wiped out in the bubonic plague of 1645. The street, reputed to be the haunt of headless phantoms, still survives below ground. It can be seen from Cockburn Street, its entrance barred by a gate.

Stories of witchcraft abound in the lore of Edinburgh, where hundreds of women were burned at Castle Hill during a Scottish national frenzy that took 17,000 lives between the years 1479 and 1722. Most were tortured and put to death for allegedly possessing magical powers, including in one instance the supposed ability to sink a royal ship.

But inevitably to the forefront of Edinburgh truth-legend is the case of the body-snatchers William Burke and William Hare, Irish labourers who strangled at least 16 paupers in 1827 and sold the bodies to surgeons for medical research. Hare testified against his companion during a sensational trial and escaped the gallows, but Burke was hanged on January 28, 1829. The story still grips the imagination of Edinburgh people more than the city's most supernatural tales.

Below The grave of Bobby's master 'Auld Jock' is in Greyfriars Churchyard **Left. Above** Nearby is the pub named after Bobby.

The Church

Centuries of bitter struggle established Scotland's spiritual capital

The hundreds of church buildings in Edinburgh give the visitor an immediate impression of a city in which religion has played a vital role – a role which at various times has brought both turbulence and reassurance.

From the year AD 563, when St. Columba established his monastery on the small island of Iona, Scotland was known as Christian, although it took three centuries to convert the native tribes. By the middle of the ninth century Scotland was ruled by a Roman Catholic monarchy, and it remained a

omic decline, created a nation ready for change. That change came through the Reformation, led in Scotland by one man – the often controversial John Knox.

Knox's dream was not only to create a reformed Church in Scotland, and banish 'popery' from her shores, but also to strengthen democracy and to set up a system of comprehensive education. But it was to take almost 130 years of bitter struggle to achieve the religious transition.

Between 1559 and 1689 various monarchs attempted to re-establish the Catholic Church,

but the seeds of reform had been deeply sown, and the Covenanters, as they came to be called, fought steadfastly and determinedly for Knox's principles.

James I and VI and his son Charles I sought to make Scotland's ministers bring their Church more in line with the English Church. In 1637 Charles I attempted to introduce Archbishop Laud's new Service Book, based on the English Book of Common Prayer. As soon as the Dean of Edinburgh began to read from it he was bombarded with folding

Catholic nation until the Reformation in 1559.

The Catholic Church of early sixteenth-century Scotland has been described as the most corrupt and disorganized in Europe. Its wealth was far in excess of the country's and the taxes it demanded to maintain its establishments had nurtured a growing bitterness. This, combined with growing econ-

Right Central to the city's religious turmoil, St. Giles' Cathedral is over a thousand years old.

Above 1787, a meeting of the General Assembly.

stools, Bibles and anything else the congregation could lay hands on. Jenny Geddes, who made her living selling cabbages outside St. Giles, ensured herself a place in history by throwing the first stool and screaming 'Daur ye say mass in my lug!'

The heirs of Knox's reforms were determined that their religious freedom should not be jeopardized by a London monarch. In 1638 they gathered in the small churchyard of Greyfriars that was to become so closely associated with their fight and signed the National Covenant, swearing loyalty to the King but rejecting his rulings on the Church. And in 1643 the Solemn League and Covenant was signed, pledging its subscribers not only to preserve the reformed religion, but also to advance it in England and Ireland.

Meanwhile in England Cromwell deposed and executed Charles I and defeated the exhausted Scottish army. The Restoration of Charles II in 1660 again meant the reformed Church was threatened. It was not until the Dutch Calvinist William of Orange took the English throne in 1688 that Protestantism was assured of its survival. When in 1707 the two crowns were joined by the Act of Union, Scotland was granted its independent legal system, judicature and Church – the Church of Scotland.

But the Church was to suffer yet another blow to its confidence. At the 1843 meeting of the General Assembly nearly 500 ministers walked out to form the Free Church of Scotland, an action which became known as the Disruption.

In 1900 most of the Free Church and other Presbyterian groups joined to become the United Free Church and in 1929 the United Free Church reunited with the Church of Scotland, which had agreed to

Left Near the church where he so often preached is John Knox's House, reputed to be the oldest dwelling place in Edinburgh.

Above In the room where he died on November 24, 1572 is a stained-glass window of the fiery reformer.

abolish patronage by influential landowners. However, there was still a small minority who remained outside the union, commonly known as the 'Wee Frees'.

It wasn't until the Emancipation Act of 1829 that Roman Catholics were free to worship openly again, although Catholicism had survived quietly for the many intervening years.

During the potato famine of the nineteenth century thousands of Irish fled their homeland to settle in Scotland, most of them in the west. For this reason the Catholic Church of Scotland is administered from Glasgow.

But for the Reformed Churches, to which 80 percent of the people belong, Edinburgh has always remained the spiritual capital of the country.

The beautiful 18-year-old Catholic widow of the King of France, Mary, returned to Scotland in August 1561 to this civil and religious upheaval. She was given a tremendous welcome by the people while John Knox protested.

The sad catalogue of trouble with her nobles and her people; her confrontation with Knox and his followers on religion; her marriage to Darnley – by whom she bore James VI and I – and her husband's subsequent murder in an explosion at Kirk o' Field in 1567; her unpopular marriage to Bothwell (who was suspected of Darnley's murder) – were some of the ingredients in the period of turmoil that finally saw Mary imprisoned in Loch Leven Castle. She escaped to England, only to be imprisoned by her cousin Elizabeth, on whose orders she was beheaded.

After Mary's flight a group of nobles formed a coalition known as the Queen's Lords who resented the power of Regent Morton who ruled on behalf of the infant James. Civil war ensued: the governor of Edinburgh Castle, Sir William Kirkcaldy, allied himself with the Queen's men against the Regent. As a result the city suffered badly – the castle was under siege for five years.

It was finally defeated by the guns of the Earl of Morton. Five batteries of English guns opened simultaneously and the David Tower crashed down with men and guns to the rocks beneath, the debris choking the draw-wells of the Castle. Even so 13 hours of hand-to-hand fighting followed before Kirkcaldy surrendered the Castle and was hanged.

So, with the support of Elizabeth I of England, Morton had taken Edinburgh. But the Castle was destroyed and the city was thus undefended. Never knowing who might attack he had the Half Moon Battery built on the foundations of the ruined tower.

Morton was coerced into resignation in 1578 by a group of hostile nobles and James VI took the throne at the age of 17. But his mother, Mary, was still alive, although imprisoned.

The situation in Scotland was attracting international interest. Both Spain and France were uncertain whether to deal with Mary or James. Mary did not want to give up her part as champion of the Catholics but equally her staunchly Protestant son was the one with the power.

Fearing that France was deserting her she promised in 1580 to put herself and her son and the realm under the protection of the Spanish King Philip II – none of which endeared Mary to her English cousin who feared Mary's claim to the English throne. The result was that no one viewed Mary's death in 1587 with any great sorrow – apart from her diminishing band of Scots supporters.

James, well-educated and intelligent, very aware of his position, tried to bring peace to his nation by encouraging his feuding nobles to join forces. But he was also determined to cast himself in the Elizabethan mould and have power over Kirk as well as government.

He was soon in deep trouble with Knox's successor Andrew Melville who declared that there were two kingdoms in Scotland and that James was a subject of the realm of Christ.

The royal argument with the Kirk about power, political and religious, lasted until 1603 by which time James had determined to make the Scots Kirk conform more closely with the English pattern, with the monarch as head of the Church.

Despite his erudition and intelligence, James had a firm belief in sorcery and it is claimed that more witches were burned and strangled on Castle Hill than in any other area of Scotland.

The story of Elsie Peat, in 1589, was not an unusual one. She was an elderly woman who was often seen muttering to herself and so it was suspected that she was in league with the Devil and conversed with him. A 'dookin' was demanded.

It involved the suspected witch being thrown into Nor' Loch with her thumbs and toes tied. Her innocence would be assured if she sank and drowned but if she floated it would be proof that she was bedevilled. Poor Elsie's voluminous skirts filled with air and she floated – which gave the crowd the excuse they wanted to drag her to Castle Hill to her death.

---

*D*ucking in Nor' Loch was the punishment for fornication in these times. The tongues of perjurers were bored; drowning followed conviction for theft and when the Loch was drained in 1820 workmen found a large coffin containing the skeletons of a man and a woman, thought to be a brother and sister who were drowned in 1623 for incest.

Although punishments were hard on transgressors, measures were taken to help the poor. The problem of what to do with them came about with the dissolution of the monasteries which had provided alms and hospitals. The town council, carefully distinguishing between the 'deserving and the undeserving', issued badges to the former, authorizing them to beg, and banished the latter from the burgh.

James's capital also had the unsavoury distinction of being the filthiest city in Europe. The houses were crowded closely together round the Castle for protection and because of the terrain which restricted building on the eastern slope.

Streets were narrow, dunghills piled up and, as swine were kept by many householders in pens under the outside stairs, it was little wonder that the plague was rife.

George Heriot's School

And yet this century saw a new building for the twelfth-century high school and the foundation of the university in 1583; the Scottish Mint was moved from Holyrood and erected in the Cowgate; in lighter vein, James licensed comedians.

It also saw the rise of an Edinburgh goldsmith and friend to the King, George Heriot. He was symbolic of an age of building and of business. The war-torn capital was settling down and fear of invasion was a thing of the past. Foreign trade was increased enormously and goods coming into Edinburgh included fine woollens from England; luxury dress materials from France, Flanders and Italy; wine from Bordeaux and La Rochelle; fruit vegetables, spices and salt.

Heriot, meanwhile, was making his fortune too. He lent money to the impoverished King and his Danish Queen. 'Jingling Geordie', as he was called, was appointed goldsmith to the Queen in 1597.

When the childless Heriot died in 1612 he left his fortune to the municipality and clergy of Edinburgh to found and endow a hospital for the maintenance and education of fatherless boys and sons of freemen and burgesses in the town.

The school was started in 1628, completed in 1659, and is still one of the most striking buildings in the city, now the co-educational George Heriot's School. His example in founding the hospital for scholars was to be followed by many other prosperous citizens – notably George Watson, James Gillespie, William Fettes, Daniel Stewart, John Watson and Mary Erskine.

In 1603, a dramatic event changed the course of Scottish history. Elizabeth I of England died and James succeeded as her nearest heir. He took the road south and Scotland's capital lost its permanent royal presence and its court. He had promised to return every three years but involvements in England meant that he came back only once, in 1617. His departure meant loss of prosperity to many in the city.

There followed, however, a period of comparative peace until the ascension of Charles I in 1625. Charles celebrated his Scottish coronation in Holyrood in 1633, welcomed lavishly by the town council.

But the few following quiet years ended at a service in St. Giles after Charles, who had learned little about the Scots during his visit, had insisted on the use of the English Episcopal service book in the fiercely Presbyterian country.

On July 23, 1637, a crowded congregation in the cathedral – a title Charles had imposed which was to hold officially for only 50 years despite which it is still popularly called that – heard the new Dean of Edinburgh start to use the revised prayer book of the Anglican Church.

Uproar followed. And in the following year the National Covenant, calling on its supporters to renounce popery and resist all religious innovation, was drawn up and signed in Greyfriars Churchyard.

The city and the nation faced more civil war. In England Oliver Cromwell was stirring his forces to war. In 1642 the Scots joined the English parliamentarians in a league and covenant against the King.

The opposition of the Covenanters to the King had been a reaction to his hated religious policies but they were horrified at his execution. Six days after Charles was beheaded his son was proclaimed King in Scotland.

Before his barbarous execution in 1650, organized by the Earl of Argyll, the Marquis of Montrose had kept the royal banner flying in Scotland. He was hanged for three hours at the Mercat Cross in the capital, then his head was cut off and displayed on the Tolbooth; his legs and arms were removed to go on display in other towns, and the remnants of his body were finally buried.

In 1650 Cromwell invaded Edinburgh. The town's defensive wall was no match for Cromwell's military genius and the town council surrendered without a fight after the battle of Dunbar. Cromwell's troops, some of whom were billeted in the half-finished Heriot's Hospital, treated the city and its citizens with severity. But finally a working relationship between the city fathers and the Cromwellian regime emerged.

Despite cooperation with Cromwell there was a general rejoicing when Charles II was restored to the throne in 1660. However, when the celebrations were over the Scots found themselves facing a government committed to Episcopalianism with its structure of government-appointed bishops. The Scots Kirk wanted to elect its own leaders.

In 1662 an edict was issued ordering the use of Episcopal services and ministers were deposed for not doing so.

The Covenanters rose again only to be crushed by General Tam Dalyell and then by James Graham of Claverhouse. Martyrs faced death defiantly at the Grassmarket where their memorial stands, and the Covenanters were finally defeated at Bothwell Bridge in 1679.

About 1000 Covenanters were held in atrocious conditions for five months in what is now Greyfriars Churchyard. The man who led much of the prosecution against them was Lord Advocate Sir George Mackenzie, whose zeal won him the title of 'Bluidy Machenzie', the man who wrote a standard work on Scottish criminal law and founded the Faculty of Advocates' Library.

Life in the city was not entirely bound up with religious disruption: the *Edinburgh Gazette,* the city's first newspaper, started publication in 1679; two years later the Merchant Company was founded; in 1681 the Royal College of Physicians was chartered.

*J*n August 1686 James granted freedom of worship to Catholics in private houses and the following year Catholics and Quakers were allowed to worship more openly. In an attempt to counteract the unpopularity of these measures he granted the same rights to Presbyterians in June 1687.

But the proclamation failed to reduce anti-Catholic feeling; rather it increased mistrust and suspicion. It also made the Episcopalians feel that their royal support had weakened.

In the meantime, James's elder daughter Mary had married William of Orange who was himself a grandson of Charles I and, more to the point, a Protestant. Here was an alternative heir to those who hated Catholicism.

James's fate was sealed when his wife, Mary of Modena, produced a son – a Catholic heir – in June 1688. The 'Glorious Revolution' began. William's English anti-Catholic supporters encouraged him to come to Britain. James fled to France a month later.

In Edinburgh the mob showed its anti-Catholic feeling by sacking the Catholic Chapel Royal and driving the Jesuits from their school at Holyrood; they also desecrated the tombs of the Stuart monarchs buried there.

Popular feeling and the arrival of Protestant William brought about the reinstatement of the Presbyterian Church government in Scotland.

The Stuarts and their Catholic cause seemed at an end. The rightful heir, James Francis Edward, was denied the Crown – the usurpers William and Mary sat firmly on the throne. This led, in 1715 and 1745, to two uprisings by supporters in Scotland but neither achieved the return of the Stuarts.

By then the nations of Scotland and England had been joined under one parliament.

The union was partly due to a huge financial disaster in Scotland that brought the people to a psychological and monetary misery.

A company was formed in 1695 for trading with Africa and the Indies – an attempt to break the monopoly of the English East India Company. It was a cause that excited the Edinburgh imagination and in which William Patterson, who conceived the idea of the Bank of England, was a driving force. Eager subscribers put up 400,000 Scottish pounds.

A group of Scots colonists were landed on the coast of Darien, possibly the unhealthiest part of the Isthmus of Panama, and after a few years of unprofitable struggle were finally driven out by the Spanish in 1700.

The venture was the worst commercial undertaking in Scotland's history. There was no glory and the loss of pride and money were enormous. Scotland's exchequer and storehouses were empty and the challenge to English mercantilism was a mockery. Nine ships that the company had bought or chartered were lost; the huge capital had disappeared without profit and 2000 men, women and children had died in Darien, been abandoned in Spanish prison, or become indentured servants to English colonies.

When news of the Darien Scheme reached Edinburgh the mobs took to the streets to vent their fury at their lost hopes and fortunes and their wrath against the English who had failed to help the colonists in favour of keeping on good terms with the Spanish who had claimed Darien. The disastrous scheme so impoverished Scotland that many concluded the nation would only be successful financially if it had equal trading rights with England. In 1707 the Scottish Parliament cut its own throat by passing the Act of Union.

It was finally ratified in the Edinburgh Parliament by 110 votes to 67 and when the treaty passed through Westminster without opposition the Parliaments of Scotland and England ceased to exist. In their places was one Parliament of Great Britain with 513 English representatives and 45 Scottish in the House of Commons. In the Lords 16 elected Scottish peers would sit.

$\mathcal{S}$ome independence remained: it kept the Kirk, the system of education, the courts and legal code, and the royal burghs with their special privileges. However, the administration did move south and with it Scotland's political, cultural and economic force.

'Bought and sold for English gold' sang the Jacobite ballad of the day and, indeed, Queen Anne paid £20,000 to reduce the arrears of the Scottish government; bribes and inducements had no doubt passed hands during the long arguments. But without the union and the financial benefits it brought it is possible that Scotland would not have survived.

The General Assembly and the Court of Session stayed in Edinburgh, but the men of influence and talent moved to England. Streets like the Canongate, where the nobility had lived, declined.

But the city did not die: horse racing was still popular, cock fighting at Leith Links and other venues was a public obsession and concerts were held at Bailie Fyfe's Close every Saturday during the winter. Gentlemen exercised themselves playing golf, tennis and shooting bows and arrows.

The Jacobites revived Catholic hopes in 1715 and 1745 but their efforts never achieved return of the Stuarts and a Catholic monarchy. In 1715 they tried to put James, the 'Old Pretender', on the throne. A raid on the Castle was beaten off and the uprising, with little support in southern Scotland, died in spite of French backing.

It had never been easy to maintain order in Edinburgh and over the years various attempts were made to control crime and riot. At the end of the seventeenth century the city had appointed a city corps of guards, nicknamed by the people as the 'Toun Rats'.

Their reputation was never good but it sank to an all-time low, along with the name of the town's magistrates', when the Edinburgh mob took to the streets once more in April 1736.

It was then that the Grassmarket became the scene of a virtual lynching which has gone down in the history books as the Porteous Riot. Captain John Porteous was a Captain of the town guard who had the unsavoury reputation of relishing public executions. On April 14, a demonstration broke out when he presided over the hanging of a popular smuggler named Andrew Wilson. Wilson was highly regarded for having accepted full personal responsibility for robbing an excise officer, and thus allowing an equally guilty colleague to go free. Members of the town guard opened fire on the crowd, killing nine people and wounding many others. In the outcry that followed, Porteous was put on trial for murder and was condemned to death by the High Court. But on September 7 word spread through the city that he was about to be reprieved by royal decree. An angry mob broke into the Tolbooth jail, dragged Porteous out in his nightgown and hanged him from a pole which marked a dyer's premises, close to the scene of the shooting. The pole, symbolizing perhaps the most dramatic example of Grassmarket law and legend, stood in front of Hunter's Close on the south side of the rectangle. Porteous's body was laid to rest in nearby Greyfriars Churchyard. Except for a post inscribed P. 1736, his grave remained unmarked for 237 years. Then, in 1973, a headstone replaced the post, providing the extra information: 'John Porteous, a Captain of Edinburgh City Guard, murdered 7 September 1736. All passion spent.'

$\mathcal{R}$ebellion and violence came again to Scotland with the second Jacobite uprising of 1745 which sought to place Bonnie Prince Charlie, the 'Young Pretender', on the throne.

When news of his arrival from France reached the city a band of 1000 men was raised to defend the town. The 'Young Pretender's' army of Highlanders camped in Holyrood Park and a large crowd went out to meet the Catholic Prince, whose official recognition lay with the Pope.

The Highlanders easily entered the city and subsequently the Lord Provost Archibald Stewart had to face trial for failing to offer stiff enough resistance to the Jacobites. Their cause, though, died on the moors of Culloden the following year and the Prince fled into humiliating exile.

His supporters paid heavily for their loyalty. Apart from the blockades of the navy and revenge of the English army which hounded Culloden's survivors, about 120 of the prisoners were executed – peers by the axe and the others by the rope. A further 1150 were banished or transported and the fate of another 700 is still unknown.

Politically Scotland was also repressed. The office of Secretary of State was abolished and the post of Lord Advocate came to represent royal power in Scotland under the direction of the Secretary of the Northern Department.

Rigorous laws were passed against Episcopalians; the wearing of kilts and playing of bagpipes were banned. Some lands were annexed to the Crown.

Trustees were appointed to run the forfeited estates of Jacobite supporters and order was restored; schools were established; land tenure for crofters was improved; cottage industries were introduced and the Scottish economy began to flourish.

Continued on page 26

The Law

A unique tradition marries the two great schools of European law

*N*ot Proven – it's a court verdict you will not hear in any other part of the world. But it symbolizes a tradition of fiercely independent Scottish law born out of repeated wars with England and the Auld Alliance with France. Often quirky, sometimes at variance with the legal system in other areas of the United Kingdom, the law of Scotland stands proudly alone.

In no other part of Britain can a jury declare that the case against a defendant has not been proved. Such a verdict means simply that there was insufficient evidence to estab-

lish that the accused person was guilty or not. He or she leaves court without penalty but not without suspicion. It is a unique finding, in that few people who stand in the dock elsewhere ever walk away without being declared guilty or innocent.

'Not Proven' undoubtedly carries a kind of stigma – the notion that someone has been clever enough to get away with something – but the Scots regard it as merely a sign of commonsense. Perhaps there were genuine doubts back in June 1852, when a truly sensational trial took place in Edinburgh.

High-born Madeline Smith, her story re-enacted a hundred times in books and films, stood accused of murdering her French lover with liberal doses of arsenic. The verdict was 'Not Proven'–and Madeline went on to live to a ripe old age in the United States.

Between its close ties to France and proximity to England, Scotland has created its own coherent legal system – incorporating Roman law, feudal law, canon law, special customs and local practices. A wealth of experience went into the Scottish law first defined in the seventeenth century by Sir

James Dalrymple, later Viscount Stair. His formula persisted through the 1707 Act of Union with England to remain the basis of the law of the land. But that was also when Parliament in London began infusing its own flavour.

Critics still feel that acts of Parliament do not always take account of Scottish precedent, one of the mainstays of the system practised north of the border. The courts will always pay high regard to judicial opinions passed down in similar cases decided many years earlier.

Until 1820 the bulk of Scottish law owed its origin to those Roman regulations, feudal laws and ancient customs – in common with France and Germany and most of the then developed world, but distinct from the great common law systems of England, the United States and the majority of Commonwealth countries. Since then, Scottish law has moved away from its Roman base and taken a middle ground between the continental system and the common law of England.

In modern times Scotland has administered its own criminal law since 1926, although civil law ultimately comes under the jurisdiction of the House of Lords at Westminster. The London government appoints a Lord Advocate, usually a lawyer–politician, who represents the state in all criminal proceedings. These range from Scotland's supreme criminal tribunal, the High Court of Justiciary, to local hearings in Sheriff's and District courts. Most High Court cases are heard by a judge sitting not with 12 but 15 jurors – another unique aspect of Scottish law.

The Edinburgh Sheriff's Court stands north of the High Street, opposite St. Giles' Cathedral. But don't expect large-scale drama there – a two-year jail sentence is the limit they can impose.

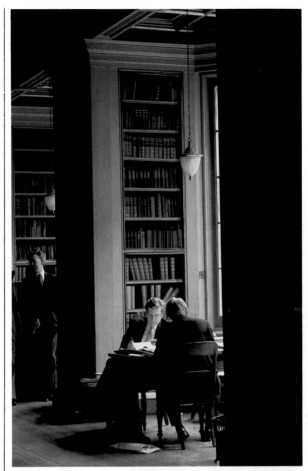

Far left The Great Hall of Parliament Hall, home of the Scottish Parliament until 1707 and now a meeting place for lawyers from the adjacent courts. The great stained glass window dates from 1532 and shows James V, one of the great protectors of Scottish law, together with Abbot Mylne, first Lord President of the Court of Session.
Above The Advocates' Library, founded in 1682. It now houses the legal collection of the National Library. **Right** Examples from the library's valuable collection of books and documents.

Literature

Great men of letters rose from the tradition of ancient Celtic bards.

Edinburgh remembers its writers and poets. And is remembered by them. Its first poet, the sixteenth-century William Dunbar, described the city as 'nobill toun'; Burns as 'Edina! Scotia's darling seat'; Scott as 'mine own romantic town' and for Stevenson, far away in Samoa, it was 'a precipitous city' whose gusty winds could make it 'scowling'.

Its characters, too, are recalled. The merchants of Dunbar's days were castigated by him for their wares which cluttered the streets and fouled the air with the 'stink of haddockis and of scattis' (skate). Allan Ramsay portrayed Lucky Spence, the madame who kept a brothel in the Canongate of the eighteenth century; Stevenson found inspiration for Dr. Jekyll and Mr. Hyde in Deacon Brodie, a respectable city councillor by day and burglar by night; Conan Doyle modelled Sherlock Holmes on the Edinburgh surgeon Dr. Joseph Bell.

The Celts have a long and revered literary heritage in their myths, legends and bardic poetry but an international seal of approval was set on the capital in the late eighteenth and early nineteenth centuries.

It was, as Smollett said, 'a hotbed of genius', when the brilliant circle of literati lived and met under the acknowledged leadership of David Hume (1711-1776), historian, philosopher, religious sceptic and humanitarian. With him were the likes of Adam Smith (1723-1790), economist and author of *The Wealth of Nations;* Adam Ferguson (1723-1816), philosopher and historian; William Robertson (1721-1793), historian and principal of Edinburgh University and Dugald Stewart (1753-1828), philosopher.

They started the popularity of literary clubs such as the Easy Club, The Cape Club and the Speculative Society, which met at the taverns tucked away in the wynds and lanes of the Old Town. They frequented the booksellers like William Creech, Burns' Edinburgh publisher, and Blackwood's 'great lounging book-shop'.

Sir Walter Scott's signature and the small statue of the author reading which marks the house in Castle Street where he moved in 1801. The printing press below is the one James Ballantyne used to print the first editions of Scott's Waverley Novels.

A segment of Burns' script of his poem 'Scots Wha Ha'e', dated 1795; the 'heaven-taught ploughman's' signature; and the statue of him that stands in Lady Stair's House, a museum dedicated to three great Scottish men of letters.

There was Robert Fergusson, born in 1750, who died of drink and madness in an asylum at 24, hailed by Burns as 'my elder brother in the Muse' and by others for his part in the revival of Scottish poetry.

Burns spent time in the city, lionized by the literati as 'the heaven-taught ploughman', amused by his landlady's complaints about the prostitutes in the flat above.

Edinburgh also attracted, over the centuries, many other writers: Daniel Defoe was here in 1710 as a government spy sent to report on Scottish attitudes to the recent Act of Union and later wrote about the 'stench and nastiness' of the Old Town; Oliver Goldsmith studied medicine here but was more interested in the social life and beauty of Scots women; Dr. Johnson visited on his way to the Hebrides with his biographer James Boswell and gave the Scots an opportunity to get their own back on him after all his insults about them.

Wordsworth, an admirer of Walter Scott, stayed as Scott's guest after a tour of the Highlands; Thomas Carlyle attended the university and trained for the ministry; Thomas de Quincey contributed to *Blackwood's Magazine* and Blackwood published his *Confessions of an English Opium Eater* in 1822; J. M. Barrie was at the university; and John Buchan became Lord Chancellor of the university.

Of all native Scots writers Sir Walter Scott and Robert Louis Stevenson are probably best known. Scott was born in 1771 and as a sickly child read poetry and romances when confined to bed. He was a prolific writer and while he wrote his old tomcat and his favourite dog, Maida, kept him company. He wrote long into the night, by hand, page after page and, in one period of three weeks, completed the last two volumes of Waverley.

Stevenson was another invalid child and his physical weakness drove him from Edinburgh to the sunnier shores of the South Pacific. But childhood memories remained with him and led to his collection of poems, *A Child's Garden of Verses*, with the much-loved Leerie the Lamplighter. He also went to university in Edinburgh and was something of a rebel, giving up his middle-class family life to spend his time with the dubious characters in the pubs and brothels of Lothian Road and Leith Walk where he was often seen with notebook and pen in hand.

The city still inspires its authors: Muriel Spark, born in 1918, was educated in Edinburgh and her novel *The Prime of Miss Jean Brodie* might well have been based on her own school – James Gillespie's School for Girls. The Scottish Renaissance Movement of the 1920s and 1930s injected new life into poetry with the appearance of writers like Hugh MacDiarmid. The Abbotsford Bar in Rose Street, the Cafe Royal near Register House and Milnes Bar in Hanover Street became meeting places for the new literati – men like Sidney Goodsir Smith (1915-1975), Robert Garioch (1909-1981) and Norman MacCaig (born in 1910), who have all written about their lives in the capital.

FOR WE ARE VERY LUCKY WITH A LAMP BEFORE THE DOOR,
AND LEERIE STOPS TO LIGHT IT AS HE LIGHTS SO MANY MORE;
AND O! BEFORE YOU HURRY BY WITH LADDER AND WITH LIGHT,
O LEERIE, SEE A LITTLE CHILD AND NOD TO HIM TONIGHT!
R·L·S

Robert Louis Stevenson

This statue of Robert Louis Stevenson stands in his boyhood home at 17 Heriot Row, and the handsome brass plaque that marks the spot is inscribed with a verse from his children's poem 'The Lamplighter.' The author died at the age of 44 in Samoa where he lived for three years presiding like a native chief in his adopted land.

Edinburgh was now beginning to burst at the seams. Around the time of 'the forty-five', conditions for the 51,000 citizens were very mixed. One estimate shows that ten percent lived in houses in the streets, 60 percent in the tight closes, 20 percent in dugouts or sheds and the remaining ten percent straggled homeless through the streets, seeking shelter wherever they could.

The city buildings of Edinburgh were still concentrated around the spine of the High Street and down the slopes of the Grassmarket and Cowgate. By the middle of the seventeenth century high tenements were standard, pushing upward, restricted from spreading outwards by the ancient city walls.

Flats of six or seven rooms were common – with a great mixture of tenants in any one building. Merchants and bankers lived in this sort of building on higher floors and the poorer people took the dark ground floors.

As a result of this gross overcrowding – one story tells of 11 adults crammed into one room – small developments were starting to open outside the walls – like Nicholson and George Squares to the south.

St. Giles and the Old Town

*T*he push came from an extraordinary visionary, George Drummond, six times Lord Provost of Edinburgh.

In 1752 he was largely responsible for drawing up 'Proposals for carrying out certain public works in the City of Edinburgh' which in 7500 words outlined the overcrowded conditions of the city and suggested an extension of the town.

He then, in September 1753, as Grand Master of the Scottish Freemasons, laid the foundation stone of the Royal Exchange in the High Street (the building later became the City Chambers). He had also been instrumental in launching in 1729 an appeal fund for an infirmary which grew into one of the world's greatest teaching hospitals, the Royal Infirmary, now standing in Lauriston Place.

Ten years after the 'Proposals' were published, Drummond managed to persuade the town council to hold a competition for a plan of a new town on the far side of Nor' Loch.

It brought in six plans and the winner, announced in 1766, was 23-year-old James Craig, son of an Edinburgh merchant, who won a gold medal and the freedom of the city – as well as overnight fame.

His plan was symmetrical; a gridiron of three main streets balanced at either end by a square. Today its shape is basically unaltered from Princes Street to George Street and Queen Street, although the houses which once lined Princes Street have all but vanished

On the original plan Princes Street was named St. Giles Street but the name was altered. In the end the whole plan was dedicated to the House of Hanover and claimed to represent the new union between England and Scotland.

The first houses of the New Town were built in Thistle Court – where they still stand – and by 1774 the foundation stone of the magnificent Register House was laid. The designs for the building were drawn by the distinguished and fashionable Adam brothers.

Robert Adam was commissioned to provide a plan and complete elevations for Charlotte Square and, in doing so, one of the world's gems of Georgian architecture was started in 1792.

The New Town was largely built of grey Craigleith stone in a neo-classical style, influenced by the Greek revival then holding the interest of the nation's intellectuals.

It gave enormous opportunities to the architects of the time – like the Adam brothers, William Playfair, William Sibbald and Robert Reid and James Gillespie Graham – whose fame spread throughout Britain.

Reid, Sibbald and Playfair made their mark on the second phase of the New Town where the grand terraces of Royal and Regent Terraces were built and the monuments on Calton Hill sprang up.

'Forty years saw the Old Town changed as respects population,' wrote Robert Chambers the publisher. 'One after another its nobles and gentry, its men of the robe, its writers, and even its substantial burghers, had during that time deserted their mansions in the High Street and Canongate, till few were left.'

The Lord Justice Clerk's house was occupied by a woman who sold furniture, the Lord President's by a French teacher, a duke's house taken over by a wheelwright – changed days indeed.

It was the town where James Boswell practised as an advocate; where Robert Fergusson died in Edinburgh's Bedlam at the age of 25 leaving some remarkable poetry and leaving another poet, Robert Burns, to appreciate its excellence and arrange for a headstone on Fergusson's grave in Canongate Kirkyard.

It was said you could stand at the Mercat Cross and take 'fifty men of genius and learning by the hand'. And yet it was a town where the household slops (and worse) were hurled from upper windows into the open gutters below.

Figures of genius were many and varied in this, Scotland's golden age, when Edinburgh earned a reputation as a brilliant intellectual and artistic centre, prompting even the cynical Voltaire to write: 'It is from Scotland we receive rules of taste in all the arts from the epic poem to gardening'.

There was the judge Lord Kames, a philosopher and jurist; William Creech, bookseller and publisher and one-time Lord Provost; David Hume, the philosopher, who went to university at the age of 12; Adam Smith, author of *The Wealth of Nations;* Henry Raeburn, the painter; Francis Jeffrey, founder of *The Edinburgh Review*, Walter Scott and Burns among the writers.

It was the time when Scotland, with a population a quarter of England's, had four universities to England's two; schools, hospitals and technical colleges were founded and produced brilliance in every direction: James Watt with his steam engine; Simpson and his discovery of chloroform – inventions and discoveries seemingly endless.

In 1790 the First Statistical Account of Scotland was under way and the publisher Creech was given his say in a comparison of Edinburgh in 1763 and in 1783.

Although he might be accused of a little exaggeration, he reported that in 1763 'five or six brothels and a very few of the lowest and most ignorant order of females skulked about the streets at night' but 20 years later 'brothels increased twenty-fold and women of the Town more than a hundred-fold'.

'Housebreaking was extremely rare' in 1763 but 1783 saw that 'housebreaking theft and robbery were frequent. Many of the crimes were committed by boys whose ages prevented them from being objects of capital punishment.'

Although bookselling was his trade, Creech was interested in all sorts of shops. 'Perfumers have splendid shops in every street. Some of them advertise they keep bears, to kill occasionally for greasing ladies' and gentlemen's hair, as superior to any other animal fat.'

Yet amid all the brilliance of the golden age which also brought a revival of pride in things Scottish and in the Gaelic language, there was still a shortage of grain in the city markets in 1800 and talk of famine among the poorer citizens as the population steadily increased. By 1811 it was 103,143 and, although the city increased in size

George Street

from its original site of 138 acres (55 ha) to several thousand acres, the Old Town was still grossly crowded and those who could not afford to move to the New Town suffered gruesome conditions.

The new century was not a peaceful one in the early years. New Year riots broke out at the end of 1811 and a policeman and clerk were killed: three youths hanged in consequence.

In 1824 one of the most disastrous fires ever to hit the city broke out. On November 15 smoke and flames burst from a house in Assembly Close off the High Street and spread rapidly to engulf the whole tenement. And before the fire was out, the entire area from the High Street below St. Giles to near the Tron Kirk and down the hill to the Cowgate was devastated. Shortly afterwards, the first municipal fire brigade in the world was founded under the direction of James Braidwood.

The city was rocked by public scandal in the late 1820s, with the Burke and Hare murders. William Burke faced trial for murdering to provide bodies for the anatomy classes run by Dr. Robert Knox. Burke and partner first filched bodies from new graves to give to the doctor but soon turned to murder to provide the anatomy subjects.

Hare turned King's Evidence and, after Burke's execution in 1829, a crowd of 24,000 went to see his body on the dissecting table at Surgeon's Hall. His skeleton is still preserved in Edinburgh University's Medical School.

The mob reacted with their customary speed and violence to the scandal and gathered to throw stones and sticks at Dr. Knox's house. They also coined a ditty:

Down the close and up the stair
But an' ben wi' Burke and Hare
Burke's the butcher, Hare's the thief,
Knox the man that buys the beef.

Through pioneers like Dr. Knox, however, Edinburgh had a huge reputation for medicine and hospitals. But balanced against this is a sorry tale of disease and neglect.

The scourge through the years was smallpox. Inoculation was practised as far back as 1745 in the city but between 1740 and 1742 a smallpox outbreak claimed 17 percent of all deaths in Edinburgh. Typhus fever also struck, and cholera outbreaks in 1831-1832 and 1838-1840 increased public concern about the squalor in the dark, insanitary houses in the Old Town.

There was pressure for the appointment of a public health officer but it was only after the collapse of a tenement in the High Street in 1861, which killed 35 inhabitants, that the town council were forced to act.

Dr. Henry Littlejohn took the post, which he

Bakehouse Close

held for the next 46 years, in 1862. Three years later he produced his first report in which he proved that Edinburgh's high death rate, for adults and babies, and all the disease was due to the insanitary and appallingly cramped conditions.

His recommendations for action were to pave and drain the closes; improve accommodation by introducing water and gas, cleaning common stairs and repairing houses; limit the number of people in each apartment; remove tenements that were in danger of collapse; and open up the worst of the narrow closes.

His ideas were backed by the Lord Provost William Chambers who did much to implement them and, by degrees, conditions improved.

The greatest impact the Industrial Revolution had on Edinburgh was probably in transport. The efforts of Thomas Telford, the engineer, and John Macadam, who invented his road surfacing, improved travel on the roads and the building of canals made transport speedier.

But it was the railways that were the most effective innovation. Edinburgh's first line was planned by Robert Stevenson to connect the coalfields of Midlothian with Edinburgh and the sea. It opened in 1831 and by 1834 passenger services were running.

Traffic on the Glasgow-Edinburgh line started moving in 1842 when the Edinburgh-Newhaven route also opened. Edinburgh and Berwick were connected to London in 1846. 'Railway mania' had begun. The Granton to Burntisland line saw the world's first train ferry – over the Forth.

Horse tramcars arrived in the city in 1871 and the system spread until, by 1891, there were 300 cars and more than 1000 horses in operation.

Cable cars were introduced in 1888 and ran down Hanover Street and Dundas to Canonmills and Goldenacre. Another opened two years later along the Stockbridge route. They were pulled by cables driven by a power station in Henderson Row.

Eventually the system, the fourth largest of its kind in the world, extended throughout the city with four power stations driving 52 miles (84 km) of cables through a 26-mile (42 km) network of routes.

Edinburgh had prospered with the Victorian industrial expansion: there was brewing, distilling, printing, baking and confectionary, the manufacture of glass and chemicals.

---

*T*he city also took to the morality and formality of the Victorians which appealed to the ethics of Knox's followers. But there was still dissension in the Kirk. In 1843 four hundred ministers took about a third of the Kirk's members to establish the Free Church because they felt that the Church of Scotland had become too liberal. And again in 1892 a group split away – this time from the Free Church to set up the Free Presbyterian Church on the grounds that the Free Church had become insufferably liberal!

Morality was also the basis for the enormous support that William Ewart Gladstone found in his father's native Scotland. He conducted his Midlothian campaign in the city in 1879, and paid for the return of the Old Mercat Cross to its present site.

Gladstone also toyed with the idea of all-round devolution for Britain and, although his energies were devoted to Irish Home Rule, the Scots responded with enthusiasm. Nationalism had already been inflamed by the vast numbers of English troops which virtually occupied Scotland after the uprisings of 1715 and 1745 and it was helped along by the intellectual interest in Scottish language and history of writers like Burns and Scott.

In the 1880s a demand was made – and met – for a Scottish Secretary to deal exclusively with Scottish affairs, and a Scottish Home Rule Association sprang up.

From 1906 onwards there was an almost annual

Pier at Newhaven

Government of Scotland Bill but it was never successful because the parties in power failed to push it through Parliament. Had World War I not intervened it is possible that the government would have been forced to honour its pledge.

The Scots started a New Home Rule Association in 1917 and by 1928 the National Party of Scotland was formed. But it did not meet with quite the popular enthusiasm its leaders had hoped for, perhaps because it was too left wing and wanted total separation from England.

The agitation over the years did lead to the move of the Scottish administration to Edinburgh from Whitehall in 1939 and gradually, after World War II, the administrative powers were widened.

The Scottish Nationalist Party won its first by-election in 1945, only to lose the seat in the subsequent general election a few weeks later. It had to wait another 20 years or so before another Nationalist sat in Westminster. In 1974 there were seven SNP members in London and it seemed that the time was ripe for a referendum on devolution. It was taken in 1979 and the feeling was such that Edinburgh spent £3 million on converting the old Royal High School, built in 1825 on Calton Hill, for the Scottish Assembly. But the vote was indecisive and the school remains empty.

While Scottish nationalism flowered, literature and the arts blossomed too. Between the two World Wars, Edinburgh was still a great city for bookshop browsing and artists and writers were busy in the city – busy enough to start a 'Scottish Renaissance' in the 1930s with poets like Hugh

Universities

Established under royal charter by James VI in 1583, Edinburgh University is the sixth oldest in Britain. Beginning with ninety freshmen, it now has over 11,000 full-time students, and over 50,000 members of its General Council (living former students). Its size is obvious: it is spread throughout the city making it the largest private owner of buildings in Scotland.

The university's founding principles were based on the firm doctrines of Calvinism and students were encouraged to attend the university to gain 'the manners of morality and virtue'. This was to be achieved by study within the college but residence 'in the presence of their friends'. Thus it was not until 1887 that Edinburgh's – and Scotland's – first hall of residence was established. This hall, Patrick Geddes (at number 2 Mound Place) was recently renovated and is occupied by students today.

The university has always been non-collegiate (there is no system of colleges) and offers no multitude of lawns, chapels and stairways. Rather, it is the buildings in which the students were taught, the austere Georgian proportions of the Old College (on the corner of Chambers Street and South Bridge) and the Medical School (in Teviot Place), that provided the architectural and educational heart of the university.

In 1582, the Town Council purchased the Kirk o' Fields on which the Old College now stands. From the outset the Council financed building and teaching alike, beginning a long involvement with the university. In 1789, the university was granted an independent coat of arms but it was not until 1858 that autonomy from the Council was achieved.

From the beginning, university students took a four year MA degree in the General Arts. Only then could they enter the Divinity School – the only other faculty. It was only later that Medicine (1705) and Law (1722) were established.

Originally, Edinburgh adopted the regent system of teaching, taken from the great university of Leyden. Each student was assigned a regent (or tutor) who taught him throughout his degree. This system was replaced in 1708 by the professorial system of today.

The demands upon the students were exacting. There were no set examinations; the regent or professor who did not examine his students daily was failing in his duty. 'Dictates' (given at dictation speed) began at five am (six am in midwinter) and continued until evening. The only break was two hours of compulsory exercise – the regent's parade – in mid-afternoon. The students were forbidden to attend the public hangings in the Grassmarket. Even funerals – except those of eminent councillors – were deemed too frivolous for attendance. Only the month of August was permitted for vacation. Calvinism reigned supreme.

This rigorous system of education did not, however, subdue all students. In 1680, Robert Brown, an Englishman, publicly burnt an effigy of the Pope in the Kirk o' Fields. This protest was directed at the Catholic heir-presumptive Duke of York who was in residence at the Palace of Holyroodhouse. The Old College and Town Guards could not prevent a student revolt from supporting Brown. The Privy Council charged the college with treason and closed it down. Brown was expelled. From this incident arose a pledge, which all students must sign today upon matriculation, agreeing to accept expulsion if

McDiarmid and Albert Mackie bringing pride back to things Scottish. And while writers wrote through the 1930s and 1940s a new idea in cultural expression came to the capital in the form of the International Festival of the arts.

It was launched in 1947 under the leadership of the Lord Provost Sir John Falconer and was an act of inspiration and faith after the gloomy days of World War II. It brought, as intended, international stars and companies to the city. Now the Festival attracts about 100,000 visitors each year and, in turn, the visitors stimulate the town's tourism, restaurants, shops and hotels.

Dr. Johnson once wrote that the best sight for a Scotsman was the road to England. It is now a road that takes the financial and trading talents of the Scots all over the world.

Edinburgh has become a major centre for banking and insurance – Charlotte Square is said to be among the richest squares in the world so many are the headquarters there. Traders like Jardine Mathieson, of Hong Kong fame, had their beginnings in Edinburgh, and the 'black gold' from the North Sea has brought more financial work for the capital.

The capital is flourishing and still has great beauty. And it retains an impression of mystery and magic of which Robert Louis Stevenson wrote: 'There is no Edinburgh emigrant, far or near, from China to Peru, but he or she carries some lively pictures of the mind, some sunset beneath the Castle cliffs, some snow scene, some maze of city lamps, indelible in the memory and delightful to study in the intervals of toil.'

---

they break the university laws or bring it into disrepute.

Throughout the nineteenth century the university continued to expand. The Divinity School, now the largest in Britain, was rehoused in the New College, where the assembly of the University meets annually each May.

The nineteenth-century Prime Ministers Lord Palmerston and Lord John Russell (son of the Duke of Bedford) studied here. Other students included Mungo Park, James Boswell, Thomas Carlyle, Oliver Goldsmith, Charles Darwin, Sir Arthur Conan Doyle, Sir Walter Scott and Robert Louis Stevenson. David Hume was refused a professorship for publicly professing disbelief in God. From 1920-1929, successive Rectors of the University were David Lloyd George, Stanley Baldwin, Sir John Gilmour and Winston Churchill. Churchill had failed in his first Rectorial election in 1905. Their predecessors included the Liberal Prime Ministers Gladstone and Lord Rosebery. University Chancellors have included the literary figures Sir James Barrie, Bt., and Lord Tweedsmuir (John Buchan). HRH the Duke of Edinburgh is the present Chancellor.

Among the eminent teachers

today is John Erickson, Professor of Politics and adviser to President Ronald Reagan on vital issues of strategic arms and defence. Professor Geoffrey Beale of the genetics department is also a widely respected expert in his field.

Today, Edinburgh University's reputation in the fields of medicine and science remain pre-eminent. The modern science complex at Kings Buildings undertakes far-reaching and invaluable research, whilst many an advocate has studied within the traditional grandeur of the Old College. If the university offers no immediately recognizable identity perhaps the answer lies in its size. For character, humour, endeavour and achievement abound here

– even if the university chooses to keep quiet about it.

The main part of Edinburgh's second university, the Heriot-Watt, stands in the woodlands of Riccarton estate on the western side of the city. Founded in 1821 as a school providing evening classes in basic science for young artisans, it later took the name of the Watt Institution and School of Arts in memory of James Watt, developer of the steam engine. From a rented hall in long-demolished Adam Square, it moved to premises in Chambers Street where, in 1885, it became the Heriot-Watt College as a result of an amalgamation with George Heriot's hospital. The college achieved university status in 1966.

Thomas Shepherd's nineteenth-century view of Edinburgh University.

Medicine

From the horrors of plague rose a city renowned for medical research

For centuries Edinburgh has had the reputation of being a great centre of medical progress – and of being one of the unhealthiest, dirtiest cities in Europe. From the earliest times disease was rife and the streets were clogged with refuse and sewage tossed at night from high tenement windows to the cry of 'gardyloo'.

In 1504, despite attempts at quarantine, bubonic plague hit the city badly. Victims were removed forcibly from the city, mass graves were excavated in areas like Bruntsfield Links. For the first time efforts were made to clean the city – the streets were cobbled and stray pigs and dogs killed.

But conditions still deteriorated and another major plague devastated the city in 1645. Ten years later Oliver Cromwell visited and was so concerned at the filth that he appointed a Town Scavenger to clear the main streets. But even that had little effect on the rat-infested closes.

By this time, though, ideas

Joseph Lister, who pioneered antiseptics, used this carbolic spray and these surgical tools. Above is the first edition of the *Edinburgh Medical Journal.*

from Europe were filtering through to Edinburgh. Robert Sibbald set up a practice with Andrew Balfour and in 1670 established a Physic Garden which had more than 1800 plants in it to supply the town's 20 or so physicians with their prescription ingredients. The garden formed the basis of the Royal Botanic Garden, the second oldest of its kind in the British Isles.

In 1681 Sibbald founded a Royal College under a patent from Charles II which became one of the focal points of medical research. Sixteen years later Edinburgh surgeons opened their first fully equipped anatomy theatre giving the public a chance to view dissection. Only hanged criminals could be used for such purposes but body-snatching soon provided plenty of corpses and became so widespread that in 1725 the enraged townsfolk rioted. The snatching went on, however, and 100 years later Robert Knox, whose dissections were well-attended social occasions, found his career in ruins when the news spread of his use of bodies brought in by the murderers Burke and Hare.

Progress in medicine speeded up in the eighteenth century: the first dispensary for the poor was opened at its start; in 1729 Lord Provost George Drummond helped physicians open a hospital which later grew into the largest voluntary hospital in the British Isles – the Royal Infirmary; and in 1737 Andrew Duncan founded a

The death mask of William Burke who, with his partner William Hare, committed between 16 and 30 murders to provide bodies for dissection. The pocket book was made from Burke's own skin.

Burke

'James' Barry, the city's first woman doctor, was awarded a medical degree in 1812. Throughout her life she had assumed the male identity necessary to achieve her goal. It was only at the autopsy that her sex was revealed.

In the early twentieth century medicine became more specialized, with the opening of the first post-graduate courses for specialists at the Royal College and the University in 1906.

Today the city's reputation for medical research is still high – particularly in the development of equipment. The ultrasound scanner, which produces pictures of internal organs by bouncing sound waves off them, was first commercially produced here and at the Medical Research Council the world-renowned brain metabolism and human genetics units flourish.

the insane and 50 years or so later the new Nightingale system of nursing was introduced to the city's hospitals. At last patients could expect care more or less in accordance with Lister's instruction to the medical profession to 'put yourself in the patient's place'.

medical students' club which later became the Royal Society of Medicine.

The teaching of medicine also forged ahead as William Cullen taught the classification of diseases by symptoms for the first time and started lecturing in English rather than Latin.

In 1805 the *Edinburgh Medical and Surgical Journal* – the first of its kind – was published with articles by the two great surgeons Robert Liston and James Syme. Syme's assistant was Joseph Lister who pioneered the use of carbolic acid in surgery to prevent wounds going septic and later was the first medical peer.

James Young Simpson discovered the anaesthetic properties of chloroform. Legend has it that his first 'guinea pigs' were guests at a dinner party at his home. His wife came in to find the assembled group literally 'under the table'.

In 1807 Andrew Duncan set up a hospital for the treatment of

Anaesthetics pioneer. James Young Simpson owned this medicine chest, pill box and primitive stethoscope.

Cooking

From Bawd Bree to Bubblyjock – a distinctive culinary repertoire

The visitor to Edinburgh who associates Scottish cooking with such deadly sounding dishes as haggis and black bun is in for a pleasant surprise. Blessed with a wealth of natural produce from its rich land and teeming waters, Scotland has developed a culinary repertoire of exceptional quality and variety. Partridge, grouse and pheasant from the rolling moorlands, venison from the red deer running wild in the mountains, salmon and trout from Highland rivers, succulent beef from the Aberdeen Angus herds, shellfish of all kinds – with ingredients like these, only a truly lamentable cook could fail to come up with a feast.

Edinburgh folk tend to look back to bygone days when the streets of the capital rang to the cries of 'oyster wives' and vendors of everything from hot peas to Het Pints – a brew of ale, eggs and whisky flavoured with nutmeg and sold from a steaming copper kettle. Those were the times when a fish dinner, including ale and perhaps a dozen oysters, cost little more than one cigarette does now. As far back as the thirteenth century, salmon was so plentiful that it was pickled for export to London to be fed to the poor, and only a hundred years ago servants in big houses had contracts stipulating that it was to be served to them no more than three times a week.

But those are bygone days indeed. The allure of traditional Scottish fare, however, has carried through to modern times in all but price. Breakfast and tea have a special place in Scottish cooking, and the visitor who might think of these meals as something light has another think coming. It was Dr. Samuel Johnson who wrote: 'If an epicure could remove by a wish in quest of sensual gratification, he would breakfast in Scotland.' Oatmeal is still a staple of the national diet, and certainly most of the older people start the day with a bowl of porridge – flavoured with salt, not sugar, please. Then come the soft warm rolls known as baps, kippered herring from Loch Fyne or smoked haddock ('smokies') from Aberdeen and Arbroath, scones and oatcakes with heather honey, jams, jellies and marmalade, claimed by Scots as their own invention. Tea is the occasion for another mammoth spread of cold meats and eggs, potato scones, crunchy shortbread and such delicacies as Dundee cake, a fruity concoction strewn with almonds.

An elaborate dinner or late supper will bring out the matchless smoked salmon, rich dark venison or feathered game, roast beef or tender mutton, perhaps lobster from the Firth of Forth. Auld Alliance, a savoury of creamed cheese laced with whisky and served with hot buttered toast, can be a superb climax to the meal.

The visitor who comes across haggis or black bun should not be put off by the unappetizing names. Haggis consists of the heart, liver and lights of a sheep, cooked with oatmeal and onions inside its stomach bag. Hard to believe, but it's delicious. Black bun, also known as Scotch bun, is a tasty cake made with raisins, cur-

rants, almonds, ginger, cinnamon and brandy.

The names of many Scottish delicacies are nothing if not colourful. A few examples: Bawd Bree (hare soup), Bubblyjock (roast turkey), Cock-a-Leekie (chicken and leek soup), Inky-Pinky (beef and carrot stew), Stovies (sliced potatoes cooked with onions and lamb) and Melting Moments (biscuits in rolled oats).

Scottish food at its best – the supreme high tea with the delights of bannocks and baps; Finnian haddie topped with poached egg for breakfast; and a fine brew from an ancient house to ease the evening.

Edinburgh Castle

The impenetrable fortress of Edinburgh Castle has been besieged and attacked numerous times in its 1300 year history but it has rarely been overwhelmed. It stands today as a memorial to the turbulent history of a nation.

This drawing of Edinburgh Castle, perched high above the Grassmarket, is by the artist Thomas H. Shepard and was published in 1829.

dinburgh Castle dominates the city below. This is no accident but a deliberate strategy of its many military designers and part of the secret of its success as a fortress. For nearly 500 years the stone edifices topping Castle Rock were regularly under siege and, though famine and maybe even betrayal led their garrisons to surrender, the Castle was never once successfully stormed.

Twentieth-century visitors can pass freely through these once impregnable defences but can only penetrate the castle's mysteries by understanding its history. It has served as a fort, palace, prison, garrison, arsenal, armoury and as a repository for the State regalia.

Castle Rock is the basalt core of one of the five extinct volcanos in the Edinburgh area. It rises 435 feet (133 m) above sea level and Ice Age glaciers made the north and south sides almost vertical. The summit can only be easily approached from the ridge on the east, and the west side, steep enough to be defended, providing grazing for animals. These factors, plus the presence of springs of good water, made it a natural stronghold.

However, though there is a wealth of evidence of prehistoric man in Holyrood Park there is none on the rock. The Romans do not appear to have made much of its potential either, although it was marked on Ptolemy's second-century map of the Roman Empire as Castrum Alatum, because of its supposed similarity to an outspread eagle. Accounts of its occupation by Picts and Saxons are mainly guesswork though this occupation lasted almost a millenium. It is widely thought the Picts held the rock until 452 when the Saxons of Northumbria took over and it changed hands frequently thereafter. A Welsh poem, the Gododdin, records a sixth-century king of the region feasting in his fortification of Dun Edin before setting out to attack the Anglo-Saxons; this probably refers to Castle Rock. Over this period the Saxons are believed to have had more influence than the Picts in this southern area of Scotland and, though the connections are hardly direct, Edinburgh is still the most Anglicized of Scottish cities.

It was the Saxon queen, Margaret, wife of Malcolm III, who can be held partly responsible for Edinburgh's development in the eleventh century. In the Middle Ages the capital moved around the kingdom with the court. Malcolm Canmore, son of Shakespeare's Duncan and successor to Macbeth, had his capital in Dunfermline but his wife thought civilization lay further south. The crude fortress on the hill was converted to a royal residence and the name Castle Rock originates from this period. Margaret's own chamber there was said to have been furnished more luxuriantly than any in Scotland at that time. She was living there when the news of her husband's and eldest son's deaths in England reached her in 1093 and she died on the rock the same year.

Her death was followed by events to be repeated frequently in the nation's history – a disputed succession and siege of the Castle. Both attempts failed and her youngest son was crowned Scotland's next king in 1124. David I is thought to have built the summit's only surviving twelfth-century structure, a chapel dedicated to his mother's memory. But he also shaped the first real settlement around the Castle which stretched as far as the present intersection of High Street and South Bridge. David I was the first to use the Castle for the assembly of earls, barons and churchmen which later became the Parliament of Scotland.

The pattern of alternating occupation of the fortress by Scots and English started in the late twelfth century. It was held by an English garrison between 1174 and 1186 but was safely back in Scots hands when their first official parliament was convened there by Alexander II in 1215. His son, Alexander III, made it a repository for the kingdom's records and regalia. On his death the succession to the throne was disputed and the English king, Edward I, called in as umpire, settled this by burning the town and seizing the castle in 1296 after a three-day siege. The Scots virtually razed the Castle to the ground in 1313 to prevent further domination by their foes from this stronghold. Only St.

Margaret's Chapel was left standing.

The Castle began to take on more of its present form in the late fourteenth century. King David II returned from captivity in England in 1356 and built a 60-foot-high tower on the site of the present Half Moon Battery to protect the Castle's east side. This defence, known as David's Tower, was so strong it withstood a major attack by Henry IV and succumbed only to the massive bombardment of English cannon in 1573.

The next monarchs strengthened David's fortifications along the east, extending them to end in the Constable's Tower. In the 1430s James I moved the royal accommodation out of David's tower stronghold to the site of the present palace block. This move did not prove as fatal for James I as his choice of Perth as a centre for his court and parliament. His assassination there in 1437 increased the importance of Edinburgh as its Castle was considered the safest in the land.

Perhaps it was safe for the nation's rulers but not for others with any claim to the throne. In 1440 when the boy King James II lived there, his regents Crichton and Livingstone lured two rivals, the young Douglas brothers, to a feast in the Castle's hall. When the food was brought to the table, the main course was a black bull's head, a symbol of death. The boys were taken from this meal, since known as the Black Dinner, to a mock trial, after which they were beheaded.

James III was so suspicious of his own brothers claiming his crown that he kept them imprisoned, holding the Duke of Albany in David's Tower in 1479 while he lived in the adjacent royal apartments. But Albany escaped after luring his guards into his chamber to drink wine before a blazing fire, killing them when they became drowsy and roasting them in full armour on the fire. Ironically, before long James III was imprisoned for two months in David's Tower, to be released by the intervention of his former captive brother, Albany. Under James III, Edinburgh was finally declared the chief town in the kingdom and the permanent seat for the Scottish Parliament.

After the crowing of James IV in 1489, life took on a brighter look at the Castle and its tournaments brought it fame throughout Europe. His building programme included the splendid Great Hall which still stands, mounted on a vaulted structure over the southern rockface. Though the Palace was also improved, the Castle was no longer used as the Royal household's main residence. This era of success ended on Flodden Field in 1513 when James IV and his army of more than 100,000 suffered, at the hands of the English, the worst military disaster in Scottish history.

James V is thought to have taken little interest in the Castle. However, during his reign the Castle's captain built a bake house and a brewery near the well house. The Flodden Wall was begun as a defence against the expected invasion of the English. But when the army arrived a full 31 years later it was still unfinished and drawings made by an English agent in 1544 show the eastern defences still dominated by David's Tower. The castle was not seriously harmed in this attack but an Italian engineer was nevertheless engaged to build an artillery bastion before the crosswall, using the latest Italian techniques.

By the time Mary, Queen of Scots began her reign, Edinburgh Castle was the nation's main armoury, making and storing gunpowder and artillery. In 1566 the armaments included at least 25 cast bronze guns, many of which were used in sieges

The huge vaults, built to create a level surface for the Great Hall above them, are best known for holding foreign prisoners-of-war. The Hall was built in James IV's time for communal living. It became a barracks in 1650 and later a hospital. The restoration, rather too romantic, was done between 1887 and 1891.

1 Esplanade
2 Statue of Robert the Bruce
3 Statue of William Wallace
4 Gatehouse
5 Gateway to the Castle
6 Portcullis Gateway
7 Disused stables
8 Forewall Battery
9 Lang Stairs
10 Saint Margaret's Chapel
11 Water reservoirs
12 Foog's Gate
13 Scottish United Services Museum
14 Dury's Battery
15 Vaults/French Prisons
16 Great Vault/Mons Meg
17 Great Hall
18 Palace
19 Half Moon Battery
20 Twentieth-century Naafi building
21 Seventeenth-century ditch
22 Crown Square
23 Scottish National War Memorial
24 The Well

The inset, on the right, shows the whole Castle, with the major buildings, in the shaded area, detailed below.

A side door, or sallyport, led from the old Castle wall to the moat that used to front the Castle in the sixteenth century. A drill hall and Tattoo storehouse were built over them in the nineteenth century.

The remnants of the tower house built by David II are here visible beneath the walls of Half Moon Battery. The tower, dating from about 1356, was knocked down in the 1573 siege. The battery, an artillery platform, was built on the rubble, overlooking the main entrance.

9

7

6

5

4

3

2

20

21

1

St. Magaret's Chapel

The Constable's Tower

David's Tower

circa 1450

The Castle walls, built on the orders of David II, were passive defences. The occupants relied heavily on the natural advantage of Castle Rock and the thickness of the walls rather than on their military skills for protection of the King's Edinburgh residence.

Kitchens
Great Hall

Portcullis Gate
The Palace

Half Moon Battery

circa 1647

The

New Barracks
Magazine and Armoury
Governor's House

Queen Anne Barracks
St. Margaret's Chapel extended

circa

around the country. Although Holyrood Palace was preferred to the Castle as a residence, Mary chose to give birth to the future king of Scotland and England, James VI and I, in the Castle, so long a symbol of the Scottish crown. The Castle was the last place to uphold Mary's cause in the most destructive siege in its history.

Sir William Kircaldy of Grange held the Castle against incredible odds for three years for the exiled Queen. There is a suspicion that he finally turned traitor as the attackers sent suddenly for help from Queen Elizabeth I. These reinforcements included 30 cannon sent by sea and by May 1573 five batteries were set up surrounding the Castle. David's Tower eventually collapsed, blocking the Castle's main well and within weeks there was no food, water or provisions. The Castle surrendered but contrary to the agreement made, Kirkcaldy and other leaders were hanged, beheaded and their heads displayed.

The Castle was put in the

Edinburgh was, by now, the capital of Scotland. More active defences, like the artillery platforms of the Half Moon Battery and the earthworks at the entrance, were needed because the Castle was a repository for state records, the Royal Mint, the armoury and the Royal Household.

hands of Regent Morton and he rebuilt the eastern defences much in their present form. Records show the massive Half Moon Battery cost £743 6s 6d and the expense led Morton to devalue the Scots currency. The Castle became a fortress seldom visited by kings, although huge sums were spent to extend and redecorate the Palace for the homecoming of James VI.

The Castle came under serious siege three times within 50 years during the seventeenth century, though no assault breeched the walls. Most impact on the defences was made by the Covenanters Army, Presbyterian loyalists,

besieging a company of English soldiers. They held out for three months and were allowed to leave with honour.

In 1649 and 1650 the Castle was made even more impregnable when the citizens of Edinburgh were used as forced labour to demolish the spur in front of it. Though the Castle, ammunition and provisions all seemed to be holding up against Cromwell's attack in 1650, General Dundas surrendered to him. The Castle's reputation was redeemed by the Duke of Gordon, holding the Castle for the exiled Old Pretender in 1689 against the forces of William and Mary. In three months the brave and steadfast Duke cost his attackers 500 lives before famine and disease forced him to give in.

The guns of the Castle fired in March 1707 then the Act of

The Unions of Crowns in 1603 and of Parliaments in 1707 had taken the Royal Court and administration south so the Castle was no longer needed for defence. The Scottish Army used the Great Hall as a barracks and Napoleonic War prisoners were kept in the vaults.

Union was read to the last Scottish Parliament; the Scottish Honours, including the Crown Jewels, were taken to the Palace building and immured. Sir Walter Scott, who played a major part in their rediscovery, said this was because 'these emblems, connected with so many galling and hostile recollections of past events, could be no safe spectacle for the public eye, while Men's minds were agitated by the supposed degradation of Scotland beneath her ancient enemy.'

The Castle came under attack only twice more, both attempts made by Jacobite forces and neither coming near to success. The first was in 1715 when a bold plan was formulated to scale the Castle's wall by night and prepare it for the Highland armies en route to England. But a combination of betrayal and bad planning turned this assault into a fiasco. Bonnie Prince Charlie fared no better in 1745. He was wel-

comed by the citizens of Edinburgh but the Castle troops fired first on Holyroodhouse, then on the houses nearby, giving one the name Cannonball House from the shot embedded in its gable. The Stuart colours finally reached the Castle, displayed as spoils of war after the Young Pretender's defeat at Culloden.

A regular army, an innovation introduced in the midseventeenth century, kept a permanent garrison at the Castle from that time. Now the fortress's main military function was as a barracks and prison, especially during the Seven Years' and Napoleonic Wars with France. At the beginning of the nineteenth century as many as 1000 prisoners of war were kept in the Castle. Most were lodged in the vaults under the Great Hall, since known as the French Prisons. Their skill in carving can be seen in graffiti on the vault walls and handiwork made, for sale, now on

The War Memorial was built and restoration work, begun by an Army officer, Gore Booth, in the late nineteenth century, was continued. Statues of the national heroes, Wallace and Bruce, were also erected and the Castle's popularity as a tourist attraction grew.

orks

rade Ground

Hospital

Military Prison

Scottish United Services Museum

St. Magaret's Chapel restored

War Memorial   circa 1930

Esplanade

view in the Castle's military museum. But they also carved mutton bones to make watermarks on forged banknotes. So skilful were these forgeries that advertisements appeared in the press offering rewards for information on the prisoners' lucrative sideline.

The prisoners were said to be kept in humane conditions but soldiers stationed at the Castle did not enjoy a much higher standard of accommodation. Up to 1000 could be lodged in barracks there at once and a 1791 census includes 159 women and 131 children. A mid-nineteenth century report described the married quarters as the worst in the United Kingdom, with no privacy and so insanitary that epidemics were rife. Even the New Barracks completed in 1799 are very austere. Troops were stationed at the Castle before serving overseas in India, North America or the Continent. The Castle was a major barracks until 1923 when the Redford Barracks south of the city were opened.

The process of restoration of Edinburgh Castle, begun in the nineteenth century, owes much to Sir Walter Scott's interest in it. He was named on a royal warrant, along with the Scottish Officers of State, allowing them to break open the oak chest in the Crown Room which was thought to contain the Scottish Honours. The Crown, Sceptre and Sword of Scotland were found inside, intact but dusty, and have only been hidden from public view twice since – during the two World Wars.

St. Margaret's Chapel was discovered by accident, as was the true nature of the Great Hall. Restoration work on the latter deviated rather a long way from its original state, but with far less damage to the Castle than would have occured if other grandiose Victorian schemes for 'improvements' had been allowed.

The age-old connection between Edinburgh Castle and military life still continues. It is the site of the National War Memorial and houses the Scottish United Services Museum. It is the headquarters for the Lowlands and the Scottish Division and the Regimental Headquarters of the Royal Scots and Royal Scots Dragoon Guards. It also has the only Army School of Piping in the country and is the real home of a few fortunate families of warders. Since 1947 the Castle has achieved international fame through its annual Military Tattoo, held on the Esplanade. But today the only invaders besieging Edinburgh Castle are tourists.

Castle Rock

Visitors to Castle Rock today need an active imagination to see why the site was an obvious choice for a defensible stronghold. The buildings of the Old Town nestle snugly up towards the defences and the North Loch has been filled in and turned into Princes Street Gardens and the railway station. But throughout most of its history Castle Rock had a far more cragged appearance and the broad terraces and sweeping approach roads are products of extensive levelling in the eighteenth and nineteenth centuries, when the fortress' working life was almost over.

The Esplanade

The Esplanade did not exist when the Castle was under siege. It was built as a parade ground in 1753 using earth from the foundations of the Royal Exchange building to level and widen the ridge formed by glacial action. The ornamental walls were added in 1812 and 1820. The Esplanade, with its

Surmounted by the Royal Arms of Scotland and flanked by statues of Robert the Bruce and William Wallace, this gatehouse was built as an entrance worthy of the Castle rather than as a true fortification.

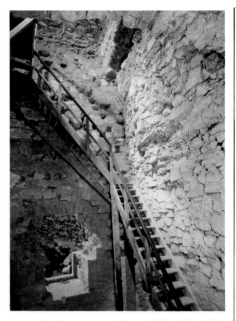

Above The cannon standing on the Half Moon Battery are 18-pounders made at the Carron Iron works near Falkirk.

Right This staircase links the remnants of the vaults in David's Tower with the battery platform above.

magnificient views of the city and its surroundings, has a blaze of glory each year when it is used for the Military Tattoo, but otherwise serves as the Castle car park.

The Gatehouse

The Gatehouse is not part of the real defences of the Castle but a symbolic entrance way built in 1887; its statues of Robert the Bruce and William Wallace were added in 1929. However, the ditch in front of it was started by Cromwell in the mid-seventeenth century, and only completed a century later. Its unusual shape allowed coverage from the walls and this three-sided form is echoed in the design of the later gatehouse. The retractable drawbridge was the last ever built in Scotland.

Eastern Defences

The rounded Half Moon Battery facing East is built over two storeys of the fourteenth century David's Tower, all but demolished in the great siege of

1573. Its artillery platform is at the same level as the principal buildings of the summit and the vaults were long used as a cistern to hold the Castle's water supply. The Forewall Battery extends northwards, incorporating a wall built in the 1540s. It ends in the Portcullis Gate, built over the gate-tower erected by Robert II. This had a residence for his constable on top and so was called the Constable's Tower.

The Portcullis Gate is also known as Argyle's Tower because the 9th Earl was imprisoned there before being beheaded. The upper part is an architectural oddity as it was added in Victorian times; it has openings for archers but artillery was the weaponry in use when the lower part was erected. Renaissance decoration on the original part of the gateway includes the arms of Regent Morton who rebuilt the Eastern defences in their present form, mainly in the late 1570s. Their commanding position can best be appreci-

ated by surveying from above the field of fire their guns command and then examining their invulnerability from the area below. Nevertheless, they did not survive the Civil War intact and needed to be repaired after Cromwell laid siege to the Castle in 1650.

Northern Defences

The Argyle or Six Gun Battery was constructed in the 1730s for Major General Wade. He had been called to the Scottish highlands to control the Jacobite insurgence and suggested also strengthening the north-western and northeastern approaches to Edinburgh Castle. Wade is well known in Scotland as many of the military roads and bridges he instigated were named after him. Mill's Mount Battery also looks north, giving fine views of Princes Street Gardens and the New Town, although when it was built these did not exist. The one o'clock gun is fired from its artillery platform every day. Below these batteries is the Low Defence, artillery outworks first built in the mid-sixteenth century but rebuilt in the seventeenth and eighteenth. This terrace was once used as the Governor's garden.

Cart-shed

The mid-eighteenth century cart-shed with its double pitched roofs has been frequently modified to serve different purposes. Formerly a barrack and an ammunition store it now serves as the Castle's tea room.

Governor's House

Several of the buildings inside the walls of the Castle are in styles pre-dating the era in which they were erected. In the case of the Governor's House with its crow-stepped gables the result is a happy one. Built in 1742 with wings to house the Master Gunner and Storekeeper, it is still in active use as an Officer's Mess while the right wing is the Governor's official residence.

Hospital

A side road leads to the Hospital, a series of buildings started in the eighteenth century but extensively remodelled as a hospital in the 'improvements' era of the late nineteenth century. The north block was then reconstructed in an early seventeenth-century style but the south block retains many of its earlier features.

Western Defences

Surrounding this range of buildings are the Western Defences built on two separate levels. The lower walls follow the natural line of the rock and mostly originate in the 1730s, although a walkway existed along this level in the mid-seventeenth century. This terrace has two sentry boxes and the northern one is named the Queen's Post. The upper terrace on the north and west sides of the Hospital replaces a simpler earlier wall. The two levels are joined by a stair inside a turret at the southern junction of these defences.

Southern Defences

The Southern Defences were built to prepare the Castle for a Jacobite attack in the early eighteenth century. They were the work of Scotland's military engineer, Theodore Dury and the highest battery bears his name. The other, Butts Battery, is so-called because the bow butts used for archery practice were nearby. These two batteries were five-gun emplacements connected to the Old Back Parade by steps. The defences were completed by 1713 and withstood the Jacobite assault two years later.

The Military Prison

The Military Prison was built about 1842 for offenders from all over Scotland. The exterior is carefully designed to fit into its historic setting and the interior

to allow all prisoners to be kept in solitary confinement. The cells are grouped around a central stairway and all can be centrally heated.

The French Prisons

When James IV wanted to build his Great Hall he obtained sufficient level ground for it by constructing a vaulted substructure on the rock face. These vaults extend under the hall and further west and have had many uses, including an arsenal, barracks, bakehouse and stores. But they are now known as the French Prisons, commemorating their use for prisoners of war in the eighteenth and nineteenth centuries. At the main entrance opening on Dury's Battery is graffiti carved in the stonework. They also put their carving skills to more practical use and an impressive ship model is currently displayed in the Scottish United Services Museum.

The vaults now contain 'Mons Meg', a huge siege gun which is one of the pair given to James II by his uncle in marriage, Phillip, Duke of Burgundy, in 1457. It consists of wrought-iron bars welded into a cylinder over a wooden core and bound with iron hoops. It was probably used as a muzzle loader and could fire a 500-pound stone nearly two miles. It was moved to sieges around the country, its wheels greased with Orkney butter and tended by more than

Left Eighteenth-century graffiti. The name of *Proyol Prisonnier nee Natiffe de Bourbouurg* is engraved for ever in the stonework of the French Prisons' west entrance.

Right Mons Meg, an iron siege-gun, was forged in Flanders in 1449. It took 100 men, five carpenters and a large number of oxen to move the five-ton Meg.

Below Foog's Gate is the only archway leading to the upper enclosure. After many names, including 'foggy' and 'fogo', the mysterious 'foog' has stuck.

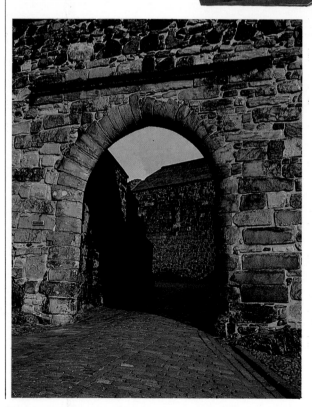

100 men. 'Mons Meg' burst while firing a birthday salute in 1681 but was later restored.

Hawk Hill

Hawk Hill is the second highest point in the Castle enclosure and came into especially heavy use in the eighteenth century. The New Barracks, which Sir Walter Scott likened to a vulgar cotton mill, was built in 1798. Earlier structures on the site included a guardhouse and artillery battery.

Foog's Gate

The road leading from Hawk Hill to the upper enclosure of the Castle passes through the protective wall by a small opening, Foog's Gate, placed so that it could be easily covered by fire from the nearby wall. This is of unknown origin but predates Charles II.

Crown Square

Crown Square is the centre of the medieval citadel but only two of its flanking buildings date from this period.

The Great Hall

The Great Hall was built by James IV and completed in the early years of the sixteenth century, but its interior has been over-imaginatively restored to the Victorian image of a medieval hall. Nonetheless it is remarkable so much survived as the building was crudely subdivided and used as a barracks and hospital for two centuries before its historic importance was realized. This hall was the meeting place of Scottish Parliaments until 1640. Earlier halls serving as communal living for the Castle household are mentioned in records but no traces survive. James IV used his hall for state ceremonial occasions and banquets. The King and his courtiers sat at the east end while the door at the west end was screened by draught-excluding timber screens. One of the hall's finest features is the hammer-beam roof, lost to view for two centuries. The restoration work done in 1887 to 1891 was financed by the publisher William Nelson.

There are many ancient and decorative features in the Great Hall.
Above The elaborate open-timbered roof.
Left A stone carving of a combined rose and thistle motif.
Below The hall has a fine display of arms and armour.

Right The Scottish Crown was remodelled in 1540 by order of James V. Together with the Sword of State and the Sceptre it is part of the Scottish Regalia.
Below In Queen Mary's Room the Old Pretender, father of Bonnie Prince Charlie, looks down from the oak panelling.
Below right The Royal Palace dates from the fourteenth century. The stair turret was turned into the Castle's main flag-staff in the early nineteenth century.

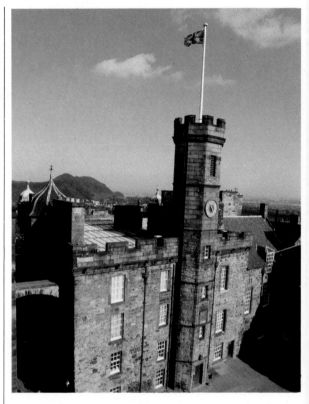

The Palace

The exterior of the Palace Block fronting Crown Square shows a compilation of styles due to the huge number of modifications made by monarchs through the ages.

Royal residences have been built on this site since James I but the basis of the present building was shaped by James IV. Two storeys and the classical windows were added between 1615 and 1617 for James VI's homecoming. The rather overbearing extension of the central turret for a flag staff was built in the early nineteenth century.

One of the most fascinating rooms inside the royal residence is the tiny bed chamber where Mary Queen of Scots gave birth to James VI of Scotland, later crowned James I of England. The entwined initials of Mary and Henry Darnley, MAH, are engraved outside the door with the birthdate – 1566. For the birth it was hung with blue velvet and taffeta but the present decorations mostly stem from the preparations for James VI's homecoming. Also of great interest is the Crown Room where the Scottish Regalia, including the Sceptre and Sword and the Crown made for James V are on display. These were walled up inside the room for over a century after the Unions of Parliaments.

The Scottish National War Memorial

The Scottish National War Memorial was created after the First World War in honour of the 150,000 Scots who died. The basic structure is an eighteenth century barracks standing on the site of the medieval church of St. Mary's which had been put to use as a munitions store. Sir Robert Lorrimer transformed the interior of the barracks into a vaulted hall with the casket holding the names of the dead at the hall's focal point. The elaborate interior includes fine stained-glass windows by Douglas Strachan. The exterior was kept simple, with most decorative detail by the entrance. The memorial was opened by the Prince of Wales in 1927 and aroused such public interest that for some months queues of visitors stretched down to the Esplanade.

The Scottish United Services Museum

The Scottish United Services Museum was founded in 1930 to house weapons, uniforms, medals and insignia of the Armed Forces, some for display and others to be kept for military historians' research. It occupies some rooms in the Palace block and also in a separate museum. This building, originally officers' quarters, was erected in 1708 over a vaulted substructure.

Saint Margaret's Chapel

St. Margaret's Chapel is the oldest building in the Castle and in Edinburgh. Its Romanesque architecture dates it as early twelfth century and it was probably built by David I in memory of his mother, Queen Margaret, who was canonized in the thirteenth century. It was a royal chapel until after Mary Queen of Scots' reign but then was linked up with other buildings and put to secular use, ending up as a powder magazine. In 1845, the garrison chaplain noticed a font-like piece of stonework which turned out to be the socket of a pillar for a chancel arch. Queen Victoria urged its restoration but the chapel became, before long, little more

The oldest structure on Castle Rock, Saint Margaret's Chapel was the only building to survive when the Castle was captured by the Earl of Moray who razed it to the ground in 1313.
Above The simple interior of the Chapel. After three centuries as a gunners' storehouse the Chapel was rediscovered in 1845 and rededicated in 1934.

than a souvenir kiosk. It was completely refurbished and finally rededicated in 1934. Though unremarkable on the outside, the interior features an arch with exquisite zig-zag ornamentation.

The Lang Stairs

The main medieval approach to the Castle's upper enclosure was a steep winding staircase which has been continued to form the Lang Stairs.

Finally, no visitor to the Castle should fail to spend time admiring the magnificent view of Princes Street Gardens, the New Town and the Firth of Forth. On a clear day Fife can be seen in the distance.

The Royal Mile

*T*he Royal Mile, a sequence of four connecting streets running roughly west to east from Edinburgh Castle to Holyrood Abbey, is the area of the city that is most steeped in history. Crossing the Esplanade below the Castle, you enter into Castle Hill, the oldest street in Edinburgh. Here you can see the development of a city from its medieval beginnings. Clustered at the start of Castle Hill and continuing along the ridge that comprises the Royal Mile are some of the most enticing sights and monuments of the city, detailing its gradual rise to one of the premier urban centres of the realm.

Castle Hill

The first building on the south side of Castle Hill is Cannonball House, built c. 1630. It derives its name from the cannonball lodged in the west wall, which tradition claims was fired from the Castle during the siege of 1745. Another explanation is that the ball marked the level to which water could rise by gravitation from the city's first piped-water system. The water was piped from Comiston Springs into the Castle Hill Reservoir, completed in 1851. It stands on the site of the first city water supply (1681) and is still in use.

To the north is Ramsey Garden, built on the site of the poet Allan Ramsay's house, which was referred to by local wits as 'Goose-pie'. Ramsay Garden is a shrine for town planners worldwide. Built in 1893 by Sir Patrick Geddes, it is the earliest example of organized town planning as we know it.

Back on Castle Hill is the Outlook Tower or Camera Obscura. Built in the seventeenth century, it was extensively altered in the 1850s by an optician who installed a camera obscura – a lens system which on a clear day projects an image of Edinburgh onto a concave white table. The lens and mirror were replaced in 1945 with a much improved system. Sir Patrick Geddes owned the house from 1892 and created one of the first museums designed to teach people about other parts of the world. Much like an old-fashioned encyclopedia, there were rooms on geography, history and natural science among others.

Opposite is Boswell's Court, a seventeenth-century tenement which is named after the uncle of James Boswell, Dr. Johnson's biographer. Just to the east of Boswell's Court is The Highland Church of Tolbooth St. John's, completed in 1844. Designed by James Gillespie Graham and Augustus W.N. Pugin, this Gothic Revival pile is topped by the highest spire in the city (240 feet/73 metres). On Sunday afternoons, services are held in Gaelic.

Crossing the street once again, you come to Semple's Close. The mansion at the foot of the close, dated 1638, was the home of Grissel, Lady Semple, widow of the 8th Lord Semple. Once a garden enclosure, these 'closes' were gradually filled in as land be-

came scarce in the walled city. The narrow lane leading from the street took on the name close.

To the east is the site of the 'Palace' of Mary of Guise, demolished in 1861 to make way for the Church of Scotland General Assembly Hall, whilst across the road at the junction of Castle Hill, Lawnmarket and Johnston Terrace is the site of the Weigh House (demolished in 1822) and commemorated by a circle of 'setts' or rectangular stone blocks. This was the place for the weighing of butter and cheese for the use of the city.

Opposite is Milne's Court, an early attempt to create some open space in the Old Town. It was created by James Mylne, master mason to Charles II in 1690. Further down and set back from the street is James' Court. Built in 1725-1727, it was once a fashionable area, with a roster of distinguished tenants. Probably the best known was the philosopher David Hume.

Continuing down the same side is Gladstone's Land. The original building dated from 1550, but in 1617, Thomas Gledstanes acquired the property and rebuilt it into a six-storey tenement. The only block of flats in Edinburgh with the original arcaded front, original painted interior decorations of the early seventeenth century still survive. Part of the National Trust of Scotland since 1935, it has recently been furnished much as it might have appeared in the last quarter of the seventeenth century.

Lawnmarket

You are now actually in The Lawnmarket (land market), originally the *agora* or marketplace of the Old Town. Here produce, butter, cheese, milk, meat and other edibles were displayed in stalls, with the exception of Wednesdays, when a special sale of linen and woollen cloth was conducted.

The close at the side of Gladstone's Land leads to Lady Stair's House, constructed in 1622 by Sir William Gray of Pittendrum. Owned in the early eighteenth century by Elizabeth, Countess Dowager of Stair, widow of the 1st Earl of Stair, it now houses memorabilia and manuscripts of three great Scottish men of letters: Robert Burns, Sir Walter Scott and Robert Louis Stevenson.

Across the Lawnmarket will be found Riddle's Close and Court, rebuilt by Captain George Riddle after 1726. David Hume lived here before moving to James' Court. In the inner court is the late sixteenth-century mansion of Bailie John McMorran, shot to death by one of the students of the high school. The Bailie's house was nevertheless of high repute, and was borrowed in 1598 (three years after his death) by the Town Council for a banquet in honour of James VI and his Queen.

Next to Riddle's Close is Brodie's Close. One of the more colourful characters in the history of Edinburgh, Deacon William Brodie (son of Francis, after whom the Close is named) was a respected cabinetmaker and member of the town council by day and a burglar by night. His success was not without hazard however. On October 1, 1788, along with an accomplice, he was hanged at the Tolbooth on a scaffold of his own design. Robert Louis Stevenson used Deacon Brodie as the model for *Dr. Jekyll and Mr. Hyde.*

Just past the George IV Bridge, you will find one of the last remaining wells in the Old City. At one time ten public wells existed in different locations.

In front of St. Giles' Cathedral is the site of the Edinburgh Tolbooth, marked by a brass plaque in the roadway and a heart-shaped design of setts. The Tolbooth may well have dated from the last years of the fourteenth century. Since then it has accommodated the Scottish Parliament, Edinburgh Town Council and the Courts of Law, as well as being used for executions and as a prison. As a jail, it was immortalized by Sir Walter Scott in *The Heart of Midlothian.*

Though a church has existed on the site of St. Giles' Cathedral since AD 854, the present structure dates, in this form, from 1829, when the exterior was clad in ashlar. However, the four central pillars date from about 1120 and the crown spire was completed in 1495. Actually, it is more appropriate to refer to the Church as the High Kirk of Edinburgh since it was a cathedral proper only for the five years following the introduction of bishops to the Presbyterian Church of Scotland by Charles I. After the Revolution of 1688, the title remained. The rather gaudy Chapel of the Order of the Thistle was added in 1911. The name St. Giles derives from a Greek hermit who settled in Provence in the sixth century.

Commemorated in the interior, amongst others, are the Regent Moray, who was assassinated, and two implacable enemies, the 1st Marquis of Argyll and the 1st Marquis of Montrose, both of whom were executed.

Behind the cathedral are located Signet Library and Parliament Hall. The Library is reached by passing through the narrow passage to the top half of Parliament Square. The Upper Hall is perhaps one of the finest bits of Georgian interior design in all of Edinburgh. The buildings themselves were finished in 1815 and are still in use by the Writers to HM Signet, now the principal body of solicitors in Scotland.

Parliament Hall was built at the behest of Charles I. It was the home of the Scots Parliament from 1639 to 1707 and the Treaty of Union. Since that time it has been the seat of Scotland's supreme courts.

The Hall contains a magnificent seventeenth-century hammer-beam roof and stained-glass windows depicting the inauguration of the Court of Session by James V in 1532. Below the Hall is the Laigh (low) Hall which Cromwell once used as a stable.

Two statues beside Parliament Hall are worth your attentions. To the west is a figure of John Knox by Pittendrigh McGillivray, erected in 1906 not far from Knox's grave; whilst to the east is the oldest lead equestrian statue in Britain, erected in 1688, of Charles II. Due east of the façade of Parliament Hall is the Mercat Cross. This marks the spot where merchants gathered to conduct business. Also the scene of assorted executions and other public celebrations, the Cross was the place from which Royal Proclamations were read. The Cross itself is nineteenth century with only a small section of the shaft left from the original sixteenth century erection.

High Street
The stretch of the Royal Mile from the Cathedral to opposite John Knox's House is known as the High Street.

The most imposing building on the High Street is the City Chambers, erected in 1761 as the Royal Exchange. It is now the meeting place of the Edinburgh City District Council. Within the arches facing the street are war memorials for 1914-1918 and 1939-1945.

New Assembly Close, opposite, leads to a courtyard containing the Edinburgh Wax Museum. From 1736 to 1784, members of 'society' staged charity balls here. Later used by the Commercial Bank of Scotland,

the building was opened as the Wax Museum in 1976. The famous and infamous figures of Scotland's past are members of the cast, alone and in historical tableaux: Mary, Queen of Scots, John Knox, Robert Burns and Burke and Hare.

Tron Church (Kirk) founded in 1637 and opened for worship in 1641, was meant for the part of the congregation for whom there was not room in St. Giles. Named after the 'trone' or salt-weighing machine standing to the north, the great fire of 1824 destroyed the spire and did other extensive damage. The present steeple was erected in 1828. Closed as a church in 1952, and with the exterior restored, Tron Kirk is still the congregation point on Hogmanay, Old Year's Night.

Further down the hill at the bottom of the High Street, next to John Knox's House, is to be found Moubray House, with traces of the structure going back to 1477. The painter George Jamieson lived here in the 1630s, and Daniel Defoe edited the *Edinburgh Courant* from here in 1710.

John Knox's House is the last house on the street to retain its top storey wooden gallery, saved by the supposed connection with the great religious reformer when plans for widening the street were proposed in 1849. Inside are displays on his life, and the architecture is a classic example of domestic structures of the time of Mary, Queen of Scots.

On the other side of the street is the Museum of Childhood, the first museum in the world devoted solely to childhood history, which contains one of the world's finest collections of toys, model dolls, hobby items and memorabilia of children.

The Canongate
The Canongate derives its name from the time when King David I gave the Augustinian canons of Holyrood permission to build on either side of their path or 'gait' between the abbey and the Royal Burgh of Edinburgh. In fact, it was a separate town, so to speak, until 1636 and did not come under the

aegis of the Edinburgh Town Council until 1856. Unlike Edinburgh proper, the Canongate was never a walled town and suffered accordingly. However, after James IV began building the Palace of Holyroodhouse, the area became increasingly fashionable as a residential sector for members of the court. After 1800, with the move to the more chic New Town, Canongate degenerated into a slum. After World War II, Robert Hurd led a crusade to save the Canongate houses, and the area has been restored and given a new life. Once again it has become a fashionable residential district,

'Chessel's Court, built in 1748 by Archibald Chessel, was advertised as 'neatly finished and fit to accommodate a genteel family'. In turn the building housed the Scottish Excise Office. A burglary here in 1788 led to the arrest of Deacon Brodie. Almost opposite is the Effigy of Moor, a remembrance of the tenement once here known as Morocco Land. The legend has it that in the early seventeenth century, Andrew Gray, the younger son of a noble family, was sentenced to death for leading a riot. Escaping to sea, he made a fortune in Morocco, returned to Edinburgh in the disguise of a Moor and threatened to sack the city. Instead, he cured the Lord Provost's daughter (his cousin) of the plague, married her and set up house on the spot where the cure had been effected.

Old Playhouse Close is named after the theatre opened here in 1747. The scene of several riots from passionate audiences, the theatre was closed in 1767. At its peak, the box office draw was reputedly as much as £70 per night. Box seats cost half a crown and the pit cost one and sixpence. The theatre succeeded in spite of clerical opposition and Sarah Siddons played here.

Smack in the middle of the Canongate outside Old Playhouse Close is the site of St. John's Cross, indicated by a circle of setts in the roadway. Charles I, making his ceremonial entrance into Edinburgh in 1633, was greeted by the provost, whom he knighted

in the time-honoured fashion on the spot.

Moray House, constructed about the time of Charles I accession to the throne, remained in the possession of the Moray family until the middle of the nineteenth century. Cromwell stayed here twice. The seventeenth-century plaster ceilings are in a remarkable state of preservation. In that same century the gardens were particularly famed. Now part of a teacher-training college, Moray House stands as one of the monuments to a more gracious age.

Across the street is Bible Land. Built in 1677 by the Incorporation of Cordiners (shoemakers) of the Canongate, the tenement is named after the sculpture above the stair entrance, quoting the first verse of Psalm 133. Also upon the shield are to be found the crown and rounding knife of St. Crispin, the patron saint of the shoemakers, who practised their craft within these walls. Note particularly the gables and termination of the stair tower.

Canongate Tolbooth, built in 1591 in the Franco-Scottish style, was the centre for the collection of public dues, the courthouse, the prison and the municipal affair centre for the independent borough of the Canongate. The motto of the armorial bearing of the Canongate is *Sic itur ad astra* (This is the path to the stars). Now used as a museum, it contains the J. Telfer Dunbar Tartan Collection, temporary exhibitions and a brass-rubbing centre. Here, visitors can make rubbings of moulded replicas of medieval brasses and Pictish inscriptions.

Canongate Church was built in 1688 with funds willed by Thomas Moodie of Edinburgh for the purpose of providing an alternative place of worship for parishioners displaced from the old parish church in the Abbey of Holyrood. The churchyard contains the remains of many famous Scots including the economist Adam Smith, the poet Robert Ferguson (the stone paid for by Robert Burns), and Mrs. Agnes McLehose, Burns' Clarinda. The Fergusson marker contains a verse by Burns:

No sculptured Marble here nor pompous lay
No Storied Urn nor animated bust
This simple Stone directs Pale Scotia's way
To pour her Sorrows o'er her Poet's Dust.

The original Canongate Mercat Cross is now located in the churchyard.

Across Canongate are located the Huntly and Acheson Houses. Built in 1570 for John Acheson, Huntly House was originally three separate houses as can be seen from the gables above. Restored in 1932, it is now the museum of the local history of the city. Located within are a splendid collection of silver and glass and the National Covenant of 1638, signed by citizens as a protest against Charles I's attempt to establish Episcopacy in Scotland and introduce a new service into the Church. Huntly House is also known as the 'speaking house', because of the inscriptions displayed on sixteenth-century plaques on the front of the building, supposed to have been placed there to answer criticisms as to the magnificence of the structure.

Acheson House, to the east, dates from 1633 and was built for Sir Archibald Acheson, a councillor to Charles I. Since 1952 it has been the headquarters of the Scottish Craft Centre. In a rear courtyard is a doorway topped with Sir Archibald's crest – a cock surmounting a trumpet – and the motto 'Vigilantibus' with the date, 1633.

On the north side of the Canongate, extending east from Canongate Church, are a number of interesting sites. The seventeenth-century garden, reached through Dunbar's Close, is a reconstruction of the formal gardens of the time. Panmure House, reached by way of Little Lochen Close, and once the town house of the Earls of Panmure, was the home of Adam Smith, author of *The Wealth of Nations,*

Reid's Court, named after an eighteenth-century coachmaker, was built c.1690 and was the Manse of the Canongate until 1832 and again from 1958. The Site of Golfers' Land was supposedly erected by a shoemaker, John Paterson, with his share of the winnings from a golf match. The game took place on the Leith Links and his partner was the Duke of York, later James VII and II. Whitefoord House, now home for veterans, was built in 1766, but stands on the site of 'Seton Palace' where Lord Darnley stayed on his first visit to Edinburgh.

Across from Whitefoord House stands Queensberry House, erected in 1681 by Lord Hatton. Now a hospital for the elderly, Queensberry House was bought a few years later by William, 1st Duke of Queensberry. His son, James, was the principal promoter of the Treaty of Union of 1707, a part played to the displeasure of nearly everyone in Scotland. Supposedly, when he was out gathering signatures for the treaty his eldest son, Lord Drumlanrig, who was thoroughly mad, roasted a Canongate kitchen boy and was found devouring his flesh

Just before the Canongate runs off into Abbeyhill stands the Site of Girth Cross, marked by a circle of setts in the roadway. Known to exist until 1750, the Cross was the scene of many executions and marked the sanctuary area (western boundary) that surrounded the Abbey and Palace

White Horse Close was named after the White Horse Inn, which occupied the building (1623) at the rear of the close. Now restored, this was the main coaching house for travellers to and from London.

Finally, before entering the precincts of the abbey and Palace you come to the Abbey Strand and Sanctuary, once the residence of aristocratic debtors. The 'Abbey Lairds', as they were known, were safe from arrest withing these precincts, including Holyrood Park and Arthur's Seat. Only on Sundays could they venture safely forth. The sanctuary was in effect from around 1128 until 1880 when imprisonment for debt was abolished.

And so, after a leisurely journey through the history of a city, you now stand at the gates of Holyroodhouse.

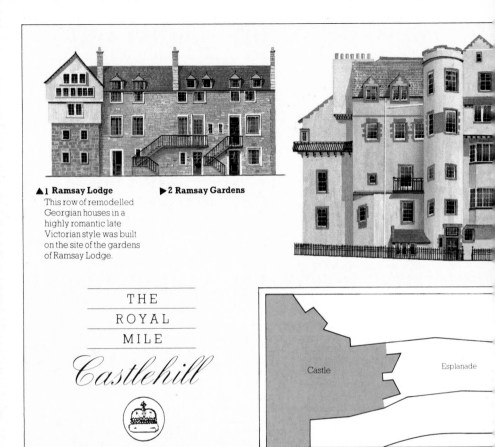

▲1 Ramsay Lodge **▶2 Ramsay Gardens**

This row of remodelled
Georgian houses in a
highly romantic late
Victorian style was built
on the site of the gardens
of Ramsay Lodge.

THE
ROYAL
MILE

Castlehill

Castle   Esplanade

◀6 Castle Gatehouse

The gatehouse was built
in 1887 to create a fitting
entrance to the Castle,
without much heed to any
military logic. The
drawbridge was the last
built in Scotland.

▶▲7 Canonball House

Legend says the ball,
lodged in the bricks, was
fired from the Castle in
the 1745 rebellion but
another theory claims it
marks the gravitation
height of the first water
supply.

▲ 3 Witches Well
The iron fountain marks the spot where hundreds of witches, 'some evil, some misunderstood', were burned to death between 1479-1722.

◀ 4 Outlook Tower
An optician, Maria Theresa Short, installed a camera obscura here in the 1850s. A new lens and mirror were added in 1945 and the camera still gives a fine panoramic view of the city.

▼ 5 Tolbooth Kirk
The kirk was built in 1842-1844 for the General Assembly of the Church of Scotland and the Tolbooth congregation. It has the tallest spire in the city – 240 feet (73m).

◄▲ 1 Wardrop's Court
In 1790 a burgess and wright of the city, John Wardrop, built a tenement here. Four dragon figures guard the entrance and Lady Stair's house rises from within.

THE

ROYAL

MILE

Lawnmarket

◄ 4 Gladstone's Land
This six-storey tenement, completed in 1620, housed burgess Thomas Gledstanes. The main rooms now show a typical seventeenth-century home and the original shopbooths display period goods.

► 5 Milne's Court
This reconstruction of the city's first open square was named after the Master Mason to King Charles II, James Mylne, who designed the extensions to Holyroodhouse and the Castle.

◀▼ 3 Lady Stair's House
Relics of the writers Scott, Burns and Stevenson are on show in this 1622 house. The latter's possessions include the riding boots, crop, spurs and cap that he wore in Samoa.

Bank Street

St Giles Street

3

1

Lawnmarket

Parliament Square

◀ 6 James' Court
David Hume and James Boswell both lived here; Adam Smith and Dr. Johnson were visitors. The court, which has three entrances, was built between 1725 and 1727 by a wright, James Brownhill. The original, destroyed in 1857, was rebuilt.

▲ 7 Deacon Brodie's Tavern
This tavern was named after the infamous William Brodie, respectable citizen by day, burglar by night.

Across the street is Brodie's Close, named after William's father, a glass-grinder and burgess of the city. William lived there before his hanging in 1788.

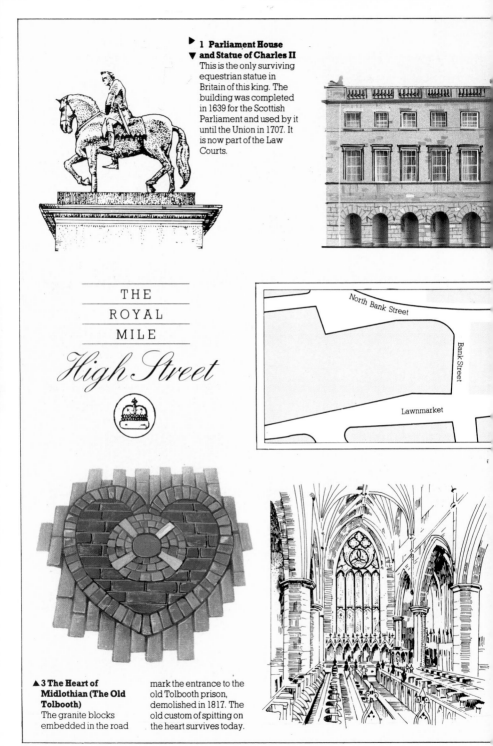

1 Parliament House and Statue of Charles II

This is the only surviving equestrian statue in Britain of this king. The building was completed in 1639 for the Scottish Parliament and used by it until the Union in 1707. It is now part of the Law Courts.

THE
ROYAL
MILE

High Street

3 The Heart of Midlothian (The Old Tolbooth)

The granite blocks embedded in the road mark the entrance to the old Tolbooth prison, demolished in 1817. The old custom of spitting on the heart survives today.

High Street

3

4

1

▲ 2 John Knox Statue
The religious reformer,
whose zeal led to the
establishment of the
Protestant faith in
Scotland, looks over the
site of his grave in what
was once St. Giles'
Churchyard.

▲▶ 4 St. Giles' Cathedral
Originally the city's only
parish church, some
parts date from 1100. It
became a cathedral in
1633.

◀ 1 City Chambers
The City Chambers were built as the Royal Exchange with coffee houses, flats and a printing press between 1754 and 1757. The Town Council took it over in 1811.

▶ 2 Edwardian placard
One of a series of enamelled Edwardian advertisements on the front of the Waverley Cameron Pen Company Building in Blair Street.

THE
ROYAL
MILE

High Street

WAVERLEY

PEN
THE WORLDS FAVOURITE

▲▶ 3 Mercat Cross
The first cross, a focus for the market where royal proclamations were read, dates from 1365. The present one, paid for by Gladstone, used the shaft of a cross demolished in 1756.

North Bridge

High Street

5

Hunter Square

4

2

◀ 5 Tron Kirk
Founded in 1637 by Charles I for those displaced when St. Giles became a cathedral, this church is named after a tron, or weighing machine, that stood on the site.

◀▼ 4 Edinburgh Wax Museum
The 1766 New Assemblies Hall now houses the city's Wax Museum based on the work of the Gems family. Mary, Queen of Scots, and a scene from *Alice in Wonderland* are included.

◀ 1 Museum of Childhood
This sign gives a taste of the charms of a large and varied collection of historic dolls, games and hobbies inside.

▲ 2 Paisley Close
These words, above the entrance to the close, were the cry of a boy trapped under rubble when tenements nearby collapsed in 1861.

THE

ROYAL

MILE

High Street

High Street

Blackfriars Street

◀ 5 John Knox's House
The house, possibly the oldest dwelling in the city, dates from 1490. It belonged to Mariota Arres and her husband James Mosman and their initials decorate the

outside. Knox may have lived here from 1561 to 1572. It was bought by the Church of Scotland, became a museum in 1853 and was again restored in 1958.

3 Netherbow Port

The brass plate marks the position of the last Netherbow Port, one of six city gates, built in 1513 and demolished in 1764. The heads of criminals and preachers were displayed there.

▶ 4 Moubray House

Built around 1462, this was a tavern in the eighteenth century, Daniel Defoe's office, and later Constable's bookshop. In 1890 the upper floors were a temperance hotel.

◀ 6 St Patrick's Church

Like many of the later public buildings of the Old Town, St Patrick's Church is tucked away in a close. Originally a Church of England chapel, it was consecrated as Episcopal Church, Cowgate in 1771; it changed its name to its present one in 1856, when it became a Roman Catholic church.

▲ 1 The Tolbooth

Built in 1591 as a council chamber, court house and jail, the tower of the Tolbooth is set with fearsome, but useless, gun ports. The clock was added in 1884.

THE
ROYAL
MILE

Canongate

Canongate

New Street

St Mary's Street

4

6

◄ 3 Bakehouse Close

A property in the close was once owned by the Incorporation of Bakers of the Canongate. The archway was formed in 1570. Records from 1851 show that 230 people lived here.

► 4 Morocco's Land

This tenement is named after the stone, life-sized figure of a Moor, which was probably a late seventeenth-century merchant's sign, but the motto has long since been erased.

▶ 2 Huntly House

Built as a row of sixteenth-century houses and remodelled by the Incorporation of Hammermen in 1647, Huntly House was rescued from ruin to form a museum in the 1930s.

Canongate

St John Street

1

5

2

3

▼ 5 Moray House

The most opulent of the early town houses, built about 1625 by Mary, Dowager Countess of Home, Moray House is now a teachers' training college.

▲ 6 Chessel's Court

Archibald Chessel, a wright, started building the Court in 1748 and Deacon Brodie was caught robbing here in 1788.

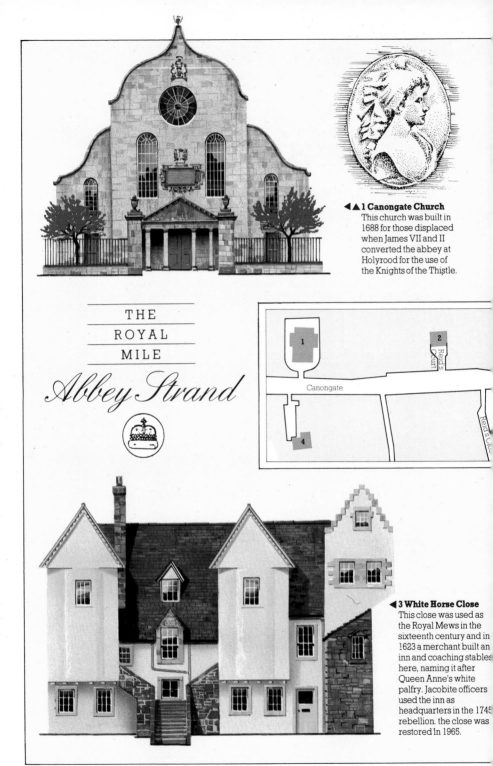

THE ROYAL MILE

Abbey Strand

1 Canongate Church
This church was built in 1688 for those displaced when James VII and II converted the abbey at Holyrood for the use of the Knights of the Thistle.

3 White Horse Close
This close was used as the Royal Mews in the sixteenth century and in 1623 a merchant built an inn and coaching stables here, naming it after Queen Anne's white palfry. Jacobite officers used the inn as headquarters in the 1745 rebellion. the close was restored in 1965.

Canongate

Reids Court

Reids

Canongate Manse

uilt in 1690 as a coaching
n, this building became
manse in 1789 and
emained one until 1832.
fter having fallen into
isrepair it was restored
1958, and once again
ecame the home of the
inister of the Canongate
hurch.

▲ 4 Acheson House
Sir Archibald Acheson,
one-time Secretary of
State for Scotland under
Charles I, built this house
in 1633. It was restored in
1937.

◀ 5 Holyroodhouse Gates
Set at the entrance to the
magnificent palace, the
wrought-iron gates were
part of the 1922 national
memorial to King
Edward VII.

At the foot of the Royal Mile stands one of the most imposing royal residences in the world. For over nine centuries Holyrood has been the scene of pomp and glory – and of bloodshed and turbulence. It is still the official Scottish home of Britain's Royal Family.

The Palace of Holyroodhouse

The splendid royal palace that conceals a gruesome and grisly past

$\mathcal{G}$littering pageantry vies with a notorious murder and a splendid but grisly funeral in the crowded history of the Palace of Holyroodhouse, official Scottish residence of Britain's Royal Family. Down the centuries, the palace has seen dark events as well as grand designs, riot combined with revelry, fire and bloodshed along with the splendours of court life.

Bonnie Prince Charlie, Mary, Queen of Scots, Oliver Cromwell and the King he beheaded, Charles I – a note of grimness and tragedy runs through many of the names so inextricably linked with the fortunes of the Palace. It came into existence as a guest house associated with the medieval abbey which was founded in 1128 by King David I after a hunting accident that he barely survived. According to legend, the King was knocked from his horse and wounded in the thigh by a stag which then tried to finish him off. But a cross miraculously appeared between its antlers, the King clutched it, and the animal slunk away, suitably crushed. In thankfulness for his deliverance, David bequeathed the land to Augustinian canons then living in Edinburgh Castle and he ordered them to build the Abbey of Holyrood, known as the 'Church of the Holy Cross'.

The guest house for royal visitors was built to the west of the now-ruined abbey. Scottish kings lodged there in its earliest use as a royal residence, and James II was born, crowned, married and buried within its walls. In 1501 James IV decided to transform the guest house into a palace fit for a king and spent large sums on new buildings. An imposing four-storey corner tower was built with a gabled roof and balustrade – it is the northwest tower of the present building and still the most eye-catching feature. After James IV's death at the battle of Flodden Field, his son carried on the work of creating royal apartments and had reception rooms and bedchambers built above the ground floor vaults.

It was on the second floor that Mary, Queen of Scots had her rooms, and some of the original decoration survives in the painted ceilings and freize of her bedchamber. Mary, regarded by Catholics as the rightful Queen of England, was dining in her small supper room authoritative work 13.9 inches thick.

Right An aerial view of the Palace of Holyrood House, with the ruined abbey in the foreground. Originally built in the forests east of the town, the Palace was much more secluded than it is today. Salisbury Crags can be seen in the background.

in the west turret on March 9, 1566, along with guests who included her Italian secretary – and hated favourite – David Rizzio. Protestant plotters accompanied by Mary's second husband, Henry, Lord Darnley, burst in over the Queen's protests and dragged Rizzio to an antechamber where they stabbed him to death. His body was left with 56 dagger wounds. A brass tablet marks the spot.

The early Palace was only about 30 years old when, in 1544, an invading English army burned down most of it – and the adjoining abbey for good mea-sure – while laying waste to the countryside around Edinburgh. The great tower survived the flames, however, and after it had been repaired and extended the Palace buildings surrounded three courtyards occupying roughly the same site as the present ones. The palace stayed largely unchanged until 1650, when an accidental fire reduced it to ruin except for the tower, whose massive walls saved it for the second time. Oliver Cromwell, who had quartered some of his troops there earlier that year while subduing the rebellious Scots, ordered major rebuilding but in a style regarded as highly inferior to the original, and it stayed that way until the monarchy was restored with Charles II.

In 1661 Holyrood saw one of the most spectacular funerals in Edinburgh's history. The royalist Marquis of Montrose, who had been executed by Cromwell for high treason and his limbs cut off for display around the country, was rehabilitated for a grand ceremony of farewell. One of his legs was brought from Aberdeen in an elaborate casket, his head from a spike in the capital, his other leg and his arms from Glasgow, Stirling and Perth, and the rest of his remains from the local gallows. After four months' lying in state in the chapel of Holyrood, the pieces of the Marquis were paraded through the crowded streets in a coffin carried by 14 earls and buried in the Kirk of St. Giles.

Although he never actually entered Holyrood, Charles II – the Merry Monarch – began building the existing Palace in 1671. It was a massive reconstruction which involved tearing down Cromwell's handiwork and erecting a new façade flanked at one end by the old tower put up by James

The Palace of Holyroodhouse.

16

15

14

13

12

The aspects of the growth of Holyrood.
Left The Abbey *circa* fourteenth century.
Right By the mid-sixteenth century Holyroodhouse had become a palace.

Two magnificent state rooms designed by Sir William Bruce for Charles II as a presence chamber and a privy chamber in the Royal Apartments.

The square closet in Charles II Tower, which looks through to the Old Council Chamber where a seventeenth-century ceiling is still intact.

The bedchamber of Mary, Queen of Scots, in James V Tower where a seventeenth-century frieze has recently been discovered. The Queen's secretary David Rizzio was dragged from one of the small chambers to his death in 1556.

1 The Outer Court
2 The Inner Court
3 The Royal Dining Room
4 The Great Stair
5 The West Drawing Room
6 The Throne Room
7 The Great Apartment
8 The Picture Gallery
9 The Lobby
10 The South Closet
11 The Bedchamber, the Inner Chamber
12 The North Closet
13 The Antechamber
14 The Outer Chamber
15 The Great Turnpike
16 The Abbey Kirk

IV more than 150 years earlier. The plans were drawn up by Sir William Bruce, a proven loyalist and fine architect, and the King's Master Mason, Robert Mylne, was called in to translate the design into stone. The total cost, sky-high for that time, was £57,000.

The Palace is built round an elegant, Italian-style courtyard quadrangle with an arcaded loggia and superimposed Doric, Ionic and Corinthian orders. On one projection there is a pediment bearing the Royal Arms, with its Scottish elements to the fore. The west front combines the medieval tower, which Charles II was anxious to retain, with the Renaissance-classicism of the grass-covered courtyard. To achieve the effect he wanted, Bruce designed a matching tower on the southwest and linked the two with a screen dominated by a grand entrance of four Doric columns surmounted by the Royal Arms of Scotland. The motto 'In Defence' is emblazoned above the crest, while at its base are the Latin words *'Nemo Me Impune Lacessit'* (No one provokes me with impunity), motto of the Most Noble Order of the Thistle. The general style of Palace architecture is French, of the time of Louis XIV. The north side of the quadrangle contains the renowned Picture Gallery, with the State Apartments on the southern side.

Work on the new Palace was well under way by 1676 and three years later it was largely completed, with the truncated abbey becoming the Chapel Royal. The clock on the cupola over the gate bears the date 1680. A variety of non-Scots took part in the interior finishing. Two Englishmen did the ornamental plasterwork, a Dutchman was responsible for the carving, and the decorative painting was by another Dutch-

Left This splendid fireplace of black veined marble is in the Morning Drawing Room. *Cupid and Psyche* are enclosed within the ornately carved wooden chimneypiece

Below The largest of the historical rooms, the Picture Gallery is still used for many state functions. Set into the panelling are the portraits of 111 Scottish monarchs.

man, Jacob de Wit.

De Wit's major legacy is to be found in the Picture Gallery – framed portraits of 111 Scottish kings and queens. A deed drawn up between Hugh Wallace, His Majesty's Cashkeeper, and de Wit 'binds and obleidges him to compleatly draw, finish and perfyte The Pictures of the Haill Kings who have Reigned over this Kingdome of Scotland... and to make them like unto the Originalls which are to be given to him'. De Wit set to with a will, but doubts have been cast on the accuracy of the likenesses he produced between 1684 and 1686 with the aid of old portraits supplied by the government. He was paid £120 a year for the work, which begins with King Fergus in the fourth century and ends with James VII – James II of England. A good deal of imagination seems to have gone into his masterpiece; more than 30 of de Wit's kings apparently never existed. Sir Walter Scott described the gallery as 'long, low and ill-proportioned, hung

Right The atmosphere of the seventeenth century is recaptured in Charles II's State Bedroom. The grand canopied bed dates from 1672.

Above The elaborate plasterwork on the ceiling is the work of Dunsterfield and Hulbert. It surrounds de Wit's *Apotheosis of Hercules*.

with pictures affirmed to be the portraits of kings who, if they ever flourished at all, lived several hundred years before the invention of painting in oil colours'. Undaunted, today's Royal Family holds state ceremonies in the gallery, which is the largest of the palace's 'historical apartments'. Representative peers of Scotland are elected in the gallery, which measures 150 feet (45 m) long,

24 feet (72 m) wide and 20 feet (6 m) high. It was here that Bonnie Prince Charlie – otherwise Charles Edward, the Young Pretender – held sparkling levees during a stay in Edinburgh in 1745.

From the Picture Gallery, the State Apartments of the James IV tower are entered through a chamber known as the Duchess of Hamilton's Drawing Room, which has ornamental ceilings and oval panels containing the cypher of Charles II. The Throne Room and drawing rooms all feature fine paintings, tapestries, furniture, panelling and ceilings. In the older part of the Palace are Lord Darnley's Rooms, consisting of an audience chamber, bedroom and dressing room with fireplaces of marble and Dutch tiles, portraits and ancient tapestry.

Queen Mary's corresponding apartments on the second floor are reached by a turnpike stair from Darnley's audience chamber. The public, by the way, has no access to a small private staircase by which the murderers of Rizzio entered the Queen's rooms on that fateful night in 1566. The supper room, where the attack on the Italian was mounted, is perhaps the most interesting of these apartments, at least for students of history. Coffered ceilings of oak are among the few fixed features left from Mary's time at Holyrood, but two panels embroidered in cross-stitch on linen canvas were genuinely

The richly carved ceiling of the Inner Chamber, or Queen's Bedroom, in James IV Tower is emblazoned with the initials of James V and his wife, Mary of Guise, mother of Mary, Queen of Scots. The panels were painted later, in the seventeenth century, and bear monarchs' emblems.

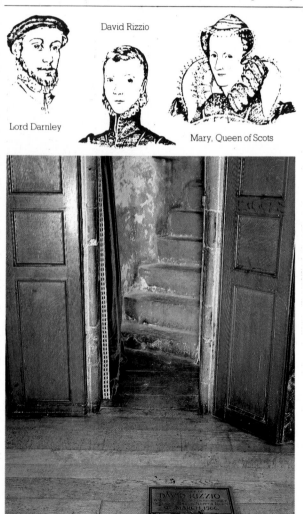

David Rizzio

Lord Darnley

Mary, Queen of Scots

The murder of Rizzio

Mary, Queen of Scots chose for her second husband in 1565 her cousin Henry Stuart, Lord Darnley. He was handsome and amusing and his claims to the English throne could bolster her own, but he was also violent, arrogant and had talents for making enemies. The royal pair soon quarrelled and when Mary was six months' pregnant with Darnley's child, he accused her of an affair with her Italian secretary. Jealous of the Queen's affection for the accomplished David Rizzio, Darnley found support for his hatred in those who thought the foreigner an undeserving, ambitious upstart. One cold night in March 1566 Darnley and his cohorts climbed the dark, hidden steps to Mary's chambers and dragged the screaming Rizzio from the Queen's supper table. In the corridor outside they stabbed him again and again. Rizzio died at Mary's feet with more than 50 wounds in his body. Darnley's dagger stood deep in his heart, left there for all to see by Darnley's accomplice, Lord Ruthven. Mary was distraught at the Italian's death but suspected that Darnley had wanted her dead too. He was killed by his enemies in an explosion at Kirk o'Field in 1567.

worked by the Queen during her imprisonment in England, where she was eventually put to death at the order of Elizabeth I. Her work is signed with her monogram, MR.

The outer room, known as Queen Mary's Audience Chamber, 24 feet (72 m) long and 22 feet (66 m) wide, has a splendid display of heraldic symbols representing the arms of James V, King of Scots; his Queen, Mary of Guise; Mary, Queen of Scots; her first husband, the Dauphin of France;

and his father, King Henry II of France. At the east end there is an oratory, and part of the freize which adorned the walls in Mary's time has been uncovered. Other panels contain the crowned initials of James V and his Queen. The initials recur in the inner chamber, called Queen Mary's Bedroom, which has panelled compartments with the emblems of Scottish sovereigns in the ceiling. The walls are hung with tapestry. More tapestry, much decayed, hangs in a small dressing room

The House of Stuart

Elizabeth Mure m(1) ROBERT II, King of Scots m(2) Euphemia of Ross
of Rowallan · d 1390

John Earl of Carrick (ROBERT III King of Scots) · Walter · Robert Earl of Fife (later Duke of Albany and Governor of Scotland) · Alexander · David Earl of Strathearn · Walter Earl of Atholl

Euphemia m Sir Patrick Graham · James Master of Atholl · Alan

Murdoch Duke of Albany

Malise Graham Earl of Strathearn · Robert Master of Atholl

David Duke of Rothesay · JAMES I m(1) Joan Beaufort m(2) Sir James Stewart 'The Black Knight of Lorne' King of Scots d 1437

JAMES II m Marie of Gueldres King of Scots d 1460 · daughters · John Earl of Atholl · James Earl of Buchan · Andrew Bishop of Moray

JAMES III King of Scots d 1488 m Margaret of Denmark · Alexander Duke of Albany · John Earl of Mar o s p · Mary m(1) Thomas Boyd, Earl of Arran o s p m(2) James, 1st Lord Hamilton

John Duke of Albany (Regent) o s p

Elizabeth m Matthew Stewart 2nd Earl of Lennox · James Hamilton 1st Earl of Arran

JAMES IV King of Scots d 1513 m Margaret Tudor m(2) Archibald Douglas 6th Earl of Angus

John Stewart 3rd Earl of Lennox · James Hamilton 2nd Earl of Arran & Duke of Châtelherault (Regent)

JAMES V m(1) Madeleine King of Scots of France d 1542 o s p m(2) Marie de Guise · Lady Margaret m Matthew Stuart ★ Douglas 4th Earl of Lennox (Regent) · John Stuart 5th Lord d'Aubigny · James Hamilton 3rd Earl of Arran d 1609

MARY, Queen of Scots m Henry Stuart Lord Darnley ex 1587

Esmé Stuart 6th Lord d'Aubigny & 1st Duke of Lennox d 1583

★ This Earl of Lennox took French nationality in 1537. From him derives the French spelling of the surname 'Stuart'.

HOUSE OF STUART
JAMES m Anne of Denmark
VI of Scotland and I of England
d 1625

Henry Prince of Wales o s p 1612 · Elizabeth d 1662 m Frederick V Elector Palatine · CHARLES I m Henrietta Maria ex 1649

Sophia d 1714 m Ernest of Hanover

CHARLES II d 1685 m Catherine of Braganza (no legitimate issue) · Mary m William of Orange · JAMES VII of Scotland m(1) Anne Hyde m(2) Mary of Modena and II of England d 1701

HOUSE OF HANOVER

WILLIAM III m MARY II d 1702 o s p d 1694 · ANNE d 1714 (no surviving issue) · JAMES 'VIII and III' m Maria Clementina d 1766 Sobieska

CHARLES EDWARD ('Charles III') d 1788 m Louise of Stolberg (no legitimate issue) · HENRY BENEDICT Cardinal Duke of York ('Henry IX') o s p 1807

o s p = died without children

which adjoins the bedroom and occupies the eastern turret of the tower. Tapestries in the State Apartments came from the looms of Flanders, Brussels and Paris in the sixteenth and seventeenth centuries, but much of the furniture dates from a later period.

Sir William Bruce's scheme for the State Apartments involved more rooms than Charles II finally decided to have. Bruce wanted to keep to the tradition of a separate suite of rooms and private stairs for the King and Queen. In each suite there was to be a guard hall, a 'presence chamber', a bedroom, dressing room and closets, planned so as to bring the bedrooms near to each other. But the King chose the eastern section for his apartments because he wanted to look out towards a garden he had made on the site of the demolished abbey's cloister. Except for her bedroom, the Queen's rooms were constructed in the southern range of the Palace. Charles also ruled out having the private chapel on the ground floor of the tower, insisting that the chapel should be at the eastern end of the long gallery where private family prayers could be said near his presence chamber.

With the building near completion, work was held up by political uncertainties and a lack of funds. The south and west quarters of the Palace were left unfinished, and a good deal of the oak panelling and plasterwork to be seen now is modern. But it fits in well with the original work – sympathetic treatment which has been credited to the Royal Family's interest since the Palace became their home in Scotland's capital.

A sun dial made in 1633 by a royal master mason graces the garden to the northwest of the James IV tower. It has carvings of various royal heraldic badges and the crowned initials of Charles I. The fountain in the palace forecourt was put up by Queen Victoria, and a small building called Queen Mary's Bath House stands in a corner of the one-time garden. She was reputed to have bathed there in wine.

During Bonnie Prince Charlie's stay in 1745, the Palace became the focus of a glittering court life, most notably the grand levee he staged in the long gallery. But then Holyroodhouse fell into disuse as a regular royal residence. The Duke of Cumberland lived there for a short time in 1746 after a punitive campaign in

Scotland, but 50 years then went by before royalty came back in the person of a refugee from the French Revolution, Count d'Artois. He lived there for four years and later returned as the exiled King Charles X, staying for three more years. James Boswell, the author and traveller, described Holyrood as 'a virtuous place where no monarch dwells'. The tide turned in 1822, however, when George IV – the first Hanoverian king to set foot on Scottish soil – held a levee in the Palace but failed to take up residence because he found it uninhabitable. Queen Victoria and Prince Albert stayed in the royal apartments in 1850 and enjoyed their visit so much that they made a habit of resting at Holyroodhouse on their travels to and from Balmoral Castle.

Repair works prevented King Edward VII and Queen Alexandra from moving into the Palace in 1903, a year after their coronation, but they delighted Edinburgh society by holding a levee there. Holyroodhouse came more frequently into royal use with the accession of King George V and Queen Mary, who paid seven state visits between 1911 and 1934. Much redecoration and renovation were authorized by the royal couple, who had several

The sumptuous bedchamber of Mary, Queen of Scots was linked to Lord Darnley's below by a private staircase in James IV Tower. The Queen's room has since been changed and the bed moved to the King's Suite in the newer part of Holyrood Palace commissioned by Charles II.

Mary worked two of these panels when she was in the custody of George Talbot, 6th Earl of Shrewsbury. The cat and mouse expressed her own situation. Bess of Hardwick, George's wife, embroidered the third.

uncompleted state rooms panelled in oak to harmonize with the original designs. The kitchens were entirely remodelled and Queen Mary personally directed the refurnishing of many rooms. More lavish and colourful ceremonial revived under King George VI and Queen Elizabeth, the present Queen Mother. They took up residence and held a whole series of state functions in the Palace shortly after their coronation in 1937. Their many further visits have been emulated by the present Queen and Prince Philip, Duke of Edinburgh, since she succeeded to the throne.

Since 1929, the palace has had the official designation of the Palace of Holyroodhouse, a title first used centuries ago. Since its triumphant return to royal favour, the days seem long past when Robert Louis Stevenson wrote in 1896: 'The Palace of Holyrood has been left aside in the growth of Edinburgh and stands grey and silent in a workmen's quarter between breweries and gas works.'

However, all that now remains of the glory of the medieval 'fair Abbey of Holyrood' is reflected in its ruined nave. Only a section of the north wall and the roofless nave are from the original twelfth-century chapel. The magnificent window of the east wall dates back to the seventeenth century, when the abbey was partially restored for the coronation of Charles I. The abbey's story is one of destruction and

violence. The transepts and choir were brought down by church order in 1569 and the vaulted ceiling of the nave collapsed during a storm in 1768, felling the main arcading on the north side. The western front is generally in the English style, with intrusions of later Gothic. Gravestones pave the floor of the nave, and among the tombs is that of Sir James Douglas, who killed the Earl of Arran in 1596 and was himself stabbed to death by Arran's nephew in the High Street of Edinburgh 12 years later.

Rioters played their part in the abbey's long descent to ruin. The trouble erupted after James II fled from his throne and William and Mary arrived from Holland in the 'bloodless revolution' of 1688. Supporters of the Dutch Orangeman overwhelmed a company of musketeers defending the Palace and rampaged through the royal apartments, tearing out all the furniture and ornaments of the private chapel. Then, in a passion to purge the abbey of Roman Catholic ornaments, they burst into the kirk and smashed it up. The lids of lead coffins in the royal burial vault were stolen for their high market value, and the bones of kings and princes were said to have been left exposed for many years. The mob built a huge fire in the outer court, burning books, images and every last symbol of Catholicism – or so they thought. In fact, the altar vessels were saved and are now held by the Scottish hierarchy of the Catholic

Church. The royal vault was restored by Queen Victoria in 1898. Occupying the east end of the south aisle, it contains the remains of such Kings of Scots as David II, James II, James V and of Lord Darnley, consort of Mary, Queen of Scots.

For almost four centuries the abbey was a haven for debtors – not only paupers but professional men like doctors and lawyers who had fallen on hard times. Even the exiled King Charles X of France stayed there at one time. Debtors began seeking refuge in the abbey in the 1530s, and a small township grew up nearby with shops, taverns and markets. Inhabitants were under strict rules: they had to secure a place to sleep and report to the man in charge, the bailie, within 24 hours of arriving, but after that they were safe from the law.

The leave was allowed between midnight on Saturday and midnight on Sunday, and one debt-ridden minister used to walk 20 miles to preach in his parish and then trudge back again within the time limit. The last debtor recorded as having entered the abbey for sanctuary was an Edinburgh solicitor in 1880.

When it was founded in 1128, the abbey was in fact part of a sanctuary stretching from the base of the present-day Royal Mile to Duddingston Loch and covering what is now known as Holyrood Park. Today, despite its ravages, it remains an oasis of peace and serenity not far from the bustle of the city.

The Old Town

The tumult of ages has bequeathed old Edinburgh a brooding appeal.

Winding alleys, dark lanes and thoroughfares steeped in history make up the Old Town of Edinburgh. It stretches from the Castle to the Palace of Holyroodhouse down the Royal Mile, main street of the medieval burgh. Romantic and picturesque, the Old Town is the very core of Scotland's capital, rescued from one-time squalor and restored to city pride. Built on a ridge ending with the towering Castle Rock, where Picts first founded a settlement in pre-historic times, it has captured the imagination of travellers through centuries of high drama. Washington Irving, the nineteenth-century American author who spent seventeen years in sojourns throughout Europe, was especially captivated. He wrote of the Old Town that '... the shadows of a thousand sad memories mingle with the light of other days upon it, sombre, sublime, silent in its age'. The antiquity and charm of this area have never been overshadowed by the New Town, the spacious and graceful city extension conceived in 1767. The main reason has to be a brooding appeal which stems from its history of violent death, of folly and betrayal, of noble patriotism and religious dedication.

Perhaps most evocative of the good – or bad – old days are the Grassmarket and the Cowgate, lying south of the Castle and the High Street. Cowgate, an extension of Holyrood Road leading from the Palace, was originally a country lane along which cattle were driven to pasture. This narrow and somewhat sombre road has known its ups and downs in the life of the Old Town. In the fifteenth century it began to be a fashionable suburb with lavish mansions and private wells to provide acceptable drinking water for the gentry. Cowgate was described by the writer Alexander Alesse in the early sixteenth century as the place 'where the nobility and chief citizens dwell and the greatest in the land have their palaces, where nothing is cheap or mean but all things are magnificent'.

Some of the rich residents apparently disliked the road's somewhat earthy name, and the street degenerated over the years to the point where traveller Alexander Smith wrote in 1865: 'The inhabitants are morally and geographically the lower orders. They keep to their own quarters and seldom come up to the light of day. Many an Edinburgh man has never set his foot in the street. The condition of the inhabitants is as little known to respectable Edinburgh as are the habits of moles, earthworms and the mining population.' At the eastern entrance to the Cowgate stands the Magdalen Chapel, which was erected about the middle of the sixteenth century and contains what are regarded as the best examples of rare pre-Reformation stained-glass windows in Scotland. The windows represent the Royal Arms, encircled with a wreath of thistles. The chapel now serves as the University Chapel of Heriot-Watt University.

Farther to the east stands St. Cecilia's Hall, which has a world-famous collection of over 30 keyboard instruments including harpsichords, clavichords, fortepianos, spinets, virginals and chamber organs.

On the south side once stood the Blackfriars Monastery, a Dominican friary founded as far back as 1230.

Cowgate then passes under an arch of South Bridge and into a valley between the Heriot-Watt University on the south and the National Library of Scotland to the north. The library, opened by Queen Elizabeth II in 1956, contains more than three million books and manuscripts, the largest and most valuable collection of its kind in Scotland.

Take note of Guthrie Street, on the south side. Sir Walter Scott was born there in 1771, in a house long demolished and now marked by a stone tablet. After passing under George IV Bridge, Cowgate opens into the Grassmarket, a stately 230-yard (210 m) long rectangle standing in splendour under the lofty heights of the Castle. The tree-lined Grassmarket is a pleasant place now, but it has to be set against a bloody backcloth of murder and execution. At the east end, a small enclosed garden marks the place where the public gallows stood until 1784, when a halt was ordered to executions in the Grassmarket. 'Common criminals' died in

their hundreds on this spot, along with high-born leaders and rebel Covenanters – of whom at least 100 were hanged between the years 1661 and 1688. The site of the gallows is marked by a St. Andrew's Cross, in rose-coloured cobblestones, which bears the inscription: 'For the Protestant faith on this spot many Martyrs and Covenanters died.' The particular irony of the inscription is that, in the complex religious divisions of that era, it was other Protestants who ordered the executions. When one Covenanter stood on the gallows and refused to recant his faith in the face of death, the Duke of Rothes is said to have remarked: 'Then let him glorify God in the Grassmarket.'

The Grassmarket's most notorious inhabitants were infamous murderers. In Tanner's Close, long vanished, William Burke and William Hare carried out their trade of supplying corpses to surgeons for medical research. They lured paupers and prostitutes to their lodging house and strangled them. Hare finally turned against his companion in crime and got away with murder, but Burke died on the Grassmarket gallows on Christmas Eve 1829. The judge who sentenced him said in court: 'I trust that if it is ever customary to preserve skeletons, yours will be preserved in order that posterity may keep in remembrance your atrocious crimes.' The judge's remark was heeded, and Burke's body was delivered to the Department of Anatomy at Edinburgh University, where many of his victims had ended up. His skeleton may still be seen there today.

Murders, riots and executions apart, the Grassmarket had an important trading role in the life of the Old Town. In 1477 King James III granted a charter for a weekly market which was held regularly until 1911, when it

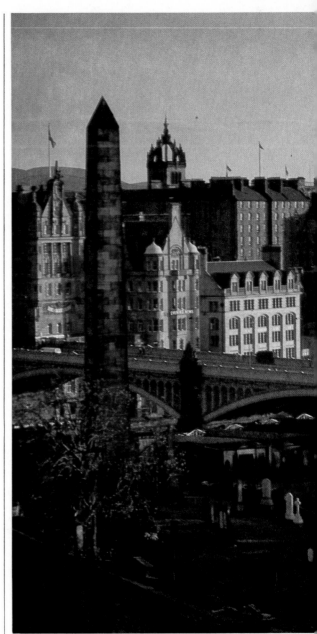

Spires emerge from the Old Town, viewed from above Calton churchyard.

was removed to Saughton in the west of the city. Circuses, cockfighting and other so-called entertainments were once a feature of the bustling market-

place nestled into a hollow at the base of Castle Rock. A plaque commemorating the 500th anniversary of the charter was unveiled in the west end of

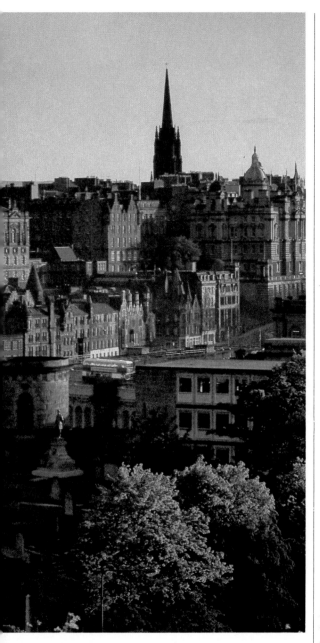

area was so crowded that travel was almost impossible between the Grassmarket and the Cowgate leading to Holyroodhouse Palace. And yet this is still the largest open space in the Old Town. From the West Bow, so named because it was within arrow shot of the Castle, it extends just over 230 yards (210 m) to King's Stables Road.

In the heart of the Old Town you find tall, crammed buildings, dating from the fifteenth to the seventeenth century and almost Dutch in appearance. But only the occasional summer fair brings back the atmosphere of the ancient market. Perhaps the best example of the Grassmarket's age and architecture can be seen halfway down the north side, before you reach Castle Wynd. A stairway entrance, only three feet (0.9 m) across, carries the inscription: 'Blessed by God for all his giftis.' Shops selling clothes and antiques are the main attraction of the Grassmarket today. Fascinating little shops abound, some offering rare books, others selling kitchen utensils, some telling visitors that it's their last chance to pick up a really good brush or broomstick.

In a passage at the southwest corner of the Grassmarket is a section of the Flodden Wall, which was painstakingly built around Edinburgh after the Scots suffered a dreadful defeat by the English at the battle of Flodden Field in 1513. Some authorities say that the legendary caution of Edinburgh folk is exemplified by the fact the wall took the best part of 50 years to build. Nevertheless, it defined the limits of the burgh for 250 years; it now serves as the western boundary of the grounds of George Heriot's School, founded and endowed in 1628 by the goldsmith to King James VI.

There is another special sight to see on the north side of the Grassmarket. It is the White

the Grassmarket in 1977.

What a marvellous place the old marketplace must have been. Printers, tanners, brewers, tobacconists, corn merchants and 'such trades as prepare cat gut from the intestines of animals' all lived, worked and sold their goods there. On Fridays, the main market day, the

Hart Inn, an early eighteenth-century hostelry which has beautiful wallhead gables to the front and two semi-octagonal stair towers at the rear. Among noted guests at the inn were the poets Robert Burns and William Wordsworth.

Before leaving the Grassmarket, do have a look at the new Mountbatten building of the Heriot-Watt University, which was erected in 1968 on the site of the old Corn Exchange.

At its southeast corner the Grassmarket joins ancient Candlemaker Row and the southern part of the Old Town; it connects with the fragment of West Bow which now runs into Victoria Street West Bow, formerly led to the heights but was remodelled in the nineteenth century to join the George IV Bridge.

At the upper end of Victoria Street stand the India Buildings, erected in 1867 and now used mostly as a magistrate's court.

Candlemaker Row was named in recognition of one of Edinburgh's great crafts, which flourished from 1488 until gas lighting emerged early in the nineteenth century. The hall of the ancient Corporation of Candlemakers can be found at the head of the row. It was built in 1722 and restored in 1929. At the road junction in front of the hall is a memorial to 'Greyfriars Bobby', the Skye terrier who kept a 14-year vigil at the grave of his master in the adjoining churchyard. The main entrance of the churchyard, once the garden of a Franciscan monastery, can be reached through a lane at the top of Candlemaker Row.

More than any other place of worship in Edinburgh, Greyfriars Kirk reflects the turbulent history of the Church of Scotland from the Reformation in 1559 to the establishment of the Protestant faith in 1689. Its his-

The old craft of candlemaking revived with a modern touch.

tory is particularly closely associated with the Covenanters. The church was opened in 1620 – the first built in Scotland since the Reformation. It owned two 'repentance stools' on which worshippers with a record of unseemly behaviour were forced to sit during services. One of these stools has survived and is now to be seen at the National Museum of Antiquities in Queen Street. During the 1650s, when Oliver Cromwell's troops occupied Edinburgh, Greyfriars was used as a barracks. The congregation was unceremoniously kicked out. The church suffered badly at the hands of the soldiers, and a collection for repairs was taken at all the places of worship in Edinburgh when Greyfriars was handed back to the congregation in 1653. The church suffered yet again in 1718, when gunpowder stored in the tower by the city fathers exploded. The event was recorded by the Court Clerk in this way: 'On Wednesday the 7th of May instant 1718, about a quarter of an hour before Two of the Clock in the morning, the Grayfrier Church Steiple was blown up, which Surprized and allaramed the whole City, more particularly the Grayfrier Congregation. By which the Gray-

frier Church sustained so great damage as it was rendered unfit for the Congregation to assemble therein for publick worship...' After fresh repairs the kirk was reduced in size and a new church was built as an extension in 1721, with a dividing wall. It also suffered serious damage in a fire in 1845. Eventually the entire church was restored, the dividing wall was removed in 1938, and now the united congregations worship in the Kirk of the Greyfriars.

Today the church is architecturally quite unremarkable, a somewhat featureless oblong with an interior in a simple Gothic style. Its unbroken nave extends for 150 feet (45 m). But it stands in an historic enclosure – the churchyard occupying a spectacular site between the George IV Bridge and the Grassmarket. Its fame is chiefly associated with the signing of the National Covenant in 1638. Here, on February 28, in what is now the churchyard, the entire congregation gathered with Edinburgh's noblemen and merchants to put their names to the Covenant, which pledged all its signatories to fight anyone trying to establish the 'papist' religion in this country.

In effect, it professed loyalty to King Charles I but warned him not to interfere in the affairs of the Scottish Kirk. The Covenant, which also called for a free Scottish Parliament, was said to have been signed on a tombstone in the churchyard – sometimes in blood. Copies were later signed in churches all over Scotland.

On the side of the churchyard backing onto Candlemaker Row is the Martyrs Monument, erected in 1688 to the memory of Covenanters who had been executed in Edinburgh more than 20 years earlier. Its inscription reads, in part: 'Here lies interred the dust of those who stood 'gainst perjury, re-

Public executions were witnessed from these windows on the north side of the Grassmarket.

sisting unto blood, adhering to the Covenants and laws... Their lives were sacrificed unto the lust of prelatists and abjur'd.'

The majority of the martyrs were buried in the churchyard, ironically not far from the tomb of the man who ordered their torture and execution. He was Sir George Mackenzie, a Lord Advocate – or royal prosecutor – who came to be known as 'Bluidy Mackenzie'.

In the southwest corner of the churchyard is the Covenanters' Prison, now barred and locked. Some 1200 Covenanters, captured at the battle of Bothwell Bridge, were imprisoned for five months here – under open skies and through the grim Edinburgh winter of 1679.

Rigorously guarded, the inmates were allowed a daily ration of one 'penny loaf', but in many ways they were better off than their leaders – who were condemned to enslavement in the American plantations.

Round the churchyard walls are a range of stately monuments and ornate tombstones commemorating famous citizens of old Edinburgh. Here are the last resting places of William Adam, the classical architect; Joseph Black, renowned physicist and chemist; George Buchanan, tutor to Mary, Queen of Scots; John and George Watson, who founded the hospitals that bear their names; Gaelic poet Duncan Ban McIntyre; James Craig, architect of the New Town; and Dr. Thomas McCrie, church historian and biographer of John Knox. But it must be said that most visitors head straight for the grave of Greyfriars Bobby, the faithful terrier. The spot is marked by a headstone provided by the 'American Lovers of Bobby'.

To the south, on the western side of the quaintly named Middle Meadow Walk, stands one of Britain's leading hospitals, the Royal Infirmary. It started in a humble way in 1729 as a 'hospital for the destitute sick', with only six beds. The site is marked by a plaque at the top of Infirmary Street. A second royal infirmary was completed in 1748, starting with about 70 beds but growing as funds increased. Between 1762 and 1765, according to medical records, 15,600 patients were admitted, of which about 75 percent were discharged as cured. The records show that about 750 patients died under treatment, and quite a few 'left of their own accord'. The foundation stone of the present building was laid in 1870 by the Prince of Wales, later Edward VII, and the new hospital was opened nine years afterwards. There was a major extension in 1939, when the Royal Simpson Maternity Pavilion was opened. Nowadays the Royal Infirmary is one of the most important centres in the country for training doctors. Thousands are treated each year at the hospital, which has a number of associated homes and clinics.

There is quite an inspiring story about the building of the first infirmary. Its true creator was George Drummond, who was elected six times as Lord Provost (Mayor) of Edinburgh and is regarded as the father of the city. Drummond struck a chord among the residents when he appealed for funds to meet this crying need in eighteenth-century Edinburgh. Money poured in from firms as well as individuals, from church-door collections and social groups who had the name of 'dancing assemblies'. Well-off citizens provided cash in response to Drummond's appeal. Landowners and quarrymasters gave stone, slates and timber. Farmers supplied carts for carrying materials to the site. Some English companies gave glass for the windows – and many Edinburgh workmen toiled there without wages for one day a month. The sacrifices were made out of a genuine desire for progress – and one wonders whether such dedication could emerge today in a different but no less traumatic climate.

The New Town

The prime mover for the New Town, its inspiration and drive, was the city's Lord Provost, George Drummond.

Drummond, who had the idea from one mooted at the time of Charles II a century earlier, started planning the extension to the city when he was first elected Lord Provost in 1725. In his biography the Reverend Thomas Somerville quotes a fascinating conversation he had with Drummond:

'I happened one day . . . to be standing at a window (in the Old Town) looking out to the opposite side of the North Loch, then called Barefoot's Parks, in which there was not a single house to be seen. "Look at these fields," says Provost Drummond. "You Mr. Somerville are a young man and may probably live, though I will not, to see all these fields covered with houses, forming a splendid and magnificent city. To the accomplishment of this nothing more is necessary than draining the North Loch and providing a proper access from the Old Town. I have never lost sight of this object since the year 1725 when I was first elected Provost.'

But it was not until 1752 that his 'Proposals' were published and 14 years later a competition for the final plans opened. It was won by an unknown 23-year-old architect, James Craig, son

Detail of a Charlotte Square window (**above**) and the Moray Estate (**left**).

of an Edinburgh merchant. Only six had entered the contest and the prize was the freedom of the city and a gold medal. For James Craig there was also overnight fame.

The cause of all the planning was the great increase in population (the Scots economy was improving) to about 50,000 who were crammed within the ancient city walls on an area of 138 acres (55.2 ha). Conditions were gruesome, disease rife and crime high. It was clear something had to be done.

Drummond, six times Lord Provost between 1725 and 1764, was met by plenty of traditionalist opposition to his visionary ideas but he was shrewd enough to push them through in well-spaced stages.

First came the publication of the 'Proposals' in 1752, setting out the intention to build on the green fields overlooking the city to the north. Then in 1765 a contract was awarded for the building of North Bridge to take a new road across the valley of Nor' Loch to the port of Leith – and at the same time give access to the New Town land (much of which had been bought already by speculating city officials).

A year later, the year of Drummond's death, the competition was announced and in 1767, only two weeks after Parliament in Westminster had passed the Act to extend the city limits, Craig's win was announced.

The first stage

Craig's plan was classic and grand, with its grid-iron pattern of squares, gardens and parallel streets. But it was simple, too, and without any detailed drawings for the rows of houses that were to come. That was left to other architects.

The street names were an integral part of the design and symbolized the parliamentary union between England and

Above Craig's triumphant design in the 1776 competition for a New Town plan. **Left** The 23-year-old winner at work. **Far right** The architect Robert Adam in profile. **Below** One of the finest examples of his genius, Register House, designed in 1772. **Right** Interior of Register House.

Scotland, glorifying George III and the House of Hanover. George Street, the main axis, linked two magnificent squares that were to be St. George's and St. Andrew's, the patron saints of England and Scotland, but Queen Charlotte thought differently and the former was soon renamed after her.

The outer streets were Princes and Queen Streets and were crossed by Frederick (George's son), Hanover and Castle. The ones in between, where the trades and craftsmen were to thrive, were Thistle and Rose Streets, named after the national emblems of Scotland and England.

There was, though, a reluctance on the part of the townspeople to build in the New Town area and the city's council soon came to the conclusion that incentives would have to be offered.

Mr. John Young, who built his house at Thistle Court, off St. Andrew's Square, was awarded £20 for being the first to make his home in the New Town. The silk merchant, John Neale was exempted from city rates when he built the first house in Princes Street in 1769.

In 1777 advertisements invited plans 'by which buildings might be erected in the most regular, handsome and commodious manner'. Plain-fronted tenements, double flats and houses began to spring up but there was no uniformity of style and by 1782 the city decided to impose a few rules. Every house on the main streets, for example, was to be three-storeyed with a sunk basement and a frontage of not more than 48 feet (14.4 m). Failure to comply meant a £30 fine and immediate removal. But the more elaborate houses were designed by the notable architects of the day and the New Town became the fashionable place to live.

By now Robert Adam had

Above Charlotte Square in detail from the air; and the original elevation plan drawn by Robert Adam for the north and south sides (only the north was built). **From the left**: The view of St. George's Church from the square; the square's surroundings; intricate old street lamps; and an elegant doorway.

made his reputation as a stylish young architect in England and had made some very influential friends. But he returned to his native Scotland (which he had left calling it 'a narrow place') for the chance to design great public buildings.

Register House, where the historic and administrative records of state are kept, was started in 1774 from designs of Robert's and his brothers James and John. Robert did not actually move to Edinburgh but, as the building progressed, John kept an eye on it and Robert visited. It took more than 12 years to build and cost the government £31,000 but it is still one of the most remarkable architectural features of the city with its huge dome and splendid frontage. The former home of Sir Laurence Dundas flanks the east side of St. Andrew's Square. This square is one of the richest in the world due to the number of banks and insurance headquarters there. In the centre is a statue of Henry Dundas 1st Viscount Melville, a powerful Scottish figure in the 1780's.

At the other end of George Street, balancing St. Andrew's Square, is Charlotte Square, the most spectacular and beautiful of Adam's achievements. It was designed by Robert Adam who had been commissioned by the town council in 1791 to produce a unified scheme of frontages for the houses in the square – something quite new to a city where only a similarity in style had been attempted.

Robert died the following year and a letter written by his brother James afterwards asks for payment on account of a promise to Robert of 200 guineas for the elevations for Charlotte Square. But, accounting difficulties aside, the building went ahead and the rectangular square, with streets entering at each corner, one side of elegant frontages mirroring its opposite side and

The beauty of the Royal Bank of Scotland, formerly Sir Laurence Dundas's home, designed by Sir William Chambers in 1772. The star shapes cut in the ceiling allow light in. Light, this time at night, illuminates the Assembly Rooms (**right**).

the gardens in the middle, is a major achievement in European civic architecture.

Princes Street, once regarded as the most beautiful street in Europe, grew up rather haphazardly, starting at the beginning of the building of the New Town and not ending until 1805. It has a glorious open view on the south side across the gardens to the Castle. But this now much-admired view was once under threat. Town officials, greedy for the profits

of development, discussed a plan to enclose the south side of the street and, after a running battle, the gardens' owners were smart enough to take out a 99-year lease on the land in 1771, which prevented any building at all.

During the building of Princes Street's north side the excavated earth from it, and other streets, was used to fill in the already drained Nor' Loch to make private gardens for the residents. These were jealous-

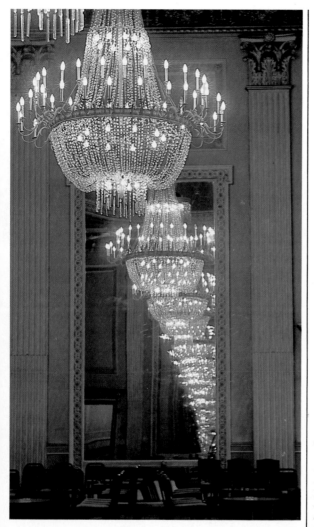

lost his fortune after a divorce and a disastrous second marriage.

It was Miss Burns' custom to take an evening walk along Princes Street where she attracted much attention. But it was her behaviour at her home that caused enormous trouble – particularly to a Lord Swinton whose back windows overlooked hers. The matter ended in court where Bailie – later Lord Provost – Creech heard the case and expelled her from the city on pain of six months in a House of Correction, a 'drumming' through the streets and further expulsion. But she appealed to higher courts and won the right to stay.

Bailie Creech's dislike of the 20-year-old beauty was well known and the matter prompted comment from many. Even Robert Burns has his say on the lady:

Cease, ye prudes, your
        envious railing:
    Lovely Burns has charms –
        confess:
    True it is she had one
        failing:
    Had a woman ever less!

The second stage

By the close of the eighteenth century the New Town had become the fashionable place to live and in the 1820s the Governors of Heriot's Hospital, who owned the land immediately to the north, embarked upon a speculative extension to the New Town. This second stage was largely residential and has remained so. The scale therefore is more homely and the downhill sloping site gave magnificent views across the Forth to Fife. The whole development was largely under the control of Robert Reid, the Master of the King's Works in Scotland, and William Sibbald, Superintendant of Works in the City, and thus has more architectural unity than the first stage.

ly guarded from the public – possibly because it was the owners who had to pay for planting and laying them out.

The garden owners were issued with keys, for £1 each, to get into the gardens but it was not long before a Rose Street locksmith was producing replicas and a builder of houses in Castle Terrace gave his buyers keys which just happened to fit the garden gates!

The Mound, which divides the gardens, was begun by a Lawnmarket clothier, George Boyd, in 1781 as a shortcut for his New Town customers. His mud brig was officially sanctioned by the Town Council and more than two million cartloads of soil from the foundation of New Town houses were dumped there in his time.

Rose Street was also the centre of a scandal which shocked the local residents. In about 1789 a young lady called Miss Burns moved to the street from Durham where her father had

It too is based on a grid system. The outward-looking Heriot and Fettes Rows flank Northumberland, Cumberland and Great King Streets, which lead onto the massive open spaces of Drummond Place and Royal Circus.

Royal Circus was the work of William Playfair, possibly the most prolific and influential of Edinburgh's architects. He was born in London in 1789, the son of a Scots architect, and when his father died in 1793, William was sent to Edinburgh to his uncle John, professor of mathematics and, later, of natural philosophy, at the city's prestigious university.

William first gained attention when he won a competition for a design which would complete the university, largely planned by Robert Adam. He went on to do a massive amount of work until his death in 1857. Donaldson's Hospital was his largest work but the others were scarcely inconsiderable: the National Gallery, the Calton Hill scheme, the National Monument and New Observatory, the Royal Institution (now the Royal Scottish Academy), the Royal College of Surgeons. The list is almost endless – even the Princes Street railway line was his design.

This phase, too, met with great opposition. Robert Chambers, writing his *Walks in Edinburgh* in 1825, says the building of Heriot Row was thought by many to be a mad speculation. And an English traveller, Sir John Carr, said the fine view from Queen Street was beginning 'to be interrupted by the recent elevation of new streets and particularly by the houses on a piece of ground called Heriot's Row'.

The lesser streets run parallel to the main ones, and Northumberland and Cumberland Streets, which have marvellous Georgian features, have been recently restored.

Another, Jamaica Street, was inferior and deteriorated so badly that it was eventually demolished. But it did have one claim to posterity. For a time, the young Thomas Carlyle tried to find the tranquillity he needed for his writing in a top flat there but his window overlooked Royal Circus and he wrote, in 1821, that 50 masons were 'chipping away'. He moved to more peaceful rural surroundings in Spey Street on the road to Leith.

The East End and Calton Hill

The area that earned Edinburgh the title of 'Athens of the North' is Calton Hill. There is an odd array of buildings and monuments, begun in 1776 and finished in 1830.

The Old Observatory came first, designed by Craig and made to look, it is said on the suggestion of Robert Adam, like a fortress. It is his only surviving building in the city and is basically a tower with Gothic windows. He planned it in 1776 but it was not completed until much later – in 1792.

Nearby is the New Observatory, Roman Doric and in the shape of a cross, begun in 1818 and designed by William Playfair. There is also a monument in Grecian Doric form to his uncle, John Playfair, who was also president of the Astronomical Institution.

William Playfair was also responsible for the monument to Dugald Stewart, another Grecian-style construction like a small circular temple. Stewart succeeded Adam Ferguson as professor of moral philosophy at the university in 1785. Both his memorial and that to Burns on the lower slope of the hill near Regent Road, designed by Thomas Hamilton (1830), were copied from the monument of Lysicrates in Athens.

Above them rises the column of Nelson's Monument, a rather Gothic design by Robert Burn

The glories of Calton Hill. **Far left**: The neo-classical memorial to the philosopher Dugald Stewart by William Playfair (1822). **Near left** Nelson's Monument (1807) by Robert Burn. **Below** The ribs of the intended National Monument, started in 1822 and never completed because of lack of funds.

The steady expansion of the New
Town over the years is marked by
distinctly separate stages of
development.

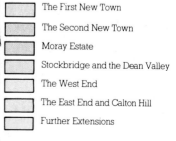

The First New Town

The Second New Town

Moray Estate

Stockbridge and the Dean Valley

The West End

The East End and Calton Hill

Further Extensions

and supposed to represent an upturned telescope. On top of the 106-foot (31.8m) tower is a time ball which drops daily at 13.00, at the same time the Castle cannon is fired.

But the National Monument which stands on the summit is the one that grabs the eye. Funds with which to complete it were not forthcoming and it stands now not as a memorial to the Scottish soldiers and sailors who died in the Napoleonic Wars as was intended but to the hasty enthusiasm of those who conceived it.

It was supposed to be an exact copy of the Parthenon to be used as a grand memorial church with catacombs beneath, a sort of 'Scottish Valhalla'. C. R. Cockerell designed it originally but Playfair was ultimately responsible.

In 1822, when part of the money had been collected, the foundation stone was laid with great ceremony but only the base and 12 columns were built – at the cost of £1000 each. Ever since, the structure has been called all sorts of names: Scotland's Pride and Poverty, Edinburgh's Disgrace and Edinburgh's Folly.

Waterloo Place, which leads from Princes Street to the hill, was conceived to give access to the new prison on the south slope. In 1815, the year of Wellington's victory, Robert Stevenson started work on the street. Old houses had to be cleared, a gorge crossed and tons of rock removed from the hill. Now all that is left of the jail is the little 'fortress' of the governor's residence and the underworks that support St. Andrew's House.

Further east is the old Royal High School. The school was founded in 1128 and originally supervised by the abbots of Holyrood. But by the early nineteenth century, when a new building was considered, it was the responsibility of the city fathers. The site at Calton Hill was chosen in 1825 after much discussion. Thomas Hamilton, a former pupil, was asked to plan it and he kept the cost down to £24,000. Building was completed in 1829 and it is generally regarded as one of the best of the city's neo-classical edifices.

The New Town to the east was mooted as far back as 1811 on ground belonging largely to Heriot's and Trinity Hospitals, and Mr. Allan of Hillside. Once again Playfair took over a project, this time from his master William Stark, who had stressed the importance of trees and landscape in his discussions. Stark died in 1818 and the following year Playfair completed his design. It is very spacious and Royal Terrace, on the north side of the hill, is the grandest part of the triangle. It is the longest continuous frontage in the city – very nearly a quarter of a mile – and was built between 1821 and 1860.

Regent Terrace, which looks south over the Old Town, is an impressive continuous block which climbs to make a grand sweep around the end of the hill. It is decorated with a wrought-iron balcony which runs the whole length.

In between, the triangular garden was designed for the proprietors' use by Joseph Paxton with the idea that it would be more attractive than the scheme at the West End.

The West End

The story of this area, bordered by Queensferry Road and Haymarket Terrace, Belford Road and Atholl Crescent, is spread over many years. James Gillespie Graham produced a master plan in 1813 but progress was confused by the feudal rights of landowners and an enormous number of architects. Building in the area went on until 1907.

Robert Brown designed most of the area from Melville Street to Coates Crescent for the Walker family in 1813. In the middle of the street, where it is crossed by Walker Street, is Melville Crescent, laid out by John Lessels in 1855 with a grandoise statue of the 2nd Viscount Melville in the centre.

At one end of the street is St. Mary's Episcopal Cathedral, designed by Sir George Gilbert Scott in 1879, a solid soaring edifice to Victoriana. It is the largest ecclesiastical building erected in Scotland since the Reformation.

The Misses Walker of Easter Coates were largely responsible for the creation of the massive cathedral. They left their grand old manor house – and the fortune they made by letting off the bulk of their estate during the latter stages of the building of the New Town – to the Church. The result was the cathedral with its two western towers, finished in 1917, named Barbara and Mary after them.

Atholl Crescent, by Thomas Bonnar (1824), was the home of William Gladstone's father, Sir John, who lived at Number 11. Across the road, in Coates Crescent, an earlier block by Robert Brown built between 1813 and 1823, is the W. E. Gladstone Memorial, moved there from its original site in St. Andrew's Square in 1955. Atholl Crescent is interrupted by Canning House, the last of the office towers to be built in Edinburgh's centre before they were banned in 1974.

The two crescents lead into Shandwick Place where Sir Walter Scott lived for two years at Number 6. He left when he gave up his post as clerk of session in 1830.

Scott was instrumental in helping his literary neighbour in Manor Place, Mrs. Grant of Laggan, acquire a pension of £100 a year from George IV. The lady, who wrote *Letters from the Mountains*, held many parties for celebrities of her time and the profits from her writing, together with bequests from deceased friends and the pension paid through the Civil Establishment of Scotland, made her later years comfortable. She died in Manor Place in 1838 at the age of 84.

Manor Place leads into Rothesay Place, built by John Watherston between 1876 and 1907. There were strange disturbances reported by one owner who had brought home a piece of wood from a friend's cottage in the north of Scotland. Drawers opened and closed of their own accord, teapots fell off the table, and a pervading smell of tobacco lingered. It was all blamed on a sailor called Merry Jack Tar who was supposed to be haunting the flat above the old Theatre Royal (now the Post Office).

In the theatre itself ghosts apparently re-enacted plays on stage after the manager and his family had retired to their upstairs flat. This story, also linked with Tar, was mentioned in a pamphlet marking the closure of the theatre in 1859.

The Moray Estate
In 1822, the same year work began on Royal Circus, Lord Moray advertised his estate for a development. It had been bought 40 years before by the previous Earl of Moray to use as the family's suburban home. It was an odd-shaped piece of land, north of Charlotte Square, bounded by the deep gorge of the Water of Leith on its further side.

The Earl, in the conditions he set for the sale of his grounds, had determined to make the new area of the highest quality. He had, in the architect's words, done 'everything in his power, consistent with his own interest, to render the plan ornamental to the City and convenient for the inhabitants'. He had ensured, equally, that none of the

expense of streets, sewers, boundary walls or pleasure gardens would fall on him but, proportionately, would be the purchasers' responsibility.

The plans for the new estate were drawn by James Gillespie Graham. For a fee of five guineas he supplied drawings of each house front, including full-size details, which would grace the newest part of the New Town. He even designed the railings which had to be of a standard pattern – a distinctive double rail with wreaths in between – for the price.

Gillespie Graham shied away from the grid-iron pattern of Craig and created instead the majestic curves of Randolph Crescent, Ainslie Place and the many-sided Moray Place, connected with short avenues to the streets of Craig, Reid and Sibbald.

All the building that was going on was quite a surprise to many of the townspeople. An anonymous diarist wrote, in March 1823, that the sale of the Earl's grounds 'which commenced last year, is likely to lead to the formation of a third grand division of our new town. The addition of from 700 to 800 new dwelling-houses in Edinburgh every year for some years past, one would think, must through time over-stock the market and lower the rents, but this state of matters has not yet taken place.'

In October he was still astonished at the progress: 'The most remarkable increase as to buildings of expensive architecture are those on Lord Moray's ground.... Now a great part of three or four sides of the Octagon are visible.'

Moray Place, the grandest of circuses, is, in fact, 12-sided. Only two sides can be seen at a time and each has a Tuscan portico, alternatively plain and pedimented. Lord Moray took one of the houses, Number 28, for his own home.

Most of the house-plots had been sold by 1827 although a few plots on the south side of Great Stuart Street and Ainslie Place remained undeveloped until the middle of the century.

On the steep, wooded slope that led from the houses to the Water of Leith, the land was planted with shrubs and pathways were made. It became known as Lord Moray's pleasure-ground. It, too, was paid for by the householders who enjoyed it and who contributed to its upkeep. Their successors still use the gardens for a stroll along the cliff whose retaining walls are now ivy-decked.

Stockbridge and the Dean Valley
Across the Water of Leith, beyond the city boundary, there was building too. The villages that had existed for centuries were swallowed up by new streets but they were not digested and still remain – black, old and incongruous in the middle of the grey eighteenth- and nineteenth-century serenity.

The earliest development of these outlying villages began in 1813 when the portrait painter Sir Henry Raeburn began to sell house-building plots in the street that he had given to his wife Ann, and named after her. It is rather grand in the middle but the houses at the two ends of the street have a doll-house charm with long front gardens, a rare thing in Georgian streets. Tradition maintains that Raeburn designed it himself but it may have been the work of the architect James Milne.

In nearby Henderson Row on July 1, 1823, the foundation stone of the new Edinburgh Academy was laid despite the opposition of the Town Council. The Council maintained that distinctions of wealth would be introduced if there were a rival to the high school where children from all walks of life had studied together. But Sir Walter Scott was behind the new school, together with other powerful voices like the judge, Henry, Lord Cockburn. Both men joined the first board of 16 directors, whose chairman was Robert Dundas of Arniston.

The Council were furious but could do nothing. There was a rumour, though, that the Council deliberately chose the site for William Playfair's massive St. Stephen's Church to block the view of the new academy which could be seen from the whole length of Howe Street.

Where Henderson Row meets Hamilton Place is the district of Silvermills. In 1607 quantities of silver were found at Linlithgow, 15 miles away from the city, and ore was refined on the banks of the Water of Leith. Traces of the mills, bought by James IV with the mines, remain on both sides of West Silvermills Lane.

In 1824 the Lord Provost Learmonth proposed a new bridge to his newly acquired estate of Dean, north of the river near the west end of town. He had ideas of development too and employed Thomas Telford to build Dean Bridge, begun in 1829, which was one of the highest of its era. But a recession had set in and it was another 20 or 30 years before the streets like Oxford and Eton Terraces were built – in Victorian style.

The old village of Dean, west of the bridge, has partly survived almost hidden in the gorge of the Water. It was, in the sixteenth and seventeenth centuries, a very busy milling centre where there were 11 mills and many 'baxters' (bakers) of Edinburgh.

City Life

The most extraordinary thing about all the energetic, speculative building and investment that went on in the whole of the New Town was that the common people were starving.

At the turn of the nineteenth century the city streets were infested with beggars, there was widespread unemployment and famine – and ugly violence followed.

War with France and poor harvest made food scarce and dear. The 'meal mobs' – famished townspeople – attacked shops to provide grain for their malnourished families. In 1800 Parliament was forced to allow the town's authorities to raise £10,000 to give food to the impoverished but it wasn't enough and further riots, in the Grassmarket and Cowgate, followed. Permanent soup kitchens and cash handouts had to be made for those in need.

In 1811 Hogmanay was, in the words of diarist W.M. Gilbert, 'disgraced by a series of riots, outrages and robberies'. Two people died in the riot and a reward of 100 guineas was offered for the arrest of the murderers. Three youths, all under 18, were hanged.

There was also the problem of professional beggars and those who refused to work in a House of Industry (the work house) were sent to Bridewell Prison and the special society formed to deal with beggars heard 622 cases in its first year of operation.

The Committee for the Relief of Workmen out of Employment helped a few with work on the roads project, costing £10,000 at Calton, and on the Union Canal to Glasgow.

Properly trained police were brought in to replace the much-criticized town guard and they were certainly well occupied by those, not finding work, who fought and looted in the streets.

Despite the problems of the city, the poverty and lack of public funds, the New Town grew to be acclaimed as a huge architectural and town planning success, much admired throughout the Europe of the era and still renowned today.

Unusual in the New Town is the rural feeling that has been captured in the pleasant development of Ann Street. The artist Sir Henry Raeburn, whose wife was called Ann, started laying out the land in 1813 with unusually long gardens in front of the rather formal Georgian houses.

The Georgian House

An English tradition brought style and quality to Edinburgh living

Towards the end of the eighteenth century the building of the Edinburgh New Town with its terraces of spacious Georgian residences permitted a style and quality of living previously unthought of in Scotland. The new residents of this extension to the city were consciously Anglophile in their admiration of all things English and wished to reproduce the high standard of living they glimpsed on their very occasional visits to London. Some of the grandest of their private dwellings stood on Charlotte Square at the west end of James Craig's New Town plan.

The north side of this square was designed by Robert Adam and its building begun before his death in 1792. It is a master-piece in the Georgian neo-classical style. Under the influence of ancient Roman architecture Adam created an impressive 'palace' façade to dominate the handsome square. Heavily rusticated at the base and decorated with a variety of light ornament on the upper levels, this symmetrical façade embraces separate houses, all of which underwent drastic interior alteration during the Victorian period. Now, one of them – No.7 – has been completely restored to the style of the late eighteenth century.

Its owners and keepers, the National Trust for Scotland, went to enormous lengths to guarantee the authenticity of the restoration. Appropriate furniture and fittings were acquired from all over the country; suitable paintings either given or borrowed; layers of paint removed from walls and woodwork in an attempt to discover the original colour scheme; floor-boards dry-scrubbed in the original style; and eighteenth-century pattern fabrics specially woven for curtains and coverings. The result for the visitor is a genuine experience of the life-style of such a house around 1800.

In every room there is a fascinating array of artefacts. The dining room, its table prepared for dinner with Wedgwood dinner service and Sheffield plate; the adjoining bedchamber (reconstructed here, as it would have been in the late eighteenth century, on the ground floor) with its wonderful four-poster bed dominating the room; and, perhaps most magnificent, the formally arranged drawing room stretching the entire width of the house. Do not miss the kitchen in the basement, and try to imagine a small army of servants needed to run such a grand, sophisticated house.

Two other features make a visit to No.7 Charlotte Square an extraordinary pleasure. The first is the absence of ropes cordoning off the valuable 'exhibits'. You can stroll freely around the house. Touching of the furniture is, of course, forbidden but the lack of obvious restrictions makes for a more relaxed atmosphere.

Right The contents of the dining room date mainly from the last quarter of the eighteenth century. Note especially the harlequin set of chairs.
Left This Wedgwood dinner service was made around 1830.

Above No kitchen was complete without a mortar and pestle. This large specimen is made from marble.
Right The kitchen was painted blue as it was believed that this colour contained something to ward off flies.

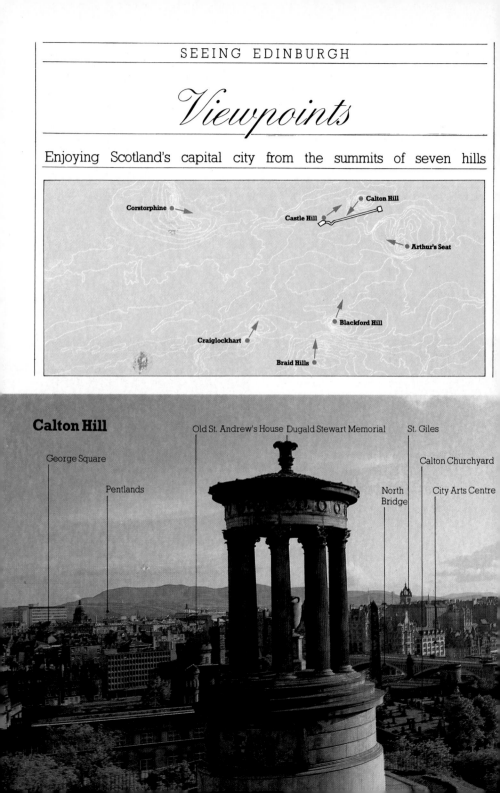

Viewpoints

Enjoying Scotland's capital city from the summits of seven hills

Corstorphine

Calton Hill

Castle Hill

Arthur's Seat

Blackford Hill

Craiglockhart

Braid Hills

Calton Hill

George Square

Pentlands

Old St. Andrew's House   Dugald Stewart Memorial

North Bridge

St. Giles

Calton Churchyard

City Arts Centre

*E*dinburgh was described by her native son Robert Louis Stevenson as a 'precipitous city'. Like Rome, she is built upon seven hills, though perhaps without the craggy magnificence of her southern counterpart. Nevertheless, Edinburgh's 'mountains' do provide an amazingly variegated panorama of street and building, close and park.

The hills are all named:

Blackford	539ft (164m)
Braid	675ft (206m)
Castle	435ft (133m)
West Craiglockhart	575ft (175m)
Arthur's Seat	823ft (251m)
Calton	328ft (100m)
Corstorphine	531ft (162m)

The highest is Arthur's Seat, named in the fifteenth century with the revival of interest in the Arthurian romances. An extinct volcano of red igneous rock, Arthur's Seat offers panoramic views over the city to the Pentland Hills and the Firth of Forth.

Calton Hill, as Stevenson noted, is the best place from which to view both the Castle and Arthur's Seat. The views along Princes Street and of the Old Town are truly magnificent. It slopes rather abruptly on the northwestern ridge.

Blackford Hill was described by Scott as the spot where Marmion stood gazing with rapt wonder and delight on the scene below. Overlooking the gentle southern suburbs of the city, it is located in a park with a pond and assorted birdlife. It is also the home of the Royal Observatory

Craiglockhart Hill, of hard basalt, overlooks the southwestern part of the city. The village of Swanston is still much as it was when Stevenson described it.

Braid Hill gives fine views of Ben Lomond to the northwest and the slopes of the Pentlands to the south.

Corstorphine Hill offers a wide panorama of the city. The Clemiston Tower was built to celebrate the centenary of the birth of Sir Walter Scott (1771). The crest of the hill figures in Stevenson's *Kidnapped* and is the site of the Edinburgh Zoo.

Castle Hill is perhaps the most commanding spot in Edinburgh. Since it was the starting point for the city, almost the whole of both the Old and New Towns are visible, and the parapets make for an infinite variety of overlooks.

For the energetic, fit and trim, the hills can be mounted over the course of a couple of days. Transport is easily arranged by bus, foot or car.

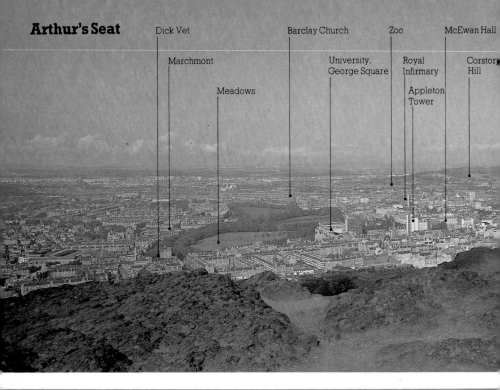

Arthur's Seat

Dick Vet

Marchmont

Meadows

Barclay Church

University, George Square

Zoo

Royal Infirmary

Appleton Tower

McEwan Hall

Corstorphine Hill

Blackford Hill

Granton

West Register House

St. G

Astley Ainslie Hospital

Edinburgh Castle

Royal Infirmary

Tolbooth St. John's

Scott Monument

North Bridge

North British
Hotel

Waverley Station

Nelson's Monument

Calton Hill

National Monument

Nelson's Monument

Salisbury Crags

Commonwealth Pool

Pollock Halls

rge
are

Arthur's Seat

Braid Hills

Forth Bridges

Corstorphine Hill

Granton

Wester Craiglockhart

Fife

Firth of Forth

Donaldson's School

St. Mary's Cathedral

Mary's Cathedral

Edinburgh Castle

Tolbooth St. John's

St. Giles

City Observatory

Calton Hill

Tolbooth St. John's

Nelson's Monument

Salisbury Crags

Arthur's Seat

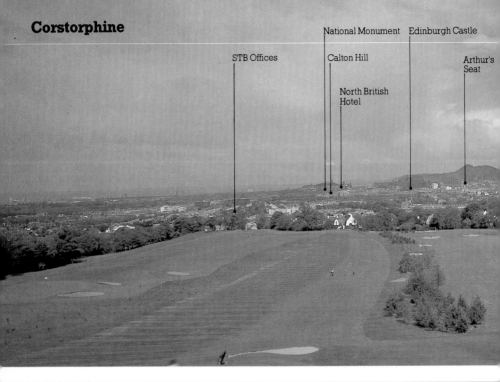

Corstorphine

STB Offices

National Monument   Edinburgh Castle

Calton Hill

Arthur's Seat

North British Hotel

Castle Hill

Princes Street

Dundas Monument

St. Andrew's House   Scott Monum

Princes St Gardens

National Gallery

Royal Scottish Academy

Ca Hil

National Monument

Nelson's Monument

Waverley Station

Royal High School

North Bridge

The Mound

Bank of Scotland

Assembly Hall

Ramsay Lodge

St. Giles

Section of Castle

Tolbooth St. John's

Villages of Edinburgh

The other Edinburgh: a patchwork of rural life, history and tradition

To most visitors, historic Edinburgh consists of the Castle and Holyrood Palace with the Royal Mile in between and the New Town to the north. Such a view does no justice to the other sections and deceives the people who hold it.

In the first half of the eighteenth century, there were as many as 46 villages spread out over the area which Edinburgh now covers. Although over the next two centuries, the boundaries gradually melted away, there are still many semi-rural communities with independent histories and traditions in existence today. Dean Village, with its riverside tranquillity, is very much a country town, while the coastline villages have a completely different character, and could be miles away. It is this blending patchwork of communities which has to be understood for Edinburgh to be fully appreciated. And without the villages Edinburgh would lack much of her charm.

Dean Village

The romantic informality of Dean Village contrasts vividly with the classic regular style of its neighbour, the New Town. Set in a valley with steep wooded slopes on either side, the distinctive red pantiled roofs of the village buildings may be seen clearly from many vantage points around it. The apparent uniformity of the bright rooftops is deceptive however and a closer inspection reveals an eclectic architectural approach to building with varied wall finishes and a diversity of period, style and condition. This is not surprising. It is natural that a village which has existed for 800 years or so has some changes.

Accessibility to the Water of Leith resulted in a milling community being established here as far back as the twelfth century and, for a long time, the city and the Incorporation of Baxters (Baker's Union) operated 11 watermills and two granaries in the area. Numerous relics of those times remain today.

Bell's Brae House, originally built as an inn in 1640, was the Baxters' meeting place and in the northeastern wall is the bakers' stone with symbolic wheat sheaves, the ripening sun and bakers' shovels.

At the bottom of Bell's Brae stands the Baxters' Tollbooth, built in the same century and the official headquarters and granary of the incorporation. It is typical of Scottish domestic architecture of the time, with stair towers and cut-away corners over the window lintels and on a wall adjoining Dean Bridge parapet is a stone with the inscription: 'Blessed be God for all his gifts' This came from Lindsay's Mill of which only three grindstones remain on its site by the riverside path formerly called Miller's Row. Jericho Mill, almost completely destroyed by a fire in 1956, is being restored as offices.

Before the building of Telford's Dean Bridge in 1832, the village was also important as a crossing point, for Bell's Brae was the main road out to Queensferry and the north. In 1751, the road was turnpiked with a toll bar at the top of the hill and some distance down it were the stables and coach houses. Both have now been restored as offices.

Many other buildings, including some houses in Dean Path and a seventeenth-century building near Dean Bridge, have also been sympathetically modernized. Others have gone completely but have been replaced by suitable worthwhile structures. Well Court, a great square of red stone buildings, designed by Sydney Mitchell in 1884, was built on the site of some old cottages to provide community housing in a highly experimental way. Dean House has also gone. In its place stands the cemetery, where Lord Cockburn and other great personalities rest.

Baxters' mills of yesteryear in Dean Village by the Water of Leith

Corstorphine

Despite rapid expansion in the twentieth century, bringing modern office blocks, shops and houses in its wake, the spirit of old Corstorphine lingers on. Situated on the southwest side of the city, Corstorphine today is clearly a residential area, surrounded and interspersed by parks and wide open spaces. But it has, like other villages, a main street and several historic features of interest.

For centuries farming was the mainstay of the local economy – mostly wheat and potatoes in the eighteenth century, then market gardening some time later. Owing to the presence of a spring of 'weak sulphurous water' reputed to have medicinal properties until it became polluted as a result of reclamation of the loch which once existed here, Corstorphine also had its day as a fashionable spa with its round of balls and concerts for the wealthy families of Edinburgh.

In 1910, an important craft industry was set up by the son of William Morris, making 'dovecot tapestries'. In 1946, it became the Edinburgh Tapestry Company and still continues in business today.

Of Corstorphine Castle, once lived in by Adam Forrester to whom the estate belonged, little remains, except a few relics found by local houseowners through the years, and an ancient stone dovecot, circular in shape, still has some 1060 nests to provide 'fresh food for the laird' and 'fertilizer for his crops' had he been there.

Not far away and probably part of an avenue of trees once leading to the castle is an old sycamore tree, 55 feet (16.7 m) high and 12½ feet (3.8 m) girth, always veiled with beautiful foliage in summer. Legend has it that the ghost of Christian Nimmo, who stabbed her lover, James Lord Forrester, by the tree in 1679, still haunts it.

Dover House in St. Margaret's Park was built in the mid-seventeenth century and displays characteristically Scottish crow-stepped gables. The ornamental gate pillars at the east High Street entrance to the park were probably once the entrance to the castle.

Corstorphine Kirk, another relic of the Forrester reign, contains some interesting early tombs of the family, with carved stone effigies and heraldic panels. A lamp, high on the building, placed there to guide travellers coming along the marsh or along the loch late at night in days of yore, has now been replaced by a symbolic electric light. In 1905, the church was successfully modernized to harmonize with some of the earlier structures and now, considered to be the 'Corstorphine Heirloom', is a source of pride to the community-conscious inhabitants.

Morningside

Traditionally a salubrious part of Edinburgh (the accent is said to have derived from Irish elocutionist, Thomas Sheridan, father of the famous playwright), Morningside actually had its origins in agriculture and it was only the advent of the railways at the end of the nineteenth century that brought about its considerable change in status.

Many years ago, the village was centred on the small area now occupied by the Public Library and the Merlin pub. The Old Tollhouse was built on the lawn surrounding Braid Church on Morningside Road and has now been rebuilt as a gatehouse at the entrance to the Hermitage of Braid Drive. Number 259, its original number, can be seen on a lintel at the rear of the building.

Later, the nineteenth century influx of wealthy people brought with it a great 'growth' in the building of beautiful villas in the district of Cluny, Hermitage and Braid. Each villa had resident servants, usually spinster ladies, and at that time the population ratio of Morningside was two females to one male.

Of these buildings not many remain, although Number 6 Morningside Place, home of the Misses Balfour, aunts of Robert Louis Stevenson, still stands complete with the author's initials which he himself carved on a cupboard door. Of the humbler and older residences, a group of old stone cottages in Springvalley Terrace remain, as do some cottages at 160 Morningside Road, one of which has an outside stone staircase. Two large square stones with holes to support gibbets in Braid Road were the scene of public executions.

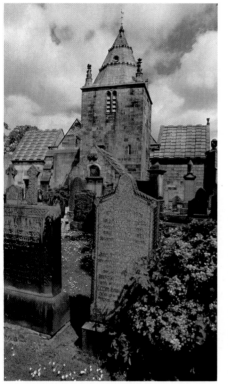

Monumental stones in the churchyard

This old dovecot houses 1060 nests

The residents also knew how to enjoy themselves, however, and Carter's Parade, on the first Friday in April, was the excuse for great festivity, usually ending up in the Volunteer's Rest (now Volunteer's Arms or the Canny Man). This pub, standing at the corner of Canaan and Morningside Lanes, has a complete range of copper whisky blending jugs and measures as well as an accounts book (dated 1892-93) in which regular customers were each allocated a page and there are such entries as 'George the joiner – glass of whisky – 4d'. One of the customers, the painter Sam Bough, presented the inn with a two-sided oil painting for use as a sign board today displayed in-

Morningside serenity

side the pub. Perhaps he did not want to see his name entered in the book. Today, Morningside is a spacious suburb which in many ways still retains the well-to-do air of the turn-of-the-century. The wide streets and well-preserved buildings reflect the comfortable standing of the residents. Trees and wide open spaces, many of them hospital and school grounds, break up the unfolding vista.

Not only does Morningside preserve this atmosphere; people also still demonstrate many of the characteristics that have made their village celebrated. The Morningside accent, for instance, with its 'refained' vowels, is still a city landmark.

Colinton

Today, the affluent 'village' of Colinton, with its beautiful villas surrounded on all sides by the serenity of the unspoilt countryside, makes it hard to believe that at the turn of the nineteenth century it seemed to be in decline. Although agriculture was the main source of employment, many people depended on the distillery, skinnery and water mills powered by the Water of Leith as a means of livelihood. The former two died a natural death, while the latter was no competition for the steam-operated machines now being used elsewhere.

The coming of the railways in 1875 turned the course of events. Now that Colinton was within commutable distance of the city centre, wealthy people started building villas here. This was not surprising. The rural beauty of the area still survives today. The Pentland Hills, the starting point of the Water of Leith, and Colinton and Craiglockhart Dells, with ivy-entwined sycamore trees, wild hyacinths and pink hedgerows

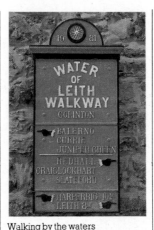

Walking by the waters

of dog rose, have always been outstandingly beautiful

Despite its expansion, many relics of Colinton's past remain, emphasizing the village spirit of the area. Colinton Brig, the main road into the village, retains much of its character, and the ruins of Colinton Castle may still be seen in Merchiston Castle School. The Parish Church, first erected in 1771 on the site of an earlier building and mod-

ernized in 1968, has many features of historic interest. An old mort safe, to prevent bodies from being dug up for medical research in bygone days still stands to the left of the entrance gates, while ancient tombstones in the churchyard provide material for perusal. James Gillespie, millowner and public benefactor, lies buried here, as does Reverend Dr. Lewis Balfour – maternal grandfather of Robert Louis Stevenson and once minister of the church. Indeed, the novelist spent much time in Colinton and his grandfather's manse and old yew tree (seen from Dell Road, over the wall and across the graveyard) are mentioned in *Kidnapped*.

Many other buildings of note are to be found throughout the village, some of them designed by Sir Robert Lorimer. Glenlyon and Almora in Pentland Avenue, distinguishable by their semi-circular towers, are two such examples. Across the road, built in 1898 but Scottish seventeenth century in style are the 'Sir William Fraser

Swanston

Separated from the rest of Edinburgh by half a mile of farmland, Swanston, nestling on the lower slopes of the Pentlands, with fields or golf courses on all sides, is in truly splendid rural isolation.

This unspoilt hamlet remains much the same as when Robert Louis Stevenson and later Edwin Muir knew it. The T-shaped wood behind Swanston, planted by a Trotter as a memorial to a descendant of the house who fell in battle, is still

green and lush. The village centre with its old-world charm has also not altered much in the last century or so.

A group of seventeenth-century white-washed cottages, with blue paintwork, black chimney pots and thatched roofs have been sympathetically restored and modernized. The old farmhouse, the heart of the village, now being used as a bothy, and the White House, the old school, are still there.

A later addition, was some

stone cottages with slated roofs, around a square. Some distance away is Swanston Cottage, described as a 'rambling infinitesimal cathedral' by Stevenson in *St Ives*. It was used as a summer cottage by the Stevenson family from 1867 to 1880 and the house on the left of the drive leading to the cottage belonged to Alison Cunningham, known as 'Cummy' to the novelist, his 'first wife and second mother'. John Todd, a Swanston shepherd provided

The parish church dating back to 1771

Rural glades surround the village

Homes', originally founded by a wealthy merchant for the rent-free use of retired ladies.

Of the humbler abodes, several small cottages are still in evidence. Those at the foot of the long steps near the church have unusual porches, rough-finished façades and moss-covered pantiles. Others of a similar ilk are on Spylaw Bank Road which also has the old station master's cottage connected by wooden steps (Jacob's Ladder) to the platform of a former station. Redhall Mill is still in use today and the Old Boag's Mill which produced bank notes in 1735, later turning to the grinding of oatmeal and barley, also still stands.

Seventeenth-century cottages in Swanston

the writer with many anecdotes of his working life and some of these stories are also depicted in the author's book, *St. Ives.*

Apart from Swanston Golf Club and the new Swanston Farm, there is little else of the village. It truly earns its reputation of being tiny and unspoilt and, now classified as a Conservation Area, it will probably remain so. Within the village, the small white houses stand out against the lush green background, while from the outside, screened on all sides by high trees, it is an oasis of quiet retreat and a delightful contrast to the vital beat of the city centre.

Duddingston

Located between Duddingston Loch and Arthur's Seat, with Holyrood Park to the west, is the village where a sense of enclosure prevails. The high walls, tall trees and remains of the old stone boundary all contribute to the intimacy of the old village centre.

At the beginning of the eighteenth century, the cottage weaving industry was the main

Duddingston Loch and the village

Portobello

It was a battle in Panama's Puerto Bello in 1739 which gave rise to the name and possibly the development of this village. A returning sailor built a house called Porto Bello in a spot where the Baptist Church in High Street now stands. He or his successor in the house dabbled in saddlery and coach repairing and the last pottery works, in Bridge Street, was moved to Crieff in 1972.

In order to attract more custom in 1753, he advertised that a horse race would be run 'at Porto Bello, in the midst of the Freegate Whins'. Thus began the growth of a community.

By the end of the eighteenth century, the village was developing in two ways. William Jameson 'Father of Portobello' started an important pottery industry using the extensive beds of clay lying on its beaches. The site soon became a service station for itinerants.

The bracing air and miles of golden sands had the potential of attracting another market which John Cairns was quick to spot. He acted promptly and, in 1795, advertised 'bathing machines on the sands'. These proved most popular and brought about the spread of the many simple Georgian houses,

Greenside

Because of its miniscule size, it is hard to believe that Greenside was ever a village, much less such an interesting one. Lying below Calton Hill's western slope and Leith Walk, and including today's Blenheim Place and Greenside Row, it was given to the sporting fraternity by James II to practise the art of mimic warfare. Thus it became a Tilting Ground and, later, in the nineteenth century was the place for holding open-air plays and revels. Until 1769, it was also a popular site for the burning and hanging of criminals and witches. Indeed, there are records showing that in 1717, a certain Robert Irvine had both hands cut off *before* he was executed here. His body was then flung unceremoniously into a quarry hole at the east end of Royal Terrace.

In the mid-sixteenth century a Carmelite monastery is said to have existed here and still to this day an official in the Convent of the Carmelites in Rome bears the inimitable title 'Il Padre Priore di Greenside'.

A hospital for lepers was established in the building left unoccupied by the nuns.

Greenside has changed much since those days and even since the 1960s a lot has means of support for most people living in the area, when the manufacture of a flaxen cloth – Duddingston Hardings – was at its peak. By 1845, severe competition had brought this to a halt and gradually the old weavers cottages on the Causeway (the main road) were also demolished. Later the pits, breweries and the mills provided jobs for the men, and where Duddingston Road crosses Braid Burn, some of the latter may still be seen, although only brewing still thrives.

The Sheep's Heid Inn, said to be the oldest licensed premises in Scotland is in the Causeway. It is said that James VI frequented the inn and in 1580 presented the landlord with an embellished ram's head. By the inn is an old skittle alley and the Sheep Heid Trotters (celebrating their centenary in 1982) meet here

Duddingston Kirk, built in Norman style, is the oldest building in the village. A watch tower, to guard against body snatchers, stands in the churchyard, and at the gate are some old jougs – iron collar and chain, to punish evil-doers – and a loupin-on-stone – to help old or obese horsemen mount.

There is a seventeenth-century building where Bonnie Prince Charlie is said to have slept before the Battle of Prestonpans. Duddingston House, designed in the eighteenth century by Sir William Chambers and surrounded by a 200-acre (81 ha) park is now Mansion House Motel and golfers make use of the grounds while famous Duddingston Loch is now a bird sanctuary.

usually used as summer homes for visitors. Between the High Street and the sea and especially at the east end of Bath Street, many of these may still be seen.

The Victorians also found Portobello a relief and they too built villas – this time large baroque ones – and also established parks and bandstands and erected a wide promenade along the sea front to 'take the airs'. Later, numerous 'amusements' were added to the existing features and so Portobello became known as the 'fun place' of Edinburgh.

Personalities of note visited or lived here too: Sir Walter Scott came to stay with friends in what is now known as Bellfield Street and it was in Portobello that he completed the first canto of *The Lay of the Last Minstrel*. The Scots comedian, Harry Lauder, lived at 3 Bridge Street for a time and the King's Road was named after George IV when he rode down the street to review his troops.

Despite its past glory, by 1967, it was evident that much had to be done to aid Portobello's deteriorating condi-tion. The Victorian mansions had fallen into disrepair and the miles of golden sand, such an attraction in former days.

By the beginning of the 1970s, the Beach Nourishment Scheme had taken effect and tons of sand from a nearby beach were poured onto Portobello's shores. This not only improved the appearance of the beach but also protected the promenade wall and sea front. Many buildings such as the George Cinema were listed for preservation, while others were at least refurbished.

been demolished. On the site of the Tabernacle, a baptist church of some repute, stands the Playhouse, first built in 1929 for use as a cinema and now a popular theatre.

Of other places and events only historic and literary records remain to fill in gaps from the past. James Nasmyth, inventor of the steam hammer, as a small boy often accompanied the servants to the bleaching green on Calton Hill and in his writings he mentions the 'blacksmiths, coppersmiths and brassfounders busy in the

'Church on the Hill'

Greenside workshops'.

Robert Louis Stevenson was also a frequent visitor. His paternal grandfather, an elder at Greenside Parish Church, the 'Church on the Hill' still standing today, once occupied the house at Number 1 Baxter's Place – of which the novelist writes in picturesque terms of its 'great size, infinity of cellars, garrets and apple lofts'. On the death of the grandfather, Robert Stevenson, his three sons bequeathed a section of their garden to the church, on which was later built chapel.

Queensferry

Situated at the narrowest point of the Forth, nine miles (14.4 km) west of the city centre, Queensferry (often erroneously known as South Queensferry) still has the feel of a Scottish east coast town with a small, tightly-knit community.

The name has ancient associations with Queen Margaret, for it was just west of the town at Brinks Rock that she disembarked in 1067 as the bride of King Malcolm. Legend has it that her footprint may still be seen on the rock on which she landed. The scene has been commemorated in the Burgh Arms.

Queensferry has been an important crossing point for many years and the friars of the Carmelite Monastery were the first ferrymen. To the north of the Church of St. Mary of Mount Carmel, built over 500 years ago and one of the oldest Carmelite Houses in Great Britain still used for Christian worship, there is a line of rocks stretching to the Firth, showing traces of cutting to form landing stages for the ferry boats. The first ferry service was not officially opened until the time of King David I in 1129, however, and Queen Elizabeth II and Prince Phillip were the last to use it in 1964, just prior to the opening of the New Forth Bridge. The Ferry Fair, which still held in the second week in August, features the Bury Man, who is completely covered in burs from the burdock plant and visits householders for donations.

A feature of Queensferry has always been its terraces and it is in East Terrace that the oldest house in the town, the Black Castle, built in 1626, still stands. Typically Scottish in character, it has crow-stepped gables and ornamental dormer windows and the narrow staircase in the east gable is reputed to be a smugglers' stair. Next door is the Forth Bridge Hotel, also dating from the seventeenth century, which was much modernized after a fire in 1910.

The Burgh Chambers, which was. once a hotel, is now the Burgh Museum.

The Tollbooth, with its pointed steeple and outside staircase was originally a prison. The four-faced clock was added to commemorate Queen Victoria's Jubilee.

The other main church in

Cramond

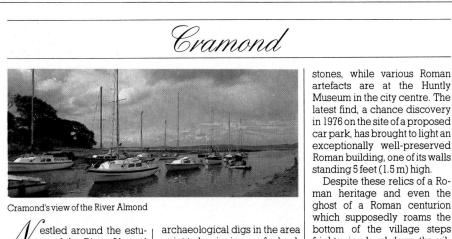

Cramond's view of the River Almond

Nestled around the estuary of the River Almond 4½ miles (7.2 km) northeast of the city centre and backed by an attractive rural hinterland, Cramond is one of the prettiest villages lying along Edinburgh's 9 miles (14.4 km) of coastline.

Conclusions drawn from archaeological digs in the area point to beginnings as far back as AD 142 when Antonius Pius established a fort here to be used as a base for his men when building the 'Antonine Wall' stretching from the Forth to the Clyde. A plan of the fort can be found next to the Kirk, itself partially constructed from Roman stones, while various Roman artefacts are at the Huntly Museum in the city centre. The latest find, a chance discovery in 1976 on the site of a proposed car park, has brought to light an exceptionally well-preserved Roman building, one of its walls standing 5 feet (1.5 m) high.

Despite these relics of a Roman heritage and even the ghost of a Roman centurion which supposedly roams the bottom of the village steps frightening local dogs, the village is predominantly eighteenth century in character. The Industrial Revolution did not pass it by. Water-driven iron-mills were put in harness for the production of iron implements such as nails and shovels, to be gradually replaced by paper

Queensferry, the Kirk, completed in 1635 but renovated in the nineteenth century, also still stands today. It had great influence within the community and parishoners were actually fined for being absent from worship or for taking a boat across the ferry on the Sabbath.

Despite the strict religious background, a distillery flourished here at the beginning of the nineteenth century. It was situated near the pier, between the present Stag Head Hotel and the Queensferry Arms Hotel, and parts of the original building still remain.

Because of Queensferry's attractive location on the Forth, it is ideally situated for pleasant walks and rambles. To the east lies Cramond, to the west, Hopetoun House, while Dalmeny, a planned estate village with great grass verges and a very fine medieval church, is only a mile away.

The old buildings of East Terrace

Newly restored house

and furniture some years later in the mid-nineteenth century. Some of these original mills still stand, as do many of the workers' white-washed cottages which, although much modernized, still retain their old-world charms.

Other buildings date from earlier times. Cramond Kirk and Cramond Tower are both medieval in origin, the latter having once been the property of the Bishops of Dunkeld when it was used as the basic part of the earliest house.

Cramond Inn, is a popular watering hole, reputed to have connections with Stevenson's *St. Ives,* while Cramond House is said to have provided the setting for his *House of Shaws.*

The bridge crossing the River Almond carried traffic between Edinburgh and nearby Queensferry and one of the old tollhouses still stands today. Legend has it that King James V was once being attacked by gypsies on the bridge when a local miller, Jock Howieson, came to his aid. Howieson's reward was the land of Braehead, on condition that his descendants would wash the hands

and feet of all new sovereigns on their first visit to Scotland. In 1952 Elizabeth II was the last to have been the recipient of this quaint gesture.

Interesting though the history is, it is the scenery which first catches the eye and there is a wide variety of walks in the area made all the more enjoyable by the bracing sea air. Northwards towards Hound's Point (so called because of the dog which supposedly haunts it) and Queensferry, a walk passes several interesting features en route, one of which is the first Gothic Revival building in Scotland – Dalmeny House. At low tide one can walk to Cramond Island, inhabited only by birds and mammals. A wide, open promenade leads to Granton and Silverknowes, while a delightful route through leafy glades along the river goes to Barnton.

Newhaven

To many people New-haven still conjures up images of traditional fish-wives, clad in colourful costumes, their cry of 'Caller Ou' resounding through the streets. Unfortunately, these ladies, immortalized in Sir Walter Scott's *The Antiquary* are no longer there, the last one having retired in 1977 at the sprightly age of 89. The village, undergoing extensive re-development, survives, however, and much has been preserved for the appreciation and enjoyment of many generations to come.

Newhaven was originally established at the beginning of the sixteenth century when James IV, at war with England, decided to build a Scottish navy of his own. Its flagship, to be called the *Great Michael*, could not be constructed in Leith owing to insufficient depth of water and so new dockyards were laid out at 'Novus Portus de Leith' (Newhaven) and

Vessels in harbour

Flemish, Dutch and French workers brought in to build the ship. The death of James at the Battle of Flodden brought an end to the ship-building industry which had started to flourish here but soon afterwards the Society of Free Fishermen was founded, adding fuel to Newhaven's increasingly significant standing as a fishing village.

As an offshoot of this industry, a reputation for the preparation of sea food was established in the eighteenth century and in 1767, a wine merchant, Thomas Peacock, petitioned Edinburgh for a few of the links and cottages where the food was prepared. The Peacock Hotel, named after him, still stands.

For a short time in the late 1700s, Newhaven also became the most important ferry and packing station in Scotland, although competition from nearby Granton, established in 1835, soon put this to an end.

Fishing again came to the rescue, this time in the unlikely form of oysters. A bowl of them cost 6d – 2½p – and that included the bowl. Newhaven Fish Market came into being in 1896 and the stalwart Newhaven Fisherwomen's Choir was established during the First World War.

Today, the tramlines and old

Leith

Despite its proximity to the city centre, Leith has always been entirely distinct from it and some animosity has prevailed between the two. Today, many locals bemoan the changes which have taken place here, but it's vital – if chequered – history more than compensates for the steps it has taken under the name of progress.

In the fourteenth century, Logan of Restalrig was allowed to establish the little village of Leith as a burgh of the barony, with fewer privileges than a royal burgh, but holding the right to have incorporations (trade guilds). Even then, trade rivalry between Leith and the city existed and was not improved when, desperate for money, the laird finally sold the superiority of the shore and harbour to Edinburgh. The powerful Leith incorporations were not recognized by the city and friction prevailed until 1833 when Leith gained its independence only to lose it again just after World War I.

Because of its standing as a port and nearness to the city centre, Leith was often the first glimpse of Scotland many royal visitors ever had. It was here that George IV landed with such pomp and ceremony. Mary of Gueldres, Queen Madeleine, Mary of Guise and of course Mary Queen of Scots also arrived on its shores and it was in Lamb's House (now used as a centre by the Edinburgh and Leith Old People's Welfare Council) that the latter rested.

The royal procession would go through Kirkgate, the main street, passing the Church of St. Mary (today, South Leith Church in the churchyard of which are recorded the names of Leith's merchant princes and

Fisherfolk's cottages in the old port

towering lamp-posts which were still in the Main Street in 1948 are no longer there, and most of the buildings have either been restored or completely demolished and new ones put in their place. This on the whole has been done with taste and the cottages on the north side of the Main Street have been restored to retain many of their original Flemish features, with red pantiled roofs and external staircases. Other restored areas include Lamb's Court, Fishmarket Square, Peacock Court and the fishermens' burial ground.

Victoria School, not much altered since 1875 when it was built, has twisting stairs and meandering corridors, as well as an interesting museum of Old Newhaven. Among its exhibits is a copy of the 'Newhaven Sculptured Stone' dated 1588. Local legend has it that this commemorates the part played by the village in the defeat of the Armada. Few would have thought that such a tiny place could have been so influential in its day.

mariners in great days of sail). Some stayed for a time and Charles I played golf in what is now known as Leith Links.

Leith was once a popular bathing resort with a bathing machine on the sands as early as 1750. Shipbuilding was also important and *Sirius*, the first British steamship to cross the Atlantic, was built here in 1837.

Trinity House, belonging to the guild of the sea-faring community still stands today. Part of it is a Maritime Museum and a Raeburn portrait of a famous Leith admiral hangs on one of its walls. The original Custom House in Commercial Street is also still there as is the Boundary Bar, halfway up Leith Walk, complete with brass plate

Leith's Custom House

marking the boundary between Leith and Edinburgh, before 1920.

Indeed, many old buildings have been restored. The Old Leith Bank at the corner of Bernard Street and Constitution Street; King's Wark, an early eighteenth–century tenement building nearby.

Much has also disappeared. The Auld Gaiety, a music hall, is no longer there and neither are the fiddlers, organ-grinders and beggars, including Commodore O'Brien who sat daily on the east side of Leith Walk, in a little masted boat given him by order of George IV.

Perhaps mistakes have been made in the past, but interest has been recently revitalized in preserving that which remains and the tarnished gems of historic Leith are at last being polished for posterity.

The National Gallery of Scotland

Scotland's premier collection of Old Masters and indigenous artists

*I*n contrast to immense galleries like the Louvre in Paris and the National Gallery in London, with their labyrinth of rooms and endless corridors, the National Gallery of Scotland, designed by W.H. Playfair, is entirely accessible and human in scale.

The collection of paintings is not enormous although it contains the most important group of Old Masters in Great Britain outside London and is studded with rarities and masterpieces from almost every major period in Western art. The collection was begun in the 1830s by the old Royal Institution and given its international significance in 1946 by the loan of the Duke of Sutherland's collection – one of the finest collections in Great Britain – containing major works by Raphael, Titian and Rembrandt. In recent years the quality of the collection has been further augmented by the gallery's well-conceived and perspicacious buying policy which has recently enabled it to acquire major works.

A new wing on a lower level houses a Scottish collection which may well surprise the visitor. It has its fair share of curiosities but also includes the work of Scottish painters of international interest: Ramsay, Raeburn and Wilkie.

The following selective tour through the gallery traces the major European artistic movements illuminated by the most important and interesting pictures in the gallery. The easiest and most logical way to gain a good overall impression of the collection is to make your way to the rear of the ground floor after turning left through the entrance. Beginning in Room 7, walk in an anti-clockwise direction around the main floor and then mount the staircase at the rear of the gallery to view the nineteenth-century and Impressionist collections. The comprehensive Scottish wing is downstairs.

Upper Floors

Ground Floor

New Wing

Entrance

The *Bridgewater Madonna* by Raphael, part of the collection on loan to the Gallery from the Duke of Sutherland.

Room 7

This room houses some of the earliest paintings in the gallery. If they all look very different from one another it is because they were painted during the Renaissance, one of the most revolutionary periods in the history of art.

The Renaissance was a dramatic cultural upheaval – literally a rebirth of learning – and affected every sphere of Europe's creative life. In the great city-states of Italy – Florence, Rome, Sienna – scholars rediscovered the literature of ancient Greece and Rome. The Christian ethos of the medieval world was gradually replaced by a new confidence in man's ability to organize his own cosmos. The repercussions on painting were enormous. The flat, decorative late medieval style was abandoned as artists struggled to represent mankind in a believable, naturalistic way. To this end they studied anatomy and practised drawing from life. By 1500 an artist's ability was judged by his skill in painting the figure. A new discovery, scientific perspective, was used to create the illusion of three-dimensional settings.

The medieval tradition of artist as craftsman is exemplified by the thirteenth-century *Tuscan Triptych* displayed in this room. Painting was only one of the artist's skills. His aim was to create a valuable and awe-inspiring object of worship. In this case a large amount of gold-leaf has been employed; the small figure scenes stand out like jewels against the rich background. An altarpiece like this was meant to be closely observed – the scenes of Christ's Passion on the side-panels, for example, are clear

Verrocchio's *Madonna and Child*

and very detailed.

The small late fifteenth-century panel fragment depicting the *Death of St. Ephraim* attributed to Giuliano *Amedei* presents an interesting stylistic contrast with the much earlier triptych. By the time this small panel was painted, artists were studying their environment far more closely. The painter of the triptych made no attempt to place his small figure groups in naturalistic settings but, here, the artist has surrounded his group of mourners with a believable, if stylized, landscape. The figures interact one with another; one can almost hear the murmur of conversation. Unlike the consistently stylized drapery in the triptych, their

robes fall into natural folds.

The stylistic contradictions of Lorenzo Monaco's *Madonna and Child* are the result of an incomplete assimilation of Renaissance ideas. The Madonna herself is of an older tradition – rather like a Byzantine icon – but the child is much more believable. The artist attempts to model the faces and hands but he treats the Madonna's robe in the stylized medieval way. Incidentally, the strange colouring of the Madonna's face was not intentional. Centuries of kissing by the devout has worn away the surface to reveal the green underpaint.

There is no painting here by the greatest Renaissance genius, Leonardo da Vinci.

However, a *Madonna and Child* by his teacher, Andrea del Verrochio, is a particularly tender treatment of this subject. The Madonna gazes down at a very life-like baby fidgeting and sucking his finger. Behind her, Verrochio displays his knowledge of the new perspective in his depiction of an ornate Roman ruin. The drawing of the Madonna's hands for which Verrochio was particularly noted is beautiful. This kind of sweet Italian painting was especially appreciated in Victorian England and this example was owned by John Ruskin.

The background of Raphael's *Bridgewater Madonna* has been overpainted at some time, but the figures show why Raphael was considered one of the greatest Renaissance painters. Not only are they beautifully drawn but they are juxtaposed in perfectly harmonious balance.

The only non-religious work in this room is a portrait by a Florentine contemporary of Raphael, Andrea del Sarto. Raphael and Leonardo had exploited all the subtle effects of oil paint to make the portrait into a penetrating study of the sitter's personality. Following their example, del Sarto employs sensitive brushwork and a restrained tonality to create a very intimate portrait.

Room 8
The main centres of the Renaissance in Italy were Florence, Rome and Venice. Michaelangelo, Leonardo and Raphael worked mostly in Florence and Rome where accurate observation and fine drawing were valued above all else. However, in Venice there was a greater emphasis on colour and the free handling of paint. Absorbing the achievements of Florence and Rome, the Venetians used them to create a far more sensuous style of painting

and the great master of the sixteenth century was Titian. He dominated the scene for most of the century, and no major painter could escape his influence. The five Titians which hang in this room are on loan from the Duke of Sutherland and span the artist's long career.

The Three Ages of Man was painted when Titian was in his early twenties. It is typically Venetian in concept – a poetic work in which landscape is combined with figure painting. A master of the nude, he painted the male figure with an absolute sureness of touch. Titian also invented a new type of female nude exemplified by the *Venus Anadyomene*. Voluptuous and potentially erotic, she recurs in the work of every painter to specialize in the nude from Rubens to Renoir.

In the 1570s Philip II of Spain commissioned Titian to paint a series of mythological subjects. Well aware of his patron's erotic tastes, Titian took the opportunity to show off his mastery of the female nude. The two pictures from that series which hang here represent scenes

from the legend of Diana the huntress. In *Diana and Actaeon* the youthful Actaeon accidentally interrupts the goddess while she is bathing at a fountain in a forest glade. It is an essentially voyeuristic scene. The intruder strides in from the left plunging Diana's naked attendants into disarray while the goddess herself raises a cloth in a gesture indicating anger rather than modesty. Through the arch on the distant horizon a little hunting scene foreshadows Actaeon's fate – Diana turned him into a stag and his own dogs tore him to pieces.

Vengeance is once more the theme in *Diana and Calisto* where the goddess chastises her pregnant handmaiden for her carnality. Here Titian has evolved in style from the smooth finish of *The Three Ages of Man* towards a much more impressionistic and free approach. Paint is applied unevenly over the picture – in some places it is just skimmed over the canvas while in others it is applied densely. The movement and drama are underlined by the immediacy of the technique.

Diana and Actaeon by Titian

Room 9

Scotland lost nearly all of its religious art during the Reformation and the *Trinity Altarpiece* is almost unique in its survival. Nobody is sure of the original function of the two remaining panels though they were once thought to be organ shutters. More likely, they are the flanking wings of a triptych, the central section of which was destroyed. We do know that they were specifically painted for the Collegiate Church of the Holy Trinity, which stood, until the railway came, on the present site of Waverley Station. We also know that they were not painted by a Scottish artist but by the fifteenth-century Netherlandish painter Hugo van der Goes. He was greatly esteemed for his draughtsmanship and fluid use of oil paint, a technique which had recently been refined in Flanders. The commissioning of such a work by a major artist says a great deal about the cosmopolitanism of fifteenth-century Scotland.

The panels are painted on both sides and mounted on a mechanism which turns them at 30-minute intervals. In their closed position, Sir Edward Bonkil, first provost of the Collegiate Church, is depicted kneeling in front of the patron saint of music, St. Cecilia, conventionally portrayed at the organ. The Bonkil portrait is astonishingly realistic and full of character, and was probably painted from life when he travelled to Ghent to arrange the commission.

The panels open to reveal King James III of Scotland and his wife Margaret of Denmark kneeling in front of their country's respective patron saints –

St. Andrew and St. Canute. The fine painting of fabrics and the rich opulence of the backgrounds are typical of Flemish painting though the execution of the royal portrait heads suggests that they were inserted by a local artist after the paintings were shipped to Scotland. It was undoubtedly because of the royal portraits that the panels survived the Reformation. The subject of the missing centrepiece remains a mystery and one can only guess at its splendour.

Room 10

Typical Venetian works by Titian's younger contemporaries are hung in this room.

The recent cleaning of Jacopo Bassano's *Adoration of the Kings* has revealed its brilliance – real Venetian colour. Its exuberance is also typical of Venice – the nativity is just an excuse for a full-scale costume pageant. Everything – colours, patterns, texture – conspires to produce a gorgeous spectacle, but don't be too dazzled. The young Bassano also excelled in portraiture and there are a number of fine portrait heads set into the tumult of robes and accessories. Bassano's attempt at an architectural setting is little more than a caprice.

Tintoretto is most famous for his large-scale mural decorations in which he attempted to combine the drawing of Michaelangelo with the colour of Titian. His *Deposition of Christ* really belongs in the dark of a chapel in the Venetian church of St. Francesco della Vigna. There the candlelight in which the scene takes place would have appeared even more eerie. Tintoretto has managed to give Christ's limp body a real feeling of weight and one can sense the struggle involved in manoeuvering it down from the Cross. The two crouching figures in the foreground are derived from Michaelangelo's

sybils from the ceiling in the Sistine Chapel.

Spanish painting is poorly represented in the collection.

Of the works by El Greco only *The Saviour of the World* truly shows his visionary power. But even this has a certain sweetness which detracts from the potency of the image. Christ has the hieratic appearance of the icons from El Greco's native Crete, combined with the elongated and mannered drawing style of Tintoretto whose work influenced the young Greek when he was studying in Venice. By the time he executed these paintings El Greco had been settled for

El Greco's *The Saviour of the World* painted in the 1590s

many years in Spain where his heightened emotionalism was sympathetic to the religious fervour of the Spanish people.

Velazquez painted *An Old Woman Cooking Eggs* when he was only 19 years old. He was to become one of the greatest portrait painters of all time and, although this picture is a genre piece, the realism of the head painting is quite remarkable. Spanish tradition was essentially realist and Spanish painters excelled at the depiction of surface textures. The still-life in the foreground rivals the best Dutch still-lifes.

Bassano's *The Adoration of the Kings*

Room 11

Painting north of the Alps was always quite distinct from Italy. Painters in Germany and the Low Countries were more pragmatic and their figures are individual, not generalized, types. They were less inclined to experiment than the Italians and medieval traditions persisted longer. But by the beginning of the fifteenth century, Renaissance ideas began filtering through.

Bernard van Orley was a Brussels painter who did his best to imitate the new southern style. He may have visited Italy and certainly saw Raphael's tapestry cartoons which came to Brussels to be woven. His work may not look much like Raphael to today's viewer, but in his day he was known as 'The Raphael of the Netherlands'. The bulky figure of Christ in *Before the Crucifixion* is similar

to Michaelangelo's male on the Sistine ceiling and it fits awkwardly with the grieving women who are still treated in the nothern manner.

Quentin Massays, a leading Antwerp portrait painter, obviously knew about Raphael's and Leonardo's accomplishments. *Portrait of a Man* has an intimate naturalistic air to it. The notary (if that is what he is, for nobody has explained his halo) sits in front of an arcaded window behind which recedes a beautiful rocky landscape similar to Leonardo's in the *Mona Lisa*.

Hans Holbein the younger is also best known for his portraits, especially those of the court of Henry VIII. The unusual *Allegory of the Old and the New Testaments* is a small-scale work executed before he left his native Basle to settle in England. Although it is propagan-

dist in nature – it proclaims the superiority of the new Protestant religion over the old order – the figures are treated with the same realism as his portraits.

Massys' *Portrait of a Notary*

Room 12

Here are works by the two greatest Flemish painters of the seventeenth century: master and pupil – Sir Peter Paul Rubens and Sir Anthony van Dyck. Both worked in England for the ill-fated Charles I and were knighted for their services.

Rubens was a multi-talented genius: diplomat, courtier and linguist, he is one of the most attractive personalities in art history. As a young man he travelled throughout Europe, and he thoroughly absorbed the grand Venetian decorative manner, imbuing it with his own passionate temperament. The result was a colourful ebullient style – full of energy and movement. Rubens satisfied the demands for his work by organizing his workshop on factory lines. Though he was responsible for the overall design of the pictures much of the work was carried out by assistants.

The *Reconciliation of Jacob and Esau* is the sort of small oil sketch Rubens always made for a larger painting. The colour and brushwork is fresh and spontaneous and his composition is full of exotic detail – note the camels in the top right-hand corner.

The full-size *Feast of Herod* is a hugely enjoyable banqueting scene. Rubens has converted one of the most horrific of biblical tales into a brilliant costume piece. Salome sweeps across the picture carrying the head of John the Baptist. After his assistants had completed their tasks it is likely that Rubens himself worked over his canvas, for the bravura brushwork bears his unmistakable stamp.

Van Dyck's *St. Sebastian*

Rubens' *Feast of Herod*

Bound for Martyrdom is an early work painted in the exuberant baroque manner of his master. However, his reputation was made in England as a portrait painter to Charles I and his court. The painting of the Genoese Lomellini family was done in Italy before he settled in England. He was never averse to flattering his subjects and they look down on us with amused disdain.

If you are acquainted with the work of the Dutch painter Vermeer, *Christ in the House of Martha and Mary* may come as a surprise. It is the earliest of his

The Lomellini Family by van Dyck

known works and its biblical theme and large scale make it quite unlike the tranquil domestic interiors for which he

is so famous. The existence of one religious picture caused art historians to presume that Vermeer had done others which have since been lost. This prompted the famous Dutch forger van Meegren to produce a number of fake Vermeers in the style of the Edinburgh picture. The sombre tonality of the picture is characteristic of a group of Dutch painters who imitated the dramatic contrasts of light and shade of the Italian painter Caravaggio. A more typical example of this school's work is Hendrik Terbrugghen's *Beheading of John the Baptist* – possibly the most depressing picture in the gallery.

Room 13

This room is devoted to seventeenth-century artists working in Rome.

It is dominated by *Landscape with Apollo and the Muses*, the largest landscape ever painted by the French-born artist Claude Lorraine. Claude worshipped classical Rome and at an early age decided to spend his life among her ruins. His pictures are not depictions of actual places but idyllic dreams of perfect landscapes peopled by mythological figures. But the figures are

Il Contento by Elsheimer

almost incidental to the composition, and Claude can be seen as the father of pure landscape painting. His work had an enormous influence on succeeding generations of artists.

Two of the smallest and rarest pictures in the gallery are the work of a German expatriot living in Rome, Adam Elsheimer. Elsheimer worked in oil paint on a copper surface – a technique which gives his colours a striking luminosity. In *The Stoning of St. Stephen* the shiny metal underneath makes the bloody gash on the martyr's forehead horribly vivid. *Il Contento* is his masterpiece. An agitated crowd is trying to prevent Zeus abducting the goddess of happiness, unaware that he has replaced her with the goddess of discontent. The picture is filled with movement and dramatic contrast. In spite of the miniature scale of his work and his early death at the age of 32, the vitality and atmosphere of Elsheimer's style inspired a

Elsheimer's *The Stoning of St. Stephen*

host of younger painters from Rubens to Rembrandt.

Even as early as the seventeenth century, Italian artists were looking back to the achievements of the High Renaissance. Domenichino, Guido Reni and Poussin aspired to the calm of Raphael.

The effectiveness of Domenichino's design in his *Nativity* relies on the clear surface pattern formed by the arrangement of his figures. In this he was an important influence on Poussin for whose *Seven Sacraments* the whole of Room 15 is set aside.

You are here

Room 14

This room is upstairs and contains paintings of academic and historical interest rather than those of great artistic merit. Except to students and art historians it is of little interest and the general visitor is advised to pass it by. But the gallery is lucky enough to possess a work by Giotto's pupil Bernardo Daddi which is kept here.

Triptych with Crucifixion is a small private altarpiece. Fourteenth-century artists were craftsmen as well as painters and Daddi has combined painting with delicate wood-carving and a lavish use of gold-leaf to create a visual jewel. The small-scale scenes are treated very theatrically and the little figures are convincing actors. Their tiny faces – especially in the Crucifixion – are filled with grief. Like all works of this period – 100 years before the introduction of oil paint – the triptych is painted in tempera, coloured pigment mixed with egg.

Room 15

A Frenchman, Nicholas Poussin spent his working life in Rome where he was influenced by antique friezes and the figure style of Raphael. He dedicated his life to developing a detached unemotional style through which he could express his deep religious and philosophical convictions.

The Seven Sacraments is a second version of this unusual subject. By freezing all action and subduing the colour, he aimed to induce a quiet, contemplative response. The meaning of each of the sacraments is emphasized by the symmetrical composition

Detail of Poussin's *Baptism*

Detail of Poussin's *Mystic Marriage of St. Catherine*

which focuses attention on the central action – in the Baptism for example, the pouring of the water onto Christ's head.

Room 16

Sixteenth-century Holland was a thriving trading nation and the art of the period reflects the Dutch bourgeois preoccupation with everyday life.

Dutch landscapists were the first artists to paint naturalistic landscapes. Avercamp's atmospheric *Winter Landscape* is thronged not with classical figures, but with ice-skaters. There are no antique ruins in *The Banks of a River* by Jacob van Ruisdael, only a real Dutch town in the distance.

Peter de Hoogh shared Vermeer's interest in the depiction of ordinary rooms and objects. His simple picture of a *Court-yard with an Arbour* (in the corridor leading to Room 17) would have been unthinkable to the Italians.

Frans Hals of Haarlem was almost exclusively a portrait painter. The pair of *Portraits of a Gentleman and His Wife* are extremely fine examples of his mature work, the figures clearly proclaiming in confident poses their wealth and security.

Hals' deftness of touch was second only to Rembrandt's. Rembrandt's earlier portraits are very tightly painted – *Portrait of a Young Woman with Flowers in Her Hair*, wearing a minutely detailed lace collar, shows how precise he could be. However, he was not satisfied only to represent the surface appearance of things and his later work – particularly his self-portraits – shows his obsession with inner character at the expense of expected standards of finish. The *Self-Portrait* is alive with his brushwork.

But Rembrandt was also much moved by biblical stories and often used them as subjects for his paintings. The sentiment of *Hannah and Samuel* is touching because of the tender relationship between the old woman and the boy – the more convincing because the model was probably the painter's own son. The picture on the easel, *Woman in Bed*, was probably meant as part of a larger biblical composition. The model is thought to be Geertje Dircx, who lived with the artist.

At the height of his fame Rembrandt had many pupils, not all of whom were to develop the same free technique as their master. Gerrit Dou was intrigued by light and reflections and painted exquisitely detailed little pictures such as *Interior with a Young Violinist*. Very different from Rembrandt's later work, this is obviously a young man's painting, carefully detailing the usual paraphernalia associated with students. Books are strewn around and there is an upturned beer tankard lying on the floor – things haven't changed much in 350 years.

Self-Portrait from 1657, one of several painted by Rembrandt

Room 17

Back to Italy again, this room is mainly dedicated to the eighteenth-century painters who worked there. At that time no gentleman's education was considered complete unless he went on the 'Grand Tour' and visited the artistic centres of Europe. Rome was the highlight of the trip and the painters resident there profited from the lucrative tourist trade. It was the height of fashion to have one's portrait painted while in Rome – often with a typical Roman background such as the Colosseum. Pompeo Batoni's portrait of *Princess Benedetto Guistiani* lacks the fashionable landscape backdrop, but in the strong characterization and delicacy of handling you can see why he was the most popular portrait painter in the city.

The Scots painter Gavin Hamilton worked on a grandiose scale and one cannot imagine even the most enthusiastic tourist carrying home his *Achilles Lamenting the Death of Patroclus*. Hamilton was a dealer in antiquities who spent most of his life digging up Rome. His unparalleled knowledge of ancient Roman art was the main influence on his painting, though his figure style owes a great deal to Poussin.

In complete contrast to the academicism of Hamilton is *The Finding of Moses* by the Venetian painter Giovanni Battista Tiepolo. There is nothing pedantic about this bravura romp by one of the greatest decorators of the eighteenth century. Tiepolo makes absolutely no attempt at historical accuracy. Although this scene is sup-

Achilles Lamenting the Death of Patroclus by Hamilton, 1763

El Medico (The Doctor) by Goya

posed to have taken place in ancient Egypt, he has dressed Pharaoh's daughter in sixteenth-century finery and her attendants – especially the dwarf – are straight out of a Renaissance court.

The style of the Spanish painter Francisco de. Goya also owes something to Tiepolo although he lacks the Italian's frivolity. Indeed his later work was exceedingly dark and pessimistic. *El Medico* is an unusually light-hearted picture of a doctor on his rounds warming himself over a brazier and is a tapestry design meant for a decorative scheme in one of the Spanish royal palaces.

Room 18

During the eighteenth century the English aristocracy developed a passion for portraiture, and many gifted painters specialized in giving the public what it wanted. Perhaps the greatest was Thomas Gainsborough who gave his clients good value for money.

The Honourable Mrs. Graham was only 18 when she sat for Gainsborough, so we can be sure that her youthful bloom had nothing to do with flattery. But young faces present even the finest painter with a difficult problem – they can so easily appear bland and characterless. Gainsborough has coped by making a great play of the costume – a dazzling piece of work. Mrs. Graham was shown at the Academy in 1777 and we can be sure that she outshone her rivals.

Gainsborough's chief rival

Detail of Gainsborough's
The Hon. Mrs. Graham

Chardin's *Still Life*

Constable's *The Vale of Dedham*

was Sir Joshua Reynolds, first President of the Royal Academy and one of the most respected figures in English art.

In matters of theory Reynolds was the most erudite man in the country, but when it came to painting portraits he lacked Gainsborough's vitality though his pictures of women and children have an attractive sweetness. The *Ladies Waldegrave* – three fashionable sisters – are portrayed with an appropriately flattering eye.

In France, J.B.S. Chardin is distinguished from his contemporaries by this unaffected and direct approach to subject matter as can be seen in his *Still Life: The Kitchen Table*. Neither could anything be simpler than *Vase of Flowers*, his only surviving flowerpiece. It is a minor masterpiece.

In contrast fellow Frenchman Antoine Watteau has painted supremely artificial works. His imaginary scenes of costumed ladies and gentlemen cavorting in prettified pastoral settings are really *bon-bons*. This is not to belittle his talent, for Watteau was a fine draughtsman and kept albums of his beautiful drawings from which he selected the figures for his compositions. *Fêtes Venitiennes* is not only one of his finest pictures, it is also one of the best preserved.

Rooms 19 and 20

The room to the left at the top of the stairs is mostly dedicated to early nineteenth-century English painting, so Frederick Edwin Church's *Niagara Falls from the American Side* is decidedly out of place. Church was one of the leading lights of the emergent nineteenth-century American landscape school which sought to celebrate the natural wonders of the New World. He could hardly have found a more awe-inspiring subject than Niagara and represents the full force of its torrents on a suitably enormous canvas.

John Constable's *Vale of Dedham* is positively serene by comparison. It is based on a classical composition by Claude Lorraine though it does contain precise features of Constable's local landscape such as the tower of Dedham Church and the meandering River Stour. This is a highly finished exhibition picture worked on at length in the studio and quite different from the loosely treated little sketch *On the Stour* which was probably executed in a few minutes direct from nature.

However, the most magnetic picture in the room, far outshining Church's bombastic Niagra, is J.M.W. Turner's *Dream of Italy*, the paint surface of which seems almost dissolved in light. Unlike Constable who adored the English landscape, Turner was besotted by Italy. His pair of Roman views, *Modern Rome* and *Rome from the Aventine*, are full of topographical details such as the Colosseum, yet they remain poetic evocations of a golden Mediterranean world.

In the early nineteenth century pure landscape was considered a minor art and Turner was obliged to include mythological or historical figures to make his pictures acceptable to the Royal Academy. Constable refused to compromise his authentic view of rural England and, unlike the successful Turner, he gained little official recognition. Despite these differences, in Turner's and Constable's freedom of handling and preoccupation with light effects they can be seen as precursors of the Impressionists.

Eugene Delacroix, the greatest romantic painter of nineteenth-century France, admired both Constable and Turner although he was preoccupied with monumental figure composition rather than pure landscape. Like all romantics, he was intrigued by exotic Eastern subject matter and *The Chessplayers* gives us a hint of the opulence of his colour and technique.

Upper Rooms 21, 22, 23.

All the paintings hanging in these rooms are the work of men who, in one way or another, rejected the authority of the French Salon. Their experiments and investigations were to transform people's ideas about painting and sow the seeds of an aesthetic revolution they could have scarcely foreseen.

Gustave Courbet's small canvases, *View of Ornans with Church Tower, River in Mountain Gorge* and *The Wave* may look harmless enough – even conventional to modern eyes. But in the 1850s their painter represented all that was revolutionary in French art. Courbet waged war against the Academy and all it stood for. When his works were accepted for exhibition in the annual Salon, they incurred bitter criticism on account of what was seen as their vulgarity. If his work failed to be accepted he characteristically set up an alternative show – erecting a tent and charging admission! Courbet offended against official taste both in his choice of subjects and the way in which he painted them. He chose 'down to earth' things – a local burial or men breaking stones for example. Not for him historical or mythological subjects, false sentimentality or overt moralizing. Something of this direct approach can be seen in these three small pictures; especially in the simplicity of his sea composition with its broad use of palette-knife. The unprettified, sober townscape is a view of Ornans – the artist's hometown. Courbet's attitude to his art was influenced in no small way by his political idealism. A convinced socialist,

perhaps the most bizarre episode of his extrovert career occurred in 1871 when he was held responsible for the destruction of the Vendome Column during the Paris Commune of that year. His last years were spent in exile in Switzerland.

The other small landscapes hanging here alongside the work of Courbet represent another – less violent – anti-Academic trend in mid-nineteenth-century painting. *Soleil Couchant* and *Cottages at Barbizon: Evening* by Charles Daubigny and *Pool in the Forest* by Narcisse Diaz are both typical, in their freshness and intimacy, of the pictures produced by a group of landscapists working in the Fontainbleau woods south of Paris. Centred on the village of Barbizon, they have become known as the Barbizon School and anticipate the Impressionists in their dedication to working directly from nature out of doors.

They admired Dutch seventeenth-century landscape painting and the work of John Constable and the spontaneity of many of their small pictures recalls that of the English artist. The charming picture *Entrance to a Wood* was painted by the group's chief mentor, Camille Corot, and is a fine example of the subtle, poetic type of landscape which made him the most popular and influential landscape painter of his generation. Building up a picture with small areas of soft tone, Corot produced a very indistinct romantic effect, paying scant attention to precise line-drawing and concentrating on the atmosphere of a subject. This aspect of his work not only endeared him to the Impressionists but also made him a favourite with generations of forgers who made sure that Corots continued to come onto the market long after his death in 1875.

Pictures by the Impressionists are so often reproduced

that the shocking effect they must have had on the public in the 1870s can easily be forgotten. But, even here, where they rub shoulders with the pictures of the Barbizon school, their brightness – the high pitch of their colours – produces a shattering contrast.

The spirit of the group is epitomized by Auguste Renoir's *La Promenade*. Such a delightfully casual subject would have been unthinkable earlier in the century. The naturalism of the picture is a result of Renoir's acute observation of the effect of light filtering through the trees and dappling the strolling couple. And it was light and the difficult technical problem of rendering its transitory effects that obsessed the Impressionists. Claude Monet spent his whole life grappling with the problem. In the 1890s he painted entire series of works – almost scientific studies – of the same subject seen at different times of day and in different weather conditions. *Poplars on the Epte* and *Haystacks: Snow Effect* are from two such series. The picture of haystacks is a very good example of the Impressionist belief that the shadows of objects are tinged by the object's complimentary colour.

In the painting of poplar trees the form of the trees is broken up by the shimmering light rendered with small agitated brushstrokes. These small dabby brushstrokes became a hallmark of Impressionist pictures. Alfred Sisley produced some of the prettiest of them. *Mosley Weir: Hampton Court* was painted when, along with several other Impressionists, he fled to England during the 1870s in order to escape the political turmoil of France.

Together with Monet, Camille Pissarro was to become one of the most dedicated and consistent practitioners of Impressionism, but his large *River*

The Wave by Courbet

Haystacks by Monet

Landscape hanging here was executed before he had fully developed his ideas. *The Kitchen Garden at the Hermitage, Pontoise* is a more typical work.

Edgar Degas' *Portrait of Diego Martelli* displays all the characteristics which set him

Degas' *Diego Martelli*

apart from other Impressionists.

The picture's greatest strength is the superb drawing of Diego Martelli (note the delineation of the crumpled trousers). Degas was a magnificent draughtsman, traditionally trained, and this love of drawing always tended to make him antipathetic towards the Impressionists' overwhelming preoccupation with light. For Degas light was a dramatic tool with which to compose arresting pictures in the quiet of his studio and not something to be slavishly copied out of doors. But in spite of his more conventional attitude towards picturemaking, he was in many respects an innovator. One of the first painters to use the camera extensively in his work, he became fascinated by the unusual appearances of things seen from unexpected angles. Extending the Impressionist range of modern subjects, he painted the races, women in hat shops, laundresses. The ballet, in particular, gave him endless scope to compose interesting groups of contorted figures and the artificial theatre lights

prompted him to explore exciting, unnatural combinations of colours. Note how deftly Degas is able to contrive a composition like *Group of Dancers* from a severely limited palette of greens and oranges. While some of the Impressionists

escaped to England to avoid the deprivations of Paris under seige by the Prussians in 1870-1871, Degas stayed on, enduring dreadful hardships. As a result he soon began to lose his sight. *Nude Study for 14 Year Old Dancer, Dressed* is a bronze taken from one of the sensitive wax models he made when his almost total blindness prevented him from painting.

A comparison between Paul Gauguin's *Vision of the Sermon: Jacob and the Angel* and the previously discussed Impressionist pictures will give some idea of the extreme reaction against Impressionist naturalism which occurred in the 1880s. Before he found his very personal voice Gauguin worked in an Impressionist style, exhibiting with the group in their later exhibitions. *The Vision* is his first overwhelming antinaturalistic picture – an imaginary subject painted in flat brilliant colours. The convoluted

shapes of the Breton women's headdresses are silhouetted against a field of strident vermillion. The diagonal thrust of the tree across the picture plane is inspired by similar compositions found in the Japanese prints popular in

Gauguin's *The Vision of the Sermon (Jacob Wrestling with the Angel)*

France at this time. The overall effect of Gauguin's picture is closer to that of medieval stained glass than the work of the Impressionists and it was, indeed, the emotional impact found in medieval work with which Gauguin wanted to imbue his picture. Gauguin continued his visionary painting in the South Seas. The serene mood of a picture like *Three Tahitians* gives no indication of the inconveniences and hardships he suffered there.

Gauguin eventually abandoned the small brushstrokes of the Impressionists to paint in flat areas of vivid colour but van Gogh chose to develop them into a violent personalized calligraphy. *Olive Trees* vibrates with the artist's disturbed personality. The brushstrokes of colour writhe over the surface of the canvas. What might have been a rather charming scene in the hands of one of the Impressionists has become an emotional expression of the artist's state of mind. Like Gauguin who fled from the bourgeois life of a stockbroker to dedicate himself to art, van Gogh came to painting late in life. For a very short period in 1888 the two painters even tried applying paint, Seurat's art is in almost every other respect alien to that of the Impressionists. Unlike them he had no interest in capturing the fleeting moment but wanted to compose harmonious classical pictures. The small study hanging underlying forms of nature – the solidity of an apple or a mountain. In his later years he lived a hermit's life near Aix en Provence, constantly analysing a very narrow range of subjects. The underlying structure and shape of *Mont St. Victoire* was a

Van Gogh's *Olive Trees*

living together but this experiment was not a success. .

The Impressionist method of building up an image with small strokes of paint of precisely the right tone and colour had always been a more or less instinctive process. George Seurat investigated the actual scientific basis for the theories vaguely espoused by Monet and the other Impressionists. Under the influence of various optical theories current in the 1880s, he developed a way of placing small dashes of pure colour alongside one another, intending them to fuse into correct areas of tone to the eye.

Apart from the similar way of

here is a free sketch for the monumental depiction of a contemporary bathing scene in the National Gallery, London.

Whatever the virtues of Impressionist painting, it could never really defend itself against the criticism that it was lacking in form. Impressionist pictures were painted quickly in an effort to capture a particular moment – the transitory effects of light on things. The structure of things was more or less irrelevant. Paul Cezanne began by painting in a more formless manner than any of the Impressionists but gradually became obsessed by the problem of describing the simple

source of constant fascination for him. Using the natural brush-strokes and a limited palette, he repeatedly tried to find some equation for its form on canvas. Many of these attempts are unfinished, like our example here, almost, as if the task was too daunting to be successfully accomplished. Cezanne's single-minded dedication to solving this problem influenced a generation of artists. The first great movement of the twentieth century, Cubism, developed as a result of his research and he is now generally regarded as one of the most influential artists of the last 100 years.

1   2   3   4   5

The Scottish Collection

The new downstairs extension houses the gallery's Scottish collection. These few rooms offer a quick survey of eighteenth- and nineteenth-century Scottish painting which should not be missed. It is an uneven group of paintings but the best pictures certainly rank alongside many of the masterpieces of European painting upstairs.

Keeping company amidst a number of undistinguished early portraits we meet with the haunting eyes of the French philosopher *Jean-Jacques Rousseau*. The painting is by Rousseau's friend Allan Ramsay who exemplifies the sophisticated, cosmopolitan, eighteenth-century Scot. Ramsay made a considerable reputation in London, eventually becoming court painter to George III. This was an appointment much resented by Reynolds

whom contemporary critics considered superior in male portraiture. Reynolds never produced anything quite so perceptive as this characterization of the quicksilver Rousseau. Rousseau was upset that Ramsay had made him look too 'shifty'. Reynolds' admirers, however, conceded that Ramsay was without equal in the portrayal of female beauty.

The other great eighteenth-century Scottish portraitist, Sir Henry Raeburn, made his reputation entirely in Scotland, immortalizing the leading lights of the eighteenth-century cultural revival. Had he shown more in London perhaps his international reputation might now stand higher, for at his best he has the freshness and fluidity of Goya. A portrait like *Sir Patrick Inglis* shows Raeburn at his most natural. Executed quickly and simply in broad brushstrokes of fresh colour without fussing over unnecessary detail, in it he has captured the whole character of his sitter.

In contrast his magnificent portrait of *Colonel Alastair*

McDonnel of Glengarry in full highland dress seems rather over-worked. But it is a costume piece and must have looked very dramatic high on the wall of some dark baronial hall.

On a less serious note, who can fail to be charmed by Raeburn's portrait of *The Rev. Robert Walker Skating on Duddingston Loch*. The ludicrous sight of this dour minister skating is one of the most memorable images in the gallery.

Sir David Wilkie's reputation was made in London where he became a member of the Royal Academy. The honest realism of his early work comes straight from Dutch art. The narrative and attention to detail in such story pictures as *The Letter of Introduction* and *Distraining for Rent* made him enormously popular in his own day. However, in later life after suffering a breakdown of health he visited Spain where he came under the influence of Spanish painting. These last pictures are the antithesis of all his early work – large in scale and loosely painted. Unfortunately, he mixed bitumen with his paint to make his dark colours richer and this has caused these pictures to crack dreadfully.

The remaining rooms are filled with a plethora of lochs, beasties and elders of the Church. Enjoy wandering through for they are great fun, if not exactly high art. Marvel at Noel Paton's enamelled fairy paintings crammed with hundreds of tiny female nudes – in reality, Victorian soft pornography. Thrill to the drama of James Drummond's costume pieces, starring the ill-fated Mary, Queen of Scots. Do not miss the tiny tempera panels of William Dyce whose exact technique and sincere approach to religious subject matter influenced the English Pre-Raphaelites.

Finally, as you are leaving, note the large Impressionistic pictures of the West Coast of Scotland by Sir William McTaggart. He understood the Impressionist's theories before any other British painter and his brushwork and fresh colour points the direction of modern Scottish painting.

Far left *The Quarrel of Oberon and Titania* by Paton, 1849.
Above *Rev. Robert Walker Skating* by Raeburn.
Below *The Storm* by McTaggart, dated 1890.

National Gallery of Modern Art

Masterpieces of twentieth-century painting, sculpture and graphic art

The Scottish National Gallery of Modern Art enjoys one of the finest settings in the city. It stands on a small hill in the middle of the Royal Botanic Garden, Edinburgh's most delightful park. The location is perfect. There is a remarkable view – the best to be had – of the city skyline from the lawn in front of the gallery and the surrounding gardens guarantee just the right atmosphere in which to look at pictures. It is a pity there is not more sculpture displayed in the grounds; Henry Moore's two reclining figures are particularly impressive, silhouetted against the backdrop of the city.

Recently, however, the gallery has been considering a move to larger premises in a less romantic quarter of town. The present building's only drawback is its size. Limited wallspace allows only a fraction of the collection to be shown at any one time. To ensure choice works get a regular airing, the exhibition needs frequent rehanging; over-exposed works are returned to the store; neglected pictures are resurrected. Consequently it is not a gallery where you can become accustomed to seeing 'old friends' hanging in the same position. The Matisse you examine so carefully on one visit is absent on the next; occasionally the entire upper floor is given over to a special exhibition. A room-by-room guide is, therefore, impossible but certain works by the established masters of the modern movement are usually on display somewhere in the gallery. In spite of the inflated price of modern art the Scottish National Gallery of Modern Art has succeeded in building up a very respectable collection since its founding in 1960.

The core of its collection is a small group of works by the pioneer artists of the twentieth century. *Candlestick* by Georges Braque is a very good example of the work of the Cubist movement he developed along with Picasso in the years leading up to World War I. There are pictures from the various phases of the career of

Artistic tradition in Scotland

The long traditions of Scottish art are linked with those of Europe in certain respects, but, in others, they are unique. The national tradition of painting really begins with the Renaissance – or, rather, the lack of it, for the Renaissance spirit of artistic independence totally failed to spread to Scotland at the time. Unlike England, where itinerant Continental painters such as Holbein and Van Dyck took the place of the monkish artists expelled by the Reformation, Scotland had little such imput. The chief reason for this was the sheer distance from the centres of European art, though the climate and the dour Scottish character may have had something to do with it as well.

Thrown back on their own resources, the Scots developed their own native art style. Mostly, Scottish painters worked in portrait – a tradition that was to expand and flower until it reached its peak in the work of the eighteenth-century artists Allan Ramsay and Henry Raeburn. These were the painters of the first great Celtic revival, even though Ramsay made his reputation in London and eventually became Court Painter to George III.

As this tradition reached its peak with Raeburn, another tradition was being founded with the work of the young David Wilkie. His development marks the beginning of a new movement in art which was not just of Scottish, but also of European, importance. Wilkie's adoration of the Dutch and Flemish schools led him to adopt the genre style in his painting. This, sometimes in a slightly debased form, became a cult in Victorian times. Wilkie was described by Millais as the greatest Scottish painter; he became so fashionable that, when his painting showing the return of the veterans from Waterloo was exhibited at the Royal Academy, London, barriers had to be erected to keep back the crowds.

The style became part of the

Pablo Picasso – probably the most universally acclaimed artist in history: a tiny canvas *Mother and Child* from his famous 'Blue Period', and two still-lifes, *La Table de Musicien* and *The Soles*, both painted in later contrasting styles. Do not miss *La Leçon de Peinture* by Henri Matisse. It is an uncharacteristically sombre picture by a painter famed for his bright colours: a picture composed of simplified decorative shapes. There are a number of fascinating Surrealist works: pictures by Rene Magrite, Joan Miró and Max Ernst. The works of German and Russian artists – often greatly influenced by avant-garde French developments in the early years of the century – are displayed alongside the French work. Note the chilling nude by Otto Dix.

Perhaps the gallery's greatest strength is its comprehensive selection of British twentieth-century painting. All major figures are represented from Matthew Smith, with his very personal interpretation of French Fauvism, to David Hockney, one of the most popular artists in Britain today.

A unique feature of the Scottish National Gallery of Modern Art collection is its group of works by Scottish painters. Relatively unknown in the rest of Britain, painters in Scotland at the beginning of this century were often closer to continental developments than their counterparts in England. They form a specifically Scottish school known as the Colourists. Their brightly coloured work is often on view. Look out for paintings by Peploe, Cadell Hunter and Fergusson.

Reclining Figure 1951, in bronze, is one of two by Henry Moore in the grounds

Scottish Academy tradition, together with good portraiture, following Raeburn's example. By the mid-nineteenth century, the former was becoming steadily more romantic – subjects included scenes from Scott's novels, border ballads and the like – and centred on landscape.

It was at this time that yet another tradition started, which has deeply influenced Scottish art down to the present day. This was a painterly version of the Auld Alliance, demonstrating the continuing Scottish love of things French and of French culture in particular.

In reaction to the conservatism of the Scottish Academy, a group of young painters started looking to France and, in particular, to the work of the Impressionists. Gradually, the link grew. Sir William McTaggart, for instance, was the first notable painter in Britain to work in the Impressionist tradition.

McTaggart was joined by a group known as the Colourists. This group was Glasgow- and Edinburgh-based (the first Academy rebels had been from Glasgow). Scotland's painters today still show the influence; it is notable, for instance, in the work of Joan Eardly, one of Scotland's most important painters.

The story of Scottish art is made up of many strands and themes. Some Scottish artists took the prosperous road south; others, like Raeburn, have been neglected in Britain, though acclaimed on the Continent and in the USA. One factor remains constant – the fact that individuality has been preserved in Scottish art. Its great flowering was almost as much a reaction to external circumstances as the result of the gifts of the painters themselves. The guiding light, in art as in much else since the Union of Parliaments, has been the determination to make painting an integral part of an independent national heritage. In pictorial form, this shows itself in the free handling of paint; in attitude, it shows itself in a spirit of fierce independence which has persisted to the present day.

Royal Scottish Museum

A celebration of the skills that powered the Industrial Revolution

As might be expected of the capital of a proud and ancient nation, Edinburgh's many museums are treasure-houses of national, as well as local, importance. Full coverage is given in the directory section of this book, but, because of their unique importance, two – the Royal Scottish Museum and the National Museum of Antiquities of Scotland – are singled out here.

The Royal Scottish Museum, Chambers Street, has many

claims to distinction. First, it is the only national museum in the UK to house its main collections under one roof. Second, it is housed in one of the finest Victorian buildings in the country; its light, spacious galleries, arranged around a striking main hall, make an ideal setting for the varied collections. These range from celebrated

mammal and bird exhibitions through practically every artistic and scientific field.

It appears, however, that such diversity was not necessarily the intention of the museum's founding fathers. The forerunner of the Royal Scottish was the Industrial Museum of Scotland, founded in 1854; since that time, industry, invention, science and technology have always been given major emphasis.

Such emphasis is natural

The huge natural history section displays elephants, the skeleton of a blue whale (**left**) and the dodo of the Indian Ocean (**above**). The attractive iron galleries of the Main Hall are shown on the opposite page.

enough, for many of the leading lights of the great days of the Industrial Revolution were Scots themselves, or had links with Scotland. James Watt, whose skill and ingenuity made the steam engine into a practical proposition, was born in Scotland; Robert Stephenson, with his father, George, a pioneer of the railway age, was educated

at Edinburgh University. These are only two examples from the host of Scottish inventors and entrepreneurs, many of whom are now forgotten but whose achievements played a major part in the shaping of our modern industrial world.

On the ground floor, the sheer scale of the Hall of Power and the exhibits within it aptly set off the importance of its chief theme – the development of steam as the power source which set the wheels of industry turning. Here, Scottish ingenuity combined with Scottish pragmatism to major effect; it is often forgotten that James Watt's first backer, John Roebuck, was Scottish and that it was only after the latter ran into financial difficulties that his share in Watt's patents was sold to Matthew Boulton.

Dominating one end of the Hall of Power is a giant industrial waterwheel, made in Manchester in 1826 for a firm of millers in Aberdeen. Close by it stands another major exhibit, the locomotive *Wylam Dilly*. This dates from 1813 and, with its twin, *Puffing Billy*, is the oldest locomotive in existence. Next to the locomotive is a working model. Scale models are a major feature of the Royal Scottish's engineering and scientific collections; in many instances, recorded push-button commentaries are also available.

In the southeast corner of the hall is the enormous black cylinder of the Boulton and Watt Double-Acting Beam Engine

(1786). This is an early example of Watt's work. Contrary to popular belief, Watt did not invent the steam engine; he took the existing Newcomen model and vastly improved it, making it far more efficient, as well as cutting down on fuel consumption. The resulting engine was the work-horse of the Industrial Revolution. It was long-lasting, reliable and, with appropriate modification, could be used in mines, iron works, mills, pumping stations and breweries. Many Watt engines continued in service until the end of the nineteenth century; the museum's engine worked for 99 years before being replaced.

Like many great ideas, Watt's was simple in concept. While repairing a Newcomen-type model, he realized that it was extremely wasteful to first heat the cylinder to produce the steam and then to cool the cylinder to condense it. On a Sunday afternoon walk, it came to him that a separate condenser and air pump was the answer. The latter was the key part of the invention. It sucked the air out of the condenser to produce a partial vacuum. The steam from the cylinder rushed into this vacuum, where it was immediately condensed. The surrounding steam at atmospheric pressure then moved the engine's piston.

The size of the Boulton and Watt engine is in keeping with its importance in the annals of the Industrial Revolution. To the north of *Wylam Dilly*, however, is another exhibit, which, though far smaller in scale, was just as important to the world of agriculture as the work of Watt was to the growth of industry.

In 1750 the Scottish millwright Andrew Meikle produced his version of the 'fan-tail' gear for automatically keeping a mill facing the wind. This was one of the greatest advances in windmill engineering ever recorded, for it meant that the miller no longer had to alter the position of the mill's sails manually when the wind changed direction. Meikle went on to apply his inventiveness to adapt the windmill as a 'windengine' for the driving of farm machinery as well as the grinding of corn. The museum's model may have been an inventor's model, or it may have been made to demonstrate advances in windmill design.

Agriculture, however, was rapidly overhauled by industry as the prime source of the nation's wealth and a host of new inventions flooded onto the market to make that industry more efficient and productive. As always, Scottish pioneers led the way. James Nasmyth's

Museum floor plan

Second floor

First floor

Ground floor

Entrance

Some of the fascinating encounters that await the visitor to the Royal Scottish Museum are pictured here. They are representatives from the four main departments of the museum – art and archaeology, geology, natural history and technology

The departments generally are not restricted to one area but have exhibits on several floors.

Scottish silver box 1736

Fish fossils, 350 million years old

Relief of Pharoah Akhenaten 1365-1348 BC

Model of Bell Rock lighthouse 1833

Locomotive Wylam Dilly 1813

Percy Pilcher's *Hawk* 1896

Western lowland gorilla 1868

Stirling's Hot Air Engine 1816

The huge Hercules beetle
is the size of a
man's hand.

Industrial waterwheel 1826

steam hammer (1842) – a model by the west wall – made it possible to forge large pieces of iron. Nasmyth was also a pioneer of machine tools, the life blood of modern industry. His fertile mind encompassed many fields, including an intriguing anti-invasion floating mortar, designed to destroy 'by one masterly blow, the largest ship of an invading enemy'.

Scottish inventiveness was not confined to the large or monumental. Hanging in the Hall of Power is Percy Pilcher's 'Hawk' glider, dating from 1896. This is the oldest flying machine in Britain and, though its inventor was born in Bath, it was built and flown in Scotland. Pilcher was working on a powered airplane when he crashed to his death in 1899; had he survived, it is an open question whether Scotland, rather than the USA, might not have given birth to the flying machine.

A last intriguing exhibit is the Stirling Hot Air Engine (1816), directly across from the Pilcher glider. Invented by Robert Stirling, a Perthshire minister, the engine used hot air, rather than steam, as its driving force. Its special feature was a regenerator to absorb and store heat that would otherwise have been wasted. A similar type of engine is being used in space

experiments today.

Through the south door of the Hall of Power is the Hall of Shipping. During the nineteenth and early twentieth centuries, Scotland was the centre of the world's finest shipbuilding industry and its Clydeside yards produced literally thousands of ships for all nations, ranging from humble tugs to sleek warships and vast ocean liners. The museum's shipping exhibits are divided between this hall and the Hall of Victorian Engineering, but here note the models of the armed merchantman *Yellow Carvel* (1480) and the warship *Great Michael* (1511). These demonstrate that the Scottish maritime tradition stretches back over centuries.

There is yet another example of Scottish invention. By the middle of the south wall is the screw propeller invented by Robert Wilson of Dunbar in 1826. Though there is fierce dispute – as there was in Wilson's own lifetime – as to whether he was first in the field, his screw is very similar to modern design.

Directly above the Hall of Shipping on the first floor is the gallery of Lighthouses and Bridges. Both of these were among the principal Scottish achievements in the nineteenth century; in the Edinburgh area alone, there are the Dean

Bridge and the Forth Rail Bridge, the latter being joined today by its road equivalent. Leith Docks were another major civil engineering achievement.

Just in front of the east entrance is a model of the Bell Rock lighthouse. This was designed by Robert Stevenson, grandfather of the author Robert Louis and the principal lighthouse engineer of his day. It was completed in 1811. The model not only shows details of the lighthouse itself, but of how the men who built it went about the task.

The Stevenson family influenced Scottish lighthouse design for several generations. Near the Bell Rock exhibit, in a case against the east wall, is an elaborate oil lamp of considerable candlepower, designed in 1842 by Alan Stevenson, eldest son of Robert.

However, the chief glory of Scottish civil engineering in the nineteenth century was undoubtedly the construction of the Forth Rail Bridge. On a pillar beside the open well looking down to the Hall of Shipping is a series of photographs showing the construction of the bridge. Work on it began in January 1883 and the opening ceremony was on March 4, 1890. During the intervening

Scotland's Oil – 1851

Say 'Scotland's oil' to the man in the street and he will immediately associate the statement with the towering oil platforms of the North Sea. Yet the true story of Scottish oil begins in 1851, years before the first US oil well was drilled.

The Scottish oil industry was founded by one man, James 'Paraffin' Young. He discovered the secret of extracting oil from a special coal, called Torbanite, found in West Lothian, and in 1851 he established the

James 'Paraffin' Young, founding father of the modern oil industry, and the chemist Robert Angus Smith.

world's first commercial oil works. With the exhaustion of Torbanite supplies, he found a subsitute in oil-shale and the Scottish oil-boom began.

By 1865, some 120 companies were in the field, though the number soon dwindled. Nevertheless, even with the growth of the giant oil industries of the USA and the Middle East, Scottish shale oil survived until 1962, when the price of it finally became economically exorbitant and the last shale working closed.

Dunlop's first pneumatic bicycle tyres, made in 1888. The Royal Scottish has the front wheel and tyre.

years up to 4600 men worked on it at any one time, while the bridge cost approximately £3 million to build. Nearby, the stages of building the Forth Road Bridge (1964) are shown. This cost considerably more than its Victorian predecessor, even allowing for the changing value of money.

The pick of the Victorian engineering collections is now housed in the Hall of Victorian Engineering. Here, the exhibits cover every aspect of Victorian endeavour. Compare the presentation models of notable locomotives – note in particular the early Stephenson-type *Edina* (1840) – with that of the cruiser *HMS Terrible*, built on Clydeside in 1898. It was the most powerful warship of its type in its day, its 48 boilers

driving it at a top speed of 22 knots. Its builders, J & G Thomson, gave the model just as much attention as the ship itself.

Yet another controversy has raged over two juxtaposed exhibits in the hall – an interesting reminder of how jealous our business-like Victorian forefathers could be. The dispute over who developed the first pneumatic tyre was bitterly contended at the time and the exhibits here demonstrate the work of the two Scots who laid claim to the invention – John Boyd Dunlop and R. W. Thomson. Today, it is clear that Thomson invented the principle of the pneumatic tyre in 1845 at the staggeringly early age of 23 – it is shown here fitted to an 1845 Brougham – but, because of practical difficulties, the idea languished until 1887. Then Dunlop married his skill to new techniques to produce the first durable pneumatic tyre.

Thomson, however, was ac-

tive in many other fields. As well as being a pioneer of steam road traction, he contributed greatly to the development of the gas industry, as his rotary exhauster, used to pump gas, shows. Gas lighting itself was pioneered by yet another Scot, William Murdock, in 1798. The importance of the Scottish contribution to the gas industry is commemorated by the Royal Scottish at its outstation at Biggar, 29 miles (47km) southwest of Edinburgh.

Naturally, the Royal Scottish contains much else of absorbing interest to the visitor, whether tourist or resident. This brief glimpse of one aspect of its contents, however, should serve to demonstrate how much we owe today to the extraordinary breed of men produced by Scotland, who combined the willingness to experiment with practical sagacity and a stubborn belief that nothing was impossible.

The National Museum of Antiquities

The gift of an eccentric Earl preserves Scotland's national heritage

Edinburgh's other notable museum is the National Museum of Antiquities of Scotland, in Queen Street, which, unlike the Royal Scottish, restricts its exhibits to those of Scottish origin. The emphasis has always been on archaeology – it is Scotland's premier archaeological museum, housing an internationally important collection – but other exhibits cover almost every aspect of Scottish life from earliest times to the present century.

The museum was founded by the 11th Earl of Buchan (1742-1829). Buchan was one of the great eccentrics of his day, free with his advice on practically every issue. Amongst those he bombarded with correspondence were George III and George Washington, both of whom he rather surprisingly addressed as 'cousin'.

Though the Earl's eccentricity and vanity undoubtedly put some people off – one letter reads simply 'I beg you will send me no more intimations respecting the meetings of the Antiquarian Society' – his creation flourished. It moved to its present home, which it shares with the Scottish National Portrait Gallery, in 1891.

Today, the exhibits are arranged on three floors, with temporary exhibitions on the stairs from time to time. Many of the major displays have been redesigned recently, while alterations and additions are constantly being made. There is always something new to see, particularly at the entrances to the various galleries, where new discoveries and recent acquisitions are put on special display.

The ground floor is devoted

to exhibits of sculptured stones, medieval and later antiquities. The sculptured stones are in their own gallery and represent a unique collection of sculpture, dating from the Roman withdrawal from Britain to AD 1050. They are a surviving memorial to the great and dramatic changes which swept Scotland during this period; on one hand, the collapse of Pictish society in northern Scotland and the decline of Romano-British culture on the Scottish border and, on the other, the growing influence of waves of invaders who sought to conquer. Chief among these were the Angles, of Saxon origin, the Irish, particularly that group known as the Scots, and the Vikings, otherwise referred to as the Norse. The stones also mark the great change from paganism to Christianity, which eventually served to link all the various artistic styles and produce one of the greatest artistic flowerings Scotland has ever seen.

There are also permanent exhibitions in the main gallery, including, towards the back, a display of Scottish costume. Although small, the collection shows the dress of both the grand and the humble. The late seventeenth century and early eighteenth century male suits look particularly rough and uncomfortable to wear; they are in interesting contrast to the adjacent silks and satins.

However, for many the chief interest of the ground floor lies in the fascinating juxtaposition of objects in the various areas of

This museum has permanent displays on three floors and temporary displays may be found on the stairs. The ground floor gallery contains a variety of material ranging from sculptured stones to silver and costumes. The first floor gallery is largely devoted to archaeology and the second to the Romans.

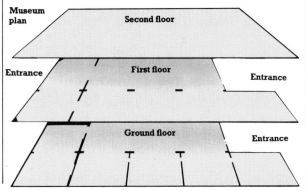

Museum plan

Second floor

First floor

Ground floor

Entrance

Entrance

Entrance

On this page are some of the interesting treasures to be found in the Museum.

1 Two beakers 2000-1600 AD
2 Two silver-gilt chapes, part of the St. Ninian's treasure
3 The Hunterstone Brooch *circa* AD 700
4 Roman iron helmet mask with traces of silver plating, late 1st century AD
5 Pictish symbol stone 7th-8th century AD
6 Three carved stone balls and a macehead *circa* 2000 BC
7 Gold collar and earring *circa* 2000-1700 BC

the main collection. The silver and plate exhibits – both religious and secular – are of outstanding national importance. So, too, are the displays of weapons, including pistols and swords. Though the former were largely made in Scotland, the blades of the latter, in the majority of instances, came from southern Germany.

Yet some of the most interesting exhibits might escape a casual glance. In one case, for instance, is a collection of Communion tokens from the various Scottish churches. They had to be presented to the minister to show that their holders were worthy to take part in the service; after it, the tokens were handed back to the minister for future re-use. The churches also licensed beggars in a similar fashion; as the beggars' badges show, this continued until the late nineteenth century. The right to beg was strictly confined to a single parish, whilst the churches also kept a watchful eye on how much the beggars were receiving.

The importance of religion in Scottish national life is demonstrated in exhibits as diverse as the copy of the National League and Covenant and the stool of repentance, from Old Greyfriars, Edinburgh. As its name implies, this was an instrument of penitence. The offender sat in the stool in front of the congregation and was publicly rebuked by the minister's thundering tones.

More serious transgressors met a more dire fate. Situated towards the rear of the gallery is the grim structure of the Maiden, a Scottish precursor of the guillotine. This example was made in 1564 and continued in use in Edinburgh until 1710, being used for public executions on Castle Hill, in St. Giles and the Lawnmarket. Among its most notable victims was Regent Morton, executed in 1581, who is said to have

helped to design it.

Scottish life had its cultured side, however, during even the grimmest periods of its history. At the time the Maiden was claiming its victims, Edinburgh's goldsmiths and clockmakers were creating some of the best examples of their work. Though many of the best craftsmen, such as Heriot and Ramsay, moved to London with the Scottish court after the Union of Crowns, others continued the tradition. This was particularly the case as far as bookbinding and printing were concerned. An early copy of Milton's *Paradise Lost* shows the skills of the Scott brothers, a celebrated firm of Edinburgh bookbinders. And it was in Edinburgh in 1725 that William Ged, a local jeweller, invented the principles of stereotype printing. Two early plates, dating from 1739, are on show, together with the pages of Sallust they printed. Close by are a collection of book-lettering tools, some of which were used for the binding of Scott's Waverley novels.

Another major attraction is the fine collection of Scottish coins, from the time of David I onwards. These, too, can be used as something of an insight into Scottish history. At one time, Edinburgh's mint was one of 21 in Scotland, but these were the victims of the process of centralization started by the Act of Union. By the end of the eighteenth century, trade tokens had to be introduced to meet the demands for small change.

The museum's unique collection of personal relics is also fascinating. These range from mementoes of the days of witchcraft and sorcery to a coconut cup, made by Alexander Selkirk, the original for Robinson Crusoe, and Deacon Brodie's dark lantern and skeleton keys, together with a chest of drawers, a product of his more re-

spectable days rather than his nights. Near the priceless Lewish chessmen, a set of exquisitely carved whalebone chess pieces, is another relic of particular interest to Edinburgh. Eight miniature coffins, with carved figures inside and probably dating from the 1830s, are part of a collection of 17 found in a cave on Arthur's Seat. No one is certain what their purpose was, although there are various theories ranging from witchcraft to burial by proxy of victims of a shipwreck.

The first floor gallery contains the museum's great hoard of prehistoric and Viking antiquities. The word 'hoard' is a literal description of quite a few of the treasures, many of which came from burial sites located throughout Scotland. The exhibits relate to the period from the first appearance of man in Scotland to the Norse settlements in the late Dark Ages.

Among the earliest exhibits on show are a collection of Neolithic polished axes. These stone axes date from between 4000 BC and 2500 BC. They were not just functional tools; the examples here demonstrate that such axes could rise to the status of minor works of art in their own right. They were made of specially selected stone and some even came from as far away as the Alps. They probably did not reach Scotland directly; it is thought that they were passed from tribe to tribe as gifts until they eventually reached their northern home.

In the centre of the gallery, there is a reconstruction and linked exhibits from one of the most important late Neolithic village sites in the world – Skara Brae, Orkney. The museum's links with this site are extremely close; not only does it house the material found in the celebrated 1920 excavations, but it has also mounted a subsequent expedition there.

Note also the elaborate jet necklaces that are on display. This easily worked stone was frequently used to make objects for personal adornment in the late Neolithic and early Bronze Ages; as well as necklaces, buttons and toggles were carved in it. From the same period come the carved stone balls, which are a prominent feature. Modern research has succeeded in dating them, but it is still not clear what they were used for.

Gold is also an important part of the collections. The two most significant displays show a variety of ornaments made in the Bronze Age; these include the recently discovered hoard of late Bronze Age armlets and bracelets from Easter Ross.

The gift of craftsmanship persisted over the centuries. In later times, the Celtic metalworkers became renowned for the skill with which they worked and decorated their products, particularly those made of bronze. The earliest noteworthy piece is the Toors Chamfrein from Kircudbright, which dates from the second to third centuries BC. The second is the famous Carnyx, a Celtic war trumpet, from Deskford, Banffshire. This is the only example to survive in Britain. On a much smaller scale, the Hunterston Brooch is one of the finest examples of Celtic jewellery to survive. It bears a Norse inscription and dates from the eighth century AD.

The Vikings were jewellery-makers too, though they preferred silver to gold. As it was Viking custom to bury the dead with their earthly riches, the museum has amassed a large collection of Viking jewellery. Among the most striking – and certainly the largest – examples are the Thistle brooches, so-called because of the decoratio at the end of the pin.

The most spectacular treasure of recent years, however, is undoubtedly the hoard of late Pictish silver, found on St. Ninian's Isle, Shetland, in 1958. The carefully decorated objects had been placed in a wooden box and hidden beneath the floor of the church in about AD 800, probably to protect them from being stolen in a Viking raid. The artistic motifs displayed on the hoard are similar to those seen on the sculptured stones in the ground floor gallery.

On the second floor, the gallery is devoted totally to exhibits demonstrating the Roman presence in Scotland. From the first century to the fourth century AD, southern Scotland was a buffer zone between the hostile tribes north of the Forth and the rich Roman province to the south of Hadrian's Wall. Thus, Scotland never knew the full benefits of the Pax Romana, but, in purely military terms, the Romans left a wealth of material behind.

The exhibits here record the military facts of the Roman presence – from the building of the Antonine Wall to scenes of the domestic life of the legions – and the native reaction to it. The Bridgeness slab came from the eastern end of the Antonine Wall at Bridgeness, West Lothian, and dates to approximately AD 140. The left-hand panel forms one of the most remarkable images of Roman Scotland to survive. Roman parade armour, from the principal fortress in southern Scotland, is also on display, plus a collection of military tools. Examine the tools in particular, for it is interesting to note how the basic shapes of some of them have remained virtually unchanged up to the present day.

Another interesting Roman survival is the huge collection of iron nails that were apparently buried deliberately at Inchtuthill, Perthshire. The fort there was abandoned even before it was completed, as the troops intended to make up its garrison were needed elsewhere.

A reconstruction of a Celtic chariot provides an interesting insight into the type of weapon the Celts used to oppose the deadly legion. But the gallery's greatest treasure is the hoard of Roman silver known as the Treasure of Traprain, discovered in 1919 during the excavation of Traprain Law, Scotland's largest hill fort and capital of a tribe known as the Votadini.

The hoard largely consists of silver plate, but the four coins which were found indicate that it was buried between AD 410 and AD 425. The objects are of particularly fine quality and come from a table service, a lady's dressing table, an army officer's uniform and possibly a church, as some of the objects are stamped with Christian symbols.

Most of the objects, however, are crushed or cut into pieces. The mystery is how such a treasure found its way into a native settlement in the first place. The first theory is that the hoard represents loot captured on a raid south of Hadrian's Wall, which was subsequently cut up so that the spoil could be divided. The second is that the silver was given to the leader of the tribe as a bribe to stop him raiding into Roman territory.

These are only some of the treasures of the museum and, although, as has been said, the collections are rotated regularly, there is much of interest that there is simply not room to display. New buildings on the opposite side of the road are scheduled to open at the beginning of 1982 and it is planned that they should house four new galleries. One of these will be for furniture, one will be for costume and a third for more prehistoric material. The fourth will be used to house visiting exhibitions.

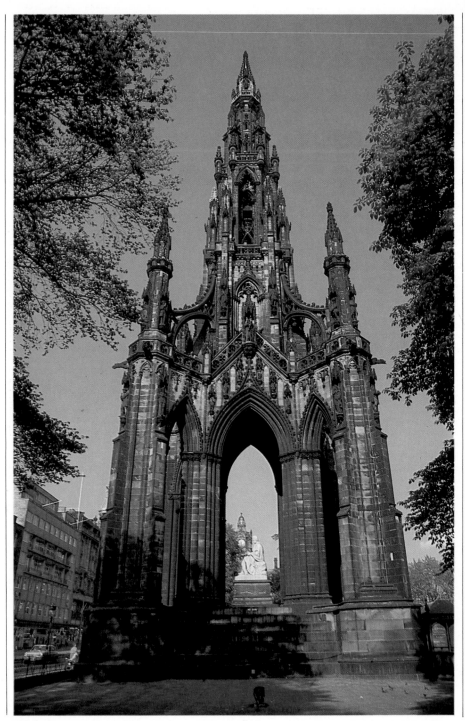

Statues and Monuments

A miscellany of the many memorials Edinburgh has raised to heroes

The Gothic fantasy of Sir Walter Scott's monument dominates east Princes Street, towering over the gardens at the foot of St. David's Street.

Designed by George Meikle Kemp, a joiner and draftsman, and with a twice-life-sized statue of the seated Sir Walter by the sculptor Sir John Steell, it is a legacy to the romantic Gothic Revival popularized by Scott.

The competition for the design of the monument, announced in 1836, caused, enormous controversy over the design and the winner: Kemp was accused of plagiarism – and he was an unknown from the lower classes. But his monument was inaugurated after interminable squabbles and delays on August 15, 1846, and immediately became one of the major attractions of the city.

Kemp designed the monument, inspired by Melrose Abbey and Gothic memorial crosses, in only five days and it was chosen by the Memorial Committee despite designs submitted by illustrious architects like William Playfair

The monument is 200½ feet (601.5m) high, and the 55-square-feet ($5m^2$) base rests on a foundation of solid rock 52 feet (15.6m) below street level.

Above the foundations, rising seven steps on each side, is a quadrangular platform where the statue of Scott and his dog, Maida, rests. It is carved from a solid block of Carrara marble that originally weighed 30 tons and was, in fact, the first marble statue in Scotland.

At each corner of the platform, four massive piers of clustered shafts are joined by pointed arches and the space above is vaulted over with ribbed arches. The vaults are supported by four external buttresses, rising 90 feet (27m). A gallery surmounts the four principal arches and contains a central room, the Museum Room, completed in the 1870s.

Above the gallery the main tower rises steeply and contains a further three galleries with connecting stairs. The uppermost gallery is a climb of 287 steps but the view from the top is spectacular.

The exterior is highly decorated with 64 characters from Scott's novels and a further 16 statuettes are of Scottish poets.

Extensive restoration was undertaken in the mid-1970s at a massive cost of £154,000 – a sharp contrast to the original cost of the monument of £16,000.

David Livingstone

At the Waverley Bridge entrance to East Princes Street Gardens stands this statue to David Livingstone, the nineteenth-century explorer and missionary. After discovering the Zambezi River and Victoria Falls, he was awarded the Gold Medal by the Royal Geographical Society, shortly after which he was made an honorary burgess of Edinburgh. Livingstone died in 1873 while searching for the source of the Nile, and his body was returned to Britain to be buried in Westminster Abbey. Three years later this bronze statue was erected. It is the only statue in the gardens sculpted by a woman, Amelia Robertson Hill. Although it was said to be an 'admirable likeness', many present at its inauguration thought this statue to be too small for the open air and more suitable for the interior of a building.

Allan Ramsay

The marble statue, showing this eighteenth-century wigmaker turned poet wearing a silk nightcap, was sculpted by Sir John Steell, who carved it from a solid block that weighed 18 tons. Ramsay, who moved to Edinburgh from his native Lanarkshire, became a great success in the capital through

his writing and bookshop and was among the pioneers of lending libraries, opening one in the High Street in 1725. This, and his involvement with the theatre which he fought to have legalized in Scotland, made him very unpopular with the Presbyterian Church.

The statue, erected in Princes Street Gardens West in 1865, was commissioned by one of his descendants, Lord Murray, who appears on one of four medallions on the plinth. General Ramsay, the poet's grandson, the poet's wife and two great-granddaughters are depicted on the others.

Charles II

In Parliament Square the Merry Monarch, Charles II, prances near the grave of the Gloomy Reformer, John Knox, whose remains were buried here when it was St. Giles graveyard. Charles's statue is the oldest in Edinburgh and the oldest equestrian statue, dated 1685, in Britain. It is thought to be of Dutch origin but the sculptor is unknown. No one knows quite how much it weighs but when it was built no supporting struts were inserted. As a result the horse is buckling at the knees and has to be repaired frequently, the last time in 1972 when it was injected with a specially prepared plastic resin.

The statue was removed during the nineteenth-century renovations to St. Giles and was put back again in 1835 when Robert Mylne, the King's Master Mason in Scotland, added the plinth.

John Knox

An ironic memorial to the reformer of the Scottish church, John Knox, stands against the wall of St. Giles in Parliament Square. 'He sleeps,' wrote Robert Louis Stevenson, 'within the call of the church that so often echoed to his preaching.' The bronze statue of Knox, who campaigned tumultuously against 'graven images' in churches, was designed by Pittendrigh MacGillivray in 1902 and cast in 1906. The statue marks the approximate site of the dour man's grave (this area used to be St. Giles graveyard) and seems to look accusingly at the nearby statue of the Merry Monarch, the libertine King Charles II.

George IV

Designed by Chantrey in 1831 to commemorate the King's glorious visit in 1822, this statue stands in Hanover Street. George's visit was very popular and he was rapturously welcomed, even though he wore pink silk tights under his kilt. The royal tour, the first since the Scottish defeat at Culloden, was seen as a recognition of Scottish participation in the union as a partner rather than a vanquished nation.

Melville Monument

This 150-feet-high (45.7 m) stone column, topped with a statue of Henry Dundas, 1st Viscount Melville, has a rather turgid history. Building began on the column, a copy of Trajan's Column in Rome, in 1821. The money, £3,500, was raised by officers, petty officers, seamen and marines who served Melville during his time as First Lord of the Admiralty, but it ran out before completion, and the city was forced to help out financially. However, it is still not certain that building debts have been cleared.

There was also a squabble over the siting – first it was to be at Calton Hill then its present site in St. Andrew Square was chosen; followed in 1823 by hot debate whether or not it should be completed at all. Others suggested it should be rededicated to William Pitt. Finally, in 1837 after 14 years of argument, Melville, so powerful in his day that he was nicknamed King Harry the Ninth, triumphed and a statue was designed by Sir Francis Chantrey and carved by Robert Forrest.

Dundas, a man of indefatigable industry, was Solicitor General for Scotland at the age of 24, Lord Advocate between 1775 and 1783, Treasurer to the Navy, under William Pitt, from 1784-1800 and then First Lord of the Admiralty.

Scottish American War Memorial

The Scottish American War Memorial Committee dedicated this statue to 'the Scottish effort in the Great War' in 1927. The bronze cast had taken the designer, Professor R. Tait Mackenzie, of Philadelphia, three years to complete and it is entitled 'The Call'. It shows a kilted soldier on a plinth looking at a frieze where volunteers from all walks of life are represented. Above the frieze are two interwined wreaths, one with a shield of the Stars and Stripes and the other with the shield of St. Andrew's Cross.

At the beginning of World War II the statue, in Princes Street Gardens West, was covered in sandbags to preserve it. The bags were ceremoniously removed during a memorial service on May 30, 1942.

Alexander and Bucephalus

Sir John Steell first modelled this huge statue 50 years before it was finally cast in bronze – the first cast in Scotland – in 1883, the cost paid for by subscribers. It shows the Macedonian king Alexander taming his warhorse Bucephalus as a representation of 'mind over brute force' and was unveiled in 1884 on the west side of St. Andrew Square. In 1916 it was moved to its present position outside the City Chambers in High Street, because it was a traffic hazard. The Gladstone Memorial Committee paid the cost of the move as they replaced it with a statue of Gladstone but this, too, had to be moved in time.

Earl Haig Memorial

A Bombay parsee, Sir Dhumjibhoy Bomanzi, commissioned this bronze statue of Earl Haig and his horse 'in admiration of the services rendered to the British Empire by the Field Marshal'. Haig was Commander in Chief of the British Army in World War I. The statue was designed by George Wade and unveiled in 1923 on the northern edge of the Castle Esplanade, alongside a parade of memorials to Scottish soldiers and regiments.

Adam Black

The politician and publisher was Lord Provost of Edinburgh from 1843 to 1848 and is depicted by John Hutchison, the sculptor, in his robes of office. Black, who also represented the city as a Liberal Member of Parliament, refused the knighthood normally offered to retiring Lord Provosts, with the words, 'I have no need of a title for my wife to be called "my lady" (she was already a Lady) and I have enough heirs to do without airs and graces.' He was one of the city's most prominent publishers, founder of A & C Black, and had acquired the copyright for some of the early editions of the *Encylopaedia Britannica* and Scott's Waverley Novels. The statue, cast in bronze, was erected in Princes Street Gardens East in 1877.

Duke of Wellington

This statue, outside Register House in Princes Street, so pleased the Duke of Wellington that he wanted a copy for his London home. But as the complete equestrian sculpture weighed 12 tons, he had only the bust cast.

Known as the 'Iron Duke in bronze by Steell', it was among the first successful models of a

prancing horse, cleverly using the tail as means of support. The Duke's war horse, Copenhagen, was unavailable as a model for the sculptor, Sir John Steell, so he borrowed a horse of a similar breed from the Duke of Buccleuch's stables at Dalkeith Palace, to which he again resorted for models for the Albert Statue in Charlotte Square.

Sir William Chambers

When the Town Council commissioned a statue of their former Lord Provost William Chambers there was heated argument about the suitability of the design – a recumbent figure that was to have lain in St. Giles Kirk. But the Kirk authorities objected and the council were forced to find an alternative site. A competition for a new design was launched and the sculptor John Rhind won with his model of Chambers, brother of the publisher, standing in his Provost's robes. The bronze statue was erected by the Town Council in 1891 and unveiled by the then Lord Provost John Boyd in Chambers Street at a cost of £1400.

The Royal Botanic Garden

The largest section of the Royal Botanic Garden is the Arboretum, where visitors can wander or rest in the shade of trees and shrubs from all over the world. Some of the most brilliant flowering is in the nearby Rhododendron Walk.

Few cities in the world can boast a park or garden of over 70 acres (28 ha) only a 10-minute bus ride from the centre. As you pass through the East Gate, Inverleith Row, you can see what makes Edinburgh's Royal Botanic Garden different; the emphasis on woodland and wild areas contrasts completely with the formality of mansion gardens.

The quiet sanctuary of the Royal Botanic Garden contains exotic orchids, Amazon lilies, a fossilized tree from thousands of centuries ago, an excellent collection of Scotland's heathers and five giant beds of all types of azaleas which from the beginning of June are a blaze of colour.

The Botanic Garden is best known for its collection of rhododendrons and as a scientific establishment. In 1980 the garden, the second oldest botanic garden in Britain, was voted the best garden in Europe, for its collections and contribution to science and education.

The magnificent gardens are the result of two Edinburgh physicians establishing a physic garden in 1670. Medicine at the time relied largely upon herbs and, from the Dark Ages to the early Middle Ages, upon the work of monks. The use of plants until about the beginning of the nineteenth century was central to medicine and, until the creation and development of physic gardens in the sixteenth and seventeenth centuries, it was the monastic communities that maintained interest in herbs and their healing potential. Even today plants are used as starting materials for semi-synthetic drugs or, indeed, as pure drugs.

Physic gardens were always associated with universities where medicine was taught because medicine relied upon plant life and its study. Dr. Robert Sibbald, the first Professor of Medicine at Edinburgh University, and Dr. Robert Balfour, an eminent physician, recognizing the unsatisfactory state of medicine in the city, decided to establish a physic garden for the cultivation of medicinal and other plants.

The site the two doctors secured was just 40 feet (12 m) square, a small plot of land not far from Holyrood Abbey. The venture was successful, with the assistance of James Sutherland, the first Intendant of the Garden, but they could not have dreamed that such humble beginnings would result in today's renowned Botanic Garden of some 70 acres (28 ha).

In 1676 Balfour and Sibbald realized that more land was required and they took over the garden attached to Trinity Hospital — on the site of which Waverley Station stands today. James Sutherland was responsible for both gardens and in 1695 was appointed Professor of Botany at the university and in the same year took control of part of the Royal Garden at Holyrood. Four years later Sutherland was appointed King's Botanist and in 1710 he became Regius Professor of Botany.

The Royal Botanic Garden was extremely fortunate both in

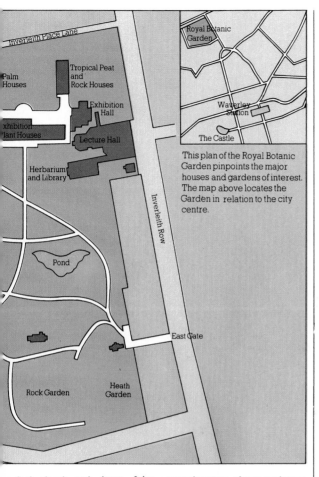

This plan of the Royal Botanic Garden pinpoints the major houses and gardens of interest. The map above locates the Garden in relation to the city centre.

Sutherland and, later, John Hope. Sutherland's reputation for skill and learning coupled with exceptional energy earned him the monopoly on botanical teaching in the city.

It is to Hope's eternal credit that he was able to restore and develop the Botanic Garden afterwards. Hope had originally entered the University of Edinburgh as a medical student but his interest in botany took him over. He went to Paris to study under Bernard de Jussieu (1699-1777), Professor of Botany at the Royal Garden in Paris, one of the strongest supporters of the Linnaean system of plant classification. It is today a universal system of nomenclature and classification.

In 1763 Hope carried out his greatest achievement from the point of view of the garden's history. The Trinity Hospital Garden was in 1763 moved to a larger site of about five acres (2 ha) off Leith Walk, to a site where Haddington Place now stands. At the same time, Professor John Hope, the Regius Keeper, obtained a permanent income for the new garden from the Crown, from which time the Gardens came under the Commissioners of Her Majesty's Works and Public Buildings.

John Hope's period as Super-intendent of the Garden was one of great activity. His two great interests were plant physiology and systematic botany and these studies and his teaching contributed greatly to the science. He encouraged his students to research in the field and it is now acknowledged that he and his pupils were the pioneer investigators of Scottish plant life, collecting not only from the mainland but from Arran, Mull, Orkney, Shetland and Skye as well. His name has been commemorated for all time in the genus of trees from South China, South-east Asia and Indonesia and Malaysia – Hopea.

Hope was succeeded in 1786 by Daniel Rutherford who, as a chemist, was more interested in plants as objects for his experiments in determining the chemistry of the atmosphere. Of his six principal gardeners during his 33 years as Professor and Keeper of the Royal Garden, John Tweedie was notable. Tweedie had worked at Dalkeith Palace Gardens, and later, in 1825 at the age of 50, left to explore the reported botanical splendour of South America. Tweedie introduced several species of Verbena, the Chilean Jasmine and a number of other exotic and colourful plants which can be seen in the herbarium at the Gardens.

Rutherford was responsible too for appointing John McKay of Edinburgh as Principal Gardener in 1800. He removed old trees, exchanged plants with the Gardens at Kew, London, and embarked on botanical excursions with a number of dedicated students. McKay died in 1802 but in 1810 Rutherford was again lucky in his gardeners; this time he appointed William McNab, a leading horticulturalist from Kew.

McNab showed immense enthusiasm in his task of developing the Botanic Garden. He introduced many new and rare plants and carried out the culture of aquatic plants such as Egyptian water lilies and other water-living plants from Bengal, south and east Asia, the United States and India.

McNab was the organizer for the move to Inverleith, the home of the gardens today. Transporting and transplanting well-established trees and shrubs has never been easy and the collection was a considerable one. McNab invented a transplanting machine to allow the removal of mature trees. The operation took over two years and it is McNab who should be credited for the fact that virtually nothing died.

Up until this time specimens from abroad had been introduced in a rather haphazard way; most of the botanical excursions were concentrated on native Scottish plant life.

Naturalists had accompanied expeditions: the group of monkey puzzle trees between the Pond and the Azalea Lawn, for example, were introduced in 1795 by Archibald Menzies, a student under Professor John Hope. He had accompanied Captain Vancouver in the *Discovery* in 1790 and returned with the specimens from Chile. Later expeditions included that of Captain James Clark Ross's *Erebus* to the Antarctic in 1839. Many specimens were introduced, however, by an informal

system of exchange with other gardens, notably Kew.

The Universities (Scotland) Act of 1889 proposed that the Botanic Garden should be transferred to the University of Edinburgh. Balfour resisted for a number of reasons. As a result the gardens were handed over by the Treasury to the First Commissioner of Works and the gardens had to be open on Sundays. The public showed their approval: 27,000 visited over four Sundays while the Free Church Presbytery denounced the arrangement as 'a most wanton desecration.

The following year, 1890, the Right Hon. the Lords Commissioners of HM Treasury set up an enquiry to consider the role of the Keeper and the outlay for the gardens in the future. The beginning of the Royal Botanic Garden as it is today at last began to take form.

Towards the end of the 1830s more formal transactions on a large scale were contemplated, and by 1844 the first volume of *Transactions* had been published. But the scheme was on a small scale until the period from 1905 to 1925 which was especially rich in the introduction of foreign species – in particular the collections of George Forrest from western China. Their classification by bontanists on the university and garden staffs re-

sulted in botanical papers on Asiatic rhododendrons, primulas, gentians, lilies, conifers and other groups of plants which were to completely transform the gardens. Exchanges of seeds are now made with gardens all over the world, and trust funds, such as the Rock Plant Trust Fund, sponsor botanists on collecting trips.

But to return to the last century: in 1864 the Experimental Garden of the Royal Caledonian Horticultural Society was transferred to the Botanic Garden and in 1876 a further 30 acres (12 ha) of ground surrounding Inverleith House were added. The gardens were at this time under the supervision of Isaac Bayley Balfour, who had succeeded his father John Hutton Balfour.

New accommodation for botanical research and teaching was built, laying out of the Rock Garden started and new glasshouses were constructed – some of which survived until 1966. Edinburgh became an important centre for taxonomic research, especially on the plants of China and the Himalayas which included the famous rhododendrons. This work owed much to the naturalists who accompanied expeditions of exploration, and in particular to the plant collector, George Forrest, who brought from China many important horticultural plants and over 40,000 dried and living specimens for scientific research.

Isaac Bayley Balfour quickly realized the need for extensive modernization and reorganization of the gardens themselves and the way in which they were controlled. Up until 1889 the Botanic Garden was under the dual control of the Treasury and the Commissioner of Works. Balfour saw that dual control led to inefficiency, more money was needed for maintenance and development and research should be furthered.

The Winter Palace in the late nineteenth century

A walk through the gardens

The Rhododendron Walk

Edinburgh's Royal Botanic Garden now contains the largest collection of rhododendrons in Britain. The most beautiful display is in the Rhododendron Walk which extends from the West Gate entrance, and many others are dotted around.

Thickets of the largest leaved of the hardy bamboos provide shade and protection for other plants, which include specimens of *Bergenia*, mainly Himalayan and Chinese, and plantain lilies

Shrubs from New Zealand have found the protection from wind and frost and the full sun they need on the south and west facing walls of Inverleith House. These include *Sophora tetraptera*, the kowhai, with its curious golden yellow flowers that appear in June and *Hoheria sexstylosa* which flowers profusely in July and August.

To the north of Inverleith House and along one side of the *Rhododendron x praecox* hedge is a collection of *Enkianthus* species. Their clusters of white, pink or reddish flowers appear in spring, and in autumn their foliage turns magnificent hues of orange and crimson.

Near the *Enkianthus* are several plants which would be considered delicate when grown on the east coast of Scotland: the evergreen *Desfontainea spinosa* from Chile produces yellow-lobed scarlet flowers during the summer and *Mahonia lomariifolia* blossoms yellow flowers in November.

Several plants in the Rhododendron Walk produce either fruits or flowers as late as November and, in the case of the hellebores, in December and January. The spectacular Corsican hellebore, for example, produces pale green flowers from a mass of toothed foliage well after the New Year. On the east side of Inverleith House is a collection of magnolias which, as well as producing large, attractive flowers in spring, also contribute to autumn colour.

The Arboretum

Much of the original planting in the Arboretum, south of the Rhododendron Walk, was carried out on the basis of assembling all the species of a single genus as near together as possible. The introduction of new species, especially from the Himalayas, western China and North America, and the need to plant some species to give shelter to others, has made it impossible to adhere strictly to the plan. The main collection of oaks, for example, is on the lawn to the north of Inverleith House, but some fine specimens are found near the pond, to the east, as well.

The Arboretum, the Latin name for a botanic garden of trees, has been added to continually since its founding in 1877. The lawns include a varied sampling of trees of the rose family, such as the flowering crabs and rowans, hawthorns, and of the maple and lime families. There are also willows, poplars, silver birches and alders. The extensive collection of barberries is located principally on the lawn between the conifers and the main collection of oaks.

The Peat Garden

It was under the direction of William Wright Smith that the Peat Garden, the first in Britain, was constructed in 1939 at the north entrance of the Woodland Garden. A series of raised borders, rich in peat, has allowed the successful cultivation of plants like dwarf rhododendrons, primulas, gentians, lilies. An immense variety of creeping shrubs and dwarf shrubs provide winter cover so that ground penetration by frost is reduced. The dwarf lilies and the terrestrial orchids, notably the North African *Dactylorhiza elata* and the Madeiran *D. maderensis* are particularly interesting. *Primula whitei* and *P. gracilipes* are two of the primulas that attract visitors in such numbers, from spring onwards, that the surrounding turf is often worn bare. Ferns, such as the native Adder's Tongue, thrive in the peaty conditions.

The Woodland Garden

The Woodland (or wild) Garden is the least formal of the sections: the illusion of remoteness is achieved by introducing large masses of evergreen shrubs which shut off the surrounding buildings, and by

Spring

Summer

Autumn

Winter

trees which provide partial overhead shade.

Grassy paths wind through the woodland and the area is enlivened with evergreen shrubs to provide a leafy background and masses of colour in season.

Shade and shelter for the woodland vegetation is given in part by conifers such as cypress, thuja, fir and pine. Owing to atmospheric pollution, unfortunately, none of these is really splendid but at least they help the survival of other plants.

As well as an abundance of rhododendrons, the shrubs include hydrangeas, viburnums, eucryphias, camellias, magnolias and cotoneasters – as well as many others. Shade-loving plants include the striking may lily, with its heart-shaped leaves and small, white flowers, the wood anemone, greater celandine, the North American bleeding heart or Dutchman's breeches, the plantain lily of Japan, with its beautiful foliage, and, not least, bluebells and poppies.

The Rock Garden

To the east of the conifers in the Woodland Garden, lies the Rock Garden with plants from Europe, India, China, Japan, Australia, New Zealand and the Americas.

James McNab, as principal gardener, conceived and constructed the Rock Garden in 1871. He used the well-worn steps and landing of the old School of Arts in Adam Square, carried stones from the old Bank of Scotland buildings, basalts from Giant's Causeway and Staffa, and large masses of granite and quartz, black hecla or lava stones. Isaac Bayley Balfour, however, wished to make improvements and the reconstruction work, which took until 1914, produced a rock garden that is fundamentally the one you see today. Large pieces of conglomerate from the slopes of Ben Ledi in Perthshire and red sandstone from Dumfries were used.

The spaces between the rocks harbour plants from many mountainous parts of the world – which are sometimes incorrectly thought to provide all rock garden plants. High mountain, or alpine, plants are found in great numbers in the Rock Garden, together with species from the varied environments of the warm Mediterranean shores and the cold permafrost regions of the Arctic.

There is a collection of mainly Scottish alpine plants in the centre of the Rock Garden; there are saxifrages, campanulas, alliums, gentians from Europe, America, Asia Minor, the Himalayas, China, Turkestan; a variety of species from Spain, Portugal, North Africa and the Americas; and the plants with white flowers from New Zealand include the celmisias with silvery, often sword-shaped, leaves and great daisy-like flowers and *Ranunculus lyallii,* probably the most beautiful buttercup in the world.

Miniature waterfalls and pools give the area added interest as well as ensuring sufficient moisture. Much of the rock is covered by prostrate or creeping shrubs. Species of *Cotoneaster* from the Himalayas, southeast Tibet and western China, for example, carpet the rocks and provide decorative fruits as well. The cotoneasters are best seen in the autumn, while shrubby potentillas and several species of broom provide bright colour during the summer. The dwarf rhododendrons are invaluable for colour and cover and vary from the carpeting *Rhododendron forrestii* var. *repens* (named after its collector, George Forrest) and the taller species such as *R. lapponicum* which may reach three feet (about 1 m) in height and flower profusely in May.

Apart from the many creeping shrubs and the mats of herbaceous plants, conifers such as juniper help to hide the slabs of rock with the evergreen dwarf conifers adding colour and interest during the winter.

The Heath Garden

In the southeast corner of the gardens is the Heath Garden. There are over 30 varieties of heather which flower at different times from the beginning of June until the end of October. With colours ranging through gold, dark red and mauve and the varying colours of foliage, the heath garden is attractive at any time of the year.

In the 1830s, in the time of William McNab, a spendid collection of heathers from South Africa was cultivated. By the 1930s, however, heathers had become less popular with the public and only a few of McNab's specialities remained. Heaths from all over Britain and continental Europe gradually became more popular and so in 1935 a new Heath Garden was laid with thousands of plants being propogated. Species included the many forms of the variable ling or heather *Calluna vulgaris,* and the bell-heather *Erica cinerea,* from the Scottish highlands and other parts of Great Britain and

Europe; the many forms of *Erica carnea* from the mountains of central and southern Europe together with many other species of *Erica* from southern Europe, the Mediterranean and North Africa.

Thousands of these plants were introduced and planted informally with junipers, pernettyas and brooms as well as crocuses and squills to provide colour in every month of the year.

The Pond

North of the Rock Garden, past the East Gate, is the area where the Pond is the focal point. Several hardy aquatic and marsh plants can be seen here: the yellow water lily, *Nuphar lutea,* and the American species *N. advena*; groups of reed mace, also known as bullrushes, are especially conspicuous after the appearance of their cylindrical brown fruiting heads. Emerging well above the surface of the water in summer and autumn is the marestail, *Hippuris vulgaris*; the Cape pond weed, with its curiously branched white flowers, floats all over the surface; and during the summer the water lilac, native to Scotland, can be seen.

The first glimpse of colour around the Pond in spring is the Himalayan primula and in summer the most conspicuous plant is *Gunnera manicata*. This plant is the largest leaved plant hardy in Britain and resembles giant rhubarb – in a good season its leaves will grow to more than five feet (1.5 m) across. Moisture-loving plants such as primulas, irises and astilbes flower in summer and the bright

scarlet flowers of species of *Lobelia* continue into the autumn. Winter colour is provided by the royal fern, *Osmunda,* and the leaves and fruiting heads of reed mace.

Trees framing and overhanging the pond area include the golden weeping willow, the Austrian pine, a weeping ash and a group of Japanese maples to the west. The Pond is the main source of water for the Rock Garden and for the animal life seen in the gardens. Two families of foxes, grey squirrels, birds and smaller creatures all inhabit the gardens.

The Azalea Lawn

Northwest of the Pond, in the centre of the gardens, is the lawn devoted to azaleas – part of the genus *Rhododendron* which start to flower in May. Azaleas are among the most popular of flowering shrubs with an astonishing variety of flower form, colour and perfume.

The Lawn includes both deciduous types from eastern Europe, the Caucasus and Belgium and evergreen types from Japan. *Rhododendron x albicans* yield an exceptional scent from their white, pale pink or pale yellow flowers. They are the last to bloom, extending the season into July.

The Lawn is dominated by beeches and there are also numerous birches which include the two North American species, the canoe birch and the river birch.

At the foot of the Lawn there are rhododendron hybrids and several beautiful examples of the rose family. The hybrid

crab-apple of the family *Rosaceae,* for example, produces bronze leaves and an abundance of purplish crimson flowers.

Plant Exhibition Houses

The glass houses today at Edinburgh's Royal Botanic Garden are, it is to be hoped, the last in a long line. The first was opened in 1834, restored in 1858, the buildings reconstructed in 1893, another range added in 1898 and in 1965 all were demolished, the new complex being opened in 1967. The houses are constructed with no internal supports, but are suspended on external pylons.

Cactus and Succulent House – No 1

Cacti come from deserts and survive with very little water. They show special adaptations, such as waxy coatings on leaf or stem and small leaves to minimize evaporation.

The plants have been arranged geographically to show convergent, or parallel, evolution: plants develop similar characteristics in similar climates although they are geographically separated and are not related to each other. Examples of this phenomenon are the African *Euphorbia*, with its characteristic shape of tall, ribbed columns, and the similar American cacti, *Echinocereus*.

Adaptation for survival is shown, too, by the stone plants of the *Lithops* genus. These small plants avoid detection by grazing animals, which frequently resort to succulent plants as the only source of water, by resembling pebbles.

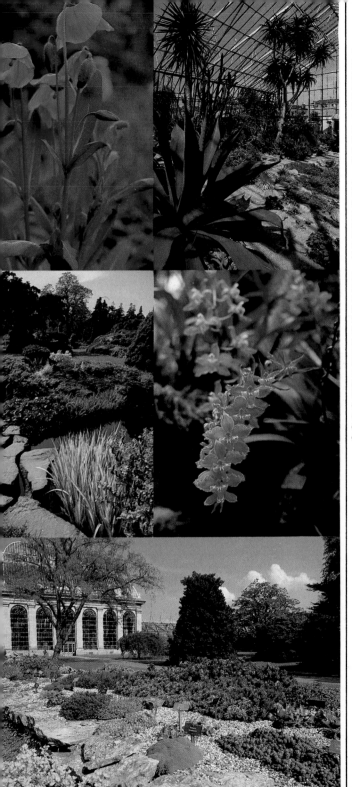

The many glorious trees, flowers, shrubs and plants found in the Royal Botanic Garden are represented on the left-hand page by *Trillium sessile*, which prefers to live in the shade (**top left**); *Trillium grandiflora* in the Peat Garden (**middle left**); the 150-year old palm *Sabal blackburniana* from Bermuda (**main picture**); a mauve dwarf rhododendron (**bottom left**); and the immaculately kept pond near the Gallery of Modern Art.

On this page are Himalayan poppies, also found in the Peat Garden (**top left**); exotica in the Cactus and Succulent House (**top right**); the tranquillity and miniature plants of the Rock Garden (**middle left**); a hybrid orchid of the *Odontonia* genus (**middle right**); and, near the Palm House, the delights of the Heath Garden where one bush or another flowers in every season.

Not only are they the right colour, but they are speckled as well so that they merge with their background.

The window succulents are unusual in that their leaves are normally buried in the sand. Only the flattened tips are exposed and these act as converging lenses to transmit light to the leaf. It is here that chlorophyll is stored for photosynthesis, which takes place when sufficient light is received.

The Warm Temperate Aquatic House – No 2

The pool and several water-living plants dominate this house, but there are also some succulents which require a moister atmosphere than that of the Cactus and Succulent House. Specially interesting are the species of *Selenicereus* and *Hylocereus* which in summer produce huge flowers of great beauty and an attractive scent.

The East Indian waterlilies, sacred in India and China, have bright pink flowers which are associated with the Buddha. Their leaves are held high out of the water.

The blue dawn flower, *Pharbitis learii*, blooms for the longest time of the plants in this house. Like most of the morning glories, to which group it belongs, it is best seen early in the day since the flowers which open in the morning lose their brilliance in the afternoon and fall in the evening. There are also large growths of sugar cane and species of *Hibiscus* and *Cinchona*. Quinine was isloated from *Cinchona* in 1820.

Tropical fish have been put in the pool to create as natural an environment as possible – and these are paid for by visitors who drop in coins from the bridge. After every weekend, the coins are collected – with just a few left to stimulate further contributions – and used to buy more fish.

Temperate Plant House – No 3

Here are plants from the warm temperate regions of the world, in particular those which would not do well in Scotland's cli-, mate, arranged geographically. Many of the trees are from Australia and include several species of *Acacia*, colourful in early spring, and *Eucalyptus*. *Callistemon*; also from Australia, has small flowers and dramatic scarlet 'bottle-brushes' made up of numerous brightly coloured stamens. Species from the cooler regions of Africa, the Canaries, China and Japan are also grown.

Cobaea scandens, growing over the railing, is a climber which gives off a smell of rotting fruit. The odour attracts fruit-eating bats who, in the wild, are deceived into pollinating it.

The locust tree (*Ceratonia siliqua*) has long pods which are used as animal fodder in Mediterranean countries. Its seeds were used as the original carat weights by goldsmiths.

At the west end of the house the Tropical Aquatic House pool can be seen from below from a special chamber and there is a collection of aquatic plants and many species of tropical and cold-water fish.

Tropical Aquatic House – No 4

The gigantic leaves of the Victoria waterlilies from tropical South America are the main attraction here. In their native habitat they would grow to about 15 feet (4.5 m) in diameter, but as this would be impracticable to allow in the plant house, they are removed each year and regrown from seed. Even so, they grow to such a size and strength that it is possible for one to support a baby. The base and sides of the lilies are covered in spikes, nature's solution to the threat of hungry fish. The sides are raised as an adaptation against turbulent

water which would overflow the leaf. The leaf structure of these plants is one of nature's wonders: as it cannot be seen properly from above, there is an underground viewing chamber beneath the pool, entrance to which is in the Temperate Plant House.

The strongly scented flowers of the Amazon lilies are as impressive as the plant itself and are produced from June to October, each one lasting just two days. When they first open in the late afternoon, they are a creamy white but by the second evening they change to a deep purplish-rose. They then become submerged and after the fruit ripens the seeds fall to the bottom of the pond.

Marsh plants include the Egyptian paper-reed, *Cyperus papyrus*, from which the ancient Egyptians made paper, and rice, *Oryza sativa*.

The southeast corner of the house is devoted to a group of plants which live for their mutual benefit with ants.

One example of this phenomenon is seen in the trumpet tree (*Cecropia peltata*). The ants pierce the hollow stem and live in the internal cavity, and in return for shelter the ants, which tend to bite or sting on sight, protect the plant from insects.

The Fern House – No 5

Over 300 species of tree ferns create the illusion of a forest. In nature many grow on tropical mountains, up to an altitude of 1000 feet (300 m), while others have come from temperate regions such as New Zealand, Australia and South Africa. The tallest in the house, *Cyathea australis*, can grow to nearly 66 feet (20 m) in the wild.

As well as the collection of tree ferns, there are many other low-growing varieties and fern allies, such as *Selanginellas*, which are grown here for ground cover.

Cycad and Orchid House – No 6

The cycads with their huge, palm-like leaves dominate the house, and some are thought to be almost 200 years old. Cycads are not related to palms but to a family which is thought to link the ferns and the flowering plants.

Some of the 20,000 species of the orchid family are the other central feature. These most exotic of flowers are found in all parts of the world and are most abundant in the tropics.

Orchids vary enormously in shape – and for a purpose. The flower of each species resembles one kind of insect, so that insects may be drawn to the plant where they will unwittingly pollinate it. The unsuspecting insect, perhaps a bee or a fly, is attracted both by colour and scent whose resemblance is close enough for inexperienced male insects to attempt copulation with the flower.

Tropical Peat and Rock Houses

This is a separate house, divided into two sections, and shows some of the research activities carried out by the Royal Botanic Garden. One of the three main families under study is the *Ericaceae*, which includes heathers and rhododendrons, but there are also a number of unfamiliar genera. The other two families, *Gesneriaceae* and Zingiberaceae, are principally tropical, the former including rock garden plants. Many of the plants have been collected only recently, while others are in cultivation for the first time.

Exhibition Hall

To the east of the Plant Exhibition Houses lies the Exhibition Hall where more detailed information can be presented than in the rest of the garden. The Hall opened in 1970. Various aspects of plant biology are shown by text, audiovisual units and plants and the displays are changed at regular intervals.

The Palm Houses

The Tropical Palm House was opened in 1834 and in 1858 the larger Temperate Palm House was opened. A minimum night temperature of 46°F (8°C) is maintained in the Temperate House, while in the Tropical House it is never below 64°F (18°C).

The palms are of more economic importance than any other plant family, providing food, shelter and clothing for people all over the world.

There is an astonishing variety of species. The size of the stem and the structure of the leaves vary enormously, while some are altogether stemless. Their flowers are not usually particularly attractive, but the talipot palm from India and Ceylon, *Corypha umbraculifera*, has achieved distinction in producing an inflorescence about 33 feet (10m) long with about 60 million flowers.

The fruit of the palm varies much more than the flowers, ranging in size from a pea to the double coconut which can weigh over 30 pounds (13.6 kg).

. The outstanding palm in the Temperate House is *Livistona australis*, of which there are several specimens of different ages, one almost touching the roof. In the centre of the Tropical Palm House grows the remarkable *Sabal blackburneana*, the fan or thatch palm of the West Indies. This specimen was transplanted by William McNab's machine from Haddington Place in 1822. It is well over 170 years old and every May it produces an abundance of black pea-sized fruits.

Alpine House

This was designed to house some of the more tender species of alpine plant which would not find the conditions of the Rock Garden suitable. The plants in the house and its surrounds are constantly changing, but in spring there are crocuses, tulips, narcissi and fritillaries. There are always some dwarf primulas, and the saxifrages are usually found in flower for a long period. Some saxifrages form low cushions of foliage, so that water loss in the wild is reduced.

The Frames, adjoining the Alpine House, accommodate those species which would find conditions in the house itself too hot in the summer. Within the house, the floor is overlaid with moist sand in which the pots are plunged to avoid excess evaporation and to maintain a constant root temperature.

The Copse

West of the Alpine House, and the other Plant Exhibition Houses, is the delightfully informal Copse, similar in style to the Woodland Garden. Here in the Copse are birches, pine and eucalyptus, which are especially striking during the winter, while the *Acer palmatum* 'Senkaki' provides colour in spring and autumn.

Situated on a knoll overlooking the Palm Houses, the Copse is protected by belts of holly and pines. Winding grassy paths are lined with bushes of rhododendrons, magnolia, meconopsis, lily and many others. The collection of viburnums extends beyond the Copse on to a grassy slope. Of special note is the rapid growing Japanese *Magnolia obovata,* whose large creamy-white flowers are conspicuous in June not only on account of their size but also because of their heavy perfume which, on a still evening, is noticeable many yards away.

Northwards from the Copse is the most magnificent herbaceous border. The planting has been carried out with the aim of a succession of flowering, so that when one end has finished flowering the other is still in full bloom, making the border a constant attraction.

Near the western end of the herbaceous border is the Monterey cypress, one of the best specimens in Britain of this species native only to California. Continuing round to the West Gate entrance, outstanding among the trees are the maples and yews.

The Demonstration Garden

The informative role of the Royal Botanic Garden is served by the Exhibition Hall and the Demonstration Garden, as 'classrooms for the public'.

The display of annual plants shows the gardener what he can grow at home. The layout is changed each year, but it may include pansies, marigolds, wallflowers and dahlias. Hedges, too, are exhibited so that the intending gardener can select with a better idea of what he may expect.

There are a number of other informative displays. The display of plant family relationships shows the horticultural development of several popular plant groups – for example, species of the *Brassica* genus, such as cabbage, cauliflower and kale, are grouped to show their various relationships to one another.

Plantings include culinary and medicinal herbs, grasses including the South American pampas grass, while others illustrate aspects of plant biology.

A place of learning

Training the botanists of the future is an important part of the work carried out at Edinburgh's Royal Botanic Garden. Former students include today's head gardener at Tokyo Palace and the Director of the Botanic Garden in Ghana. Some 42 student gardeners are employed in the gardens, and they attend a three-year diploma course in amenity horticulture.

The primary function of a botanic garden is botanical and horticultural research, and in particular the accurate identification and classification of plants. The gardens, the glasshouses and the herbarium (a collection of preserved plant specimens from all over the world) house the plant material for such research. A comprehensive reference library with over 75,000 volumes, augmented by an extensive collection of prints, photographs and manuscripts, supplements the herbarium.

There is a ten-acre (4 ha) experimental ground which serves both for training and for grafting and experimental cultivation. Four students and one curator are employed here, with 100 people employed in the herbarium and 250 in the gardens.

It has been proposed, as part of the garden's commitment to the dissemination of knowledge and a concern for safety, to mount a permanent collection of plants that are poisonous. The two species of deadly nightshade, for example, are a particular hazard for the unwary as one can be confused with the cherry and the other with damson. Other common causes of child illness or fatality, laburnum pods and green potatoes among them, would be exhibited.

The Royal Botanic Garden, since its humble beginnings as a Physic garden under three inspired men, has achieved a major place in the botanic gardens of the world. In 1980 over 592,000 people enjoyed the results of the work of dedicated men for three centuries.

Zoological Park

A marvellous menagerie where education and research are paramount

The deceptively narrow entrance to Edinburgh Zoo gives way to the 80 acres (30 ha) which contain some of the world's rarest and most beautiful animals in an area of natural beauty which, at its northwestern tip, fades into the woodland of Corstorphine Hill.

Edinburgh Zoo is in a constant state of development with its energetic programmes of breeding from stock, the introduction of new species from other zoos and the continuous schedule of new buildings and enclosures on the areas acquired for development. With such activity, it is difficult for the zoo itself to keep pace with the location of each species. The map contained in their otherwise most informative booklet is therefore sometimes out of date. The map that appears on the opposite page, however, records the species to be seen in the zoo in the summer of 1981.

With so much to see in such sympathetic surroundings, it is wise to allow at least half a day if not more for a tour of the zoo. As you enter through the main gates, taking the path to the right, you will see the Californian sealions on your left. There are one male and two females, one bull being on loan to London Zoo for breeding purposes. The pool was cut from natural rock in 1914 and sealions have always been happy in it. Sealions can move very fast in water, achieving nearly 20 miles per hour (32 km/h) by planing across the surface. Feeding time, at 15.00 in the summer and

14.30 in the winter, sees them diving and leaping for fish.

Deer are to be seen on the right, followed by the Brunton aviaries and the pheasants. Pheasants have been hunted so extensively in the wild that the group now numbers several of the world's most endangered birds among its 48 species. These rare and beautiful birds are high on Edinburgh Zoo's list for its commitment to breeding and reintroducing into the wild.

North of the aviaries is the Orchard Paddock, with its small pond and overhanging apple trees. The Paddock usually contains a collection of mammals, such as the South American capybaras and Australian wallabies, and large birds, such as cranes and peafowl.

As the path bends to the right, you will see the cassowaries, which are not unlike the emu in appearance. They can inflict extremely unpleasant wounds, however, and the male, whose responsibility it is to incubate the eggs and rear the chicks, can become ferocious during the breeding cycle.

Past the cassowaries to the right, you will come upon the Tropical Bird House and the Reptile House. The birds are exotic both in colour and name and include small parrots, parakeets and long-tailed Paradise whydahs. Of the tortoises, turtles, snakes, lizards, crocodiles and frogs, toads, newts and salamanders in the Reptile House, the stately Mississippi alligator cannot be missed.

They live for about 60 years, growing about one foot (30 cm) each year for the first ten years of their life after which growth slows. It is only the gently heaving scales of this 15-foot (4.5 m) monster which prove it is alive. In the summer, some of the collection is moved outside to the Reptile Rock, where they can be seen in a more natural environment.

One of the very small tree frogs cannot always be spotted because of its camouflage coloration. It is a bright rich green just as the leaves of its natural habitat would be, and it has a brownish stripe running through the eye the length of its body. In the natural world, it is the eye that is most easily recognizable to would-be predators; the stripe obscures the eye and disrupts the form of the body, one of nature's many deceits to promote survival.

The Parrot Garden houses several species of parrot, the Australian cockatoo and the South American macaw. The smaller birds include tanagers, cardinals, weavers, whydahs, finches and quail. One aviary is devoted to the mynahs, whose powers of mimicry are undisputed but for which there appears to be no scientific explanation.

From the shrieks and whistles of the mynahs, you will find little respite in the Chimpanzee House. A constant display of screaming, clapping, gesticulating and hurtling down the slope to their enclosure to land, full face, against the 1¼-inch

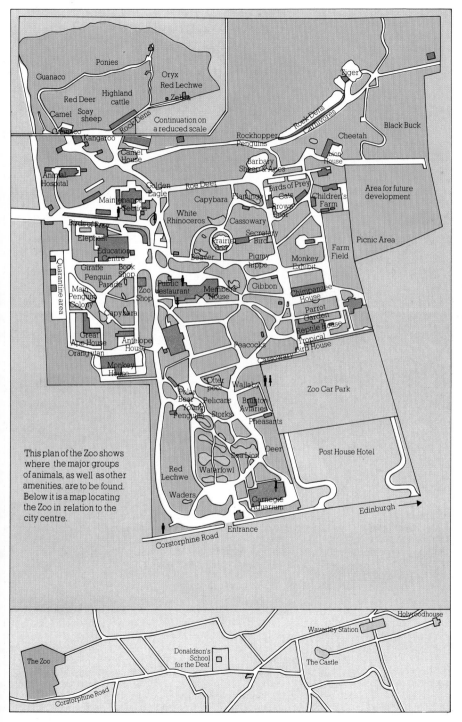

This plan of the Zoo shows where the major groups of animals, as well as other amenities, are to be found. Below it is a map locating the Zoo in relation to the city centre.

thick (32 mm) armoured glass is all part of a chimpanzee's fun. In fact, such displays indicate a continual competitiveness found in any group of chimpanzees, since their society is founded upon a dominance hierarchy. The zoo has installed a simulated ant hill, filled with honey, in the enclosure in the hope of encouraging them to use sticks to dig it out, as they would in the wild. Such projects are part of the zoo's programme of research, often undertaken with other establishments, such as St. Andrews University in this particular case.

A brown bear (**above**) takes a nap. Goat kids and other domestic animals are a popular feature of the Children's Farm. Barbary sheep, (**right**) survey visitors from their rock ledges, while a tiger sits brooding and a leopard either yawns or snarls. The leopard is the smallest of the 'big cats' and the most agile.

The Children's Farm, at the east of the zoo, has been set up to encourage children to handle animals and to be at ease with them. The domestic and farm animals include lambs, rabbits, goat kids, Shetlands, Vietnamese pot-bellied pigs which are animals of great character and amenable nature, calves, guinea pigs and poultry. Children can also be taught, under supervision, to handle stick insects and snakes. There are chipmunks and weasels on display. The principal aim of the Farm is to encourage children's awareness of animals, as part of the conservation programme. The success of the children's

scheme, started in 1975 and helped by volunteers, has inspired the zoo to start one for families from 1981. Attendance during the entire month of January can sometimes be the same as just one day in the summer – but it is worth remembering that spring and early summer are the better times to visit the Farm and the zoo, for this is when the animals are perky and at their most alert.

Next to the Children's Farm is a picnic area, which if you want to make a day of it is a perfect setting overlooking the rest of the zoo.

West of the Farm is the brown bear enclosure. Brown bears

were once common in Scotland, but they have been extinct here for many hundreds of years. They are now found only in remote mountain ranges from Alaska to the Atlantic, across Europe and Asia. They are easier to breed than polar bears, which tend to be rather solitary animals. The species from Kodiak Island of Alaska can weigh as much as a ton and, when upright, measure an awesome eleven feet (3.3 m).

Next to the brown bear is the Scottish wildcat, which looks like an ordinary tabby at first sight. It has bolder markings, particularly on the club-shaped tail, however, to distinguish it from its more peaceable relative. Its predilection for small mammals and birds has provoked gamekeepers and crofters practically to eliminate it. It has been saved, however, by the replanting of Scotland's forests by the Forestry Commission.

Edinburgh Zoo is noted for its success in breeding Snowy owls, to be seen with buzzards, eagles and other owls in the Birds of Prey enclosures. In the wild, the Snowy owl is a winter visitor to northern Scotland and further north still. Its feathers are basically white with brownish-black markings. In its natural environment of snow-covered areas, it is camouflaged most effectively from a potential predator: if it were completely white, it would be far more noticeable.

The Birds of Prey enclosure leads you to the Barbary Rock which is a most impressive home for the Barbary macaques (of the monkey family) and Barbary sheep. Steep layers have been hewn into the rock, which towers many feet above the path – and shows the animals together, as they would be in their natural environment. Continuing eastwards, you will come upon the king of all animals, the lion, who is happily located in a large enclosure interspersed with crags of old Midlothian farmhouse stone. On to the cheetah, which in the wild would be able to achieve speeds of 70 miles per hour (113

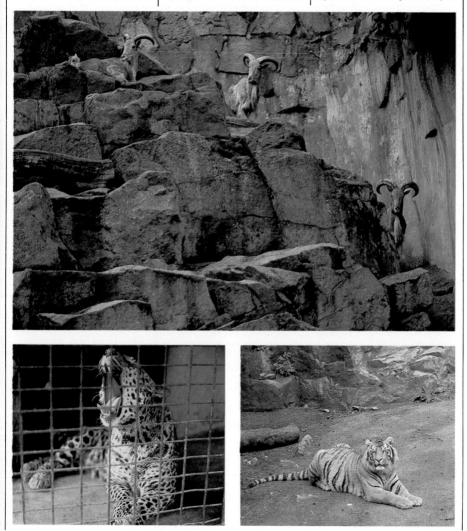

km/h) in short bursts. The cheetah's large enclosure slopes upwards into a mass of long grass and trees where the animal bounds about.

The uphill path past the cheetah's enclosure takes you to the tiger enclosure and the Rock Dens, which house several species of jaguar, leopard, hyena and puma. The puma used to be a common feature of zoos, and, for that reason, breeding was halted – a short-sightedness which has resulted in the puma becoming rare. Edinburgh Zoo has four females and one male and is hoping to breed them.

The northwestern area of the Edinburgh zoo simply does not look like a zoo. The eye moves over fields containing zebra, red lechwe, highland ponies, soay sheep, red deer and guanaco – each having the freedom and space to graze and move around in peace. Many theories have been advanced to explain the zebra's brilliant black and white stripes: one theory, which it would be difficult to justify when the animal is viewed in an enclosure, suggests that the stripes disrupt the form of the animal from a distance and at dusk, when predators in the wild would be hunting, merge together to form a uniform grey. The theory seems convincing when you see the zebras in Edinburgh's zoo, silhouetted in the dusk on the horizon.

It is known that there is a badger sett in the north of the zoo in the area of open country, but since they are nocturnal and, in any case, extremely retiring animals, you will not spot them.

A sense of freedom is not entirely lost when you leave the fields and the kangaroo enclosures as you wind your way down to the camels. They appear not to be enclosed at all – in fact their enclosure is surrounded by a dyke which is concealed by a slight rise in the ground. The Arabian camel or dromedary has one hump and is found only in a domesticated state. The Bactrian camel has two humps – so identification is simple. Camels can tolerate extreme heat and cold and can survive days without water.

The southern part of the northern zone of the zoo contains the European crane, the golden eagle and roe deer which roam in the Whitson Wood. The golden eagle is found throughout the Scottish highlands and is Britain's largest bird of prey. Although they are long-lived in captivity, breeding has only rarely been successful.

The white rhinoceroses, towards the centre of the zoo, are fascinating to watch as they indulge in mock battles. Their agility belies their great weight, as does their name their colour. It is thought that 'white' came from the Afrikaans *wijd* meaning wide.

Next to the white rhino is the Beaver Pool, which is another excellent example of how a zoo can exhibit animals in a happy and natural environment. Beavers are aquatic mammals which use their paddle-shaped tail as a rudder. It is also beaten on the ground or on the water to indicate alarm, and is used to flatten mud when they are building dams. The Beaver Pool is usually a scene of frenetic activity with the animals engaged in a continuous process of gnawing branches to suitable lengths, ferrying them across the pond and positioning them, using mud as their mortar.

The prairie dog builds enormous underground townships in the prairies of North America, consisting of intricate networks of fairly deep tunnels. The keepers have to be vigilant in preventing the prairie dogs emerging all over the zoo. The prairie dogs are social animals and co-operate in warning of approaching danger and 'console' any animal that has been frightened by a would-be predator.

Edinburgh Zoo has four pairs of Chilean flamingoes, all of which have bred successfully. These graceful birds with rosy-pink plumage are particularly interesting to watch when they are performing courtship displays before mating: the elegant rose-peach tail feathers are raised in a fan as the male bird struts and circles.

From the Flamingo Pool, past another cassowary enclosure, the secretary bird (said to derive its name from the crest of black and grey feathers resembling the quill pens of Victorian secretaries) and the small and rare pygmy hippopotamus, the gibbons come into sight. Although they look like monkeys, gibbons are more closely related to the gorilla, chimpanzee and orang utan. Agile and extremely noisy, they swing from branch to branch faster than a human being can run.

Moving directly westwards from the gibbons, you will find the western zone of the zoo, which houses the elephant, giraffe, tapir, apes, monkeys and, most important of all, the penguins.

Edinburgh Zoo is well known for its splendid collection of penguins, which is the largest and most successful group anywhere in captivity. A king penguin was first reared in 1919 as a result of the shipping company, Christian Salvesen, bringing back large numbers from South Georgia. The main breeding pool numbers about 40 king penguins and 90 of the smaller gentoo penguins.

Penguins are found mainly on the islands around the Antarctic and some in tropical waters – and so it is astonishing that they have bred so successfully in Edinburgh. Penguins cannot fly, but they more than compen-

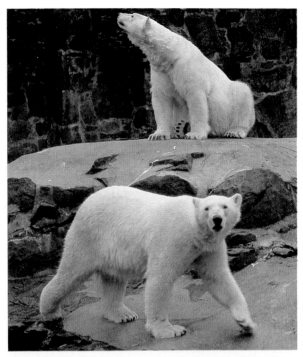

Flamingoes and storks lend their own particular grace to the Zoo, and polar bears always draw the crowds as they clamber from the water and recline on rocky islands. The penguins – of three kinds – are the largest group in captivity.

sate for this by using their wings as paddles so that they speed through the water at up to 25. miles per hour (40 km/h). They are able to emerge, bullet-like, from the sea and land on their feet on ledges or ice-floes as much as six feet (1.8 m) above the water.

King penguins have a slate grey back and white underside, with brilliant orange patches on the sides of the head, throat and upper part of the breast. Young birds are covered in a thick brown down. The king penguin does not make a nest but holds a single egg on the feet with a fold of the skin and feathers of the abdomen. Both males and females help to incubate the egg, which takes about eight weeks.

The gentoo, basically black and white, has distinctive white markings on the crown and sides of the head which resemble earphones. Gentoos lay two eggs, which in the wild would be protected in a nest of pebbles and twigs and other pieces of vegetation. In the zoo, they are presented with nesting rings filled with pebbles on March 15 each year. Gentoo courtship involves the exchange of pebble 'gifts', as well as stealing pebble-nesting material from neighbours. By the end of March, 80 to 90 eggs will have appeared and by the end of April they will have hatched. Only one chick in every two is reared by the penguins, but the second chick is usually fostered with other birds with the result that gentoos are sent to zoos all over the world.

When the young penguins are about six to eight weeks old they are removed to a crèche or nursery pool for one year. They are then moved for a further year to an enclosure adjoining the main colony. When they are two, they are allowed to rejoin the flock.

At 15.30 every summer after-

King penguins in conference.

noon just before feeding time, the penguins embark on a voluntary parade around the paths of the central area of the zoo. The spectacle of the penguin parade began in the late 1940s, quite accidentally, when a keeper left the enclosure gate open. The inquisitive penguins – and they are of a generally inquiring disposition – followed by an equally curious keeper, walked down the drive and along the pavement of the main road until the keeper judged it wise to turn them.

The penguins are fed at 15.45, after the parade, and at 18.00 in the summer, and 14.30 in the winter. Just near the penguins, you can also see the grey seals fed: 15.00 both summer and winter.

The Monkey House, the largest of the animal buildings in the zoo, houses ten different species of monkey. The cages are fronted with armoured glass rather than bars, as the zoo has discovered this prevents the animals from begging and showing off and it prevents the public from disrupting a carefully controlled diet by indiscriminate feeding.

East of the Monkey House, in the southern zone, you will find the polar bears who are to be seen clambering in and out of

the water and reclining upon rocky islands. It was not many years after the zoo was founded in 1909 that the water level enabled one of the polar bears to escape. He did return – after heavy persuasion – and the water level is now maintained with an eye to safety. Unlike other bears, the polar bear is mostly carnivorous, favouring seals. In its native habitat around the fringes of the Arctic icecaps, its off-white colouring affords effective camouflage so that it may sneak up on its unsuspecting prey.

The rest of the southern zone is devoted to red lechwe, pelicans, gannets (the emblem of the Royal Zoological Society of Scotland) and storks, which are all fed after the sealions; the shy and wary otter, an aquatic mammal that lives on fish; the raccoon, noted for its habit in captivity of washing all its food; the South American Maguari stork; the sealions (mentioned earlier); and a splendid series of shrub-covered terraces with three large pools and waterfalls for the collection of ducks from all over the world, swans, and wild birds such as the waterhen.

Back near the entrance to the zoo, you will see the Carnegie Aquarium, which was built in 1927. It cannot rival modern oceanariums, but the colourful and dramatic tropical reef fish from the coral reefs of the Philippines, Persian Gulf and Indian Ocean are particularly eyecatching. Marine turtles, crabs and conger eels, as well as trout, perch and pike from Scotland's streams and lochs, are all housed here. Of special note are the fish that give birth to live young, rather than eggs, such as guppies, swordtails and mollies. Feeding time is at 16.30 during the summer and 15.00 in the winter.

The Zoological Society of Scotland was founded in 1909 as a non-profit making organiza-

The Californian sealion

zoologist has been heard to comment on the intrinsic dullness of the giant panda despite its great popularity with the public and continual exposure by the media.

The zoo's staff of 100 is supplemented by volunteers, who, in the summer, bring the number up to about 200. Much of the building work has been carried out as a result of the government's Job Creation Programme. The zoo, in this way, has been able to save thousands of pounds on labour, which would otherwise have substantially reduced the funds available for the development of the zoo, and at the same time is combating unemployment with its resulting boredom.

The zoo is financed by admission fees, Society subscriptions and by the Adoption Scheme. The need to adopt zoo animals resulted from the conditions of war prevailing in 1940, when food was scarce. Anyone can now adopt, for example, a kangaroo for £90 a year, a tiger for £1000 a year or a weaver bird for £5 a year.

The zoo's philosophy has always centred on the need to educate as well as to entertain. Each enclosure is clearly labelled, with a description of the animal's habitat and its life and behaviour in the wild. The Education Centre, which in 1980 saw 47,000 children from infant age upwards, runs properly structured programmes of education as well as producing the necessary topic sheets and literature. The Centre contains a well-stocked bookshop with books on all aspects of natural history

A visit to the zoo is something that should not be missed when you are in Edinburgh. The tranquillity and beauty of this huge park is rivalled only by its variety of animal life – a kaleidoscope of diving sealions, talking mynahs, chortling chimpanzees and stately king penguins.

tion devoted to the study and conservation of wildlife. It became increasingly disenchanted with its inheritance of undersized, old-fashioned cages, which are often the trademark of an urban zoo.

The zoo acquired royal patronage in 1948 and in the 1980s the dedication and energy demanded by a far-seeing programme of acquisition of land, new buildings and enclosures is clearly demonstrated.

New species are usually acquired from other zoos on the basis of exchange – the introduction of animals from the wild is something of the past. Breed–

loan schemes are in operation with zoos all over the world, so that Edinburgh, for example, may send out a male sealion to another zoo that has only females and receive in return one of the species it needs to continue it own breeding programmes. These co-ordinated schemes are based on mutual co-operation – how, in any case, would it be possible to assess the financial worth of a male sealion versus a female gentoo?

Plans for the introduction of new species to Edinburgh Zoo include red pandas, a smaller and more interesting relative of the giant panda. More than one

The Edinburgh Festival

For three weeks in August the festival city plays host to the world

For three weeks every year Edinburgh is besieged by the top talent of the world – yet the identity of the city remains impregnable. Seen in full Festival regalia, this Athens of the north might well have been custom built for just such an explosion of a diverse mixture of culture – for even as the Old Town lives in harmony with the New, so do the activities of the Festival merge the artistry of great names with new, young, experimental talents. Visitors of all nationalities give the city a boost of adrenalin which can be felt in the spring of each step along Princes Street, suddenly frivolous with bunting and hanging baskets of flowers. Old hands feel superior watching the awe of newcomers as yet unaccustomed to the one o'clock gun.

It was not always thus. The first year of the Festival – 1947 – was a grey year. Britain was still in the grip of austerity. Rationing did not end until 1952. Dior's New Look was in fashion with its nipped waistline and flowing skirts succeeding years of utility clothing and coupons. Platform shoes clumped precariously over the cobbled streets of the city and trams still clanged their cheerful way along Princes Street.

Edinburgh was not renowned for her contributions to culture at this time, although there was talent in plenty to be found in the Rose Street pubs, with writers, painters, poets vying to capture the accolade of the wittiest, pithiest *bon mot* of the evening. From a theatrical point of view, there was little beyond the occasional visiting pre-London show, pantomime at Christmas and the semi-professional resident Gateway Company Theatre. Yet it was out of this post-war malaise that Rudolf Bing, then with the Glyndebourne Festival Opera, had the courage to persist in his vision of a British festival comparable in stature to those of Salzburg and Bayreuth.

Rudolf Bing became the Festival's first director. His world-wide connections proved invaluable in contracting Bruno Walter, reunited with his Vienna Philharmonic, Sir John Barbirolli and the Hallé, Arthur Schnabel, Pierre Fournier, Joseph Szigeti, William Primrose and the Louis Jouvet Company. A spirit of alliances recreated was behind the rebirth of artistic vitality in Europe urged to life by the uphill task of creating the very first Edinburgh Festival. It was with this concept in mind that the honour of playing the opening concert was given to the Orchestre des Concerts Colonne, Paris.

The sun actually shone – for three weeks. Visitors complained of the heat. The critics were impressed. The new Festival was a success. Later, of course, there were niggles about the predominance of music at the expense of drama. Criticism was made about the proportionately small Scottish contribution, despite the participation of the prominent Glasgow-born violist William Primrose, the Scottish Orchestra and the Scottish Singers. Over the following years the situation was to be rectified, aided by a mercuric rise in the standards of Scottish performers. This gave rise to the eventual formation of a Scottish Opera and Ballet Company, a Scottish National Orchestra, Chamber Orchestra and the Scottish Baroque Ensemble – all developed to an internationally accepted level.

It is hard to remember today that in the late 1940s Scottish television was in its infancy, there was no stereo, and the Scots were isolated from first-hand knowledge of the standards of cultural activity in other countries until the Festival brought it all to their doorstep. It was particularly thrilling in those early years to listen to orchestras from Europe or the United States and to their interpretation of the works of great composers.

The Usher Hall, in Lothian Road, is Edinburgh's main concert hall. Within its Edwardian elegance, audiences have been privileged to hear the best soloists in the world, to listen to leading orchestras performing under the contrasting influences of various distinguished conductors.

Live theatre

The Mound snakes southwards up that great castle-bearing glacial rock, both floodlit each festive night to dominate Princes Street. It is a stiff climb to reach the Gothic-style dignity of the Assembly

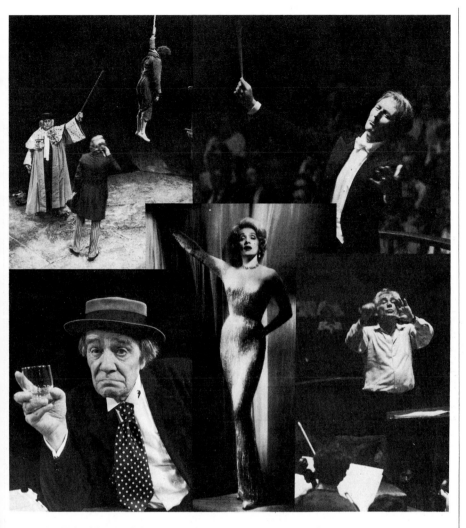

Hall of the Kirk of Scotland. It seems as though the Mound has had to bend to go respectfully round it, yet this was to become the unlikely home for the Scots breakthrough into their own festival with a bawdy play in 'the auld tongue' which satirized and challenged the very authority of the Church. Much to the astonishment of all, the Church authorities gave consent to Tyrone Guthrie's production of *The Thrie Estaites*, although mildly suggesting that nails should not be knocked

into the Moderator's throne. No restriction was made against singing or dancing or even against the provision of a bar.

In 1948 the play had its first performance since the original seven-hour version of 1540. Robert Kemp adapted it to a more acceptable length and under Guthrie's magic touch it became a recurring feature, giving Scottish actors their vehicle in many future Festivals. Few who saw the production will forget the exquisite gyrations of the late Duncan

A taste of the variety the main Festival offers: the Scottish National Opera's *Hermiston;* Carlo Maria Giulini and Leonard Bernstein conducting; Dietrich in cabaret and Max Wall as Buster Keaton.

Macrae as Flatterie, the droning of James Gibson's Deceipt, the resonant power of Tom Fleming and the vigour and pageantry of this ancient satire. The supporting music was by a Scottish composer, Cedric

In daytime rehearsals for a main Festival concert conductor Daniel Barenboim relishes the challenge of sorting out a difficult passage of music with his principal violinist and goes on to lead the field in a tea-break football match.

Thorpe Davie, who later set the music for another Scottish triumph, *The Jolly Beggars.*

During the three years of Rudolf Bing's directorship, he commissioned *The Cocktail Party* by T.S. Eliot. He brought to Edinburgh Trevor Howard, Bernard Miles and Patricia Burke in *The Taming of the Shrew*; Alec Guinness in a production by Ralph Richardson of *Richard II*; Margot Fonteyn, Beryl Grey and Frederick Ashton with the Royal Ballet, then known as Sadlers Wells; Leslie Caron and Jean Babilée with Les Ballets des Champs Elysées. Naturally the Glyndebourne Opera was well in evidence. Mozart's *Le Nozze di Figaro* and Verdi's *Macbeth* were presented. The late, incomparable Kathleen Ferrier sang with the Vienna Philarmonic one year and with the Hallé another. Her *Das Lied von der Erde* still haunts the Usher Hall and those fortunate enough to have been there. Even doubting Sir Thomas Beecham

was prevailed upon to conduct with his Royal Philharmonic Orchestra in 1949, Bing's final year as director.

Over the years the Festival has benefitted enormously from the widely varying influences imposed upon it by its six very different directors. Each built upon the work of his predecessors. Each had something new and individual to contribute.

Ian Hunter became the second director in 1950 for a period of seven years. He will be remembered particularly for his promotion of exhibitions – a new feature in the Festival programme. He initiated exhibitions which were acclaimed throughout the art world and which became an important aspect.

Art shows

These collections were shown at the National Gallery of Scotland and the Royal Scottish Academy, neighbouring buildings at the foot of the Mound.

Planning and organization of these major visiting exhibitions were in the hands of a committee representing both galleries and the Arts Council. Paintings from the principal art galleries of the world were gathered in Edinburgh in order to mount a unique collection of the featured artist – the Cézanne year, the 78 Gaugin paintings shown in 1955, 86 paintings by Braque in 1956, Corot in 1965, Derain in 1967 were memorable examples.

The first exhibition, the Rembrandt, had perhaps the greatest impact. Thirty-six of his paintings were on view in the Scottish capital, giving additional prestige to the Festival and exciting art lovers who had probably never had the opportunity to study the development of Rembrandt's genius over his lifespan.

Military Tattoo

Another stroke of genius, in 1950, was to add the tattoo to the ever-widening field of Festival activities. Although independent of the main administration, the Tattoo has become an inseparable part of the festivities. The performance – a highly polished, well-rehearsed military event – takes place in that quiet hour before dusk on the esplanade of Edinburgh Castle which provides a dramatic backdrop to historic tableaux, gymnastics, highland dancing, pageantry, mock battles and other popular entertainment devised by the military. It has all the attractions of the Royal Tournament, from horses to the occasional elephant. Each year visiting military groups display colourful regimental costume and custom, some appearing to have come straight out of Ruritania. Perhaps most popular of all is the stirring sight and sound of the massed pipe bands.

As dusk falls, the floodlights dim and a spotlight picks out a solitary piper on the battlements. In the sudden silence of the summer evening, he pipes a farewell lament.

Music

In that same year of 1950, the Castle was the setting for an after dark, open-air performance of Handel's *Music for the Royal Fireworks*, complete with firework display and live cannon obligato from the Castle battery. The conductor was Beecham himself, a figure of rare distinction in tails and a steel helmet provided by the Quartermaster's Stores as a protection against sparks.

Sir Thomas's proximity to the Tattoo may have given rise to a story about his advice to a mother who wanted her son to learn a musical instrument which would not offend the parental ear in the early stages. Sir Thomas advocated the bagpipes, saying they sounded no worse at the beginning than they did when one had learned to play them.

The administration

In 1952, the Festival administrators faced up for the first time to the inherent problems of in-

viting an overseas opera company to perform at the King's Theatre. The exterior of the theatre, built in 1906, is undistinguished but the interior is a gem of plush and gilt baroque – like an opera house in miniature. Its smallness was the main problem for the first visitors, the Hamburg Opera Company, which was accustomed to its own vast stage. For one thing, the scenery would not fit. All in all, the size of German operas presented at the King's looked a trifle shabby that year. The problem persists, but years of experience have taught ways and means of making the best of it. Measurements are sent well ahead to visiting companies so that they may plan their compromises.

Robert Ponsonby, 6 feet 6 inches tall, took over from Ian Hunter in 1956. It was he who encouraged and developed the late night satirical aspect of the Festival which spread on to TV screens with such success. Anna Russell was allowed to make a little fun of the hallowed Festival itself. Then, in 1959, Michael Flanders and Donald Swan appeared in *At the Drop of a Hat*. *Beyond the Fringe* hit the boards in 1960.

Ponsonby's interest in ballet was clearly marked by 12 new works especially commissioned for 1958. Until then the major balletic contribution had come principally from the Sad-

from Madrid, the Royal Ballet and the new excitement of Jerome Robbins with his Ballet USA.

Robert Burns had his 200th anniversary at that time, an event which inspired Iain Hamilton to create his *Sinfonia for Two Orchestras*. There were intensive Burns readings and the premiere of *The Jolly Beggars* to boost Scottish

Russian performers was exciting and justifying. For other tastes there were thrilling appearances by Rex Harrison, Martha Graham and Marlene Dietrich; in the theatre there were new plays by Dylan Thomas, Lawrence Durrell and Nigel Dennis.

It was during this phase of the Festival's growth that conductor Alexander Gibson formed

The colourful costumes of singers in Don Giovanni at the King's Theatre and a group from the Scottish National Orchestra playing in the Library of the Signet.

ler's Wells Company, which had presented a varied classical and modern programme ranging from *Swan Lake* to early works by the talented young choreographers John Cranko and Scotland's Kenneth MacMillan. There had, of course, been other visiting companies – Ram Gopal with his Indian ballet, Les Ballets de Champs Elysées, the Yugoslav Ballet and the American Ballet Theater.

In 1959 and 1960 there were performances at the Royal Lyceum by The National Ballet of Finland, Les Ballets Babilée, the Little Ballet Troupe from Bombay, The Ballets Européens de Nervi, Susana y José

morale.

The Ponsonby period was also distinguished by his introduction of Maria Callas to Edinburgh. She took the Festival by storm as Amina in *La Sonnambula* with the La Scala Company from Milan.

Lord Harewood's reign – 1961 to 1965 – was both stimulating and controversial. He introduced the concept of featuring a particular composer each year, and Edinburgh was treated to 24 performances by Schoenberg in the first Harewood Festival. Subsequent years were saturated with Boulez, Tippett and Janácek. Some critics felt, however, that such a policy was departing somewhat from the original concept as expressed by Lord Provost Sir John Falconer in the inaugural year: '...the programme should be for the delight of the average listener'. But Shostakovitch played by

the Scottish Opera Chorus, later to become the Edinburgh Festival Chorus and the basis of the Scottish Opera company.

The first appearance of Scottish Opera at a Festival came in 1967 with productions of *The Rake's Progress* and *The Soldier's Tale*. By this time, Peter Diamand had been appointed as director and was continuing the policy of featuring composers each year. It was Schubert and Britten year in 1968, during which the new national opera company presented *Peter Grimes*. At that time a performance of Britten's *War Requiem* underlined the emotional intensity aroused by the Soviet-led invasion of Czechoslovakia which had reached its climax during the Festival. Drama was transferred to the streets in the form of pickets and demonstrations outside the Usher Hall where the State Orchestra of the USSR was playing.

During the 13 years of Peter Diamand's control the Festival had its 21st birthday. In its maturity the proportion of younger artists invited to take part was increased. The new policy demonstrated that the Festival was now sufficiently established to become a patron – perhaps too it was aimed at reducing the gap between the official events and the essen-

operative venture in which there were no stars and '...all decisions were made through mutual discussion'. The cast included Moira Redmond, Ian McKellen and Frank Middlemas. The new company contributed lunch-time and evening performances and was highly praised. Londoners subsequently became familiar with *Joseph and the Amazing Tech-*

ger afford to do it. Art galleries are increasingly reluctant to risk letting valuable paintings out of the country. The sale of tickets covers less than half the outlay and the balance of the burden falls on the Edinburgh City and District Council, the Scottish Arts Council and the Lothian Regional Council. Between 1947 and 1977, thirty Festivals had been subsidized to

Performing for the Fringe Festival in a former municipal poorhouse overlooking Greyfriars churchyard a company of Polish actors provoke their audience.

tially young Fringe movement which had been developing alongside.

Among the highlights of this prolonged administration was an adaptation of Ariosto's *Orlando Furioso* by the Teatro Libero Rome, which took place in 1970 at the Haymarket Ice Rink using the open-stage technique to bring the audience into the performance as Guthrie had done with *The Thrie Estaites*. At the Assembly Hall the Prospect Company enlivened Shakespeare's *Much Ado About Nothing* with John Neville playing Benedict. The Royal Lyceum Company – Edinburgh's new Civic Theatre – presented *The Changeling* by Thomas Middleton, and thus established itself as a company able to hold its own.

The actors' cooperative

In 1972 came the birth of The Actor's Company, a co-

nicolour *Dreamcoat*, with music by Andrew Lloyd-Webber, which was playing at the Haymarket Ice Rink along with and in striking contrast to the Japanese Hosho Noh Theatre. These few examples reflect the care and skill with which an interesting mix of content was planned for each year's programme in the face of ever-increasing costs. It had taken £60,000 to launch the 1947 Festival. Towards the end of the Diamand administration, the figure had risen to £190,000.

John Drummond took over in 1978 for the 1979 Festival. Formerly head of the BBC Television Music and Arts Department, he may be remembered as the director who preserved the Edinburgh International Festival through the years of world recession. At one time visiting companies had subsidized part of the cost of coming to perform, but they can no lon-

the tune of £4,335,986. This included £773,866 given in private donations. The question of whether the Festival can survive is repeated annually.

Typical of the Festival's esteem is that even in the hard times of 1981, contributions from private sponsors and donations increased by 30 percent from 1980 to a total of £200,000. Add the Edinburgh District Council grant of £400,000 and the Arts Council grant, increased by 10 percent to £360,000, and the total becomes £960,000. This leaves box offices to find £540,000 to meet the estimated 1981 Festival cost of £1.5 million

One of 1981's economies was to refrain from renting the fine eighteenth-century Assembly Rooms in George Street as the Festival Club premises. The Festival Club still exists; however, membership is open to those aged over-18 holding

Festival tickets. Season tickets for the club are available from the Festival Office at 21 Market Street, using the ticket order form in the Festival brochure. A 21-day season ticket is a modest £9, seven days for £4, or £1 daily. The club is open from 09.00 until 01.00, providing cafeteria, snack bar, lounges, bar and restaurant. University buildings provide social facilities for both Festival and Fringe.

The Film Festival

The Edinburgh Film Festival has been an event in the capital since the Festival as a whole started in 1947.

At first it was confined to one week of documentary films, but it has grown in size and prestige to compare with the festivals at Cannes and Berlin.

Humble beginnings are concealed by the fine Georgian façade of the Film Society's present premises at 3 Randolph Crescent, which houses a film theatre, reception and lecture rooms and a restaurant. Even though the programme now spreads over all three weeks, presenting hundreds of feature films, documentaries, cartoons, retrospective and educational films, the unit is still run on a shoestring. It is independent of the Festival Society and therefore receives no financial assistance.

An august amateur body, the Edinburgh Film Guild, established the first festival with the aim of showing 'unusual films not normally seen in the ordinary cinema' such as the documentaries pioneered by Scottish-born John Grierson. By the second year, feature films had been introduced as well and the programme extended to three weeks to cover over 100 entries from 25 countries.

Film directors were soon appearing personally to explain their work to the public. Flaherty, Grierson, Michael Balcon, Vittorio de Sica,

Charles Frend, Samuel Fuller, John Huston, Douglas Sirk, Joseph Losey and Peter Ustinov are a few who have appeared over the years to help clarify new trends and techniques for filmgoers.

As the range of films shown widened, so audiences increased. As a result of the 1955 Festival Conference on Making Films for Children, an international centre was set up. Since 1956, a magazine, *The Living Cinema,* has been produced annually to report on each year's activities in the film world and record the contributions to each Festival. An International

Art Film Competition has also been organized.

Since the Film Festival by policy is free from the pressures of box office commercialism, it is unrestricted in the range and scope of films it may present. New controversial films such as *The Trip* can be shown without fear of public censure. The format usually includes a retrospective selection of films of a particular director – possibly one of the Hollywood greats – while not neglecting Andy Warhol and other contemporary contributors from Godard to Corman. Fernandel is as important a part of

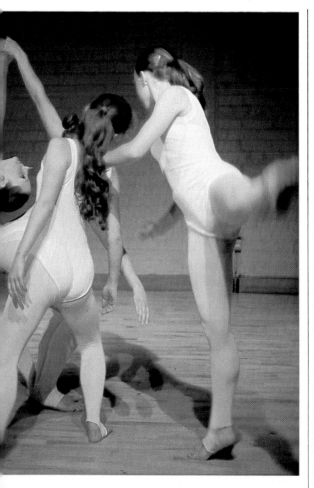

the Festival as Bergman, *The Running, Jumping and Standing Still Film* is taken as seriously as *Dr. Zhivago.*

Television films of merit are shown, but the documentary, past and present, is never allowed to lose its predominant place.

The major Festival programme is often enhanced by linking an opera or theatre production to a film presentation of the same work: a surrealist exhibition is accompanied by surrealist films from the same country; the experimental films of Eduardo Palozzi are the more interesting because his sculp-

ture may be seen in the Scottish National Gallery of Modern Art.

In such ways the Film Festival has added an extra dimension to the rich tapestry of the Festival as a whole, while making a major international contribution to increasing public knowledge of the art of film.

The Fringe

Can 392,000 people be wrong? That was the astounding number of tickets sold for Fringe events in 1980 when 391 companies presented 624 shows, plays, concerts, reviews, dance, mime, recitals, exhibitions and even operas. The Ox-

ford Dictionary defines 'fringe' as an ornamental bordering of threads left loose – a fairly fitting description of this colourful embellishment to the official Festival. It was born 'spontaneously' in the same year as its more staid parent, by virtue of eight theatre companies which simply set out to do their own thing. The university theatre companies of Oxford and Cambridge were early on the scene, using small halls in the Old Town. By the end of the fifties the bordering had grown to some 30 groups spread all over Edinburgh, a central box office had been organized, a programme published yearly and a Fringe Club opened.

Today's printed programme has grown to a 48-page booklet. Each listing gives some idea of what the event is about. In 1981, for instance, the programme includes 297 companies offering a huge variety of entertainment. If the main festival boasts of bringing Bayreuth to Edinburgh's doorstep, the Fringe may justly claim predominance in world premieres – 180 in 1980 – many to appear later in London's West End theatres at three times the admission price. Visitors may be tempted by a stage autobiography of Harpo Marx as performed by the California State University Fresno; *The Wonderful World of Maggie Thatcher* by the AAV (Actors Against VAT) Company; or the Cambridge Mummers in *Rubble,* an Irish myth brought up to date.

By direct contrast, Marlborough College, a leading British public school, selected William Blake's only known complete drama, *The Ghost of Abel,* as its contribution. The National Student Theatre Company adapted Anthony Burgess's novel *The Clockwork Orange* to follow their successes of previous years.

Visitors are often surprised at the world-wide success of the Fringe; its story is an interesting one. It was in 1960 that Jonathan Miller, Alan Bennett, Peter Cook and Dudley Moore first captured international attention with their show *Beyond the Fringe*. They were allocated four performances in the official venue of the Royal Lyceum theatre, put new life into British humour and are now part of an unorthodox establishment of their own making. They also set beyond challenge the Fringe's early reputation for the quality of its late night shows.

The Oxford Theatre Group's premiere of *Rosencrantz and Guildernstern Are Dead* brought Tom Stoppard the attention he deserved and the controversial Traverse Theatre Club, with stimulating interpretations of Shakespeare, was founded in Edinburgh in 1963 as a result of Fringe events.

Joan Littlewood, already well known for her theatre in east London, was quick to see the advantage of taking her Theatre Workshop to the Fringe. *Hinge and Bracket*, now nationally famous, first charmed Edinburgh in 1974, and a 1977 production of *Writer's Cramp* by John Byrne transferred successfully to London's West End.

A wealth of experience can be gleaned by all the young participants gathered together in one compact city whose normal population is under 500,000. The Fringe Club in the university union building, Bristo Square, provides a social meeting place for actors and audience. There are two restaurants open until 01.00 and four bars, all of which are open till 02.00 and serve snacks. Club membership is a modest £5 for the three-week season and this includes early mailing of the following year's programme. Membership for a shorter period costs £1 a day.

Many other unscheduled events take place in pubs and hotels, mainly poetry readings and jazz groups. There is a healthy traditional jazz movement in Edinburgh all year round, and a Jazz Festival evolved out of it, sponsored by a brewery. There is a Jazz Festival Ball at Tiffanys in St. Stephen Street on the evening of the opening day. Concerts are usually free, but players will be happy to accept a drink.

The Fringe supports as many as 25 exhibitions, many of them free. The scope is wide and varied. There might be British glass at the Scottish Crafts Centre in Canongate or an ambitious Impressionist exhibition at the MacIntosh Gallery, Johnston Terrace. The opening of the Richard Demarco Gallery in 1966 was an important event in Fringe history. In defiance perhaps of the established giants on show at the official exhibitions, this new gallery concentrated on twentieth-century art. In its second year, with the assistance of Edinburgh University and support from the Arts Council, it encouraged contemporary artists to submit work for prizes of £1000 to be awarded to each of nine artists. Out of 1500 entries, 100 works were selected for exhibition at the Festival and became known as the *Edinburgh Open 100*. This was followed by *Canada 101*. The Demarco Gallery continued to make a contribution to the overall picture of artistic endeavour by introducing the work of contemporary Rumanian and Polish artists. Objects USA at the City of Edinburgh Art Gallery took up the theme in 1973. By the following year the official Festival had caught on and mounted an exhibition in the Scottish Arts Council Gallery called *Eight English Artists 1924-1940*, among them Barbara Hepworth, Henry Moore, Paul Nash and Ben Nicholson

The Demarco Gallery had its origins in the Traverse Theatre which in turn evolved out of a paperback bookshop run by an enthusiastic American, Jim Haynes. In the early 1960s Haynes had presented a dialogue there during the Festival. This developed into an all-year-round intimate theatre in Fringe style, relocated in the Lawnmarket in premises once known as 'Kelly's Paradise', one of old Edinburgh's more notorious brothels. In its new home, the stage traversed the audience – hence the name – and Richard Demarco organized a small gallery in the theatre.

The Traverse Theatre has become a permanent and important feature of Edinburgh's culture. The capital certainly needs entertainment between Festivals, although its citizens maintain a characteristic reserve over supporting anything new and experimental.

How then does the Scot in the street react to the Festival after all these years? As far as the expense of supporting it is concerned, it may take a few pence out of his sporran but it returns pounds to his wallet in terms of tourist spending and side benefits from publicity. He may still feel a little wary about all these foreigners swarming in each summer, but his deeply inbred sense of hospitality never wavers.

The Stately Homes

*A*lthough Edinburgh has its fair share of fine houses and architecture commissioned by the rich and aristocratic inhabitants, some of the greatest displays of wealth and grandeur are outside the city.

Many of the stately homes were built as impressive edifices to money and power on massive estates within a few miles of the capital. They contain superb collections of every conceivable art form and, indeed, their architecture is some of the finest to be seen in Scotland.

There are those, the majority, built after the Union with England in 1707 when Scotland, at last, could trade freely and fill the coffers. But others are the ancient seats of families who led Scotland long before peace with the southerners. These stand, steeped in history and memories of Scotland's turbulence, without any pretentions to the mighty ostentation of the newer houses.

Of the mansions around Edinburgh there are four which represent the many styles, periods and riches of Scottish architecture.

Traquair, home of the royal Stuart family, has its roots in the previous millenium and has been constantly occupied ever since – at times by some of the most romantic figures in the realm's history, like Mary, Queen of Scots

In sharp contrast, there is Hopetoun House, founded on the huge new riches (of the Leadhills mines) acquired by the 1st Earl of Hopetoun. It was designed to display the family's new social status and almost aspires to the Sun King's Palace of Versailles, near Paris.

The original house was begun in 1699, drawn up by William Bruce and added to, 20 years later, by the illustrious Adam family, William and his sons Robert and John. It is possibly Scotland's most magnificent mansion.

Nearby is Dalmeny House, the home of the 7th Earl of Rosebery. It was the first Tudor Gothic revival house in Scotland, designed by William Wilkins in 1815 on the open country of the shores of the Firth of Forth.

Here are two of the nation's finest collections – the Mentmore Collection from Baron Meyer de Rothschild's Buckinghamshire estate; and the Rosebery Collection based on the historical, literary and artistic interests of the 3rd Earl.

Lastly there is Sir Walter Scott's Abbotsford, 40 miles southeast of the capital on the banks of the Tweed. Bought as a farmhouse and transformed into a grand Scottish Border Laird's residence by Scott on the profits of his writing, it stands as a tribute to all that is, and has been, Scotland.

Traquair

This head of Bonnie Prince Charlie is engraved on a glass that is part of a rare collection of Jacobite mementoes kept at Traquair. Legend says the Prince visited his loyal kinsmen while making preparations for the uprising in 1745.

Left Among the many relics of Mary, Queen of Scots at Traquair is this bed in which she slept and the silk counterpane she and her 'four Maries' so carefully worked. In the cradle (**below**) she tended her infant son, the future King James VI and I, of Scotland and England.

Above This harpsicord is now restored to working order. It was made in Antwerp by Andreas Rucker in 1651 and is the only one in Britain with the original decoration.

*T*raquair is perhaps the most romantic house in Scotland. Only 28 miles (45 km) south of Edinburgh, it is also the oldest inhabited dwelling in the realm. Traquair has grown from the original foundation which legend dates back to AD 950, and is filled with the memorabilia of one family.

That family is the Stuarts, related to the Scottish Royal Family, who have lived here since 1491. In fact the three most tragic members of the House of Stuart – Mary, Queen of Scots, Charles I and Bonnie Prince Charlie – are inextricably connected with the story of the house.

The famous Bear Gates, the main entrance to the tree-lined drive, have remained closed (so the story goes) since Bonnie Prince Charlie passed through them on his way to defeat in England. Family tradition says that they will remain closed until a Stuart King sits on the Scottish throne.

From the castle forecourt, you can see the development of the house which began life in its current form in about 1100 as a royal hunting lodge. It grew into a fortified tower house in the fifteenth century, and was extended into the present structure in the mid-seventeenth century. Its castle-like appearance, with corner turrets and tiny ground floor windows, reflects the times of border feuds and years of political and religious unrest in Scotland.

Pass through the nail-studded seventeenth-century door, make your way to the end of the ground floor corridor. The last room was part of the original hunting lodge, later becoming the basement of the tower house. The walls are immensely thick, the windows mere slits. During a border raid, the family would have brought their cattle in here.

The first-floor sitting room is part of the seventeenth-century addition. Partially exposed in the ceiling are seventeenth-century painted beams which, along with medieval-style wall paintings, formed the original decoration of the room.

The room was remodelled in the eighteenth century when the ceilings were plastered and the paintings covered with wood panelling. There is still a fine, unusual wall painting in the museum room directly above.

More sophisticated decorative painting was done by the Norries, an Edinburgh firm of decorators, and a seascape was inserted above the fireplace. The furniture is mostly eighteenth-century, too. This room is still used, and has a lived-in, cluttered air about it.

The beautiful harpsicord is by Andreas Ruckers, Antwerp, 1651, and is the only known example from this workshop with its original paintings and decoration. It is also in perfect working order, and it is possible to hear a tape of music recorded from it.

The dressing room next door is arranged to show off Victorian clothes discovered in the attics, including two wedding dresses and a pair of the last Earl's stockings.

The King's Room, in the Old Tower, is the most atmospheric room in the house. This was the room Mary and her husband, Lord Darnley, occupied when they visited Traquair on a hunting trip in 1566. The cradle at the foot of the bed was the one she used to rock her infant son, the future James I. The beautifully embroidered white silk bedcovering is said to have

The chapel was built after the Catholic Emancipation Act of 1829. *Joseph Flying to Egypt* (**above**) is one of 12 sixteenth-century wood panels in the chapel. The figure of Mary and the dead Christ (**right**) is in front of the altar.

been worked by the Queen and her ladies-in-waiting, the 'four Maries' of the song.

The portrait between the windows is of Anne, second wife of the 2nd Earl of Traquair. She was descended from the same family as Mary Seton.

The Earldom of Traquair was created by Charles I and the 1st Earl supported him in the Civil War. Upon the defeat of the Royalists by Cromwell, he was imprisoned for four years. John, the 2nd Earl, also fought against Cromwell and his family suffered severe harassments from the Presbyterians. Catholicism was banned, and though the Earl was an Episcopalian, he was fined £5000 for marrying Henrietta Gordon, a Catholic.

Henrietta died young, and his second wife, Anne Seton, was also an ardent Catholic. Her husband died soon after their marriage, and she is portrayed here with a widow's peak. After her husband's death, she was continually persecuted by the local presbytery, who often searched the house for 'popish' objects. At this time she converted the topmost floor of the tower into a private chapel with a secret stair, hidden in the cup-

board, so that the priest could escape into the woods.

Her eldest son, William, was taken from her to be educated against Catholicism. He, however, died young, and his younger brother Charles succeeded as 4th Earl and continued to practise Catholicism which remains in the family to this day.

The Earls of Traquair were also ardent Jacobites. A portrait in the Library depicts the 5th Earl wearing the end of his neckerchief tucked through his buttonhole – a secret Jacobite sign; and the museum contains some fine examples of Jacobite glass including the 'amen' glass with the inscription:

God bless the Prince of
    Wales,
The true-born Prince of
    Wales,
Sent us by thee;
Send him soon over
And kick out Hanover,
And soon we'll recover
Our old libertie.

Though the 4th Earl was not imprisoned for his part in the 1715 uprising, his brother-in-law, the Earl of Nithsdale, was

incarcerated in the Tower of London under sentence of death. His escape from the Tower disguised as a woman – aided by his wife – was the only escape ever from the Tower and is yet another of the romantic stories connected with the family.

The 5th Earl was also imprisoned in the Tower for two years after the 1745 rebellion. His wife voluntarily joined him in his Tower apartments. It was he who made the dramatic gesture of closing the Bear Gates.

The family fortunes have been less adverse since then, and with the passage of the Catholic Emancipation Act of 1829, the family was able to practise their faith openly. Then they built the present Chapel, furnished with an Italian marble altar and 12 sixteenth-century Flemish-style woodcarvings bought by the 5th Earl.

The last of the direct line was Lady Louisa Stuart who lived to be almost 100. An acquaintance of Burns and friend of Sir Walter Scott, she founded the local Catholic Church of Peebles and Innerleithen which commemorate her centenary.

Hopetoun House,
a mansion built
on the wealth of lead
mining interests to
bolster the social status
of Charles, the 1st Earl.

Hopetoun House

Nathaniel Dance painted this portrait of the 3rd Earl and his brother Charles with their tutor William Rouet, in Rome where they stayed on their Grand Tour of Europe. It hangs in the Red Drawing Room designed by Adam.

Left The Yellow Drawing Room was created by the Adam family. The silk brocade on the walls was made around 1850.

Above Hopetoun's back door, the visitors' entrance, was part of the first phase of the mansion, started in 1699, designed by Sir William Bruce.

opetoun is the most magnificent house in Scotland, something of an equivalent to Blenheim Palace or, in a much smaller way, to Versailles. Built in the eighteenth century for the Hope family, approximately 10 miles (16 km) west of Edinburgh, it was consciously designed to proclaim their newfound wealth and social status.

The 1st Earl's grandfather had married well – the heiress to the Leadhills mines – So the family fortune was made. The Earldom was only created in 1703, most probably through the ambitions of Lady Margaret Hamilton, mother of Charles, the 1st Earl. It was she who commissioned William Bruce to begin work on the original mansion in 1699.

However, the Bruce House was not quite grand enough for Charles and his wife, Lady Henrietta Johnstone, the sister of the cultured and cosmopolitan Marquess of Annandale. She inherited his extensive collection of Italian art in 1721. Perhaps it was to house this collection that the most fashionable architect of the day, William Adam, was engaged to enlarge the house.

He designed the great façade with its colonnades and flanking pavilions. After William Adam's death in 1748, the remodelling and decoration were completed by his sons, Robert and John. Their main contribution was to the interiors and, in particular, to the magnificent suite of state rooms on the ground floor.

Perhaps the best way to see Hopetoun is to start in the oldest part of the house. Pass through the neo-classical entrance hall by Adam with its antique roundels from the Annandale Collection set high into the walls, and enter the original Bruce House. The restrained decoration and wooden panelling give these rooms a warm and intimate character. You can imagine a family actually living here, something a bit more difficult to do in the more imposing Adam rooms. The ground floor rooms are not exactly as envisaged by Bruce. The Library has been made by joining two bedchambers, and the Bruce bedchamber was painted in the eighteenth century to give a lighter, more decorative effect. The marvellously theatrical bed was designed for the Adam

State Bedchamber.

If you mount the original staircase, encrusted with exquisite wood-carved friezes (the murals were painted in 1967 as a memorial to the present Marquess' first wife), you enter rooms which Lady Margaret Hamilton would still recognize and feel at home in. Her portrait by Karel de Moor hangs at the top of the stairs.

The tapestries depicting pastoral scenes were specially made by the John Vanderbank Soho Tapestry Company as were a series of decorative paintings extolling the Virtues by the Dutch painter Tideman.

It is quite a psychological and decorative jump from the cosy West Wainscot Bedchamber to the rather ostentatious Yellow Drawing Room. This is the first room of the Adam Suite, originally laid out as Dining Room, Drawing Room and State Bedchamber.

The Yellow Drawing Room was originally the dining room and much of the furniture is Adam-designed and made by James Cullen, the 'Scottish chippendale'. The elegant mirrors between the windows were meant to reflect candlelit

Right The Red Drawing Room, with a ceiling by Robert Adam and the 10-foot-long marble fireplace by J. Michael Rysbrack.
Below A London craftsman, Mathias Lock, supplied this bed of gilt

dinner guests, and the two beautiful plump commodes on either side of the Adam fireplace come from the State Bedchamber.

In the early nineteenth century, the 4th Earl, who was a professional soldier and knew little of the arts, delegated Andrew Wilson, an Edinburgh art dealer, to take care of the Hopetoun art collection. Though some of the most spectacular pictures were bought by Wilson, he also sold important works, taking a commission on all his transactions, much in the manner of a present-day stockbroker. Wilson's attributions were often inaccurate; for instance, the *Doge of Genoa* in the Red Drawing Room, purchased by him as a Tintoretto, is actually a *Doge of Venice* and most certainly not painted by Tintoretto. However, he must be given credit for the purchase of the *Adoration of the Shepherds* in the Yellow Drawing Room. Though not by Rubens himself, it is a very fine product of his school and may well have been done under the master's supervision. Note also the rather fine School of Rembrandt of an old woman and the

little Teniers *Temptation of St. Anthony* with its nasty Bosch-like demons.

The Red Drawing Room is the only room in the house which retains its original function. Its furniture was designed to be kept against the walls so guests could promenade and show off their finery. It is the grandest room in the house. The elaborate Robert Adam ceiling is wonderfully elegant and the grand fireplace by Rysbruck is particularly impressive.

Apart from the misattributed *Doge* above the fireplace there are some good Italian pictures from the Annandale Collection. Passerotti's *Brothers of the Manaldini Family* is a particularly fine example. But the two most interesting paintings in the room are the full-length portraits of James, the 3rd Earl, and his brother, Charles, by Nathaniel Dance. These were done in Italy while the brothers were doing the 'Grand Tour', and include details of Roman architecture in the background to prove their literary and artistic cosmopolitanism.

Also by Dance is the little conversation piece which

shows the two boys with their tutor in the Borghese Gardens with St. Peters Cathedral in the background. It is a particularly charming and intimate rendering, lacking the bombast of the full-length portraits.

The final room in the suite is the State Dining Room, originally the State Bedchamber. Apart from Versailles, State Bedchambers were never really very practicable, and the 4th Earl had the room converted into a dining room in 1820. It was here in 1822 that George IV dined on turtle soup and three glasses of wine before knighting the painter Henry Raeburn. There is, in fact, a Raeburn portrait of the 4th Earl hanging here, as well as fine portraits by Ramsay and Gainsborough. The most interesting, if not the best, picture is David Allan's posthumous portrait of the 1st Earl shown at his desk with the plans for the house, while the actual building of it goes on in the background. Painted 40 years after the Earl's death in 1792, this portrait underlines most succinctly the importance which the family attached to their own little Palace of Versailles.

A late portrait of Sir Walter that shows clearly his high-domed skull which was possibly the result of the poliomyelitis attack he suffered as a child.

Abbotsford

The baronial mansion of Sir Walter Scott, overlooking the Tweed, is a dream come true. Writing brought Scott, one of 13 born to an Edinburgh solicitor, a baronetcy, fame and a fortune which he used to build his Gothic fantasy.

Left The view from the dining room turned bedroom where the dying Scott could enjoy his favourite sight of the lawns by the Tweed.

Above Scott found sitting for artists tedious but admirers constantly demanded his likeness and dozens were made: this one by Raeburn.

To visit Abbotsford, about 40 miles (64 km) southeast of Edinburgh, is to step directly into the life of Sir Walter Scott. Scott, who began his career as an Edinburgh lawyer, became, during his own lifetime, one of Europe's most successful novelists. With his sudden rise to fame he became obsessed with the idea of becoming a Border laird and in 1811 he bought the little farm of Carthyhole with the intention of creating himself a country seat. At first he only made additions to the existing building but in 1822 he had the old farmhouse entirely pulled down to build the main block of Abbotsford. Sir Walter had paid just 4000 guineas for the 110-acre (44.5 ha) property standing on the right bank of the River Tweed. The land had at one time belonged to the monks of Melrose. This, plus the fact that there was a ford across a nearby stream, prompted Scott to change the name from Carthyhole to Abbotsford.

The tour of Abbotsford begins in Scott's book-lined Study. One would not be at all surprised to see the white-haired old man walk through the little door in the gallery which leads from his bedroom. It was in the comfy leather armchair at this desk that Scott wrote the famous Waverley Novels. Despite their phenomenal success Scott's life story became a romantic tragedy worthy of one of his own novels. At the height of his fame, in 1826, his publisher, Constable, went bankrupt leaving debts of over £120,000. Scott, with his immense sense of pride, took on these debts and worked himself almost to death to honour them. It is a tribute to his tenacity that he virtually paid the debt in full.

Among the masterworks produced at Abbotsford were such classics as *The Heart of Midlothian* and *Rob Roy*. In response to public demand, Scott turned to English history as well, notably with *Ivanhoe*, though with *Redgauntlet*, the last of his novels, he returned to the Scottish theme with which he was always more at home.

The desk at which he wrote was made from pieces of wood from the wrecked ships of the Spanish Armada. And wooden panels line the Study which contains part of Sir Walter's collection of 9000 books. Here too is a portrait of the hero Rob Roy.

Move through to the Library which is surveyed by the idealized bust of Sir Walter by Chantrey. As in the Raeburn portrait in the Sitting Room he appears every inch the Border laird he tried so hard to become.

He was a magpie of a collector with a passion for anything to do with Scottish history, particularly objects with romantic connotations or associations with his own novels. The heavy moulded plaster Gothic ceiling is copied from Roslin chapel which features in several of his novels. If you look in the glass case in the window you will find Bonnie Prince Charlie's quaich, Rob Roy's purse and a tumbler with a few lines of poetry scratched on it by Robert Burns. As well as Scottish romantic novels Scott wrote a scholarly life of Napoleon and also on display is Napoleon's cloakclasp, in the form of two golden bees, found in his carriage after Waterloo.

Many of the objects in the house were presents from admirers. The two elaborately carved Italian chairs, said to

The dirk of Rob Roy whose real name was Robert McGregor. He was a highland outlaw with Jacobite loyalties who was romanticized by Scott.

Right Scott's carefully kept writing materials and notes are still at Abbotsford where he worked himself to death trying to pay off his publishers' debts. Apart from his many novels Scott wrote poems, ballads, reviews and histories.

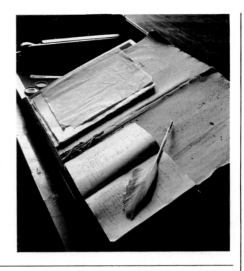

The original keys to the Old Tolbooth in Edinburgh hang on a wall in the entrance hall, one item in Scott's massive collection.

have come from the Borghese Palace in Rome, were donated by his publisher. The beautiful handpainted Chinese wallpaper in the sitting room came from Sir Walter's brother-in-law, while the ebony roll-top desk was a present from King George IV and the silver urn in the niche beside it was a gift from Byron.

The walls of the Armoury are encrusted with weapons of great beauty as well as those of historical interest – note the superbly inlaid ivory butt of an Austrian rifle. Rob Roy's broadsword, dirk and gun also hang here.

In the Anteroom to the Armoury hangs a painting of Ginger, one of Sir Walter's dogs, by Sir Edward Landseer.

A glass case in the Dining Room contains an important relic of Scottish history – the sword of James IV, later given by Charles I to the Marquess of Montrose. It was here in the Dining Room that Sir Walter lay on his deathbed propped up by the window so that he could see his beloved River Tweed.

The Entrance Hall is panelled with oak from the Auld Kirk of Dunfermline. The two semi-circular cupboards were constructed out of the pulpit and, rather irreverently, Sir Walter kept wine in them. The walls are adorned, baronial style, with antique weapons and suits of armour – echoes of *Ivanhoe*.

On the exterior wall just above the entrance porch is set the condemned criminals' door of the Old Tolbooth of Edinburgh and in the centre of the Courtyard is a fountain which once formed part of Edinburgh's Mercat Cross, which in 1660 ran wine for the citizens at the Restoration of Charles II.

Sculptured medallions from the same cross are set into the south wall of the court alongside antique Roman reliefs from Hadrian's Wall. Maida, Sir Walter's favourite dog, is buried near the front porch beneath a stone effigy (Maida's likeness also appears on the Scott Monument in Princes Street Gardens). An inscription in Latin runs around the marker. Scott translated it as:

Beneath the sculptured form
which late you wore
Sleep soundly, Maida,
At your master's door.

The garden archway leads to the family's private apartments through the Chapel, with its fifteenth-century Flemish altarfront and painting of *Madonna and Child* by Ghirlandaio. This is also open to the public. Cardinal Newman was a friend of Scott's descendants and frequently celebrated Mass here.

This wing was added in the mid-nineteenth century and Scott's two great-great-granddaughters still live here. They see the house very much as a shrine to Sir Walter who they would like to think would still feel perfectly at home here since hardly a thing has been changed since his death in 1832.

Indeed electricity was installed scarcely 20 years ago; Sir Walter was an amateur scientist and until then the family made do with a gas lighting system of his own design. (Abbotsford was one of the first gas-lit houses in Britain.)

The whole house testifies to the personality of the man whose romantic view of Scotland caused the whole world to take note of Scotland's unique contribution to European culture.

The splendid home of the
Earls of Rosebery on the
Firth of Forth has some of
the world's greatest
treasures in two collections.

Dalmeny House

John Millais's sensitive portrait of the 5th Earl was painted in 1886. The Earl was a great scholar, writer and politician who became a Liberal Prime Minister and was an avid collector of works of art, books and objects that are now on view.

Left Treasures of the Mentmore collection - stately French furniture, tapestries, clocks and other 18th century works of art.

Above Mementoes of Napoleon, including his shaving stand and harpoon gun, are arranged in the room devoted to the Emperor.

*J*ust seven miles (11 km) outside Edinburgh stands one of the area's most celebrated historic houses – Dalmeny House, the home of the Earls of Rosebery. Dalmeny is important for two reasons; first, because of the role played by the 5th Earl as Prime Minister and leader of the Liberal Party in the 1890s and second because it houses some of the principal items from the fabulous Mentmore collection. These came into the family through the marriage of the 5th Earl to Hannah Rothschild, heir to Mentmore, the Rothschild's rambling Buckinghamshire mansion.

But the links between the Roseberys and Dalmeny go much further back than this – in fact, to 1662, when the estate of Dalmeny and Barnbougle was bought by Sir Archibald Primrose – Primrose is the Rosebery family name – when he was Lord Clerk Register of Scotland. He and his family lived in the thirteenth-century castle of Barnbougle, right on the shores of the Forth, which had belonged to the English Moubrays, Knights Templars in the Crusades. It was to Barnbougle

that the smuggling Moubray descendants brought contraband to be stored in the castle cellars.

Sir Archibald's son, who followed in his father's legal footsteps, became the 1st Earl of Rosebery in 1703 in Queen Anne's Coronation honours. He, too, continued to live in the cold and primitive castle.

It was the 3rd Earl's family who began to complain bitterly about the old castle but the Earl would have none of it. 'What was good enough for my grandfather, is good enough for my grandchildren,' came the reply. It took a huge wave, crashing through the dining room window, knocking him off his feet, to overcome his obstinacy and convince him that the castle did need rebuilding.

He commissioned Robert Adam to redesign the ancient castle but the results were not acted on, since the thrifty Earl considered them too extravagant.

When the 3rd Earl died, at the age of 88, in 1814, however, the 4th Earl acted quickly. He commissioned William Wilkins, whom he had known at Cambridge, to set about plan-

ning Scotland's first Tudor Gothic Revival house, a little way up the hill from Barnbougle Castle. The new house became, after its completion in 1817, a model for many nineteenth-century Scottish country houses, being noted for its comfort and modernity.

Though the Roseberys had always been important Scottish figures, it was the 5th Earl who was the first to take the national stage. He had three overwhelming ambitions: one was to marry the richest woman in England, another to become Prime Minister and the third to win the Derby. He achieved them all – he married Hannah Rothschild, heir to Mentmore, in 1878; followed Gladstone as Liberal Premier in 1894; and eventually won the Derby three times, with horses bred at Mentmore.

This Rosebery was a complex character. As well as being a politician, he was also a scholar, with a fascination for Napoleon, on whom he wrote one of the classic books. He also collected objects and portraits with Napoleonic connections and these, with the eighteenth-century portraits that also in-

Left Dalmeny House contains an unsurpassed collection of furniture. **Above** Wilkins, architect of the House, designed this table. **Middle** A Scottish bible box. **Below** An eighteenth century chair.

Right The joys of childhood is the theme of Goya tapestries adorning the hall stairway. A rare art form for the Spanish master, the works demonstrate an uncommonly lighthearted style.

terested him, formed the basis of his great collection.

His marriage to Hannah, the only child of Baron Meyer de Rothschild, brought him the exceptional collection at Mentmore in Buckinghamshire. The Baron had bought largely French eighteenth-century works of art between 1830 and 1850 – at the same time that the Wallace collections were put together – classic examples of which are now at Dalmeny. He also amassed a vast amount of Victorian works which were not brought to Dalmeny but were auctioned at Mentmore.

The 5th Earl thus set the pattern of Rosebery life over the years. Six months of the year was spent at Dalmeny and the rest of the time in the south. The treasures were similarly divided. The classic collections – notably the French furniture – remained at Mentmore, while Dalmeny was filled with pieces in the Scottish baronial style.

The decision to sell Mentmore and its collection completely changed this. The family decided what to keep according to a deliberate philosophy. This was that Dalmeny should remain a home and not become a museum. The fine pieces from Mentmore, therefore, were chosen just as much for personal reasons as for their financial or artistic value, though the last factor also played an important part. The care that has gone into selecting what the visitor sees at Dalmeny today thus reflects the love the Roseberys have for their home and their possessions.

Inside the Gothic entrance hall, beneath the hammer beams and a fan-vaulted ceiling, is a large and impressive portrait of the assiduous 5th Earl by Millais. It is one of Millais' best portraits, with the figure dramatically set off against a dark background. The Earl's face is painted in sensitive detail.

On the stairway hang some of the rarest treasures of the house: the very unusual Goya designed tapestries. They were made by the Royal Tapestry Factory to fit into decorative schemes for Spanish royal palaces. They are four lighthearted, merry scenes of lovers and children and, apart from being a rare art form for Goya, they are also distinguished by their jollity compared to Goya's more common gloominess.

On the top landing is Hogarth's *The Painter's Wife*. Like the Goya works it is untypical of the painter who was largely concerned with social comment. This is a personal and honest portrait, direct and concerned with the person beneath the image.

The Library, rebuilt in the 1950s following a wartime fire, is still used by the Rosebery family as a sitting room. It houses the book collection the 5th Earl, who collected books all his life.

Among the portraits in the room is one of the 6th Earl who inherited both Mentmore and Dalmeny and, justly, divided his time between the two. He was an all-round sportsman and a very keen racehorse enthusiast. He had a distinguished career with Allenby in World War I and as military governor in Egypt, and in World War II became Regional Commissioner for Civil Defence in Scotland. Racing mementoes are also on display.

The 6th Earl's wife, a pianist, was very involved with the arts and much of the planning for the

Edinburgh Festival was discussed in the Library. Indeed, Lady Rosebery was on the Programme Committee of the Festival for 25 years.

In the neo-classical Drawing Room are the greatest treasures from the Mentmore Collection. They are the pieces selected lovingly and carefully from the Buckinghamshire house by the present Earl of Rosebery and his wife before the sale in 1977, forced on by heavy death duties when the 6th Earl died.

They are largely French works made between 1680 and 1780 during the reign of the Sun King Louis XIV, Louis XV and Louis XVI. On the floor are the earliest Savonnerie carpets, from a series of 900 made for Louis XIV's palaces, which have taken the Roseberys more than two years to restore – with the help of the Rosebery children soaping them with sponges on their feet.

The Beauvais tapestries, designed by Boucher, were also under the caring eye and hand of the restorers for two years. They now clearly show the original design of François Boucher from about 1740, showing the European fascination with life in China at the time.

In the Drawing Room are some stately examples of French furniture, like the desk with the dolphins at the corners designed for the Dauphin in rococo style in about 1756; or the beautiful Louis XVI Secretaire designed by Oeben and finished by his son-in-law Riesener, the best and most expensive French cabinetmaker of his time.

The safe in the room weighs a ton and takes six men to move it. Baron Rothschild bought it as one belonging to Louis XV. The story is that Louis XVI, when Dauphin, helped to make the safe and helped the locksmith forge and fit the locks. When, as king, he was imprisoned during the Revolution, he had locks and clocks sent in to work on.

There are many priceless pieces in the Drawing Room and the Roseberys plan to open a further room for French furniture and so demonstrate stately and more homely furniture and the changes in style over a hundred years. With it will be displayed a large collection of Sevres and Vincennes porcelain that is not yet on show.

On the way to the Napoleon Room, along the Scottish Corridor, is a portrait of a 76-year-old man attributed to Rembrandt. The man, dressed in a sweeping, dark cloak and black cap, is Joannes Uytenbogaert and it is similar to a portrait that hangs in the Hermitage in Russia.

When the corridor was restored with the splendid Gothic tracery overhead and the fan-vaulting, it was furnished with a few pieces of Scottish country-house furniture. The Roseberys discovered more of the 5th Earl's collection of Scottish furniture from the fifteenth and sixteenth centuries in Barnbougle Castle and brought it into the Corridor, where it now stands as an authentic reminder of its period in a neo-Gothic setting.

The 5th Earl, who was a renowned expert on the life of Napoleon and wrote a definitive work about the Emperor, also collected pictures, objects and furniture associated with him. The works have been arranged by the present Earl and his wife in one room – the Napoleon Room.

This room also contains David's sketch of Napoleon's coronation ceremony with the new Emperor snatching the crown from the Pope, so that he could crown himself. A bust of Napoleon stands in a corner and the shaving stand he used when in exile on St. Helena is here. There are also portraits of his wives, Josephine and Marie-Therese, and his brothers, Joseph, Louis and Lucien, whom he made rulers of lands he conquered.

Among other memorabilia is a model of The Northumberland, which took Napoleon to exile; watercolours of St. Helena; furniture used by him in exile; and a portrait of him as a sad old man with his sun hat on.

When the Roseberys organized the Dining Room, which the family still use during the holidays, their idea was to hang portraits of people who lived at much the same time and who might well have dined together.

There are several Reynolds' works – of Dr. Johnson, compiler of the famous dictionary; the politician George Selwyn; the opera singer La Contessa della Rena; and of Edward Gibbon, the historian.

Thomas Gainsborough's Lord Rodney, who beat the French at the Battle of the Saints in the West Indies; his painting of Lady Mary Fordyce; and a portrait of the powerful Henry Dundas, 1st Viscount Melville, by Sir Thomas Lawrence hang nearby.

Neil, 3rd Earl of Rosebery, painted by Henry Raeburn, shows the old Earl at the age of 84 with thick, curling hair – in fact he went bald very young in life and had three wigs, a short, a medium and a long one so that he could go to Edinburgh in the long wig and pretend to have a hair cut, next appearing in the shorter wig.

Dalmeny House has four principal rooms on show to the public at present but there are plans to open more to display additional parts of the magnificent collections. These will include Rothschild family portraits and more relics of the 5th Earl.

Dalmeny, with its surrounding estate, is one of the greatest pleasures in its area and contains some of Scotland's unique treasures.

Scottish Products

A wealth of goods results from the blend of tradition and innovation

Scotland, and especially its capital, offers a treasure trove to the shopper. Everyone will be familiar with the country's well-known products such as smoked salmon, oatcakes, haggis and kilts. But Edinburgh's shops and workshops offer an infinite variety of handmade and manufactured goods which should not be overlooked. Bagpipes and Edinburgh rock are just two of the products still made in Edinburgh itself, while there is a thriving coterie of craftsmen producing local wares.

Arts and crafts shops are generally located in areas around the Grassmarket and the High

Street. The directory section at the end of this book lists a selection of shops which specialize in local or unusual items. Appointments should be made to visit most workshops, which often work on a commission basis rather than holding a large amount of stock.

The Scottish Craft Centre exhibits and displays selected Scottish craft work, and the Scottish Tourist Board produces a booklet entitled *See Scotland at Work* which lists craft workshops and industrial concerns in Edinburgh, the rest of mainland Scotland and the Islands. All of these can be visited, some require an appointment to be made in advance and others not.

Edinburgh's crafts include candles, ceramics, dolls, embroidery, furniture and woodwork, glass, pottery, jewellery and silversmithing, knitwear and crochet, leatherwork, musical instruments, textiles, weaving.

Products which are still made in Edinburgh or for which a significant number of retail outlets and stockists exist in Edinburgh include kilts and all the elements of highland dress, tweeds, woollens such as cashmere and Shetland, bagpipes, whisky, Drambuie, Glayva, smoked salmon, oatcakes, kippers, haggis and cheeses. The articles on the following pages describe their origins and processes of production.

Away from shops and craft workshops, browsing around Edinburgh's two main markets will prove entertaining if not rewarding. The largest is at Ingliston behind the Royal Highland Showground on each Sunday of the year. Take the road to the airport, the A8 towards Glasgow, and turn off at the sign 'Ingliston, Airport'. The site has 1400 stalls where you can buy anything from a jacket to a catamaran; and you can visit a chiropodist, the mosque, the funfair or give the children a pony ride. The traders offer excellent bargains.

Edinburgh's own market, the Lane Sales, has existed for over 100 years and is especially useful for household goods. Old books and photographs are sold too, among a welter of interesting items. The market is situated between Hanover Street and Frederick Street on Thistle Street Lane Southwest Tuesdays and Fridays at 11.00. Since parking space is restricted, it is better to walk.

A wealth of goods results from tradition and innovation

Antiques

A rare Bohemian liquer glass from about 1720 and a traditional pewter 'tappit' hen.

*T*he Scots have always been great travellers – sometimes for pleasure, more often through necessity – and they have always sent or brought back to Scotland a most remarkable variety of antiques from all over the world. From Chinese porcelain to Peruvian pottery and American Indian and Eskimo artefacts, antiques continually make their way onto the market. But apart from such international treasures the visitor to Edinburgh is more often looking for items which are distinctively Scottish.

When antique-hunting, the conventional bagpipe and tartan image, so often fostered by the Scots themselves, must be discarded. This aspect of Scotland's past was largely confined to the Gaelic, clan-based society of the northwest, although it is true that the highland drover, with his pistols and broadsword and dressed in short kilt, was once a familiar sight in the Old Town.

The famous highland pistols with their all-steel construction and ball-shaped triggers are now largely to be seen only in museums, but good eighteenth-century broadswords can still be found.

Another nationally distinctive antique is high-quality Scottish pewter. The famous 'Tappit Hen', a tankard with a distinctive nobbed lid, derivative in shape from the French 'Pichet' used in Normandy for cider, is perhaps the best known and most sought after of all Scottish pewter objects. The Scots pint was equal to three Imperial pints and the 'Hen' was made both in this size and in intermediate sizes of 'Chopin' (about two pints), 'Mutchkin' (just under a pint) and 'Half Mutchkin'. It also appeared in Imperial capacity, with and without a crest, and even in a lidless form, so its permutations are many.

As a poor country Scotland had little church plate or silver but it had a great many churches, each with its pewter flagons and chalices and alms plates. All of these are distinctively Scottish in shape and many bear attractive makers' marks or 'touches'.

Despite comparative poverty the Scots loved fine silver and it was worked in most of the royal burghs. Early Scottish silver, even the humblest of articles, is distinguished by a respect for the metal, a severity of line which is very much reflective of the national character. While fine examples from the seventeenth and early eighteenth centuries fetch very high prices, most Scottish silver from the later period is priced about the same as its London equivalent. Edinburgh silver bears the attractive hallmarks of the city, the Thistle denoting the sterling quality of the metal and the Castle derived from the city's coat of arms. Most Scottish silver was made and assayed in Edinburgh and there is no better buy for the discerning visi-

The present Edinburgh assayer's mark stamped on silver.

tor today than Edinburgh silver of the late Georgian period, even if only a modest set of spoons.

Edinburgh during the eighteenth century was a centre for the production of fine quality goods of all kinds. Apart from silver, glass and pottery, much fine furniture was made, marked by a particular robustness in design which set it off from London-made furniture, particularly during the neoclassical period. Earlier Scottish furniture – chests, coffers and chairs and tables from the seventeenth century – exists in surprising quantity. It is usually made of oak.

The eighteenth century was also a halcyon time for the Scottish clockmaker who, at least in the larger towns, often doubled up as a maker of barometers as well. Almost every village or town boasted its clockmaker and these country clocks, often with attractive painted faces and usually of the longcase or 'grandfather' variety, are much preferred to English-made clocks of the same period. Scottish clocks always have a movement of eight days' duration while the country-made English clock had a simpler movement without a second hand and had to be wound daily.

Country-made French furniture from the eighteenth century can also be found easily in Edinburgh, and this is undoubtedly an additional attraction for the many continental dealers who travel here regularly.

Other collectors' items of Scottish type which are easily found include snuff boxes, or 'Mulls', made in great variety from sheeps' horns and traditional Scottish brooches and other jewellery.

Edinburgh is a compact city and most of its antique shops tend to be centred in two areas within easy reach of each other.

Start in the Grassmarket, in the Old Town below the Castle. The Grassmarket was the original centre of the antiques trade in Edinburgh, for the area was in decline and property was cheap. Today it is still the place where the 'knockers' and the 'runners', those casuals of the business, unload their goods, and from time to time a real discovery can turn up here.

The second area is scattered through the New Town. Queensferry Street off the west end of Princes Street contains a group of quality shops and the street runs down to Dean Village where there is a large cabinetmaking and antique furniture warehouse.

Situated on George Street are some of the oldest auction rooms in Edinburgh and there are many antique shops at the junction of George Street and Hanover Street, some overflowing to Thistle Street. Dundas Street, the northern continuation of Hanover Street, runs down to St. Stephen Street where several intriguing shops may be found.

The opportunites which exist in Edinburgh for the antiques' enthusiast are indeed rich and varied. The lack of specialized outlets make the opportunities for the buyer much less predictable, but by the same token the fun and the chance of making a real discovery are even greater.

Furniture

Over the years cabinet-making in Edinburgh grew from a rough trade to a fine art, the brilliance of which was not to be submerged until the onset of the Victorian Age. Its early history features criminal episodes quite uncharacteristic of the staid image of this craft.

Edinburgh was a centre for furniture-making by the mid-fifteenth century when the Incorporation of Wrights was formed, admitting only those who made their living working in wood. However, for almost three centuries their products were crude copies of English and French designs. The business ethics of these early craftsmen seem to have been equally crude for in the 1670s they seized and closed down the workshop of a colleague whose only crime was making superior furniture.

The renaissance of design and craftsmanship in England which followed the Restoration of Charles II in 1606 was not mirrored in Scotland. The first step towards such a boom north of the border was taken by Alexander Peter, considered by some experts to be Scotland's finest cabinetmaker. There are records showing he supplied furniture to George Dundas of Dundas Castle in 1734 and a flood of orders from other aristocratic clients followed. Among these was an order for some 150 pieces for Lord Dumfries.

He also commissioned Edinburgh's second outstanding cabinetmaker, Peter's ex-apprentice William Mathie, to

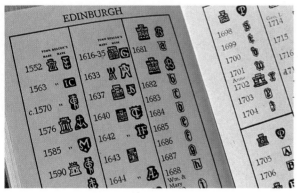
The Scottish capital's hallmarks, used between 1544 and 1792.

make a series of carved mirrors for his castle. As Lord Dumfries had been made a Knight of the Thistle in 1752, Mathie varied his usual rococo and Chinese style of decoration to include a naturalistic thistle and the entire insignia of the Order on certain mirrors.

was probably financed by Rannie, Chippendale's partner, who came from Leith. His brother was a prosperous wine and spirits merchant there and Chippendale and Rannie received many orders through this connection.

The Director's illustrations of

cess, and from Hamilton's cabinetmaking skills. Within a few decades it had changed from a small upholstery and soft-furnishings importing business into a major furniture supplier for the burgeoning New Town and statelier homes in the area.

Antique dealers' shop front with neo-classical sculptures.

However, fine as the work of these craftsmen was, they did not create an Edinburgh style. Indeed, among the Dumfries furniture is a side table which so meticulously copies a Chippendale design that only Peter's account for it convinces experts it is local work. The source of this design was Chippendale's book, *The Gentleman and Cabinet-Maker's Director*, first published in 1753 and subscribed to by many Edinburgh cabinetmakers including Peter. The book had tremendous impact on furniture design throughout Europe but there was a special reason for its popularity in Edinburgh. It

Chinese-style furniture undoubtedly contributed to the thought behind the popular Cockpen Chair, so-called because several early examples stood in the Dalhousie pew at Cockpen Church. But the actual creation of this charming chair, with its lattice-work back resembling a Chinese puzzle, is now attributed to James Hamilton. He was employed by a firm called Young and Trotter founded in 1751. The first records of his activities there date from 1774 but he became a partner very soon after, probably as a result of the enormous success of the Cockpen Chair. The firm also benefited from its suc-

The rapid rise of Young, Hamilton and Trotter can partly be attributed to the even more abrupt downfall of the Brodie family's business. Francis and his son William were both Deacon of Wrights and sat on the Town Council, thereby cornering the market for civic furniture and fittings. While in the mid-eighteenth century the Brodies continuously supplied furniture to the Town College, as the university was then known, tradesmen's accounts show that Young and Trotter only picked up minor work such as stripping wallpaper and replacing it with rat-proof material in the paste.

The Royal Scot Hotel

111 Glasgow Road
Edinburgh, EH 12 8NF
Tel: 031 334 9191

All 265 bedrooms are double glazed, centrally heated and equipped with bath and shower, colour television, radio, tea/coffee making facilities, telephone and alarm call system.

The spacious reception area provides an ideal welcome for the tourist and the business-man.

The intimate atmosphere of the restaurant is enhanced by a choice selection of traditional Scottish Fayre and international cuisine.

The Royal Scot has courtesy transport available to and from Edinburgh Airport and direct link free-pone is in the terminal building.

The ample car park and the easy accessibility of the city centre make THE ROYAL SCOT your first choice when staying in Edinburgh.

The Golden Circle
Bathgate, West Lothian. Tel: (0506) 53771
The Golden Circle is a fine modern hotel and is the perfect centre both for the tourist visiting Edinburgh, Stirling and the beautiful Trossachs and for the business visitor to the rapidly expanding and important industrial estates in this central Scotland region.

The Swallow Hotel
Invergowrie, Dundee. Tel: (0382) 641122
Dundee is an important city for both the business and holiday visitor. Demand for good accommodation has never been higher and so the Swallow Hotel has been specially extended and redesigned to meet it.

SWALLOW HOTELS
for friendly service and value for money

But in 1788 a bungled raid on the Excise Office revealed that William (Dean) Brodie, libertine and gambler but a very competent cabinetmaker, was less capable in his second-string occupation of burglar. His execution brought disgrace to the firm.

The other factor promoting the success of Young, Hamilton and Trotter was William Trotter, a descendant of John Knox who became sole proprietor of the firm in 1809. Despite active involvement in public life, in-

in Paxton House where he furnished the library and picture gallery in 1815. He also supplied furniture to the university, the Assembly Rooms and the Parliament.

There are survivors from the 100 cabinetmaking businesses in Edinburgh in 1812. The firm of Whytcock and Reid founded in that year still flourishes in Belford Mews, Dean Village, and it supplies and restores furniture for Holyrood House. But the death of William Trotter in 1833 brought the golden era

years were to pass before Edinburgh entered the stage. And it was not until the sixteenth century that a native school of craftsmen emerged in the capital. By 1600, however the art had reached a fairly advanced stage, as is evident from the work of David Ramsay, watchmaker to James VI. Originally from Dundee, he possibly worked for a while in France before coming to Edinburgh and then finally travelled to London in the wake of his royal patron as 'Clockmaker Extraordinary' to the King. Ramsay's skill was rewarded by James, who made him Page of the Bedchamber in 1627, while in 1631 he became one of the founder members of the Clockmakers' Company of London.

Throughout the seventeenth century the development of the craft accelerated. By the middle of the 1600s there were sufficient clockmakers for them to be recognized as a distinct branch of the locksmiths' trade and thus form part of the Edinburgh Incorporation of Hammermen. The first qualified 'knokmaker' to be admitted to this august body was a George Smith, on September 6, 1649.

One of the earliest members of the Incorporation, an example of whose work has survived, was Humphrey Milne or Mills who became a freeman in 1660. He has left a very fine example of a brass lantern clock. This type of clock, so called because of its lantern-like shape, was introduced in England around 1620 and continued in popularity until the first half of the eighteenth century. Such clocks usually stood on wall brackets and normally had one hand. They were probably among the first clocks produced in Scotland to meet the demand for individual time pieces.

During the second half of the seventeenth century there began the development of what was to become the most popu-

This perfect mahogany swing-top table with satin wood cross-banding was made c1820 by Trotter's firm.

cluding being Master of the Merchant Company and Lord Provost of Edinburgh, he created the version of Regency furniture known as the 'Trotter' style. From his premises in Princes Street with its workshop in Waverley Market he did a roaring trade by supplying the local customers with value for money and a distinctively Scottish style.

This furniture can be recognized by its air of masculine solidity, the use of high quality materials including wood and brass inlays and most notably by the carved lion's paws which frequently replaced the Engish Regency brass feet. One of the largest collections of his work is

of Edinburgh cabinetmaking to a sudden close. The pleasing and distinctive designs of the eighteenth century disappeared as cabinetmakers turned to producing much heavier pieces. These conformed with Victorian standards of taste but have certainly not found such favour with twentieth-century furniture connoisseurs. It is the older pieces which are sought after.

Clocks

*T*hough clockmaking in Scotland started in Aberdeen in the 1400s, a hundred

Above Brass lantern clock by Humphrey Milne, 1660-1692.
Right Engraved silver and brass pocket watch by David Ramsay, 1600-1650. **Far right** Marquetry longcase clock by Paul Roumieu Jnr, 1682-1712.

lar type of clock in Scotland – the longcase or grandfather clock. Humphrey Milne is thought to have produced some early longcase clocks and one of his apprentices, Andrew Brown, made several very beautiful clocks of this type. By far the most famous clockmaker of the late seventeenth century was Paul Roumieu. His father, Paul senior, arrived in Scotland from France sometime before 1677 and, after David Ramsay, is the earliest watchmaker recorded in Scotland. He passed on his skill to his son, who became a freeman of the Incorporation of Hammermen in 1682. The Roumieus' French

connection is a good example of the close economic links which existed between the two countries, and no doubt both father and son introduced technical advances which originated in France. The Roumieus' shop and house is thought to have been in the clockmakers' land at the top of the West Bow. Dr. Chambers in his *Traditions of Edinburgh* records that on the fourth floor of this house, which was demolished in 1835, were the remains of a curious piece of mechanism, namely a gilt ball representing the moon which was made to revolve by means of a clock.

By the middle of the eight-

eenth century Edinburgh clockmakers' skills could be compared favourably with those of clockmakers in any other part of Britain as the clockmakers responded to the demands accompanying economic prosperity.

By this time the craftsmen had perfected the movements of ordinary clocks and were becoming more adventurous. This manifested itself in a profusion of 'performing' clocks which could play complicated series of tunes or had ingenious automata. This development reached its climax in the production of extremely complicated astronomical clocks. One such was made by John Scott, who worked in Princes Street and East Register Street between 1779 and 1798. He was described as clockmaker to the Prince of Wales, and certainly he must have been a craftsman of the highest order.

The final phase in the development of the longcase clock began during the period of the painted or white dial clocks, which were popular from about 1790 to 1870. They were made in their thousands by clockmakers in virtually every town and large village in Scotland to satisfy the increased demand for a good quality 'knok' at a reasonable price. This was the era when the possibility of owning a clock came within the reach of the ordinary man. The earlier dials were decorated rather sparsely with much of the white enamelled underpainting showing, while the later dials tended to show much more flamboyant and picturesque painting. One of the reasons for the comparative cheapness of these clocks was that the faces came from clock face factories – firms specializing in making the painted dial plate and supplying them to the local clockmakers who fitted them to their own movements. Edinburgh was in the forefront of this trade, with several firms producing these dials, including Bell and Meundell, Russell and Clark and Dallaway and Son. Because of the numbers produced, this type of longcase clock is the one that has survived best and has become synonymous with the term grandfather clock.

Books

Edinburgh has a long tradition of books and bookselling. The city has even erected statues to the memory of some Allan Ramsay, bookseller, wig-

maker and poet, stands in Princes Street Gardens, and Provost Chambers, bookseller and publisher, looks down from a pedestal in the street named for him.

The early history of the business is obscure but when James IV was encouraging the spread of the European Renaissance into Scotland, two printer–

The bookseller's shop sign has the same gentle charm as the appealing jackets and pages of old editions.

booksellers called Chepman and Myllar were setting up a little shop in the Cowgate. Their books, which appeared around 1508, are the earliest dated works known to be printed in Scotland – only a few decades after Gutenberg's invention of moveable type.

Bookselling and publishing tended to be in the same premises right up to the beginning

of the twentieth century and even now a few of Edinburgh's secondhand booksellers have their own presses.

In the eighteenth century when Adam Smith and David Hume were revolutionizing economics and philosophy, the literati met in Edinburgh bookshops in the way they now do in pubs. Allan Ramsay had a shop, first at Netherbow, then by the Luckenbooths, where he combined bookselling and poetry with hairdressing and wigmaking. He was, he said, attending to both the inside and outside of his customers' heads.

In 1777 there were 98 hairdressers and 20 bookshops in the city but by 1867 the balance had changed to 43 hairdressers and 128 booksellers. One of the

FINEST SCOTTISH KNITWEAR

BY APPOINTMENT TO
H.R.H. THE DUKE OF EDINBURGH
MANUFACTURERS OF UNDERWEAR AND KNITWEAR
LYLE & SCOTT LIMITED, HAWICK, SCOTLAND

Lyle & Scott

HAWICK SCOTLAND

best of these was run by William Creech, the first Edinburgh publisher of Burns. Creech was Lord Provost from 1811 to 1813; it was remarkable how many of those involved in bookselling won high office in the city in the nineteenth century. Bookselling was very big business indeed.

In fact, one of the world's largest publishing houses started in a small Edinburgh close at the end of the eighteenth century – the *Encylopaedia Britannica*. Its publisher, Archibald Constable, who also produced the *Edinburgh Review*, was also the publisher of Walter Scott's first novel, *The Lay of The Last Minstrel*, which sold 44,000 copies between 1805 and 1830.

Ballantyne, Adam Black, John Blackie, William Blackwood, William Collins, William and Robert Chambers, Archibald Constable and Thomas Nelson are just some of the big names of nineteenth-century Scottish publishing and bookselling. Some, like Bartholomew the mapmakers, specialized; others leant more heavily towards bookselling, like Thins or the now ubiquitous John Menzies which began in Princes Street in 1833.

If you are a book collector, Edinburgh can still surprise with its great treasure trove of old books. The city has dozens of bookshops, spread through both the Old and New Towns, selling second-hand books by the thousand, from cramped quarters that can take hours to scour for titles.

It is still possible to spot a good bargain – perhaps a first edition Scott or Stevenson at the very best – in among the many more common volumes that line the shelves and those that are displayed with pride within the shops.

Books are very much loved in Scotland and there is a busy trade in them, so the turnover,

even in some of the smaller bookshops, can be faster than you think. If you find nothing the first time around, visit again, talk with the bookseller, make your wants known, and you may well walk out with the very volume the next time you visit.

Prices vary greatly, of course, with the condition and scarcity of the book in question, but it is usually possible to strike a good bargain with a bookseller. And it is certainly worthwhile having a chat with the bookseller and showing your fascination for the subject. He will certainly be interested and knowledgeable about his books and it is possible that he will open up for you an intriguing world of literary back-alleys.

Bagpipes

This shop has dealt in kilts and bagpipes for nearly 150 years.

*I*t is said that there is no inhabited continent where the Scottish highland bagpipe is not played, and certainly most people are familiar with its distinctive sound. Bagpipes are an essential part of Scotland's national heritage and their long history is indefinably embodied in the awe-inspiring sight of the pipers in full highland dress in the streets of Edinburgh.

Bagpipes consist essentially of a bag of skin which is inflated under pressure from the arm to produce a stream of air to the pipes. The invention of the bag did not represent a new musical instrument but merely an addition to pipes blown by the mouth. Reed pipes were known well before the time of Christ, particularly in hill countries where shepherds and cowherds played the pipes during their long hours of solitude.

The earliest surviving examples of the reed-sounded pipe or pipes have been found in Babylonia and ancient Egypt, but it is likely that the principle was discovered independently in innumerable countries all over the world, and certainly they were known in ancient Greece and Rome. Reeds or pieces of straw when pinched flat and blown with compressed lips yield a crude musical sound, and this principle was named the double reed after the two surfaces created by compression. The single reed is constructed by a cut a short way along the straw, which when played produces a musical sound.

Today's bagpipes comprise a bass drone (the longest pipe), which is essentially the single reed type; two tenor drones (identical in appearance) both of single reed type; a blow pipe (the short pipe which narrows at the end for use as the mouthpiece); and the chanter, which with its finger holes enables a tune to be played according to the double-reed principle. The bag acts as a reservoir and pump to supply air to the pipes. The modern version is basically the result of adding a bag to the hornpipe, the generic name for double, single and parallel pipes.

Although the double pipes existed in ancient Britain, it is known that the Romans introduced them after their invasion of Britain in the first century AD. The National Museum of Antiquities, Edinburgh, possesses the Roman stone found at Bridgeness in East Lothian which has carvings of the double pipe.

The pipes of ancient Britain however are thought to have developed from the Egyptian model, the parallel pipes, as a result of the earliest Mediterranean migrations between 2000 and 3000 BC. This theory is supported by the fact that the highlanders did not adopt the Romans' double pipes.

Up until the twelfth century the pipes comprised the hornpipe, a type of chanter fitted with a bag or skin and the blowpipe. It was not until the fourteenth century that a drone was added.

James I of Scotland (1424-

An array of drones, chanters and reeds used in sets of pipes.

1437) played the pipes, and bagpipes were the national music of England during the reign of Henry V (1413-1422). James II of Scotland (1437-1460) passed an act for the suppression of the pipes in 1449, but they were restored by James III, (1460-1488) and James IV (1488-1513) had English pipers playing at the gates of Edinburgh Castle until 1507. Up until this time pipers had traditionally been associated with the English Court from the reign of Edward III (1327-1377) but by the end of the fifteenth century there were town or burgh pipers as well. The bagpipes acquired battle status in the mid-sixteenth century in Scotland, being associated with Scottish armies, and the clans employed their own pipers. The English Court dispensed with the pipers in the 1660s, from which time bagpipes in England were relegated to folk music. It was about this time that the third pipe, the base drone, also known as the great drone, was added.

After the Jacobite Rebellion of 1745, the second (and far more vicious) Disarming Act was passed. It was judged in the High Court that bagpipes were an instrument of war, being associated with armies, and, together with weapons and symbols of nationalism such as tartan, were banned.

The result for the piper was disastrous – and furthermore there was far less employment by the clans owing to their own impoverishment because of the forfeiture of their estates. In 1757, however, the new highland regiments were formed in response to troubles abroad, and they were allowed once more to play the pipes. The Disarming Act was repealed in 1782 from which time Scotland enjoyed its piping tradition without interruption to the present day.

There is now a College of

Piping in Glasgow, and Edinburgh, like other towns in Scotland, has its own bagpipe makers. The water reed gave way first to cane and then to hard woods such as laburnum, cocus, rosewood and, in this century, African blackwood or Canadian maple. The hardness of the wood is essential, since the harder the wood, the better the tone. If Canadian maple is used, it has to be specially treated, it 'works' better than the other woods and can be bored without the need for mounts. Square sections of about ten inches (25.4 cm) in length and two inches (5.1 cm) in width are turned on a lathe into pipes. Plastic, ivory or silver are used for the embellishments and so is the traditional horn. A set of pipes will cost not less than £300 and a full-mounted silver set with hand engraved family crest or runic devices may be £2000. The pipes will last for ever, except for the bag which is made of sheepskin or cowhide and needs replacing every year or two. If the pipes are not played regularly, the skin will harden within two months.

William Sinclair has been making bagpipes in Edinburgh since the 1920s and started his own business in 1963. You have to wait several months after placing an order for the authentic article. Sinclair & Son produce about 100 sets a year mostly for professional pipers in Edinburgh. They have also exported to South Africa, Canada, the United States, Australia, France, Norway, Sweden and Finland. The United States is one of the biggest importers but the continental countries are apparently increasing their orders.

Allistair Sinclair's advice to the hopeful piper is to start learning by the age of ten and he emphasizes the importance of a good ear since you have to tune the instrument yourself.

The pipes are pitched at B flat to play with brass bands and possess just eight notes – which do not represent a true scale. The notes relate to the white notes of the piano which means there is no minor key. The instrument is tuned by rotating the two ends of the pipe, decreasing or increasing the space from end to end according to the desired sound.

The sound of the bagpipes is a uniquely haunting one which compels the ear and, with its evocation of Scotland and its history and traditions, perceptibly moves every foot.

Tartan

*O*f everything that is exclusively associated with Scotland, tartan is the most vivid and the most instantly recognizable particularly in the form of the kilt. But the tartan has an uncertain history and the misconceptions are many.

Many writers claim that the word tartan is English, the Gaelic being *breacan* but, it now seems accepted that tartan derives from *tiretaine*, French for a coloured woollen material. Scotland has produced lengths of cloth since medieval times. The basic garment for both nobleman and peasant until the end of the sixteenth century was the *leine croich*, a linen tunic. Over this was worn a woollen mantle, which developed into a large tartan blanket, the *breacan filleadh*, or folded plaid.

The wearer would lay it flat on the ground, pleat it to reduce the width, leaving a short length at either edge unpleated. He would then lie on it, with the lower edge in line with his knees. The two unpleated ends were folded across the body, overlapping, and the whole garment held in place with a belt at the waist.

The excess of fabric above the belt was either raised and draped over the head and shoulders or draped around the torso where it was fastened on the shoulder with a brooch, button or pin.

The garment was obviously an encumbrance, and towards the end of the sixteenth century the forerunner of today's kilt emerged: the lower section of the plaid had pleats stitched in place and the upper half was cut away. This became the length of plaid that today is worn over the left shoulder and fastened with a decorative brooch.

Claims that the clansmen adhered rigidly to one particular tartan so that they would not kill their own clansmen in disputes and retaliations are clearly insupportable: you would be unlikely to cross someone else's territory wearing an outfit that marked you as a target for assassination.

Some experts on the subject say that it was an Englishman, Thomas Rawlinson, manager of a Glengarry ironworks, who invented the little kilt, as it was then known. He felt his workers were too restricted in the belted plaid and so, in about 1727 he dispensed with the plaid, had pleats sewn in the lower part of the garment and hence the kilt was born.

But there are references and engravings well before 1727 which show the little kilt, and so the story of Rawlinson's invention must have been embroidered.

The tartan chosen for the kilt depended largely upon where the wearer hailed from and was not necessarily related to his clan. Since chemical dyes did not exist, vegetable dyes were used in the making of the cloth: so it was a matter of personal preference combined with the plants available that would determine the colours of the kilt. And if a great many Macdo-

KEEP IN TUNE WITH RADIO FORTH

200	240	280	320	350	kHz

94	96	98	100	104	108	MHz

700	1000	1400	kHz

Radio Forth broadcasts on medium wave 194 metres,
1548 kHz and on VHF stereo 96.8 MHz.

Radio Forth
194
Close to you

East Central Scotland's Independent Radio Station
**Radio Forth Ltd., Forth House, Forth Street, Edinburgh. EH1 3LF.
Tel. 031-556 9255.**

Radio Forth doing it all for you.

nalds, for example, existed in one area, then no doubt many of them wore kilts of the same or similar colours.

Although there was no rigid organization concerning a clan's tartan, there were personal preferences and tartan had become a symbol of the highlander.

requiring six square feet in which to read it) was a response to the revival in popularity of Scotland in general and tartan in particular due to George IV's visit to Scotland in 1822 and his fascination for it – rivalled only by Queen Victoria's interest and affection.

By the 1850s and 1860s, the

advise you on the selection of a tartan. If you know which area either you or your ancestors are associated with, Kinloch Anderson will be able to arrange the design of a new tartan according to the predominant colours of the plant life in that area.

Men normally wear the kilt,

The tartan marks the clan of each child here but not until the 1840s, when the Sobieski Stuart brothers published their disputed works on the classification of tartans, did each clan adhere to one pattern.

After the Jacobite Rebellion of 1745, all such symbols were banned under the Disarming Act of 1747. Tartan was not worn, legally at least, until 1782 when the Act was repealed.

Fragments of the old tartans that exist today, and these include those in Edinburgh's Museum of Antiquities, show that the later tartans conceived in the nineteenth century bear little or no relation to those worn before 1745 and must have been the product either of misguided historians or imaginative entrepreneurs.

Two such entrepreneurs, the Brothers Allan, also known as the Sobieski Stuart brothers, produced *The Costumes of the Clans* in 1842. The brothers claimed to be grandsons of Bonnie Prince Charlie and thus party to information known to no one else.

Their astonishing publication (weighing 22 pounds and

tartan industry was thoroughly established and the vogue for Scotland and its symbols was at its peak.

There are now over 500 clan tartans and it is accepted that if you have links with a particular clan, then you may assume its tartan – and, if not, you should not really wear any tartan.

If you wish to establish your crest or any other heraldic device, the Lord Lyon office in Edinburgh can advise. If you wish to establish whether you are descended from a particular clan, you should contact the Scots Ancestry Research Society in Edinburgh. The terms in 1981 are a £10 (plus VAT) non-returnable registration fee and an authorization for research to be carried out up to a maximum of £80.

Shops such as Kinloch Anderson operating from its historic site in Edinburgh's Royal Mile will then be able to

while women wear kilted skirts. The women's version usually takes about six to seven yards (5.4-6.4 m) of cloth, while the kilt proper requires eight to nine yards (7.3-8.2 m). The kilted skirt is complemented by a coordinating blouse and a tam.

There is nothing to rival the kilt as a symbol of Scotland. Parades and ceremonies with Scotsmen in full highland dress are an awe-inspiring sight – a reminder of Scotland's chequered history.

Tweed

*E*dinburgh is one of the best market places you can find for tweed and Harris tweed.

Tweed comes in an infinite variety of colours, weights and in herringbone or check.

The weight is selected according to the garment the tweed is destined for and the use it will receive. Men's suits, women's suits, coats, jackets, skirts and trousers can all be made up in Edinburgh once you have selected the preferred colour from the roll, or you can buy ready-mades.

Tweed was made in southern Scotland from about the 1840s and the main centres of production, in a textile industry that was otherwise depressed, included Galashiels, Jedburgh and Hawick in the Tweed river basin. The Border towns found a ready market for the tweeds in the south. Demand increased with Queen Victoria's affection for Scotland and all things Scottish.

It was the English that unwittingly gave tweed its name, rather than the river of the same name. *Tweel,* the Scottish version of the French word for cloth, *toile,* was misread – and so tweed was born.

The best quality tweed is Harris tweed, a 100 percent wool cloth, which is handwoven on the islands of the Outer Hebrides, notably the isles of Harris and Lewis. It is usually a heavyweight cloth, and it is legally protected from imitation.

The traditional cloths come in subtle shades of browns and greens. Its internationally recognized standard of durability makes tweed an attractive investment.

Cashmere

*C*ashmere is sheer magic. With its uniquely soft and velvety touch, it has become a supreme symbol of luxury and opulence. And the hardwearing quality, colours and design of cashmere clothing produced in Scotland have given it undisputed leadership

in the world's knitwear markets. Some designers, such as Bonnie Cashin, will work only with cashmere made in Scotland.

Expensive – of course. Just 2.2 pounds (1 kg) of cashmere is worth £72 today, even before any garment is produced. The reason for its high cost lies partly in the difficulty of obtaining the raw material.

The word cashmere is an anglicization of Kashmir, the province of India where the goats that supply the wool were found. Nowadays, however, the necessary undercoat of the fleece is provided by goats from China, Iran and the Soviet Union. Great expense is involved, not only because the animals roam high up in the mountains, but also because much time and skill are required in the manufacturing process.

The development and availability of cashmere can be traced most recently to the conglomerate known as Dawson International. Joseph Dawson in 1901 invented a machine which could separate the hair of the goat, a process that had previously been done entirely by hand, in preparation for yarn-spinning. As a result, Dawson's were one of the largest cashmere processors anywhere. It was not until the 1950s, however, that cashmere became the status symbol it is today.

Towards the end of the 1940s, a mixed textile company named Tood & Duncan started making lambswool yarn and, subsequently, single ply cashmere as well. By 1960, Todd & Duncan were using 70 percent of Joseph Dawson's production. Dawson, by then a public company, bought Todd & Duncan which meant that the world's largest cashmere buyer and dehairer had joined the largest cashmere spinner. One year later, the spinning strength of the company was increased by the

acquisition of Laidlaw & Fairgrieve, the firm which had pioneered in Shetland yarns in the 1950s.

Dawson's then acquired a variety of good quality Scottish knitwear manufacturers between 1966 and 1970: Barrie, Pringle, McGeorge, Glenmac, Ballantyne Sportswear and Braemar – the oldest name in Scottish knitwear. Dawson's injected the companies with capital, the principal aim being to update the machinery which, in some cases, was hopelessly antiquated.

Dawson's chairman, Alan Smith, recognized that irregular supply of the raw material was a continual problem and so, in the early 1960s, he began visiting mainland China. Between 1961 and 1971, he established a unique relationship with his suppliers, on the understanding that Dawson would buy all the cashmere they could offer, even in excess of need, in return for price stability.

The Dawson group, based at Kinross on the shores of Loch Leven, now occupy a market – the top 5 to 10 percent in price and quality – which is quite unaffected by low-cost imports that have hit the manufacturers of less luxurious knitwear.

Direct exports exceeded £40 million in 1980, with Italy being the largest individual market, followed by Switzerland. Export represents about 75 percent of their total production, but much of the remainder is exported as well: large quantities are sent to London and sold on, and this is classed as invisible export.

The six different companies comprise a huge range of colours and styles in women's suits, skirts, jerseys, cardigans, twinsets, scarves and men's ties. A plain Ballantyne jersey retails in 1981 for about £60 to £75, while an intricate intarsia design may well cost over £150. Top designers, such as Karl

Diamond Classics

Anna & Cowan
intarsia diamonds in 100% Pure Lambswool

From Pringle of Scotland stockists throughout the U.K.

Lagerfeld, are commissioned to produce designs, and certainly the tailoring is enviable.

Inlaid design, or intarsia, is one of the features of the group. The word has been borrowed from the woodworking craft of marquetry. Of the many intarsia designs, the original Argyll remains popular, while flowers, birds, butterflies, diamonds and geometrics are much in demand.

Ballantyne's intarsia knitters are based just outside Edinburgh in a large, modern factory. Their training takes two years, after which time they can produce a diamond pattern jersey front on a single bed machine in about three and a half hours – the more complex designs may take as much as eight hours.

Assembly of the fronts with the backs and sleeves produced in Innerleithen is carried out here as well. The stitch length selected on the different machines ensures that the hand-knitted intarsia front matches exactly the machine-knitted sleeves and back.

The matching and seaming carried out during assembly is a skilled process, subject to several quality checks at each stage. Assembly training takes about one to one and half years.

Batch numbers will have been attached to the collars and other trims so that each whole garment is produced from the same batch of wool. When the garment has been assembled, it goes to the milling house with its corresponding trims.

The garments and trims are thoroughly scoured in special detergent to remove the oil, and the fibre is broken down in a milling process to produce the characteristic softness. The millman estimates just how long each batch requires in the machine: the time factor is crucial as the machine may contain £1000 worth of garments at any one time.

The garments are then spun and dried, boarded (pulled over steel frames and set to size by steaming and vacuuming), and then sent out for hand-finishing. Necks are cut out for V-necks, and collars, buttons, pockets, trimming, binding, braiding constitute the next stages. A series of examinations determines whether the garment can be passed for pressing, when it is again checked for quality.

The quality, colours and designs of cashmere garments produced in Scotland ensure that they retain a supreme position in the world's knitwear markets. Although much of the total production goes for export and invisible export, Edinburgh nevertheless offers, in its concentrated shopping area, many shops specializing in Scottish woollens and tweeds. As well as cashmere, you will find lambswool, botany wool, Shetlands from the Shetland Isles, and Fair isles which originated from the sparsely populated Fair Isle off northern Scotland. Fair isles are knitted in colours and designs which are said to be Moorish and are traceable to survivors of the Spanish Armada in 1588.

Whisky

*D*o not ask for whisky, do not request a Scotch–you are in a land where brands and blends can be as individual as the wines of France. If you apply yourself diligently to the task, you can soon become a true Scot and pick out the particular glass of golden liquor to suit your mood. It will probably be one of the scores of 'single malts', the pure and crowning glory of Scottish distilling. But it might be one of hundreds of blends, which are made from a mixture of malt and grain whiskies and account for 98 percent

of all whisky sold.

Whether the choice is a light and delicate blend or the dark, smokey tang of an island malt, what you are sampling is the Gaelic 'water of life'. That is the meaning of the word *uisge-beagh,* from which whisky got its name.

The malts are a pure product made from malted barley in a series of processes known as malting, mashing, fermentation and distillation in pot stills. The barley is steeped in water so that the germination process is triggered and rootlets start to sprout. A grain of barley is in fact a small store of starch which is insoluble. After about seven days, the conversion of the starch will have taken place and the maltster then dries it, in a kiln fired by peat.

The distiller grinds the soluble starch and adds water during the process known as mashing. A sugary liquid, maltose, is extracted and fermented with yeast. During the course of about 40 hours, the sugar is converted into a crude alcohol of about 12 percent strength, known as wash.

The final product requires two distillations in large copper pot stills. The first distillation separates the alcohol from the fermented liquid and the resulting distillate, known as low wines, is then passed to another still where it is distilled a second time. The first runnings from the second distillation, the foreshots, are very strong and are set aside. Towards the end of the distillation, the strength and quality of the spirit is reduced and these runnings, known as feints, are drawn off and, together with the fore-shots, are redistilled in the next distillation of low wines.

It is the mixture of the three elements, the low wines, the foreshots and the feints, that is largely responsible for the character of the whisky. The middle cut, the runnings that

The Magic of Malt Whisky

1 Silo containing dry ripened barley

2 Barley soaks in water for up to 70 hours

3 Drained barley germinates to become green malt

5 Grain crushed to give malt grist

6 Grist plus water produces wort

4 Green malt in the kiln

7 Yeast added

9 Dilution with pure water to 110° proof

8 Distillation produces 120° proof spirit

10 Casked whisky matures

The exacting task of producing the true malt is part of a centuries-old tradition.

are taken off between the foreshots and the feints, are pumped into casks and left to mature for a minimum of three years. It is often left for considerably longer – The Glenlivet, for example, is not bottled until 12 years later. About 1½ percent a year is lost in evaporation, but the process of maturation is an important one since it results in a smoother and more mature whisky. After about 15 years or so, the whisky becomes progressively smoother and less recognizable for what it is. One might guess that it is a cognac which is being offered. After maturation, the whisky is coloured with an infinitesimal quantity of caramelized sugar, if the casks have not already imparted sufficient colour. Once bottled, the whisky does not then change in state or flavour – so you can drink it straightaway.

Malt whisky comes from four distinct regions, the Highlands, the Lowlands, Islay and Campbeltown on the Mull of Kintyre, which together represent Scotland's total 130 distilleries, of which 116 are malt distilleries. Although generalizations can be made about the malt whiskies to come from these geographical areas, it is worth remembering that each still pro-Cardhu, Longmorn-Glenlivet, Linkwood, Glen Rothes and Glengoyne; around Dufftown and Keith, the group including Glenfiddich, very much responsible for promoting the single malt in recent years, Strathisla-Glenlivet, the oldest distillery, founded in 1786, Bal-in the production of blended whiskies. The Islay distilleries make a characteristic heavy, peaty, pungent, almost medicinal style of malt for which an acquired taste is needed. The single malts from Islay include Bowmore, Laphroaig, Lagavulin and Bruichladdich.

A whisky company has occupied this New Town building since 1799.

duces a whisky that to someone in the trade is as individual as a fingerprint. Glenfiddich and Balvenie, for example, which are literally across the road from each other and use the same water and the same barley, make noticeably different products.

The Highlanders, the largest group, can be subdivided into three areas: those around the Livet valley, which include The Glenlivet, Glen Grant-Glenlivet, Fettercairn, Blair Athol, Flenfarclas, Tormore, venie, Dufftown-Glenlivet and Mortlach; and, thirdly, north of the Spey from Inverness almost to John O'Groats, a group including Glenmorangie, Old Pulteney, Dalmore and Clynelish.

The Highland malts have traditionally been regarded as the best, with the Speyside products, from around the River Spey, and the whiskies from the Glenlivet area being regarded in the trade as excellent malts. The Lowlanders are much lighter and are most often used

A blender or broker can appreciate the difference between the malts sufficiently to enable him to identify its age and area of origin and to pinpoint it to one of three or four. An Edinburgh broker, with many years in the trade, said in 1981 that of all the malts, those that commanded high prices included Aultmore, Glen Grant-Glenlivet, Longmorn-Glenlivet, The Glenlivet, and Mortlach, all of them Highland malts. He added that Glenmorangie, one of the best sellers, is a very

234

There is nothing like owning <u>the</u> original.

The Glenlivet.

The original, unblended malt whisky from Scotland's oldest licensed distillery is widely acknowledged to be the finest in the world.

The supreme malt with a unique character and exceptional smoothness, The Glenlivet is unchanged since 1824.

There is nothing like <u>The</u> Glenlivet.

<u>The</u> Glenlivet

<u>The</u> malt.
12 years old and the finest in the world.

fine malt – but, naturally, no one in the trade will commit themselves to naming the best.

Your own tasting is probably best carried out with a selection of miniatures, a good range of which are carried by Lambert Bros., 9 Frederick Street, and William Cadenhead Ltd., 172 The Canongate. Lambert's stock a huge range of whiskies, both malts and blends, carry books about whisky and have their own export service. Cadenhead's specialize in old and rare malts, and also have their own export service as well as mail order.

Whereas the malt whiskies are made purely from barley, the grains are made from a mixture of malted barley with unmalted cereals such as maize. The process, which is far less costly, is a continuous one, with the distillation carried out in a Patent or Coffey still, rather than a pot still, and the spirit is collected at a much higher strength. Since the whisky can be run at a much higher strength, and continuously, the Coffey stills can produce as much as 14,000 gallons per hour. Grain whisky is not influenced by geographical factors and it has a less pronounced aroma and flavour than the malts.

The well-known brands of blended whisky, exported all over the world, make up 98 per cent of Scotland's total whisky, and so it is to the manufacture of the blends that much of the malt and grain production goes. A blend may contain between 15 and 50 different whiskies, the process of blending being known as vatting. Blending is an art, in which the malts and grains are selected to complement their respective flavours, so that the best qualities of each are brought out. Once mixed in a blending vat, after a battery of testing, they are returned to the cask to 'marry' for several months before bottling. Some are vatted separately and only combined during bottling.

Blending was pioneered by Andrew Usher in Edinburgh in the early 1860s. It was only when this practice became common that a taste for Scotch whisky spread first to England and then throughout the world. Pot still malt whisky, although its popularity has increased greatly in the last 20 years, is inclined to be rather strongly flavoured, particularly for those in warmer climates and sedentary occupations.

To the Scotsman of the cold, rugged hills in centuries past, however, the pure malt must have been more than welcome. It is thought that distilling started in the East many centuries ago; the fact that eastern civilizations had bamboo tubes which would have been good for conducting vapour when the West had only crude implements seems to support this assumption. From the Far East the practice seems to have spread through India and the Middle East with the Crusaders to the monastic houses of Europe in the Middle Ages. The centres of learning were keeping the practice alive by distilling medicinal preparations of herbs and perhaps by making something akin to whisky for their own consumption, a practice which spread to Ireland and then to the west of Scotland. A fifth-century Welsh song refers to 'strong liquor', while the first recorded reference in Scotland is an entry in the Exchequer Rolls of 1494: 'eight bolls of malt to Friar John Cor wherewith to make aquavitae' – eight bolls is well over 2645 pounds (1200 kg), so it is clear that Friar John Cor was involved in the distillation of

Window-shopping — a parade of Scotland's matchless whiskies

rather more than would be required for one monastery.

It seems that the monasteries constituted a cottage industry, and the crofters in the highlands, too, would have been producing their own fire-water. After centuries of illegal distillation, 1823 saw the imposing of a £10 tax on stills of over 40 gallons' capacity. Although illicit distillation continued, the industry was eventually brought under control.

Scotch whisky can only be made in Scotland. It is not, by law, Scotch whisky otherwise. The words whiskey and whisky used to be confused, but whiskey is now confined to Irish whiskey, which is subjected to three distillations and uses a wider range of cereals. Before the product can claim to be called whisky, it has to mature in wooden casks for a minimum of three years.

The casks used were traditionally, and until recently, the sherry casks that are imported from Spain. These would impart a certain flavour and colour to the whisky depending on which type of sherry the cask had been used for. Other factors are involved, however, in the production of a drink that has not been repeated successfully anywhere in the world. (Much whisky is now matured in bourbon casks from the United States.)

The natural elements of water, peat (which is introduced in the malting process) and the climate, affecting the crop as well as the final product during maturation, all influence flavour of the malt whiskies. The distilling process is crucial, too. The amount of secondary constituents retained in the spirit depends upon the shape of the still, the way in which it is operated and on the strength at which the spirit is drawn off.

Whatever its origins and whatever the secrets of distillation, whisky in 1980 represented £746 million in export earnings, accounting for 83 per cent of total production. Of the remaining 16 percent, it is estimated that about one-quarter is consumed in Scotland. When you are in Edinburgh, you should not miss the chance of sampling the range of one of Scotland's oldest and most revered products.

Drambuie

*D*rambuie owes its origins to a royal debt. Disguised as a serving maid, Bonnie Prince Charlie, head of the Stuarts, fled to Skye towards the end of the 1745 rebellion after suffering a crushing defeat at the hands of the English. Mackinnon of Straithard, ancestor of today's chairman and managing director of the Drambuie Liqueur Company, sheltered the exhausted Prince and, at the end of the Jacobite Rebellion, engineered his escape from the English.

Charles Edward Louis John Sylvester Maria Casimir Stuart, before leading his faithful followers into battle, had travelled the courts of Europe, where he had achieved fluency in four languages and a considerable knowledge of food and wines.

It is said that Drambuie was the Prince's favourite drink and in grateful recognition that he owed his life to Mackinnon of Straithard presented him with the recipe.

Drambuie uses the very best quality Scotch malt whiskies which may vary in age from 8 to 21 years. For over 150 years the recipe was handed from father to eldest son, small quantities being made for members of the Mackinnon clan. It was not until the beginning of this century that Malcolm Mackinnon decided to experiment with the treasured recipe on a commercial basis. In the first year of production, 1906, only 12 cases were sold in Edinburgh. Edwardian conservatism gradually weakened, however, and in 1916 the cellarman of the House of Lords gave it the seal of his personal approbation. By the end of World War I every British officers' mess and wardroom had its stock of Drambuie, and in the United States, sales soared once the era of Prohibition ended.

The Drambuie Liqueur Company now exports 90 percent of its production to 157 countries, the United States being the largest consumer. The company employs about 200 people, but the recipe remains a secret known only to Norman Mackinnon and his wife. The only written copy is lodged with an Edinburgh bank. On his death in 1945 Malcolm Mackinnon passed on the secrets of the Drambuie essence to his son, Norman, the present chairman, who in accordance with tradition will eventually pass it on to his eldest son.

Different ways of drinking Drambuie and recipes for its use in cooking abound, but the purists recommend that it is drunk on its own after dinner. It can be drunk at any time, as an aperitif for example, and like whisky can be drunk over ice. A Rusty Nail is said to be excellent: a good measure of Drambuie is mixed in equal proportions with a good Scotch whisky, stirred gently and served in a chilled glass.

Recipes include the addition of Drambuie to meat or fish as a substitute for vinegar in hors d'oeuvres such as avocados, in strawberry sponge cakes, and in pancakes, trifle, flans and soufflés.

Cheese

*S*cotland has a long tradition of cheesemaking, and although farm cheesemaking has virtually died out, there are still a number of creameries in the north. Edinburgh sells the full variety of Scottish cheeses and you should not miss the opportunity of sampling them. The quality is assured by the richness and fertility of the soil which provides lush pastures for the cattle.

Caboc has been made in the highlands since the fifteenth century and is made purely from cream, shaped like a thick sausage and rolled in coarse oatmeal. As it is comparatively bland, it is best accompanied by oatcakes or cheese biscuits and sprinkled with freshly milled black pepper.

Crowdie is a soft cottage cheese which is best when

"...if you're only in Edinburgh for a couple of days, I urge you not to miss it..."

"...I discovered it in the back room of an ordinary-looking pub...it had been packing them in all week..."

"...would win a Scotsman award any day of the week..."

"...in the round it was perfect..."

"...a glorious head on a beautiful, slow moving body ...a substantial experience..."

"...I immediately sat through again..."

"...rich and original... worthy of the widest possible audience..."

"...cheers all round... there wasn't a dry throat in the house..."

"...not to be hurried... even if another event clashes..."

"...may it run for ever..."

McEwan's Export
Continuous performances daily, all over Edinburgh.

Worth the little extra for the extra we put in.

BAXTERS OF SPEYSIDE, FOCHABERS, SCOTLAND.

made with fresh milk. It is regarded as the traditional cheese of the highlands.

Dunlop is one of Scotland's traditional cheeses, having been made first towards the end of the seventeenth century. Not unlike Cheddar, it is somewhat softer and more mellow.

Hramsa cheese is a soft cheese made with cream and flavoured with garlic. It is specially recommended for spreads, dips and canapés.

Orkney cheese is fairly similar to Dunlop and it can be white or red and is sometimes available smoked. Orkney was originally a farmhouse cheese produced in the Orkney Islands.

Stewart cheeses are made in two varieties: the white Stewart is something of an acquired taste owing to its saltiness, but the blue is mild and certainly worth trying.

Other cheeses to look out for include *Gaelic,* a full fat soft cheese with chopped leaves of fresh garlic coated in flaked oats, almonds and hazelnuts, *Campbeltown, Galloway, Gigha, Lockerbie* and, not least, *Scottish Cheddar.*

The Choosa Cheese chain which has several branches in Edinburgh affords the best opportunity of buying a wide selection of cheeses.

Glayva

*G*layva means 'very good' and this was the name Ronald Morrison and his partner, George Petrie, a chemist, thought the most apt christening for the liqueur they first produced in Leith, the port town of Edinburgh, in the 1940s.

Glayva is made from malts and grain whiskies which are blended by Ronald Morrison and Co. Ltd. Herbal oils, heather honey, sugar and, finally, colouring are added to the blend.

Only three people know the exact recipe for the herbal oils, and these are Ronald Morrison's· two sons, Michael and Gordon, and the blender. In accordance with the mystique of the drink trade, they are not prepared to divulge the formula.

Ronald Morrison's family were in the whisky business and he subsequently spent several years in Spain, learning the sherry trade. Before his death, Ronald Morrison passed on the secrets of the recipe to his two sons.

Michael Morrison mixes the essence and it is then passed to the blender, who has performed the task since the 1950s. From dissolving vats, the ingredients are pumped into compounding vats and are then filtered and bottled.

The company says that it is, of course, a matter of personal taste which of the Scottish liqueurs one elects to drink. They believe that Glayva is less sweet than Drambuie, for example, and thicker.

Ronald Morrison's company produces 100,000 cases each year, with about 75 to 80 percent being exported. Of the 70 countries importing, the largest consumers are those where Scots have settled – Canada, Australia and New Zealand.

Glayva is said to mix well in cocktails, particularly with soft drinks such as orange, lemon and lime, and is frequently used in cooking.

Haggis

*H*aggis is probably the most traditional and certainly the best known of all Scottish dishes. It is sometimes maligned by the foreigner, but its undistinguished ingredients amount to a flavoursome, nutritious and satisfying delicacy.

The word haggis derives

from the French *hachis,*to chop. Haggis in different forms has been known since the early Greek and Roman civilizations. Its origins in Scotland are referred to by the French who knew it as *le pain bénit d'Ecosse* in the days of the Auld Alliance, the first formal treaty of which was made in 1295 and which was renewed a number of times until the end of the fifteenth century.

Haggis has ever since been consumed in large and regular quantities both by local Scotsmen and Scots abroad. It is significant that Charles Macsween's, established in 1953, sell haggis for consumption abroad. Such is the fame of haggis that it has been immortalized many times in literature, approved of by Queen Victoria and paid tribute to by Robert Burns, Scotland's revered poet, in his eight-verse ode *To a Haggis:*

> ... O what a glorious sight,
> warm-reekin, rich!

Haggis comprises essentially the sheep's 'pluck', the windpipe, lung, heart and liver. The windpipe is removed and the rest is boiled for three hours with beef fat. The fat is then skimmed off and the liver, heart and lungs minced. Oatmeal, onion, seasoning (usually pepper, salt and spices) and gravy from the boiling are then mixed into the mince.

The basic recipe has never changed, although the casing has. A number of different cases are used today and these even include plastic. Since the casing is not eaten some people maintain it is of no significance but most Scotsmen prefer their national dish properly prepared in the traditional way.

The correct casing, if only a matter of aesthetics, is the sheep's paunch, or stomach which is filled with the mixture and then blanket-stitched with

Traditional fare — haggis with battered neeps and tatties.

cotton thread. A sheep's stomach will take anything from 10 to 20 pounds (4.9 kg) of the prepared mixture and, when it is boiled, shrinks to fit. Smaller haggises are encased in a length of caecum, known as a bung, from the ox or sheep. The caecum, part of the large intestine, is about three to four feet (1-1.3 m) long in an ox and it is therefore cut to size and fastened with string or clips.

When the sheep's stomach or bung has been filled it is replaced in the boiler for a short time. It is then simmered wrapped in foil, at home, for one to one-and-a-half hours and served steaming hot with mashed potatoes and turnips, or swedes as they are called in England. 'Bashed neeps and champit tatties' are the only acceptable accompaniment to be served with haggis, according to the traditionalists.

The haggis is served as hot as possible, slit lengthways and the mixture scooped out. Care has to be taken when splitting open the haggis or it may well rain its contents over you!

There is virtually no limit to the variations in size of the haggis. Three to four people will require about one to one-and-a-half pounds (0.4-0.6 kg) but miniatures are available.

Natural Scottish thriftiness and perhaps an element of barbarism is well demonstrated by the success and long history of the haggis. Use of ingredients which alone would not be particularly desirable ensures that very little of the animal is wasted. Plenty of Scotsmen eat haggis once a week, it is served for school lunches and, more prestigiously, features on Taste of Scotland menus. These menus are organized by the Scottish Tourist Board and include other Scottish specialities such as smoked salmon, venison and whisky mousse. Some hotels serve miniature haggis or just a slice of it as an hors d'oeuvre.

John Macsween, son of the founder, supplies not only the people of Edinburgh but the English, who he says are large consumers of haggis, and the Americans. (You should check with Customs beforehand if you wish to take haggis out of Britain for regulations relating to meat import into other countries.)

Macsween's sell haggis all the year round up to the three or four pound (1.3 or 1.8 kg) size and, on receipt of an order the day before, will supply any of the larger sizes. They produce about ten tons (18,000 kg) of haggis each year. The com-

pany also sell haggis boxed in tartan presentation packs, which show Edinburgh Castle, Burns' poem *To a Haggis* and serving instructions.

Demand fluctuates according to the time of year, since haggis is traditionally a winter dish, but it is January when consumption is at its highest. Burns Night, Robert Burns' anniversary, is on January 25 and this is marked by banquets and dinners where it is customary to serve haggis and to drink a glass of neat whisky with it. The haggis is piped in by a highlander in full regalia, and the haggis is slit with a dirk (the dagger worn with highland dress). Apart from Burns Night, other festivals and occasions where haggis is *de rigueur* include Hogmanay on December 31, St. Andrew's Day on November 30 and every meeting of Masonic lodges.

Kippers

*K*ippers were once regarded as food just for the masses, but the tasty smoked herring have long graced the tables of rich and poor alike. Few foods can beat that special breakfast flavour, a fact recognized by the perceptive French who have made a habit of importing kippers from Scotland to add to their own distinctive cuisine. One important tip – don't boil them in water as so many English people do. Let them cook gently in the oil that emerges when they are heated.

Until 1977 the kipper bought in Edinburgh would be the result of smoking home-caught herring, which has always been considered superior both in size and texture. Since then, only very limited quantities of fresh herring have been available from the Clyde fishery and Edinburgh's remaining two

The Best Way To See Scotland

When the time comes to visit new places, there's no better way to see them than by train.

Edinburgh is the perfect starting point for your visit to Scotland and getting there couldn't be easier than by rail. There's a regular High Speed Train service operating between London King's Cross and Edinburgh and with a journey time of around 4½ hours you won't find a more time-saving, relaxing way to go.

If you prefer to travel by night, our Inter-City Sleeper services will let you sleep your way into Edinburgh and make the most of your first day's holiday.

And British Rail don't stop at just getting you there. There are regular services to take you to all those parts of Scotland you'll want to see; the Highland Line between Perth and Inverness; the history of Aberdeen or Stirling; Glasgow, the heart of Central Scotland; or the beaches of the Ayrshire and Clyde Coast resorts.

We'll look after your pocket too, with a range of reduced fares to take you to these places. And there's no better way to cut your costs than with a Railcard.

With a Family Railcard, for example, up to 4 adults can travel at half price so long as between 1 and 4 children travel with them — and the kids go for just £1 each!

Whichever way you look at it, British Rail provide a comprehensive service aimed at helping you make the most of your visit. This year, it's the way to go.

This is the age of the train ⇉

kipper producers have had to rely upon importing frozen herrings from Ireland, Iceland and Canada for fear of decimating Britain's stock.

It has been recorded that herring was smoked in England in 1349, but it was not until the 1890s that Eyemouth on the east coast became a principal centre of Scotland's herring industry. Other important centres included the Clyde in the South Minch, Mallaig and Ullapool in the Minch, Peterhead, Fraserburgh, Aberdeen and North Shields.

were available, the fish had to be passed on racks by one man to another perched high up in the kiln who would hang each one up on hooks. The smoking process took eight hours and kilns varied in capability from 140 pounds (63.5 kg) of herrings to 14,000 pounds (6350 kg). Today's Torry kiln, developed by the Torry Research Station at Aberdeen, takes 1680 pounds (76.2 kg) (420 pounds on each rack) and can perform three cycles a day.

Croans sell all their produce within the United Kingdom, half

salmon has been netted or rod-caught, rather than farmed, the fins will be properly formed and the flesh will be firm to the touch. The flesh will also be coarser grained than the farmed fish with a richer colour and flavour.

Salmon are netted from the sea around the northwest of Scotland, the Moray Firth areas of the northeast or from the east coast rivers, the Tay and the Tweed. The sale of netted fish is permitted from the last week in January until September 15 or until late October for rod-

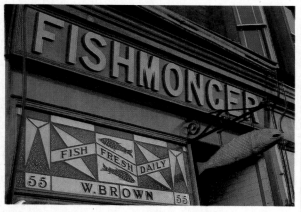

Kippers and shellfish are a speciality of Brown's in Elm Row.

Campbell's shop smoke your own salmon.

Robert Croan & Sons Ltd, one of the last two companies producing kippers in Edinburgh, started business in 1882 in the Holyrood district and still smoke herrings in the traditional way.

The fish are split and rubbed with salt. When they have been brined, they are placed on racks in a kiln and smoked over a mixture of oak chips and sawdust at 85°F (29.4°C) for about four to five hours. The temperature has to be strictly maintained because if it is too high the fish will be cooked and if too low the 'kippers' will be wet and soggy. After removal from the kiln, the kippers are left to cool and then boxed.

Before modern electric kilns

going to England and the remainder being sold in Scotland. The company believe that Loch Fyne kippers are the very best, since the fish come from inland lochs where there is a mixture of fresh water and salt which seems to produce a particularly succulent, tasty herring.

Salmon

*S*cotland's smoked salmon is world famous. Although the process of smoking has been sophisticated by chefs from London and Paris, the taste of the product remains unique and distinctive.

Either fresh or smoked, if the

caught fish. The quality of the fish deteriorates at about the end of August, with the body becoming thinner and the head larger.

Farmed fish is heavy bellied with unformed fins, and the flesh will be fine-grained with an oily texture and bland flavour.

Salmon is still smoked by the traditional cold-kiln method, whereby the fish are placed in the kiln at a low temperature for three consecutive six-hour periods. First, however, the head and tail are removed, the fish is gutted and the backbone removed. The body is split into

Oil Painting by Peter Blake, specially commissioned by Daimler Cars.

Painting by Blake.
Masterpiece by Daimler.

The opportunity to acquire a
masterpiece happens on very rare occasions.
If you have ever considered ownership of a Daimler,
this is one of those occasions.

Call your Daimler specialist for a private view.

two and placed in pickle for 12 to 24 hours, depending on its size. The average size for salmon is 8 pounds (3.6 kg) but they may be as large as 36 pounds (16.3 kg).

The pickle varies according to local taste but the traditional Scottish recipe requires demerera sugar and salt and pepper. The mixture is smoothed over the two sides of the fish and within one hour they are quite wet, the sugar and salt drawing the liquid. The salmon is left in the mixture overnight and the surplus is then washed off. The fish is removed to the smokehouse to drain and dry so that no surplus moisture remains before it is placed in the kiln. The fire is lit and another lit once it has gone out. The fish is smoked over three consecutive fires, each for a period of six hours at a very low temperature.

The salmon is left to 'set' after removal from the kiln and, once cool, is sliced by hand. After an initial period of about two months, a fishmonger can slice a 12 pound (5.4 kg) salmon into fine slices in ten minutes; a 12-pounder (5.4 kg) will yield about 5¾ pounds (2.6 kg) of smoked salmon.

Of the many fishmongers in Edinburgh where smoked salmon is available, Campbell's of Stafford Street and Dickson of West Harbour Road, Port Seton, will smoke your own fresh salmon for you.

Porridge & Oatcakes

Oatmeal, from which both porridge and oatcakes are made, has been a food staple for many hundreds of years. The grain was processed in local mills and dried out in a kiln. The old-fashioned mills provided a variation in the flavour of the meal, which is still appreciated by Scots today. It seems to be a matter of personal taste, however, whether fine, medium or coarse oatmeal is used. Today's processes of mass milling and mechanical drying are said to detract from the flavour of the meal and to reduce the nutritional qualities.

Oatmeal should be closely packed and kept airtight. It was traditionally stored in an oak chest in a dry place. If it is well packed, it may keep for over a year, and it is said to improve in sweetness and digestibility.

Of the many Scottish dishes requiring oatmeal, the best known is probably a fresh herring dusted in coarse oatmeal and served with a piquant mustard sauce and, of course, porridge and oatcakes. The list includes an endless variety of crowdies and sowans, which are somewhat similar to porridge, white (or mealie) puddings and black puddings.

Porridge

Sir Walter Scott (1771-1832) wrote to his son-in-law J. G. Lockhart: 'What meal does Johnnie want for his porridge? I will send it up from Abbotsford. I think it will agree with him better than the southern food of horses.' Scott evidently believed passionately not only in the orgin of the oatmeal but in the importance of local mills.

The sole ingredients of porridge are oatmeal, salt and water. The traditional bowl was made of a local hardwood such as birch. Horn spoons were used, and it was the custom to eat the preparation standing up. General Sir Ian Hamilton in *When I Was a Boy* wrote that 'the small nursery critics formed their most private opinions of guests a great deal on the porridge ceremonial. The worst and most deplorable giveaway was when the lady or gentleman took sugar.'

Each person should be allowed one cup of water, a handful (about 1¼ ounces/35 g) of oatmeal and a good pinch of salt. The oatmeal is added to boiling water in a steady rain from one hand, stirring briskly with the other. When the mixture is boiling, it should be taken off the heat, the lid put on and then allowed to simmer for 20 to 30 minutes. The salt is added after about ten minutes. The porridge is served very hot with cream, milk or buttermilk.

Oatcakes

In the days when oatcakes were served with every meal, each community traditionally had its own mill, grinding oats from the surrounding crofts to supply oatmeal.

Jean Froissart (1337-1404), French chronicler and poet, wrote that the Scottish soldier's equipment included a flat plate at his saddle and a wallet of meal at his back. When he had tired of meat, Froissart reported, the soldier would moisten some meal in water and lay it on the heated plate, and 'hence it is no marvel that the Scots should be able to make longer marches'.

Oatcakes are now eaten as an accompaniment to herrings, sardines, cheeses or with marmalade, honey or jams. The original oatcake was made of oatmeal and water, but it is now customary to add fat or dripping, baking soda and salt as well. Time and patience are required to make the authentic oatcake, but there are a good variety of manufactured oatcakes to choose from.

Shortbread

Shortbread owes its origins to Yule-bread, a thin bannock (circle) of oatmeal baked during Christmas and Hogmanay, and divided into farls (quarters). The ancient Yule-bannock, from the early days of sun worship, was notched, by pinching with finger and thumb around the edge, to symbolize the sun's rays just as shortbread is today.

The increasing popularity of white flour eventually ousted the ancient Yule-bannock and led to the development of the familiar rich, crisp shortbread of today.

Shortbread is eaten throughout the year now but it is still

Sun symbols in a range of shortbread.

associated particularly with Christmas and Hogmanay. It is traditionally offered to the 'first-footers' – those who call upon house after house in the early hours of New Year's Day.

You can choose from the several makes of shortbread on the market when you are in Edinburgh or make your own, since it is a quick and easy recipe. Cream four ounces (113 g) of butter and two ounces (57 g) of caster sugar together and then add a mixture of four ounces (113 g) of plain flour and two ounces (57 g) of rice flour, sieved. The resulting dough is pressed out by hand and laid on two ungreased sandwich tins. The rounds are cut into quarters or eighths with a knife, notched around the edges, pricked lightly all over and then baked at gas mark 4 (350°F/175°C) for 30 minutes.

Edinburgh Rock

*E*dinburgh rock, one of the cheapest sweets on the market, is said to owe its origins to Alex Ferguson who travelled from Doune in Perthshire to Stirling in 1822 where he tossed a coin to decide whether to set up in Edinburgh or Glasgow. Ferguson started his business in the Bow, a steep twisting street between the Grassmarket and the Lawnmarket beneath Edinburgh Castle.

Sugar, water and colouring is boiled in pans at a temperature of over 300°F (131°C), flavour is added in some cases, and the mixture is then poured onto a metal slab and partially cooled with a fan. It is then folded over, moved to a stone slab (ideally Caithness flagstone, according to Ferguson's in 1981), cooled, folded and pulled out.

The pulling-out process is basically one of extrusion whereby the huge, unmanageable, sticky mass is spun on a device of moving arms to inject it with air. The unwieldly skeins are then laid over six horizontal rotating rollers where the mass cools further and changes shape from plump oblong to tubular. The 'tube' is then passed through a half-inch (12.7 mm) space on to a slab where it is rolled by hand. A wooden measure marks off where each cut should be made, the cuts being made by tapping gently with the open blades of a pair of scissors. If it were actually cut through, it would splinter.

Ferguson's export about 5 per cent of their Original Edinburgh Rock, particularly to the United States, Canada and Australia. Flavours included in each of their presentation packs are the traditional ginger, vanilla, lemon, raspberry and orange.

While Ferguson's have the monopoly on the name 'Original Edinburgh Rock', another long-established company, Ross, have claim to 'Edinburgh Castle Rock'. Ross's was established towards the end of the nineteenth century and now produce the standard flavours of cherry, strawberry, orange, vanilla, ginger and lemon in their boxed packs.

Ross's explain that the difference between Edinburgh rock and letter rock (associated with Blackpool and Brighton) rests with the fact that Edinburgh rock is practically 100 percent sugar whereas letter rock is a mixture of sugar and glucose. In both appearance and taste it is completely different from the conventional variety.

Edinburgh rock is normally marketed in packs of five or six

A traditional Scottish sweet that is tasty and inexpensive.

different flavours in a presentation pack and in 1981 each stick was retailing at about sixpence, a comparatively low price for any sweet.

Self·drive
what you wan
in Scotland

FIESTAS, NEW ESCORTS, MINI METROS, ASTRAS, CORTINAS, RENAULTS, GRANADAS, ESTATES etc. 9, 18, 35cwt & 3 ton V/

The cars you want

More and more people are hiring from Mitchells Self Drive because Mitchells have more and more economy cars at economy rates. Fiestas, New Escorts, Mini Metros, Cortinas, Vauxhall Astras, Renaults, Granadas, Estates and other models too, all immaculately maintained and serviced. And hiring from Mitchells costs less than you think—just local rates AND NO MILEAGE CHARGE.

EDINBURGH: 32 Torphichen Street,
(near west end of Princes St.)
Tel. 031 229 5384.

GLASGOW (Car Hire): Multi-storey car park,
Mitchell Street (off Gordon St.)
Tel. 041 221 8461

GLASGOW (Van Hire): 47 McAlpine Street.
Tel. 041 248 4981

PAISLEY: Glasgow Road,
(opp. Kelburne Cinema).
Tel. 041 887 7866

HAMILTON: Miller St. (Duke St. end,
opp. corner to Marks and Spencer).
Tel. 285744

KILMARNOCK: 52 Beansburn,
(continuation of Dean Street). **Tel. 33211**

DUNDEE: Marketgait/Nethergate
Roundabout. **Tel. 23484**

ABERDEEN: 35 Chapel Street.
Tel. 50305

The vans you wan

Most people prefer Ford vans, so that's what Mitchells fleet is: all Fords. Reliable 9 cwts., 18 cwt 35 cwt. Luton and Platform vans, and three-tonne All you need is an ordinary car licence to driv Mitchells van. And you can usually have the van y want the moment you want it.

You just phone

It's so easy. Simply pick up a phone to book your car or van from Mitchells. No fuss or bother, just fast, efficient service.
Another reason more and more people are hiring cars and vans from Mitchells.
Phone, or call in and see us—we're in the city centre.

MITCHELLS
SELF DRIVE

where people come first

Directory of Essential Information

CONTENTS

INTRODUCTION

This part of Harpers Handbook to Edinburgh is designed to help the visitor enjoy his stay in the city to the full. In the first section, 'Accommodation, Eating Out and Essential Information', there are details of where to stay, where to eat and drink – from youth hostels to exclusive hotels and from top restaurants to pubs. This section also contains essential information about emergencies, health and the police and then useful information – everything from baby-sitting agencies to wheelchair hire

In section two, 'Art Galleries, Museums, Stately Homes and Town Houses', the visitor will find the addresses, opening times and descriptions of all the places of interest in and around Edinburgh. Section three, called 'Culture, Entertainment and Recreation', is a guide to relaxation in the city. Concert halls, theatres and casinos are listed and reviewed, as well as night-spots, jazz clubs and folk clubs. For the more robust, there is information on sports such as fishing.

Edinburgh is not only a city to enjoy but also a shopping centre for all that is best of Scottish produce. In section four, 'Shopping in Edinburgh', the visitor can find out where to buy traditional Scottish goods. The final section, 'Touring and Travel', is really a transport guide to the city. It tells the visitor how to get to Edinburgh, how to move around the city by bus or hired-car and how to use Edinburgh as a base to explore the surrounding countryside.

This directory should be an indispensable tool for visitors and residents alike. All the details given have been thoroughly researched and checked and are correct at the time of going to press. However, opening times, entrance fees and even addresses do change; restaurants and hotels change management and facilities, while night-spots follow the latest fashion.

Section I –
Accommodation,
Eating Out and
Essential
Information

This section of the directory gives the vital information required by any visitor to an unfamiliar city. Details of accommodation ranging from the grandest hotel to a convenient camping site; where to find the best cuisine and a good pint; and finally basic information.

Hotels

Hotels, like restaurants, arouse strong opinions. Tastes and requirements vary, and so do personal experiences. In this section we have reviewed what we consider to be Edinburgh's top 51 hotels. All have been visited more than once, and all the information given has been thoroughly researched and checked. Specific details relating to prices and facilities have been provided by the hotels themselves. Nevertheless, these details, and standards of service, food and decor do change, and it is always wise to check before confirming a reservation.

The price of a room in each hotel has been calculated according to a standard formula. It includes VAT (a Government tax) and covers the cost of a double room with bath (if bedrooms with baths are available) for two people for one night. Details of the breakfast included for this price and the service charge are given.

All the hotels included in this section have been reviewed because they have achieved a minimum standard of comfort and service. Some have been singled out and awarded stars (★) for the standard of comfort, food, atmosphere, personal service, decor, facilities, location, and value for money. A hotel that is well above average in all eight qualities has been awarded three stars; in six qualities, two stars; and in four qualities, one star.

In general, Edinburgh's better establishments tend to be slightly old fashioned, though several 'businessmen's hotels' are available. Immaculate and courteous service is a feature of the city as a whole, and certainly of its hotels. Food tends either to be slightly bland, or occasionally over-ambitious, while decor is often either modern and brash, or traditional and fading. Nevertheless, the visitor will certainly find a hotel to suit his particular requirements without difficulty – though it is advisable to book well in advance if the visit coincides with the busy Festival season.

Over £35

Braidhills Hotel

16 2C

134 Braidhills Road
Phone: (031) 447 8888
Telex: —

Set in its own extensive grounds a few miles south of the city centre, the Braidhills Hotel offers some excellent views both to the north and south of the city. A charming family hotel that is quiet, restful, and rather old fashioned—the accommodation may occasionally look in need of maintenance, but all rooms have a colour television, radio and telephone. The impressive dining room, decorated with fresh flowers from the garden, is ideal for a quiet family dinner. The Admiral's Locker, a cocktail bar, offers a selection of 65 whiskies.

52 rooms: £37.00, service and cooked breakfast included

Special Features: Night porter Car park Conference facilities

Credit Cards: Barclaycard/Visa/Access/Mastercard/Eurocard/American Express/Diners Club/Carte Blanche

The Bruntsfield Hotel

10 2C

69–74 Bruntsfield Place
Phone: (031) 229 1393
Telex: —

The Bruntsfield Hotel, ten minutes' walk from Edinburgh's West End, stands opposite Bruntsfield Links golf course (9 holes) near 'The Meadows' park. It is a medium-sized hotel, part old and part new, in which about half the rooms have a private bathroom and colour television. The remainder only have hand-basins, although all have telephones. The Grill Room in the basement, dimly lit and predominantly red in colour, serves a fairly wide range of à la carte and table d'hôte menus. Substantial pub lunches are available in the spacious bar which is also popular with local residents. The Bruntsfield is a good 'middle-of-the-road' hotel, perhaps rather expensive, that is convenient for the King's Theatre.

52 rooms: £37.95, service and cooked breakfast included

Special Features: Night porter Car park Conference facilities

Credit Cards: Barclaycard/Visa/Access/Mastercard/Eurocard/American Express/Diners Club

Caledonian Hotel

10 1C   ★

Princes Street (West End)
Phone: (031) 225 2433
Telex: 72179

The Caledonian in Edinburgh's city-centre is a hotel very much on a grand scale, and one that tends to be heavily booked during the summer months. Among the features are the elegantly decorated Pompadour Restaurant, the Versailles Room, the ballroom, and a number of impressive bedrooms and suites. All rooms have a television, radio, telephone, tea- and coffee-making facilities, a bath and trouser-press. The service in all departments is in accordance with this hotel's high international standing. The Laird's Lodge coffee house serves an interesting range of Scottish fare and is recommended for lunches, while the Pompadour Restaurant concentrates on French cuisine of a high quality. A dinner and dance is held in the Pompadour every Saturday. The choice of bars includes the American Bar, the tartan-bedecked Bothy Bar, and the Lothian Lounge—which features live jazz or folk-music on several evenings each week. The main European languages are spoken at reception.

229 rooms: £53.50, service and cooked breakfast included

Special Features: Night porter Car park Conference and function facilities Hairdressing Gift Shop Deluxe accommodation and suites available

Credit Cards: Barclaycard/Visa/ Access/Mastercard/Eurocard/ American Express/Diners Club/ Carte Blanche

Calton Hotel

10 1D

1 North Bridge
Phone: (031) 556 7277
Telex: 778125

Formerly one of Edinburgh's leading hotels, The Calton now looks somewhat out-dated, though its position on North Bridge gives many rooms a fine view over Calton Hill towards the coast and also over the east end of Princes Street. The bedrooms are in need of modernization but all have a bathroom, telephone, radio, television, and tea- and coffee-making facilities. Perhaps the finest feature of the hotel is the Carvery Restaurant with an excellent, well-prepared selection of food at reasonable prices. There are two bars—an attractively designed cocktail bar, and a public bar on the lower ground floor. Street parking is available, but is restricted and difficult to find.

97 rooms: £38.50, service and cooked breakfast included

Special Features: Night porter Conference facilities Gift Shop

Credit Cards: Barclaycard/Visa/ Access/Mastercard/Eurocard/ Carte Blanche

The County Hotel

10 1C

8–10 Abercromby Place
Phone: (031) 556 2333
Telex: —

The County is really a typical Edinburgh New Town hotel. It is set in a fine Georgian building on fashionable Abercromby Place, but the interior scarcely matches the impressive façade. Brightly decorated throughout in rather loud combinations of colour, it is larger than many hotels in the area and is suitably priced for travelling salesmen, businessmen and those on short visits to the city. Rooms with private bathrooms are available and all rooms have a telephone, radio and television. The table d'hôte lunches and dinners represent good value.

60 rooms: £36.00, cooked breakfast included, no service charge

Special Features: Night porter Car park Conference facilities

Credit Cards: Barclaycard/Visa/ Access/Mastercard/Eurocard/ American Express/Diners Club/ Carte Blanche

Forth Bridges Lodge

19 1B

South Queensferry
West Lothian
Phone: (031) 331 1199
Telex: 727430

A busy hotel nine miles (14.4 km) from Edinburgh on the main A90 road to Perth, with an attractive view over the Forth and Forth Bridges. The large Panorama Restaurant serves a range of French and Scottish food and does indeed offer a splendid view. Sunday lunch is popular, and there is a special children's menu as well as an opportunity for them to watch cartoons and film-shows. The bedrooms also have superb views, and are typically modern—fully equipped with a bath, radio, television, telephone, and tea- and coffee-making facilities. This is a hotel that aims at the broadest possible range of clientele, the whole complex resembling a motorway café on a grand scale. It is nevertheless successful, efficient and a popular venue for conferences.

109 rooms: £39.68, service and cooked breakfast included

Special Features: Night porter Car park Conference facilities Gift shop Special facilities for the disabled

Credit Cards: Barclaycard/Visa/ Access/Mastercard/Eurocard/ American Express/Diners Club/Carte Blanche

George Hotel

10 1C   ★★★

19–21 George Street
Phone: (031) 225 1251
Telex: 72570

Originally designed by Robert Adam, the famous 18th-century architect, The George is an impressive building at the east end of George Street—perfectly positioned for visitors to the centre of town. It is rated as one of Edinburgh's top hotels and the general standards of both service and decor justify this reputation. A large extension at the back of the building contains a number of smaller rooms, many of them with splendid views to the north, but there are larger and more lavish rooms in the main building. All rooms are comfortably furnished and scrupulously maintained —with a private bathroom, radio, colour television, and tea- and coffee-making facilities. There is an excellent Carvery in the impressive main dining room, an expensive French-style restaurant overlooking George Street, and morning coffee, light lunches, and afternoon tea are served in the lounge. The two cocktail bars, each with table-service, are well stocked—although less impressive decoratively than the other public rooms.

196 rooms: £50.60, service and cooked breakfast included

Special Features: Night porter Car park Conference facilities Baby-sitting service Valet service 24-hour room service

Credit Cards: Barclaycard/Visa/ Access/Mastercard/Eurocard/ American Express/Diners Club/ Carte Blanche

Greywalls

20 1C   ★★

Muirfield
Gullane
East Lothian
Phone: Gullane (0620) 842144
(Rail Station—Drem)
Telex: 727396

A pleasant 40-minute drive from Edinburgh along the coast, this distinctive and popular hotel is an impressive Edwardian country-house that was converted into a hotel in 1948. On one side it overlooks the famous Muirfield golf course and on the other a lovely rose garden and orchard. Owing to the design of the house, each bedroom has its own character and decoration, while most have a private bathroom and telephone. The large restaurant is renowned for its table d'hôte lunch and à la carte dinner, while buffet lunches on Sundays are particularly popular. After-dinner coffee can be taken in the lounge, the sun room or the library. There are a number of places of historic interest near Greywalls, such as Tantallon Castle, Dirieton Castle and Aberlady Nature Reserve. Golf enthusiasts can choose from several courses, but should note that prior arrangements must be made with the hotel in order to play the Muirfield course. Greywalls is closed from October to April.

24 rooms: £57.50, cooked breakfast included, no service charge

Special Features: Night porter Car park Facilities for small conferences

Credit Cards: Barclaycard/Visa/ Access/Mastercard/Eurocard/ Eurocard Interbank/American Express/Diners Club

Houston House Hotel

19 2A   ★★★

Uphall
West Lothian
Phone: Broxburn (0506) 853831
Telex: 727148

This beautiful hotel, 13 miles (21 km) from Edinburgh, stands in 26 acres (10.5 ha) of garden and woodland. A choice of accommodation is offered: modern rooms are available, with central heating, television, radio, telephone, and a private bathroom; alternatively, there are the more traditional rooms in 18th-century style, with wood-panelling and four-poster beds. Both types of room offer the same degree of comfort, but for the small difference in price (£6.00 more than the price given below) the traditional is recommended. The service in the hotel and the food in the restaurant are first class, the latter complemented by an exceptionally fine wine cellar—the restaurant is reviewed in the 'Restaurants' section of this directory. There is a set menu for dinner but a choice is available at lunch. The small Undercroft bar is homely and features a log fire in a 16th-century kitchen-fireplace. The Houston House Hotel is recommended without reservation for its overall excellence.

29 rooms: £40.00, service and continental breakfast included

Special Features: Night porter Car park Facilities for small conferences 18-hole golf course Cróquet lawn

Credit Cards: American Express

Howard Hotel

4 3C

32–36 Great King Street
Phone: (031) 556 1393
Telex: 727887

This quiet, friendly hotel in Edinburgh's Georgian New Town is in an ideal central position for sight-seeing trips. In spite of the rather brash entrance hall, the interior decor is on the whole pleasant, and there is an attractive 18th-century cocktail bar and two comfortable adjoining lounges. The majority of the bedrooms have a private bathroom, telephone, colour television, radio, and tea- and coffee-making facilities. No. 36, the small restaurant on the lower floor, offers a varied and imaginative selection of traditional British dishes. Also downstairs is The Claret Jug, a popular and well-run pub frequented by local residents, that serves first-class bar lunches.

26 rooms: £39.50, service and cooked breakfast included

Special Features: Night porter Car park Facilities for small conferences and functions

Credit Cards: Barclaycard/Visa/ Access/Mastercard/Eurocard/ American Express/Diners Club/ Carte Blanche

King James Hotel

10 1D

167 St. James Centre
Phone: (031) 556 0111
Telex: 727200

A large and thoroughly modern hotel at the top of Leith Walk, by the eastern end of Edinburgh's famous Princes Street. The decor is Scottish, and to some tastes rather brash and plastic. Nevertheless, it is one of the city's busiest hotels, with comfortable, clean and modern bedrooms—all have a private bathroom, radio, colour television, telephone and tea- and coffee-making facilities. There are two bars and two restaurants—all efficient, functional and somewhat over-decorated in tartan. A discotheque is held in one bar each night. The hotel is extremely efficient in all departments, and has

direct access to St. James Centre, Edinburgh's largest covered shopping area, but the bedrooms overlooking Leith Walk tend, despite double-glazing, to be rather noisy.

160 rooms: £39.50, no service charge, breakfast extra

Special Features: Night porter Small car park (but adjacent to municipal car park) Conference and function facilities Baby-sitting service

Credit Cards: Barclaycard/Visa/ Access/Mastercard/Eurocard/ American Express/Diners Club/ Carte Blanche

Ladbroke Dragonara Hotel

9 1B

Bells Mills
Belford Road
Phone: (031) 332 2545
Telex: 727979

The newest hotel in Edinburgh, the Ladbroke Dragonara opened in July 1981. Though the editors were unable to see the hotel in operation before this directory went to the printer, it seems likely that this well-designed modern complex on the banks of the Water of Leith will take its place in the top flight of Edinburgh hotels. All bedrooms have a private bathroom, colour television, telephone, radio, and tea- and coffee-making facilities, but for a payment of £5.75 (additional to the price quoted below) the 'Gold Star' bedrooms are offered: these are specially designed and contain fresh fruit, biscuits, sweets, a sewing-kit, shampoo, an electric trouser-press, and a miniature bottle of aperitif, as well as the standard features. Regular food festivals are a feature of the Water of Leith Restaurant, but normally dishes are served from a wide-ranging à la carte menu; a special 'Eastern Promise' menu is available for £12.50 per head, and Sunday 'brunch' at £6.50 per head. Bar meals are served in the The Granary Bar, a restoration of a 17th-century mill which once stood on the site, and there is also a luxurious cocktail bar. With an emphasis on service and an exhaustive range of facilities, the Ladbroke Dragonara promises to be well worth a visit.

142 rooms: £43.70, no service charge, breakfast extra

Special Features: Night porter Car park Toiletries on sale Facilities for children Two bedrooms for the disabled Facilities for wheelchairs Extension conference and function facilities, including audio-visual equipment and specially trained staff Bureau de change 24-hour room service

Credit Cards: Barclaycard/Visa/ Access/Mastercard/Eurocard/ American Express/Diners Club/ Carte Blanche

The North British Hotel

10 1C

east end of
Princes Street
Phone: (031) 556 2414
Telex: 72332

The North British, like The Caledonian at the opposite end of Princes Street, is a British Transport Hotel. It is a large Victorian building, conspicuous with 200-foot (61 m) Gothic clock tower that overlooks Princes Street Gardens and the Castle. The accommodation ranges from small, plainly furnished, single rooms to large elegantly decorated suites. Most of the bedrooms have a colour television, radio and private bathroom. Decor throughout this massive building tends to be variable and some of the colour schemes suggest a certain lack of taste. There are two modern bars, The Bannatyne and The American, and extensive conference and banqueting facilities. Dining facilities range from a reasonably priced buffet lunch, to traditional Scottish cuisine in the Cleikum Restaurant, or a full dinner in the main dining room or Restaurant des Gourmets—all are of a high standard. Regular Scottish Evenings are held during the summer, and the main European languages are spoken at reception.

193 rooms: £53.50, service and cooked breakfast included

Special Features: Night porter Deluxe accommodation and suites Gift shop Direct lift from Waverley Station Car park

Credit Cards: Barclaycard/Visa/ Access/Mastercard/Eurocard/ American Express/Diners Card/ Carte Blanche

Prestonfield House Hotel

12 3A

71 Priestfield Road
Phone: (031) 667 3479
Telex: 727396

Ten minutes from the city centre, this impressive 17th-century house stands in 23 acres (9 ha) of lawns and gardens. The interior has been astonishingly well preserved and the Italian, Tapestry and the Leather rooms are especially impressive. Surprisingly, Prestonfield only has five bedrooms and it is necessary to book accommodation well in advance. One of these, known as the Cupid Room, is spectacularly rich in ornamentation, but unfortunately only two bedrooms have running water, in the form of showers (there are two communal bathrooms) and all are reached by an old stone staircase which has no hand-rail. They are, however, centrally heated and present idyllic views of the grounds, in which sheep graze and peacocks display. The superb restaurant, the main feature of this hotel, is reviewed in detail in the 'Restaurants' section of this directory. It really appears that things have changed little at Prestonfield since the days when Doctor Johnson dined here on his return from the Western Isles.

5 rooms: £40.00, cooked breakfast included, no service charge

Special Features: No night porter (doors close 24.00 but there is a night bell) Car park Function room

Credit Cards: Barclaycard/Visa/ Access/Mastercard/Eurocard/ American Express/Diners Club/ Carte Blanche

Roxburghe Hotel

10 1C

Charlotte Square
Phone: (031) 225 3921
Telex: 727054

The Roxburghe is a traditional hotel, with the emphasis on elegance and lavish comfort, that is run with quiet Edwardian efficiency and discretion in prestigious Charlotte Square, one of the most beautiful and famous Georgian squares in the country. Tariffs are high, but the efficient, highly personalized service and subdued, formal atmosphere make it good value for money. The Consort cocktail bar and restaurant are popular venues for dining-out in Edinburgh, and the standard of catering is high. All rooms have a private bathroom or shower, telephone, central heating, a colour television, trouser-press and tea-making facilities; there is a lift to all floors. Street parking is available, but restricted.

78 rooms: £60.00, service and continental breakfast included

Special Features: night porter Conference and function facilities

Credit Cards: Barclaycard/Visa/ Access/Mastercard/Eurocard/ American Express/Diners Club

The Royal Scot Hotel

7 2A

111 Glasgow Road
Phone: (031) 334 9191
Telex: 727197

The Royal Scot is Edinburgh's largest hotel and has the distinction of being the only one with a helicopter landing pad. At first sight it appears inhospitable, but in fact offers an astonishingly wide range of services and facilities. Luxurious, but rather characterless, the Royal Scot is an excellent modern hotel—ideal for businessmen. All the bedrooms are centrally heated and double glazed, with a bath or shower, colour television, radio, telephone, and tea- and coffee-making facilities. The cocktail bar has a superb view out over the Pentland Hills and features an aquarium set on a huge marble slab; the Edinburgh Bar is decorated with pictures of famous characters from the city's past, and quick snacks are served in the Tattoo Grill. The large restaurant serves a selection of Scottish and international cuisine.

265 rooms: £37.00, service and cooked breakfast included

Special Features: Night porter Car park Helicopter landing pad Hairdresser Gift shop Sauna Car-hire desk Conference and function facilities

Credit Cards: Barclaycard/Visa/ Access/Mastercard/Eurocard/ American Express/Diners Club/ Carte Blanche

St. Andrews Hotel

10 1C

8–10 St. Andrews Street
Phone: (031) 556 8774
Telex: —

This hotel is conveniently positioned in the heart of Edinburgh. The interior is oak panelled throughout and the bedrooms have a pleasantly old-fashioned look. All are equipped with a hand-basin, telephone, radio, alarm, and tea- and coffee-making facilities. Those with bathrooms are very large and comfortable and have a colour television. Neither of the bars nor the restaurant is particularly notable but the staff throughout the hotel are noticeably courteous. Street parking is restricted, but a municipal car park is close by.

42 rooms: £36.00, cooked breakfast included, no service charge

Special Features: No night porter Facilities for small conferences and functions

Credit Cards: Barclaycard/Visa/Access/Mastercard/Eurocard/American Express/Diners Club/Carte Blanche

From £6 to £35

Albany Hotel

4 3C ★

39 Albany Street
Phone: (031) 556 0397/8
Telex: —

Winner of the Scottish Tourist Board's 'Hotel of the Year' award in 1978, the Albany continues to maintain high standards of efficiency and decor. The bedrooms are fresh, clean and tastefully furnished in pine. All rooms have a private bathroom, colour television, telephone, radio, and tea- and coffee-making facilities. The menu is interesting but the quality of the food is not as high as one might anticipate—although there can be few places in Edinburgh which offer 'bar snacks' as varied and exotic as: 'Herring Bismarck with sour cream', 'Swiss Platter', and 'Chocolate Rum Mousse'. One of the best hotels in the select New Town area, it has special winter rates, and is well worth visiting.

22 rooms: £33.00, service and cooked breakfast included

Special Features: Night porter Street parking Conference facilities

Credit Cards: Barclaycard/Visa/Access/Mastercard/Eurocard

Arden Hotel

4 3D

18–20 Royal Terrace
Phone: (031) 556 5879/8013
Telex: —

The Arden Hotel is reasonably priced, centrally situated and run with quiet efficiency. Most of the rooms have a bath or shower and all have intercom systems, central heating and hand-basins. There

are fine views to the north from several of the rooms, all of which are plainly furnished but clean and well maintained. No lunches are served but a good dinner is offered at around £6.50 per head. The hotel is fully licensed, and has an intimate cocktail bar; other amenities include a lift, a small gift shop and a television lounge. Street parking is restricted in this area.

38 rooms: £25.30, service and cooked breakfast included

Special Features: No night porter, but keys are supplied Gift shop

Credit Cards: None

The Barnton Hotel

1 3A

at Barnton Roundabout
Queensferry Road
Phone: (031) 339 1144
Telex: 727928

The Barnton Hotel is a large 19th-century building on the northern outskirts of the city. It offers a wide variety of amenities and special features such as jazz on Sunday lunchtimes, weekend dinner–dances (about £8.50 per head) and 'Fondue Nights' in the 'Ski Lodge' Bar. In addition there is a restaurant and a cocktail bar, both of which are spacious, pleasantly decorated, and provide good service. The rooms are fully equipped with a television, radio and tea- and coffee-making facilities, and all have a bath or shower. Prices tend to be high but in general the Barnton is recommended—particularly for those who look for entertainment during their stay.

48 rooms: £35.00, service included, breakfast extra

Special Features: Night porter Car park Conference facilities

Credit Cards: Barclaycard/Visa/Access/Mastercard/Eurocard/American Express/Diners Club/Carte Blanche

Christopher North Hotel

2 3C

6 Gloucester Place
Phone: (031) 225 2720
Telex: —

The emphasis in this New Town hotel in central Edinburgh is on the old-fashioned relationship between proprietor and guest. The atmosphere is genuinely friendly, the hotel immaculately maintained

throughout, and both accommodation and meals are reasonably priced. Business lunches are served in the bar and dinners in the well-arranged dining room downstairs. Most rooms have either a private bath or a shower, and all have a colour television, telephone, radio, and tea- and coffee-making facilities. There is a ground floor annex across the road from the hotel—suitable for those who would prefer not to climb the rather precipitous Georgian staircases. The residents' lounge has a subdued, drawing-room atmosphere, and one can almost imagine Christopher North, the 19th-century Edinburgh poet and satirist, at work here in days gone by. Street parking is available, but restricted.

17 rooms: £34.00, service and cooked breakfast included

Special Features: No night porter, but keys are supplied

Credit Cards: Barclaycard/Visa/Access/Mastercard/Eurocard

The Commodore Hotel

19 1B

West Mains Drive
Cramond Foreshore
Phone: (031) 336 1700
Telex: —

Overlooking the Firth of Forth, 15 minutes' drive from central Edinburgh, this hotel owned by the Reo Stakis Group has few distinguishing features other than the undeniable charm of its situation. All rooms are fully equipped with a colour television, radio, telephone, bathroom and tea- and coffee-making facilities —they tend to be small and very uniform, but comfortable. The recently renovated restaurant offers a rather predictable and expensive menu but the quality of the food and service is reasonably good. Sunday lunch represents good value, and there are two bars, both colourful and spacious.

50 rooms: £34.00, cooked breakfast included, no service charge

Special Features: Night porter Car park Conference facilities

Credit Cards: Barclaycard/Visa/Access/Mastercard/Eurocard/American Express/Diners Club

Crest Hotel

3 3A

(junction Craigleith/
Queensferry Rd)
Queensferry Road
Phone: (031) 332 2442
Telex: 72541

The Crest Hotel's prominent position overlooking Queensferry Road, about one mile (1.6 km) from Princes Street, ensures a panoramic view of the city and, looking north, to Fife. Although distinctly modern, the thoughtful interior design has helped to create a relaxed and personalized atmosphere. Light, spacious and relatively quiet, this hotel is ideal for those who seek modern conveniences but wish to avoid the hubbub of the city centre. Service is noticeably courteous, and the accommodation is simple but comfortable. All rooms have a colour television, radio, telephone, tea- and coffee-making facilities, a trouser-press and a bath or shower. The lunchtime 'Carvery' serves a standard range of Scottish and French dishes—including special 'slimmers lunches'.

180 rooms: £31.00, service included, breakfast extra

Special Features: Night porter Car park Conference facilities

Credit Cards: Barclaycard/Visa/ Access/Mastercard/Eurocard/ American Express/Diners Club

Dean Hotel

3 3B

10 Clarendon Crescent
Phone: (031) 332 0308
Telex: —

A small hotel in a tree-lined crescent that is only a short walk from Princes Street. It has recently been renovated, and rooms are plainly decorated with uniform, mass-produced furniture. All have tea- and coffee-making facilities, a shower and private toilet and colour television—shared bathrooms are available. There can be no complaints about the cleanliness, friendliness, or quality of service here and the downstairs bar, part of which is used for breakfasts and bar lunches, is elaborately furnished—a real feature of the hotel. No evening meals are served, and there are street parking restrictions.

9 rooms: £30.00, service and cooked breakfast included

Special Features: No night porter, but keys are supplied

Credit Cards: Barclaycard/Visa/ Access/Mastercard/Eurocard

Ellersley House Hotel

9 1A

Ellersley Road
Murrayfield
Phone: (031) 337 6888
Telex: 76357

Standing in two acres (0.8 ha) of walled garden, not too far from the main A8, Glasgow Road, Ellersley House is noted for both its fine exterior and well-maintained gardens. Decor throughout this comfortable and well-run establishment is of a high standard, particularly in the conference and dining rooms. The bedrooms, with more character than one generally expects, all have a colour television, private bathrooms, telephone, radio and tea-making facilities. The table d'hôte menus for lunch and dinner offer French and Scottish dishes at reasonable prices. There are two bars, one of which features live entertainment on most evenings.

54 rooms: £35.00, cooked breakfast included, no service charge

Special Features: Night porter Car park Facilities for small conferences Croquet lawn

Credit Cards: Barclaycard/Visa/ Access/Mastercard/Eurocard/ American Express/Diners Club/ Carte Blanche

Georgian Hotel

4 3C

5–6 Dean Terrace
Phone: (031) 332 4520
Telex: —

For those interested in visiting the innumerable antique and bric-a-brac shops in central Edinburgh's Stockbridge Village, the Georgian Hotel could scarcely be better placed. Dean Terrace looks out over the Water of Leith and is minutes away from Dean Path, one of the city's most pleasant walks. The Georgian is a livelier hotel than many in the area, with a consistently high turnover of guests. The lounge bar, serving good lunches, has built up a strong local clientele and has an all-day licence. The quality of the bedrooms varies, but most are comfortable—the rooms are light and spacious but not luxurious. All have a black-and-white television, radio and intercom, and tea- and coffee-making facilities; some have a private shower and a toilet. The residents' lounge is quiet, calm and furnished in a traditional manner. Street parking is available, but restricted.

12 rooms: £27.60, service and cooked breakfast included

Special Features: No night porter, but keys are available on request Facilities for small functions Baby-listening service

Credit Cards: American Express

Gloucester Hotel

4 3C

10 Gloucester Place
Phone: (031) 225 2378
Telex: —

This friendly, family hotel in the Georgian New Town has reasonable rates, and is only minutes from Princes Street. All bedrooms have hand-basins, a television and digital alarm-radio —some have private bathrooms. Only cooked breakfasts are served in the dining room, but snacks are available in the attractive and popular cocktail bar. Street parking is available, but restricted.

12 rooms: £26.00, service and cooked breakfast included

Special Features: No night porter, but keys are supplied

Credit Cards: Barclaycard/Visa/ Access/Mastercard/Eurocard

The Gordon Bruce

3 3B

15 South Learmonth Gardens
Phone: (031) 332 8248
Telex: —

A pleasant, quiet hotel in a quiet garden square minutes from the West End, with views to Fettes College and the Firth of Forth. The restaurant in the basement has an à la carte menu in the evening and there is a good selection of bar lunches in the unusually well-designed bar. All bedrooms have a telephone, colour television, fridge, tea- and coffee-making facilities and small grills for snacks. The rooms are simply decorated, clean, bright and very quiet—most have private bathrooms. Unrestricted street parking is available.

33 rooms: £34.60, cooked breakfast included, no service charge

Special Features: Night porter (the resident manager) Facilities for small conferences

Credit Cards: Barclaycard/Visa/Access/Mastercard/Eurocard/American Express

Grosvenor Centre Hotel

9 1B

9–21 Grosvenor Street
Phone: (031) 226 6001
Telex: 72445

The Grosvenor is a large, slightly impersonal hotel in Edinburgh's West End, minutes from Princes Street and close to Haymarket Railway Station. It caters primarily for businessmen and is popular for exhibitions, promotions and conferences—the hotel's central position and up-to-date facilities ensure that it is generally well booked. The bedrooms, although rather garishly decorated, are comfortable and all have a television, radio, alarm, telephone, and tea- and coffee-making facilities; rooms with a bath and shower are also available. There are three bars: 'Spats', a popular discotheque styled as an American 'speak easy' of the 1920s, and the quieter 'Georgian' and 'Stable' bars. Foreign tourists are made especially welcome in the 'Lairds Larder' restaurant which offers a wide range of Scottish food, and snacks and meals are also served in a bistro and wine bar.

160 rooms: £28.50, service included, breakfast extra

Special Features: Night porter Conference and function facilities Theatre-booking service

Credit Cards: Barclaycard/Visa/Access/Mastercard/Eurocard/American Express/Diners Club

Harp Hotel

7 2B

114 St. John's Road
Corstorphine
Phone: (031) 334 4750
Telex: —

The Harp Hotel is scarcely as splendid as its brochure claims and presents a rather uninspiring aspect from the road. Some may think the Edwardian decor tasteless, but the hotel is reasonably priced and only a short bus journey from the city centre. Bedrooms are available with or without a private bathroom or toilet, and all have a telephone, radio alarm, and tea- and coffee-making

facilities—a colour television is optional. There is a public bar, a cocktail bar, a residents' television lounge; dinner is served in the dining room and bar snacks are provided at lunchtime. Regular dinner–dances are held during the winter..

20 rooms: £29.50, cooked breakfast included, no service charge

Special Features: Night porter Car park Function facilities

Credit Cards: Barclaycard/Visa/Access/Mastercard/Eurocard/American Express/Diners Club/Carte Blanche

Lady Nairne Hotel

11 1B

228 Willowbrae Road
Phone: (031) 661 3396
Telex: —

Formerly the residence of Lady Carolina Nairne, the 18th-century Scottish poet and song writer, this building was converted into a hotel in 1969. A generally successful effort has been made to retain the character of the original house, and original furniture, wall-hangings and fittings have been effectively augumented by a variety of reproduction antique furnishings. The accommodation in the new wing is modern and rather characterless, but the original bedrooms are quite impressive and feature canopied beds. All rooms have a telephone, radio, and electric trouser-press, and most have either a private bathroom or shower. There is colour television in the television lounge—an impressive room dominated by its original fireplace—but an all-prevading tartan carpet spoils the lounge and dining room. The lunch and dinner menus are extensive, if slightly expensive. The hotel is three miles (4.8 km) from the city centre, close to Arthur's Seat and Queen's Park.

28 rooms: £26.00, service and cooked breakfast included

Special Features: Night porter (May to October) Car park Conference and function facilities

Credit Cards: Access/Mastercard/Eurocard

Learmonth Hotel

3 3B

18–20 Learmonth Terrace
Phone: (031) 343 2671
Telex: —

This hotel, set in a tree-lined Georgian terrace, caters for all tastes with 'Polly's Continental-style Cocktail Bar Coffee Lounge', a bistro and wine bar, and, during the summer, a nightly 'Scottish evening'. In general the standards are high and the accommodation has recently been thoroughly renovated. Less than half the rooms have private showers or baths, but all have a radio, television, tea-making facilities and telephone—communal bathrooms are available. The decor throughout is plain but serviceable, most attention having been paid to the bars and funtion rooms. The popular 'Scottish evening', including a five-course dinner and three hours of cabaret, costs around £12.00 per hed. Very much a 'tourist hotel' the Learnmouth is efficient, but rather impersonal. Street parking is available, but restricted.

62 rooms: £32.50, service and cooked breakfast included

Special Features: Night porter

Credit Cards: Barclaycard/Visa/Access/Mastercard/Eurocard/American Express/Diners Club

Melville Castle Hotel

20 2C

Melville Estate
(on the A7 between Edinburgh and Dalkeith)
Lasswade, Midlothian
Phone: (031) 663 6633
Telex: 727289

Built in 1788 on the ruins of Melville Castle, this hotel presents a superb aspect to the approaching guest. Seven miles (11 km) from Edinburgh and set in ten acres (4 ha) of woodland and garden, it is a curious mixture of old and new. The main hall, dominated by an enormous hanging staircase and decorated with heraldic emblems, is 18th century, but the bar and some of the rooms are perhaps less impressive. Not all bedrooms have baths but most are large and comfortable—communal bathrooms are available. Weddings are a Melville speciality; facilities include a chapel, a resident piper, a carriage pulled by Norwegian ponies and a four-poster bed for the happy couple. There is a restaurant and bar on the ground floor and the upstairs cocktail bar has an extensive range of drinks—including 200 brands of whisky. The interior does not really reflect the romantic aspirations of the façade, but the Melville Castle is nevertheless comfortable, interesting and reasonably priced.

20 rooms: £30.00, service and cooked breakfast included

Special Features: No night porter, but there is a night bell Car park Conference facilities Weddings

Credit Cards: None

Mount Royal Hotel

10 1C

53 Princes Street
Phone: (031) 225 7161
Telex: 727641

With a superb view of Princes Street which takes in the Castle, Princes Street Gardens and the Scott Monument, the Mount Royal is ideally placed for the city centre. It is, however, part of a nationwide chain—with all that this implies. There are few distinguishing features—all bedrooms have a private bathroom, radio, colour television, and tea- and coffee-making facilities. Both the large restaurant and cocktail bar have fine outlooks but the interior decor now appears slightly outdated. The lunch and dinner menus are competent but lack variety, though tea and coffee are served in the lounge throughout the day—a useful service for weary shoppers. The Mount Royal is close to Waverley railway station and the St. Andrew Square bus station. Street parking is available, but restricted.

120 rooms: £35.00, service and continental breakfast included

Special Features: Night porter Facilities for small conferences Theatre-booking service Baby-sitting service

Credit Cards: Barclaycard/Visa/ Access/Mastercard/Eurocard/ American Express/Diners Club/ Carte Blanche/Carte Bleu

Palace Hotel

10 1C

1 Castle Street
Phone: (031) 225 6222
Telex: —

Although one of Princes Street's lesser known hotels, with its entrance on Castle Street, the Palace has a number of interesting features. Both lunch and dinner, served in the Crown Room, can be chosen from an imaginative French and Scottish menu and the range of cocktails available in the bar is unusually extensive and

reasonably priced; there is also a piano bar. What the hotel lacks is character, although some rooms have views of the Castle and Princes Street Gardens; in general it is old-fashioned, but likeable, with plain decor and good service. The majority of rooms have a private bath, radio and telephone, while a television is an optional extra. The nearest car park is in Castle Terrace, a few minutes' walk away. Street parking is available, but restricted.

50 rooms: £29.00, service and cooked breakfast included

Special Features: Night Porter Facilities for small conferences

Credit Cards: American Express/ Diners Club

Post House Hotel

9 2A

Corstorphine Road
Phone: (031) 334 8221
Telex: 727103

The Post House, which stands next to the Zoo on busy Corstorphine Road, is one of Edinburgh's largest hotels. All the bedrooms, some of which offer extensive views of the Pentland Hills, are modern and comfortable with a radio, colour television, telephone, tea- and coffee-making facilities and a private bathroom. Lunch and dinner is served in the Ravelston Restaurant from a menu of Scottish and French dishes, while the 'Honey Bear' restaurant is open for snacks daily. The two cocktail bars, in keeping with the modern tone of this hotel, are spacious and efficiently run—but perhaps, like the hotel, lacking in character. The Post House, only three miles (4.8 km) away from the airport and a similar distance from the city centre, is all that one would expect from an efficient, modern hotel, and is ideal for businessmen.

208 rooms: £35.00, service included, breakfast extra

Special Features: Night porter Car park Gift shop Secretarial service Conference facilities Dogs admitted at the discretion of the management

Credit Cards: Barclaycard/Visa/ Access/Mastercard/Eurocard/ American Express/Diners Club/ Carte Blanche

Hotel Ritz

9 1B ★

14–18 Grosvenor Street
Phone: (031) 337 4315
Telex: —

Thick carpets, expensive wallpaper and chandeliers in the hall, all combine to distinguish this hotel from some of its shabbier neighbours. Centrally heated throughout, with a quiet and comfortable residents' lounge and cocktail bar, the Hotel Ritz is a quiet, somewhat retiring establishment. Most bedrooms have superb private bathrooms with a shower or bath and toilet, a telephone, radio, television, and tea- and coffee-making facilities. Breakfast and evening meals are served, to residents only, in the slightly less impressive dining room. The hotel is two minutes from Haymarket Station, in an area where street parking is restricted.

40 rooms: £29.90, cooked breakfast included, no service charge

Special Features: None

Credit Cards: Barçlaycard/Visa/ Access/Mastercard/Eurocard/ American Express/Diners Club

Royal British Hotel

10 1C

20 Princes Street
Phone: (031) 556 4901
Telex: 727661

Centrally situated in Princes Street, with excellent views of the Castle, Scott Monument and many other fine buildings from several of the bedrooms and the main lounge, the Royal British is a hotel with few pretensions but all the necessary facilities. The entrance on Princes Street has a well-worn look but the rooms are all clean and tidy, although the decor is somewhat plain. All the bedrooms have a colour television, telephone and central heating, and half of them have a private bathroom. There is a pleasant bar exclusively for residents that is open all day from 11.00, while 'The Maltings' bar, renowned for its real ale and selection of malt whiskies, is cosy and sells bar food. The hotel restaurant serves traditional Scottish fare. Street parking is available, though restricted, but the hotel is close to a multi-storey car park.

74 rooms: £34.50, cooked breakfast included, no service charge

Special Features: Night porter
Conference and function facilities

Credit Cards: Barclaycard/Visa/
Access/Mastercard/Eurocard/
American Express/Diners Club

Scotia Hotel

4 3C

5–11 Great King Street
Phone: (031) 556 3266
Telex: 727572

At present the Scotia is a strange
mixture of the brassily modern and
the outmoded. Several recent
changes of ownership have done
little to rectify this but the Scotia
remains a popular hotel in
Edinburgh's select New Town
area. Many of the bedrooms are
rather drably decorated but all
have a telephone and central
heating, and rooms with baths are
available. There is a television
room, a dining room and a spacious
lounge bar, and Scottish evenings
are held regularly at a cost of £3.00
per head. The hotel is popular with
tour operators. Street parking is
available, but restricted.

48 rooms: £32.00, service and
cooked breakfast included

Special Features: Night porter
Facilities for small conferences

Credit Cards: Barclaycard/Visa/
Access/Mastercard/Eurocard/
American Express/Diners Club

£25 and under

Buchan Hotel

9 1B

8 Coates Gardens
Phone: (031) 337 1045
Telex: —

This small 'Bed and Breakfast' type
hotel offers extremely good value
for money. The comfort and decor
of the bedrooms vary, but all are
quite acceptable and have
hand-basins and electric
blankets—communal bathrooms
are available. The evening meal at
£3.00 per head really does
represent the best of Scottish
home-cooking, and alcoholic
drinks are sold. This hotel is highly
recommended—it is small friendly
and well-positioned near the West
End.

9 rooms: £14.00, service and
cooked breakfast included

Special Features: No night porter,
but keys are available on request,
there is an emergency bell
Personal services—washing,

shoe-cleaning, special diets, care
of the handicapped

Credit Cards: None

Crammond Brig Hotel

1 2A

by Cramond Bridge
Queensferry Road
Phone: (031) 339 4350
Telex: —

With only three bedrooms the
Cramond Brig can only just be
called a hotel, but a position at the
end of the M90 motorway into
Edinburgh from the north ensures
its popularity. The bedrooms are
equipped with hand-basins,
television and tea- and
coffee-making facilities—
communal bathrooms are
available. There are three
bars—the lounge bar, where good
food is served all day, the 'Grotto'
cocktail bar, and a small public bar.
The à la carte menu in the
restaurant is reasonably priced and
there is a family room where
children can be taken.

3 rooms: £20.00, service and
cooked breakfast included

Special Features: No night porter
(doors close 23.00) but keys are
available on request Car park

Credit Cards: Barclaycard/Visa/
Access/Mastercard/Eurocard

Cumberland Hotel

9 2B

1 West Coates
Phone: (031) 337 1198
Telex: —

This small, inexpensive hotel with
few facilities is clean, comfortable
and quiet. The Cumberland is a
large house, set back from the
A8—the main road leading out to
the airport and Glasgow—with its
own garden and parking area. The
rooms are all centrally heated and
have hand-basins. The small but
inviting dining room is pleasantly
furnished and looks out onto the
garden. No evening meals are
served but the traditional Scottish
breakfast is first rate. No alcoholic
drinks are sold.

7 rooms: £18.00, service and
cooked breakfast included

Special Features: No night porter,
but keys are available on request
Car park

Credit Cards: None

Drummond Hotel

4 3C

34 Drummond Place
Phone: (031) 556 3059
Telex: —

The Drummond is a small,
family-run, establishment in a quiet
Georgian Square in the New Town
area of central Edinburgh. It has a
friendly atmosphere and tends to
revolve around the two bars that
are patronized by locals and
residents alike. All the bedrooms
have private showers, radio and
private call systems; two rooms
have private toilets. There is a
television lounge, and a machine
dispensing hot drinks 24 hours a
day. The standard of service is
consistently high. Street parking is
available but restricted.

9 rooms: £25.00, service and
cooked breakfast included

Special Features: No night porter,
but keys are supplied
Key available for Drummond Place
gardens

Credit Cards: Barclaycard/Visa/
Access/Mastercard/Eurocard/
American Express

Gillsland Hotel

9 3B

7 Gillsland Road
Phone: (031) 337 1058
Telex: —

Beautifully situated in its own
grounds 15 minutes from Princes
Street in the Polwarth area of
southwest Edinburgh, the Gillsland
is both a commercial and a family
hotel. It is a popular weekend haunt
for local families who can enjoy a
leisurely drink in the family lounge
with their children. All rooms have
hand-basins and central heating,
but none have private bathrooms.
The hotel is clean, the decor simple
and the rates are highly
competitive, with the home-cooked
evening meal good value at £5.00
per head. Baths and showers are
available on each floor. In pleasant,
natural surroundings, the Gillsland
is an ideal place for a family to stay
while visiting Edinburgh.

11 rooms: £15.00, cooked breakfast
included, no service charge

Special Features: No night porter
(doors close 01.00) but keys are
available on request Car park

Credit Cards: None

Glencairn Hotel

4 3C

19–21 Royal Circus
Phone: (031) 225 5218
Telex: —

The Glencairn Hotel is made up of two Georgian houses. It is large and roomy, and there are some splendid views over Royal Circus gardens. Apart from the busy bar it is a quiet hotel—handy for shopping in the New Town or Stockbridge Village and only minutes from Princes Street. The heavily decorated bar stocks a very wide range of whiskies and features an enormous hand-carved Elizabethan fire-surround. The only meal served is breakfast—in the downstairs 'breakfast room'. All bedrooms have showers and most have private toilets—baths can be taken in the shared bathroom. There are no telephones or televisions in the rooms, although there is a very small television room. Clean, tidy and efficiently run, the Glencairn is a pleasant family hotel. Street parking is available but restricted.

20 rooms: £24.00, service and cooked breakfast included

Special Features: No night porter, but keys are supplied Facilities for small functions

Credit Cards: None

Hailes House Hotel

14 2C

32 Hailes Avenue
off Lanark Road
Phone: (031) 441 1176
Telex: —

About twenty minutes' drive from the city centre, this hotel was originally a Scottish mansion house. Although now in the suburbs, the house has retained a degree of charm and character which seems to ensure its continuing popularity. It is efficiently run, catering for family groups, tourists or businessmen with equal facility. There are a variety of spacious and interesting rooms—all with a private bathroom, television, radio alarm and tea- and coffee-making facilities. A good four-course Sunday lunch is served in the restaurant, while the large mock-Tudor lounge bar, where bar-meals are particularly good value, has a 'happy hour' from 17.30 on weekday evenings when drinks are cheap—in the summer the large, walled Beer Garden is open.

There are also a small cocktail bar, a residents' lounge, and a number of golf courses nearby.

10 rooms: £24.50, service and cooked breakfast included

Special Features: No night porter, but keys are supplied Car park Facilities for small conferences

Credit Cards: Barclaycard/Visa/Access/Mastercard/Eurocard

Kings Manor Hotel

12 2D

100 Milton Road East
Phone: (031) 669 0444
Telex: 727037

The Kings Manor is an impressive 19th-century building, only five minutes from the beach, in Portobello, Edinburgh's coastal village, four miles (6 km) from Princes Street. It was extensively modernized in 1976 but much of the original character of the building has been retained. All the bedrooms have a telephone, television and bathroom—there are modern rooms in the extension at the rear, and more traditional rooms in the main part of the hotel. Dinner, served in the large dining room, costs around £6.00 per head and although the menu is not as varied as might be expected in a hotel of this size, the service is good. The emphasis is on a traditionally Scottish atmosphere, making the Kings Manor a popular venue with coach-tour operators. Snacks and meals are provided in the spacious bar, and regular dinner–dances are held throughout the season

70 rooms: £23.00, service and cooked breakfast included

Special Features: Night porter Conference facilities Car park Family rooms available

Credit Cards: American Express

Nelson Hotel

4 3C

9 Nelson Street
Phone: (031) 556 4344
Telex: —

A small, privately owned establishment that is both comfortable and efficiently run. All rooms have a television, radio and intercom, and most have private showers—bathrooms are available on each floor. Breakfast is the only meal served in the dining room but snacks are available in the lounge bar which is open until 01.00 at

weekends. This bar is open to non-residents, and has a predominantly homosexual clientele. The hotel has pleasant management, good service, and is centrally situated in the heart of the select New Town area of central Edinburgh where street parking is restricted.

19 rooms: £21.85, cooked breakfast included, no service charge

Special Features: No night porter (doors close 24.00 Monday–Friday, 01.30 at weekends) but there is an emergency bell) Special weekend rates

Credit Cards: None

Queensway Hotel

9 1B

1 Queensferry Road
Phone: (031) 332 6492
Telex: —

A small, friendly hotel, run by two Spanish restaurateurs. All the bedrooms have showers, (though communal bathrooms are available), and are clean and comfortable, but the main emphasis at the Queensway Hotel is on food. The menu is international, and the fresh-fish dishes in particular are to be recommended. The small cocktail bar is popular with local businessmen and hoteliers. The bedrooms overlooking busy Queensferry Road tend to be rather noisy.

6 rooms: £21.00, cooked breakfast included, no service charge

Special Features: Night porter Car park Catering for functions

Credit Cards: Barclaycard/Visa/Access/Mastercard/Eurocard/Diners Club/Carte Blanche

Suffolk Hall Hotel

11 3B

10 Craigmillar Park
Phone: (031) 667 4810
Telex: —

This is a friendly, family-run hotel set in a large Victorian mansion on the south side of the city. Its proximity to the main road means that some bedrooms are rather noisy but others, to the rear, are quiet and have splendid views over Arthur's Seat. All the accommodation is well maintained and attractively decorated and the nature of the original house is such that each room has its own character and points of interest. All bedrooms have a radio, intercom and hand-basins, and some have a private bath or shower. There is a cocktail lounge, a television lounge, a dining room with table d'hôte and a large secluded garden. The Suffolk also has its own self-contained function suite with an unusual 'Pagoda' bar.

14 rooms: £25.00, service and cooked breakfast included

Special Features: No night porter, (doors close 24.00) keys are available on request Car park Function facilities

Credit Cards: Barclaycard/Visa/Access/Mastercard/Eurocard

Thistle Court Hotel

9 2B

5 Hampton Terrace
West Coates
Phone: (031) 337 1314
Telex: —

A small, but welcoming hotel on the main, A8, Corstorphine Road approximately one mile (1.6 km) from the west end of Princes Street and near to Haymarket Station. All the bedrooms are clean, simply decorated, and comfortable—most have a private shower and toilet and all have tea-making facilities and a hand-basin. There is a friendly bar at which excellent home-cooked bar lunches are served and an à la carte dinner is available in the restaurant. The Thistle Court is one of the best of the less expensive hotels, and represents good value for money.

9 rooms: £19.24, cooked breakfast included, no service charge

Special Features: No night porter, (doors close 23.30) but keys are available on request Small car park

Credit Cards: None

Guest Houses and Bed and Breakfast

For a stay in Edinburgh on a budget, guest houses often represent tremendous value—a full, home-cooked Scottish breakfast is an experience not to be missed. Unfortunately, standards vary, and it is often impossible to know in advance whether a holiday or a short visit will be a delight or a disaster. For this reason we have selected 47 guest houses, all of which are clean, pleasant, welcoming and represent good value for money.

All of the houses listed below have been visited, and all the details given have been thoroughly checked. Nevertheless, it would be sensible to check that the guest house of your choice provides exactly what you require before your visit.

'Blairhaven'

4 3C

5 Eyre Place
Mrs. Shaw
Phone: (031) 556 3025

A moderately priced guest house, all the rooms here are equipped with electric blankets, duvets and hand-basins. There is no extra charge for the use of a shower. No evening meals are served, but there is a soup/coffee machine in the hall. It is centrally situated, on the edge of Edinburgh's select New Town, but some of the interior decor is in need of renewal. Street parking is restricted during the day.

7 bedrooms: £5.50 per head, continental breakfast included. £6.50 per head, cooked breakfast included

4 3C

7 Eyre Place
Mrs. Donaghue
Phone: (031) 556 2700

This is a pleasant guest house, run by a charming elderly lady. The decor is functional and clean but rather sombre. There is no extra charge for a shower or bath, and there is a toilet on all floors. Reasonably priced, but no evening meals are served. Street parking is restricted during the day.

8 bedrooms: £5.00 per head, continental breakfast included

'Ardenlea' Guest House

4 3C

9 Eyre Place
Mr. and Mrs. Wilson
Phone: (031) 556 2838

Open only from May until September, this is a clean well-run and airy house which has recently undergone extensive improvement. Rooms are available with private showers, and all have hand-basins and are centrally heated. Children are charged half price and there is no charge for babies. Baths are free, and each guest has his own bedroom and front-door key; there are two roomy lounges—one with television. No evening meals are served, and street parking is restricted during the day.

8 bedrooms: £6.00 per head, cooked breakfast included

4 3C

8a Great King Street
Mrs. Dickie
Phone: (031) 556 0903

Run by a couple with a young family, who only have one double bedroom to let, this guest house has a pleasant atmosphere. The bedroom has its own toilet and shower, and tea and coffee are available at any time in the lounge. Clean, well-run, situated in the heart of Edinburgh's New Town, this house is a short walk from Princes Street. Street parking is restricted and no evening meals are served.

1 bedroom: £14.00 (whether one or two people), cooked breakfast included

'Ashling' Guest House

10 1C

47 Castle Street
Mrs. Brady
Phone: (031) 225 7796

Situated at the top of a high flight of stairs, this large guest house has the advantage of being extremely central—it is literally a stone's throw from Princes Street. The interior is dominated by a vast array of paintings, although some of the rooms stand in need of redecoration. All the beds have electric blankets and duvets, and there is a small charge (20 p) for the use of a shower. All guests have their own bedroom and front-door key. No evening meals are served, and there are parking restrictions during the day.

7 bedrooms: £6.50 per head, cooked breakfast included

'Gunn' Guest House

4 3C

74 Dublin Street
Mrs. Bates
Phone: (031) 556 5032

This is an attractive and friendly establishment on the top floor of a high building in the city centre. The bedrooms are light and clean and some have splendid views out towards the Firth of Forth. None of the bedrooms have hand-basins. There is a dining room, a sitting room, and there is no extra charge for a shower. In a pleasant gesture Mrs. Bates offers guests tea and shortbread on arrival, but no evening meals are provided. There is unrestricted street parking nearby.

6 bedrooms: £6.50 per head, cooked breakfast included

4 3C

37 London Street
Mr. Mees
Phone: (031) 556 6698

This central Edinburgh flat is well positioned for both Princes Street and Waverley Station. All the rooms are supplied with kettles, metered heating, and one has its own hand-basin; there is no extra charge for a shower. The friendly and helpful proprietor creates a pleasant atmosphere, but no evening meals are available, and parking in this area is restricted.

5 bedrooms: £5.00–£6.00 per head, cooked breakfast included

10 1C

50 George Street
Mrs. Noble
Phone: (031) 225 1951

Located in one of Edinburgh's busiest and most exclusive streets, this accommodation could scarcely be more central. However, note that it stands at the top of a long flight of stairs. None of the bedrooms have hand-basins, there is a small charge (25p) for the use of a shower, and the general standard of decoration could be improved. No evening meals are served, and parking is difficult during the day.

2 bedrooms: £5.50 per head, cooked breakfast included

3 3B

67 Comely Bank Avenue
Mrs. Dignall
Phone: (031) 332 5255

There is only one twin-bedded room to let in this attractive private house. It is centrally heated and guests have the use of a private bathroom. Clean and comfortable and reasonably priced, it is in a quiet but agreeable part of Edinburgh's New Town. No evening meals are served, but unrestricted street parking is available.

1 bedroom: £6.50 per head, cooked breakfast included

'Galloway' Guest House

3 3B

Mr. and Mrs. Clark
Phone: (031) 332 3672

This guest house is clean, pleasant, and friendly—if somewhat lacking in character. Guests can come and go as they please, there is free access to the kitchen for tea and coffee, and the breakfast is substantial and well prepared. All the rooms have hand-basins and central heating, and one has a private shower. There is a separate lounge and a television. Evening meals are only available from October until June. Unrestricted street parking is available.

10 bedrooms: £6.00 per head, cooked breakfast included

4 3C

5 Dean Park Terrace
Mrs. Hughes
Phone: (031) 332 1753

There are only two rooms to let in this attractive two-storey house. The atmosphere is noticeably friendly, the prices reasonable and the landlady makes a particular effort to provide whatever her guests want for breakfast. Neither of the rooms has a hand-basin but both are comfortable and nicely decorated. There is no extra charge for a shower or a bath. Open only between April and September, with unrestricted street parking nearby.

2 bedrooms (1 twin, 1 single): £5.50 per head, cooked breakfast included

South

Clarin Guest House

10 3D

4 East Mayfield
Mrs. Stevens
Phone: (031) 667 2433

This is a quiet guest house run by a pleasant couple. All rooms have hand-basins, tea- and coffee-making facilities, heating, and some have duvets on the beds. There is no charge for baths and sandwiches can be provided on demand, but there are no evening meals. A colour television is available, and there is a car park.

7 bedrooms: £6.00 per head, cooked breakfast included Reduced rates for family rooms

Sylvern Guest House

10 3D

22 West Mayfield
Mrs. Livornese
Phone: (031) 667 1241

The tariff includes central heating in all rooms, and the use of a shower. Most of the rooms also have hand-basins. A very good evening meal is available for £2.75 per head at 18.00; afternoon tea is also served on request. A colour television is available; there is a large car park.

8 bedrooms: £6.00 per head, cooked breakfast included

Tania Guest House

10 2D

19 Minto Street
Mrs. Roscilli
Phone: (031) 667 4144

This guest house has a warm, homely atmosphere. All rooms have hand-basins and central heating, and there is no charge for the use of the showers. A good evening meal is provided at £4.00 per head, and a colour television and parking are available. Reduced rates are available during the winter for those staying a week or longer.

6 bedrooms: £6.00 per head, cooked breakfast included Reduced rates for children

Airlie Guest House

10 2D

29 Minto Street
Mrs. Hathaway
Phone: (031) 667 3562

This remarkably clean and
well-run guest house has a large
dining room and a comfortable
television lounge where coffee and
sandwiches are available from
13.00 to 20.30. Prices include
heating and showers and all rooms
have hand-basins. No evening
meals are served; a large car park
is available.

9 bedrooms: £6.00–£7.00 per head,
cooked breakfast included
Reduced rates for family rooms

Shalimar Guest House

10 2D

20 Newington Road
Mrs. Ghumman
Phone: (031) 667 0789

Run by a delightful Indian family,
the speciality here is Indian food,
which is available from £3.00 per
head to residents in the evening.
Four rooms have private showers,
and all rooms have hand-basins.
The bathrooms are clean and new,
and heating is provided in winter. A
television lounge can be used by
guests.

9 bedrooms: £6.00 per head,
English cooked breakfast included

Avondale Guest House

10 3D

10 South Gray Street
Mrs. Neill
Phone: (031) 667 6779

This pleasant house is set in a quiet
side-street. All the rooms are in
immaculate condition and include
hand-basins. There is an attractive
dining room with a breakfast bar,
and tea and biscuits are available in
the television lounge until 20.00.
There is no extra charge for the use
of the shower, but there is metered
heating in the rooms. No evening
meals are served. A car park is
available.

6 bedrooms: £6.00 per head,
cooked breakfast included
Reduced rates for children

---

10 2C

12 Warrender Park Road
Mrs. Gray
Phone: (031) 667 5160

This is perhaps more of a 'bed-sit'
than a guest house, as one of the two
rooms available also contains a
kitchen. Showers are included in
the price, but no evening meals are
available. The house is open from
June to October.

2 bedrooms: £5.00–£6.00 per head,
cooked breakfast included

Green Lady Guest House

10 2C

10 Bruntsfield Crescent
Mrs. Crawford
Phone: (031) 447 2913

Many of the original furnishings in
this large, old-fashioned house
have been retained, lending it a
quiet charm. Two of the rooms have
their own toilet, there is no extra
charge for showers or baths, and
electric blankets are available on
request; while at £1.50 per head the
evening meal represents
extremely good value. The house is
called the 'Green Lady' because of
a ghost which supposedly haunts
the area, but, this aside, there
should be no difficulty in sleeping
as the house stands at the end of a
quiet cul-de-sac.

10 bedrooms: from £5.50 per head,
cooked breakfast included
Reduced rates available for
children

---

10 3C

17 Morningside Road
Mrs. Elliott
Phone: (031) 447 7842

A feature of this immaculately clean
and delightful old house is the
wholefood cooking of the
proprietress, who caters
particularly for vegetarians, though
meat is also served. The house
stands in its own garden, is
tastefully decorated throughout
and two of the rooms have
hand-basins. The shower/
bathroom is available at no extra
cost. The meals are very
reasonable priced at about £2.50
per head; the general atmosphere
is both pleasant and welcoming
and includes a television and music
room. A car park is available.

3 bedrooms: approx. £7.00 per
head, cooked breakfast included

'Rosedene'

10 3D

4 Queens Crescent
Mrs. Gallo
Phone: (031) 667 5806

A large guest house with a kettle,
hand-basin and heating in each
room. The large, Victorian
furnishings in the bedrooms are at
times attractive but occasionally
rather imposing. The price
includes the use of showers, but no
evening meals are available. A
colour television and a car park are
also available.

10 bedrooms: £5.00–£6.00 per head,
cooked breakfast included
Reduced rates for family rooms

'Allan Lodge'

10 3D

37 Queens Crescent
Mrs. Nicol
Phone: (031) 668 2947

This is a friendly and welcoming
guest house situated in a quiet
street. The visitor's book, starting in
1947, bears witness to the large
number of satisfied guests who
have appreciated the bedrooms
with central heating, hand-basins
and duvets. Prices are inclusive of
baths, but no evening meals are
available. There is a television
lounge where a kettle is available
for tea and coffee at no extra
charge.

7 bedrooms: £6.00 per head,
cooked breakfast included
Reduced rates for children

West

Allermuir Guest House

8 2C

27 Downie Terrace
Mrs. Dryden
Phone: (031) 334 1554

A pleasant guest house, this is well
positioned for buses into town and
situated directly opposite the zoo.
All the bedrooms have
hand-basins, heating and duvets;
showers are available at no extra
charge. No evening meals are
available but coffee and
sandwiches are available on
request. There is a car park at the
rear.

3 bedrooms: £6.00 per head,
cooked breakfast included
Reduced rates for children

The Two Firs

8 2C

16 Downie Terrace
Mrs. Maxwell
Phone: (031) 334 4009

This small and agreeable guest house has one room with a shower *en suite,* but the others all have hand-basins, with heating and showers available at no extra cost. There is a television lounge and a car park, and the house is well situated for the zoo and for buses into town. No evening meals are served.

5 bedrooms: £6.00–£7.00 per head, cooked breakfast included
Reduced rates for children

Craigholme Guest House

8 2C

14 Downie Terrace
Mrs. Hennys
Phone: (031) 334 6294

An extremely well-run guest house in which the proprietress goes out of her way to ensure that the guests enjoy their stay. All rooms have a television, hand-basin and heating, and an ironing room and two bathrooms are available at no extra charge. Sandwiches and coffee are available at any time, but no evening meal is served. It is well positioned for buses; there is also a private car park.

8 bedrooms: £7.00 per head, cooked breakfast included

Wentworth House

9 2B

16 Hartington Gardens
Mrs. Hepburn
Phone: (031) 229 6459

This large house is managed with extreme efficiency by a very helpful couple. Televisions and hand-basins are provided in all rooms, and showers and central heating are available at no extra charge. There is an all-night vending machine for tea and coffee, and evening meals, at around £3.00 per head, are available on request. Car parking facilities are provided.

11 bedrooms: £6.00–£7.00 per head, cooked breakfast included
Reduced rates available for children

Kerena Guest House

9 2B

13 Hartington Gardens
Mrs. Peattie
Phone: (031) 229 6752

Set in a quiet cul-de-sac, all rooms here are equipped with kettles, televisions and hand-basins, and the beds have duvets; showers and central heating are included in the tariff. Good evening meals are served at £2.50 per head, and on-street parking is available.

5 bedrooms: £5.50–£6.00 per head, cooked breakfast included
Reduced rates for family rooms

Robertson Guest House

9 2B

5 Hartington Gardens
Mr. Sewell
Phone: (031) 229 2652

This is a well-run establishment with a helpful proprietor who takes some care to ensure that his guests enjoy their stay. The rooms are clean and bright with duvets on all the beds and a television. Central heating is available on request. One bedroom has a private bathroom. No evening meals are served but the breakfast, which includes porridge, is recommended. On-street parking is available.

7 bedrooms: £7.00–£8.50 per head, cooked breakfast included
Reduced rates for family rooms

St. Valery Guest House

9 1B

36 Coates Gardens
Mrs. Shannon
Phone: (031) 337 1893

This is a large, slightly impersonal guest house—efficiently run and reasonably priced. All the rooms have hand-basins and metered gas-fires, with a bathroom on each floor. No evening meals are served.

9 bedrooms: £6.00 per head, cooked breakfast included
Half-price for children

Kingsview Guest House

10 2C

28 Gilmore Place
Mrs. Gibson
Phone: (031) 229 8004

Although rather more expensive than some, this is an extremely pleasant guest house, run by an enthusiastic couple. The rooms, with hand-basins, are clean and bright, and the evening meal, at £4.50 per head, is recommended. There is a television lounge, and a kettle is available; use of the shower is included in the price. Kingsview is two minutes' walk from the King's Theatre and the Lothian Road area, and there is access to a car park.

8 bedrooms: £7.50 per head, cooked breakfast included
Reduced rates for children

Averon Guest House

10 2C

44 Gilmore Place
Mrs. Ellingham
Phone: (031) 229 9932

Run by a young couple who enjoy meeting people, this is a homely and well-run establishment. The rooms are clean and furnished with a mixture of traditional and new items, but none have hand-basins. All the rooms have central heating, and two have tea-making facilities; coffee or tea can be made in the television lounge and an excellent evening meal costing £3.00 per head can be provided. A car park is available.

5 bedrooms: £6.00–£7.00 per head, cooked breakfast included
Reduced rates for children

Gilmore Guest House

10 2C

51 Gilmore Place
Mr. Bain
Phone: (031) 229 5008

A clean, functional and moderately priced guest house. All rooms have hand-basins and there is no extra charge for the use of the shower, but heating in the rooms is metered. There is a television lounge, but no evening meals are provided. Parking is available nearby.

5 bedrooms: £6.00–£6.50 per head, cooked breakfast included

Kinnaird Guest House

10 2C

252 Morrison Street
Mr. Berkengoff
Phone: (031) 229 0992

This is a homely guest house, conveniently situated opposite Haymarket railway station. All rooms have a kettle, television, heating and orthopaedic beds with duvets. The atmosphere is relaxed and welcoming and prices include the use of the showers. No evening meals are served.

6 bedrooms: £6.00–£7.00 per head, cooked breakfast included

North

'Barrosa' Guest House

4 2D

21 Pilrig Street
Mrs. Pretty
Phone: (031) 554 3700

Although clean and run efficiently this guest house is slightly lacking in character. One of the bedrooms has a private shower, and all have hand-basins. Furnishing and decor throughout are standard but functional. No evening meals are served, and there is some private parking available.

7 bedrooms: £6.50–£7.00 per head, cooked breakfast included

'Balmoral' Guest House

4 2D

32 Pilrig Street
Mrs. Hinks
Phone: (031) 554 1857

This is a clean, modern, and extremely likeable guest house. All rooms have central heating and hand-basins, and showers are provided at no extra cost. Each room has tea-making facilities but no evening meals are served. Parking in this area is unrestricted.

6 bedrooms: £6.00 per head, cooked breakfast included

'Marvin' Guest House

4 2D

46 Pilrig Street
Mr. and Mrs. Ross
Phone: (031) 554 6605

A pleasant and well-run establishment which features, in the dining room/television lounge, and an interesting collection of articles from the East. All rooms have central heating and kettles, and two have private showers, at no extra charge. No evening meals are available, and there is unrestricted street parking.

8 bedrooms: £6.00 upwards per head, cooked breakfast included

'Crai Gard'

4 2D

82 Pilrig Street
Mrs. Stephen
Phone: (031) 554 7538

This attractive wood-panelled house, open from April until October, is recommended for its cleanliness and welcoming atmosphere. All rooms have metered heating and two have hand-basins. The use of a shower is included in the price, and a television lounge is available for guests. No evening meals are served. Street parking in this area is unrestricted.

4 bedrooms: £5.50 upwards per head, cooked breakfast included

Balquidder Guest House

4 2D

94 Pilrig Street
Mrs. Ferguson
Phone: (031) 554 3377

This is a small, family-run guest house in peaceful surroundings. It is very clean throughout, pleasantly decorated and a small garden is available for guests. All rooms have hand-basins, duvets on the beds, and metered heating. The dining room has a pleasant outlook over the garden, but no evening meals are served. Unrestricted parking in the street.

8 bedrooms: £6.00 per head, cooked breakfast included

Invertruin Guest House

4 2D

416 Ferry Road
Mrs. McDonald
Phone: (031) 552 4732

This is a small, well-maintained but somewhat characterless guest house. All rooms have hand-basins, kettles (with a supply of tea, coffee and biscuits), electric blankets, and

a portable television is available. The use of a shower is free, and there are reductions for those staying more than two nights. No evening meals are provided. Parking facilities are available.

3 bedrooms (2 double, 1 single): £6.50 per head, cooked breakfast included

Ashlyn Hotel

4 2C

42 Inverleith Row
Mr. Robson
Phone: (031) 552 2954

The proprietor of this successful guest house obviously aims at providing a high standard of service—and succeeds in doing so. The bedrooms and dining room are spotlessly clean and fresh, there is central heating throughout the house, most rooms have hand-basins, and there is no extra fee for a bath. There is a television lounge, all guests have their own key, and tea and toasted sandwiches can be had on request. No evening meals are served. Situated very close to the Royal Botanic Garden, the Ashlyn Hotel is recommended but bedrooms may perhaps be slightly noisy at nights. Unrestricted parking is available in the street.

9 bedrooms: £7.00 single, £13.00 double, cooked breakfast included

Annandale Guest House

4 3D

22 Annandale Street
Mrs. Wilczek
Phone: (031) 556 3392

This is a standard, average-priced guest house in which all the rooms have hand-basins, the use of a shower is included in the price, and tea and coffee are available at most times for a small charge (20 p). No evening meals are served, but parking is available in the street.

6 bedrooms: £5.50–£6.50 per head, cooked breakfast included

'Acacia'

1 3A

553 Queensferry Road
Mrs. Kerr
Phone: (031) 339 6800

All the rooms at the 'Acacia' guest house are excellently maintained and furnished and are equipped with black-and-white televisions. Two rooms have their own toilets and hand-basins, the use of a shower is free, two beds are available for children, and breakfast is served in an attractive breakfast room. The house is open only from April until October, no evening meals are served, and there are ample car parking facilities. Although slightly more expensive than is usual, this guest house is good value for money.

4 bedrooms: £7.50–£8.50 per head, cooked breakfast included

13A

467 Queensferry Road
Mrs. Findlay
Phone: (031) 336 5688

This is a nicely decorated, clean and immaculately kept guest house. Rooms have hand-basins and central heating, with no extra charge for a shower. Although no evening meals are provided, tea is served at 22.00 in the comfortable television lounge/breakfast room. Parking is available in front of the house, which is open only from April till October.

2 rooms: £5.50 per head, cooked breakfast included

East

---

12 2C

53 Milton Road West
Mrs. Laing
Phone: (031) 669 3646

Run by an enthusiastic landlady who keeps her bungalow in immaculate order as well as providing a noticeably welcoming atmosphere for guests, this guest house can be recommended. Both of the twin-bedded rooms are equipped with hand-basins, electric blankets and duvets. No evening meals are served but coffee and biscuits are provided at night on request. There is a large lounge, and a huge garden, but no facilities for young children. Private parking is available.

2 bedrooms: £6.00 per head, cooked breakfast included

---

12 2C

76 Milton Road West
Mrs. I. Hendry
Phone: (031) 669 1894

Of the three bedrooms provided by this extremely helpful landlady two have hand-basins, all are centrally heated, and there is no extra charge for the use of a shower. The dining room, originally built onto the house as a sun room, is warm and bright, and there is a homely television lounge. No evening meals are provided, and there is a private parking attached to the house.

3 bedrooms: £6.00 per head, cooked breakfast included

---

12 2D

4 Duddingston Crescent
Milton Road
Mrs. Addison
Phone: (031) 669 3390

This is a pleasant Victorian house situated opposite the Portobello golf course, on the main A1 road to Berwick-on-Tweed. The wood-panelled interior is impressive and, in general, in good condition. There are two large family rooms to let—both clean and tidy—and a large television lounge. Both rooms have views onto the golf course. Children under-ten are charged half-price and the landlady is happy to baby-sit for her guests. Private parking is available, as well as a large garden which guests can use. No evening meals are served.

2 bedrooms: £6.00 per head, cooked breakfast included

Drumore Guest House

---

11 1B

82 Willowbrae Road
Mrs. Munro
Phone: (031) 661 4349

This clean, well-run guest house with a bright and homely dining room is centrally heated throughout. All rooms have hand-basins, a television, duvets and electric blankets. There is a small extra charge for a shower (10p), and although no evening meals are provided tea and coffee are available from Mrs. Munro. A 'high chair' is available for children. Car parking is on the street.

5 bedrooms: £6.50 per head, cooked breakfast included

Caravans and Camping

Edinburgh's climate is not always ideal for camping or caravaning holidays, but they do represent a cheap way of visiting the city—particularly for families. The sites are not always heavily booked but those wishing to visit in July or August are advised to make reservations in advance. There are four main sites around Edinburgh in which the average price for a caravan (including car and passengers) is about £4.00 per night, and for a two-person tent (including car) about £2.50 per night. These prices vary according to the month and the particular site.

Little France Caravan Park

---

18 2C

219 Old Dalkeith Road
on A68, south of Edinburgh
Phone: (031) 664 4742

Touring caravans; motor caravans; tents

This site opposite Liberton golf course has space for 140 caravans and 300 tents. Facilities include toilets, showers, a launderette, playing field, public telephone and a post box. There is a bus service into town every ten minutes. No dogs are allowed.
Open April 1–September 30.
Credit cards are not accepted.

Mortonhall Caravan Site

16 3C

*30 Frogston Road East
off A720, south of Edinburgh
Phone: (031) 664 1533*

Touring caravans; motor caravans; tents

This is the best-equipped of Edinburgh's camping sites, with space for 350 caravans and 50 tents. Facilities include toilets, showers, power points, washing machines, a children's playground, television room, shop, snack bar, cafe, lounge bar, amusement arcade, public telephones and a post box. Dogs are allowed provided that they are kept on a lead. No camp fires are allowed.

Open:March 21–October 31.
Barclaycard/Visa is accepted.

Municipal Caravan Site

2 1C

*Marine Drive
off A90 north of Edinburgh
Phone: (031) 336 6874,
advance booking (031) 225
2424 ext. 6635*

Touring caravans; motor caravans; tents

This site has easy access to the beaches north of the city. There is a space for 250 caravans and 50 tents, and facilities include toilets, shower, a shop, public telephone and a daily postal collection. There is a launderette 100 yards (91 m) from the site, and the Commodore Hotel, with restaurants and bars, is nearby. Dogs are allowed provided that they are kept on a lead. No camp fires are allowed.

Open:April 1–September 20.
Credit cards are not accepted.

Pentland Park Marine Ltd

20 2C

*New Pentland, Loanhead
on A701 Peebles road, south of
Edinburgh
Phone: (031) 440 0697*

Touring caravans; motor caravans; tents

This caravan park on the edge of the Pentland Hills has 287 dual-purpose sites. Facilities include toilets, showers, a launderette, shop, public telephone and a post box. No camp

fires are permitted on the site. Dogs are allowed provided that they are kept on a lead.
Open:April 1–October 31.
Credit cards are not accepted.

Youth Hostels

Youth Hostels and YMCA's not only provide low-priced accommodation but a variety of services invaluable to those travelling on a low budget––such as meals, self-catering facilities, baths, laundries, television and games rooms, luggage storage, and booking services for other hostels.

Prices vary between £4.00 and £5.00 per night depending on age, the type of accommodation offered and the membership fee. For general information contact:

The Scottish Youth Hostel Association

10 2C

*161 Warrender Park Road
Phone: (031) 229 8660*

Hostels

Bruntsfield Youth Hostel

10 2C

*7 Bruntsfield Terrace
Phone: (031) 447 2464*

Eglinton Youth Hostel

9 1B

*17 Eglinton Crescent
Phone: (031) 337 1120*

There is separate accommodation at both hostels for men and women. Membership is required but can be obtained at the hostel. There is no age limit for membership; credit cards are not accepted.

Young Men's Christian Association (YMCA)

10 1C

*14 South St. Andrew Street
Phone: (031) 556 4304*

There is separate accommodation for men and women up to the age of 25. Membership is not required; American Express and YIEE credit cards are accepted.

Young Women's Christian Association of Great Britian (YWCA)

10 1C

*Hostel: 4 Randolph Place
Phone: (031) 225 1875*

Accommodation for women only––up to the age of 25. Membership is not required; credit cards are not accepted.

Young Women's Christian Association of Scotland (YWCA)

4 2D

*Office: 5 Casselbank Street
Phone: (031) 553 1943*

9 1B

*Hostel: 13–14 Coates Crescent
Phone: (031) 225 3771*

Accommodation for women only. No age limit for visitors, but resident single women must be between 16 and 35. Membership is not required; credit cards are not accepted.

Restaurants

Every chef in Scotland has an enormous advantage over his

colleagues in other countries. He can choose from sea-fresh sole, turbot and shellfish, trout and salmon straight from the river, an abundance of game, and beef of the highest quality––ingredients that hold the promise of a dinner to remember.

Unfortunately, Edinburgh's restaurants do not, with a few exceptions, realize this potential. Judged by the highest standards, food tends to be bland, with undistinguished sauces and vegetables that are nearly always overcooked; though on a more positive note, service is invariably courteous, friendly and efficient. However there are a number of restaurants that will be appreciated by the majority, and these are listed below. A star (★) indicates that in the opinion of our reviewers a restaurant has achieved an unusually high standard of cuisine, service, decor and value for money.

Each restaurant has been visited on a number of occasions, and the list below represents a personal selection by our reviewers. Standards, however, vary and we would be delighted to include readers' opinions and suggestions for additional listings in next year's edition of *Edinburgh*. Please write to:

the Restaurants Editor
Harpers Handbooks
Noel Collins Publishing Ltd
2 Dundonald Street
Edinburgh EH3
Scotland

The Anatolian

9 2B

13 Dalry Road
Phone: (031) 346 0204

In the warm atmosphere of this Turkish restaurant you will find some exotic and fascinating dishes to tempt you. The traditional Middle Eastern starter—meze—is a mixture of hot and cold and is very ample; there are splendid aubergine fritters; mussels and parsley fried in batter served on skewers; or borek, the spinach and feta stuffed filo pastry-pockets. More substantial courses like the varieties of kebabs, Anatolian lamb; lamb stew are delicious. If you do not want a straight two- or three-course meal you can just choose exactly what you want to have from any part of the menu and make up your own choice. For a syrupy finish try the honey cakes, baclava or kataifi and some good, strong, sweet Turkish coffee.

Open: Monday to Sunday
Last Orders: 22.30

Credit Cards: Barclaycard/Visa/American Express/Diners Club

Meal for 2, incl. drinks, service and VAT—under £22.00

Bernard's

10 1C

20 Abercromby Place
Phone: (031) 556 2270

Bernard's offers the most imaginative menu of any French restaurant in Edinburgh in comfortable and conventional surroundings. The menu reflects the real variety and interest of good French food and the cliches of French food in Britain are, thankfully, absent. Among the starters there is crêpe palais royale—two generous pancakes stuffed with asparagus, ham and mushrooms; garlicky frogs legs cooked in provençale style; escargots in wine and herb sauce and Mediterranean fish soup. Fish dishes include three small red mullet flambeed in Pernod; or fresh crayfish grilled in parsley butter. The speciality of the house is souffle in various forms, including avocado with seafood and lobster, which arrive light, fluffy and perfectly risen—an ambitious test of cooking art and a delight for those sampling it. Vegetables of the day are fresh, young and never frozen. For dessert try the coupé glacée Brêsilienne (for two people), an extravagant and mouth-watering dessert of a fresh half pineapple filled with lemon sorbet meringue and fresh strawberry.

Open: Monday to Saturday
Last Orders: 23.30 Lunch: 14.15

Credit Cards: Barclaycard/Visa/Access/Mastercard/Eurocard/Carte Blanche

Meal for 2, incl. wine, service and VAT—under £34.00

Chez Julie

2 3B

110 Raeburn Place
Phone: (031) 332 2827

Children are made welcome in this excellent value-for-money French restaurant. Do not expect particularly elegant decor but it is pleasant, with modern pine furniture and shopfront windows. The menu is short but appetizing: deep-fried whitebait; ratatouille niçoise and marvellous home-made pâté. Main courses like the duck à l'orange, cooked to perfection in a delicate sauce, or trout with cream and shrimp sauce are well-worth a try. There are plenty of continental cheeses and fresh desserts along with a modest wine list.

Open: Tuesday to Saturday
Lunches: Monday to Saturday
Last Orders: Tuesday to Thursday 22.00
Friday and Saturday 22.30
Lunch: 14.00

Credit Cards: None

Meal for 2, incl. wine, service and VAT—under £20.00

Ristorante Cosmo

10 1C

58a Castle Street
Phone: (031) 226 6743

An unostentatious and comfortable Italian restaurant with traditional Mediterranean dishes. The decor may be a bit dull but the filet mignon makes up for it—tender and beautifully cooked. Other than steak there is a range of good, well-deserved chicken and seafood dishes. The desserts and starters, although conventional, are attractive and tasty. The wines range from a moderate Valpolicella to château bottled. The service, as in many Italian restaurants, is friendly and good-humoured; regular customers are welcomed like old friends, and children are not barred or treated like monsters.

Open: Tuesday to Saturday
Last Orders: 22.15

Credit Cards: Barclaycard/Visa/Access/Mastercard/Eurocard

Meal for 2, incl. wine, service and VAT—under £32.00

Cramond Inn

11A

*30 Cramond Glebe Road,
Cramond*
Phone: (031) 336 2035

Good, plain cooking with no frills or fancy sauces: here you will find British food at its best with a Scottish flavour. The setting is cosy and comfortable, busy and popular, and rather like an inn. The speciality of the house is crab soup which really does taste like fresh crab; there are large, juicy prawns wrapped in slices of smoked salmon; and for main course is a range of simple, well-cooked choices of roast duck, pheasant, chicken and steak. The vegetables and desserts are a bit disappointing but adequate.

Open: Monday to Saturday
Last Orders: 22.00 Lunch: 14.00

Credit Cards: Barclaycard/Visa/
Access/Mastercard/Eurocard/
American Express/Diners Club

Meal for 2, incl. wine, service and
VAT—under £25.00

Crêperie Francaise

101C ★

8a Grindlay Street
Phone: (031) 229 5405

A restaurant run by French rugby fanatics does not sound like a recipe for success but the finished product is French food as it tastes in France, not its British substitute. It is a friendly, casual place with photos of rugby players on the walls. The food is not limited to crêpes: for starters there are also garlic snails, onion vol-au-vent and salade niçoise. Fish dishes include tantalizing moules marinière and scampi au Ricard; the filet de porc Façon du Chef is the best on the meat menu and the vegetables are originally and deliciously cooked.

Open: Monday to Saturday
Last Orders: 22.00

Credit Cards: Access/Mastercard/
Eurocard

Meal for 2, incl. wine, service and
VAT—under £25.00

Denzlers

101C

80 Queen Street
*Phone: (031) 226 5467 or (031)
226 5227*

No thrills but no disasters either in this high standard but unadventurou Swiss restaurant—it's perfect for those who want to play safe and for vehement non-smokers who will find a smokers and non-smokers area clearly defined. The food is conservative: starters are mainly from a cold selection that includes seafood and Swiss specialities like air-dried ham. The most interesting main courses are roast saddle of hare in piquant sauce with pears or a fondue Bourguignonne (for more than two people). The coffee is excellent and there is a choice of Swiss liqueurs and cigars and an impressive range of more than 90 European wines from £3.30 a bottle upwards.

Open: Monday to Sunday
Last Orders: 22.00

Credit Cards: None
Cheques over £50.00 by prior arrangement only

Meal for 2, incl. wine, service and
VAT—under £25.00

Dragon Pearl

43D

20 Union Place
Phone: (031) 556 4547

A well-established, reliable and popular Cantonese where large parties benefit by big helpings and a huge variety of dishes. Starters include tasty wafer-paper prawns, dumplings with roast pork and oyster sauce filling, roast turnip cake and tiny spare ribs. There is an impressive number of main dishes: crab in ginger sauce (hard work but worth it); renowned lemon chicken; various meats and vegetables in black bean sauce are some. It is licensed but pots of jasmine tea are served throughout the meal by waiters who are sometimes a bit off-hand but very efficient. The decor is very basic and informal.

Open: Monday to Sunday
Last Orders: 01.00

Credit Cards: None

Meal for 2, incl. drinks, service and
VAT—under £14.00

Edinburgh Rendezvous
(Peking Restaurant)

101C

10a Queensferry Street
*Phone: Reservations
(031) 225 3777*

The atmosphere in this 'authentic

Peking-style restaurant' is low-key but pleasant. The decor is clean and plain, with cream tablecloths, olive-green walls, and fairly bright lighting. Recommended dishes from the extensive menu include, for starters, dried scallop and greens, and among the main courses, deep fried shredded beef with chilli sauce, sweet and sour pork rendezvous, and scampi Peking-style. Service, in comparison with many Chinese restaurants, is noticeably polite and helpful, with meals served promptly. Large parties (20–40) are catered for, and meals for groups and families are a popular feature here. The wine list is quite extensive, but perhaps rather pricey. Chinese liqueurs etc. are available. This restaurant is busy at weekends and early evenings so it is best to book in advance.

Open: Tuesday to Sunday Lunches:
12.00–14.00
Last Orders: 23.00

Credit Cards: Barclaycard/Visa/
American Express/Diners Club

Meal for 2, incl. drinks, service and
VAT—under £15.00

The Engine Room

101C

7–8 Queensferry Street
Phone: (031) 225 2142

One of Edinburgh's newest night-spots where you can have a full dinner—or just a drink at the bar like an ordinary pub. Main course dishes include lemon fish tart, navarin of lamb and lobster; there is a selection of cheeses, pâtés and traditional Scottish desserts that are worth trying and generally the food is simply cooked but tasty. Alternatively customers can eat a rare beef sandwich, game pâté, or a plate of prawns in the bar while they listen to the resident jazz and blues pianists.

Open: Monday to Saturday
Last Orders: 23.30 Lunch: 14.30

Credit Cards: American Express/
Barclaycard/Visa/Diners Club

Meal for 2, incl. wine, service and
VAT—under £18.00

Houston House

192A

*Uphall,
West Lothian*
Phone: (0506) 853831

A pretty country house with the

right ingredients for an attractive and civilized eating place. It is formal and efficient but, equally, friendly and pleasant. The food is made from good, wholesome ingredients and presented swiftly on Royal Doulton china. The accent on rich food with lots of cream and butter is perhaps a bit strong but dishes like mousse piped with sorrel mayonnaise and decorated with caviar, or spinach sautéed with pine kernels are absolutely delicious. There is a good, and unusual, selection of Scottish cheeses like Caboc and Orkney and the wine list is thick as a book.

Open: Monday to Sunday
Last Orders: 21.00

Credit Cards: American Express

Meal for 2, incl. wine, service and VAT—under £26.00
£10.50 for set 5-course meal exceptionally good value

Howtowdie

9 1B

27a Stafford Street
Phone: (031) 225 6291

Definitely not for the young and down-at-heel—it is subdued and expensive and one of the city's prestige restaurants. Scottish cuisine is the speciality and some interesting recipes date back to the time of the arrival of Mary, Queen of Scots with her French, and food-conscious, entourage. Luxurious dishes include quail in champagne sauce, rainbow trout in Chablis and duck in heather honey. There are some elegant adjuncts too such as the pre-meal cocktails (on the house) and champagne sorbet served between the hors d'oeuvres and entrée to clear the palate. Some dishes may fail to live up to their full promise and the desserts are a little unimaginative. The wine list is extensive.

Open: Monday to Saturday
Last Orders: 22.30 Lunch: 14.00

Credit Cards: All accepted

Meal for 2, incl. wine, service and VAT—under £40.00
À la carte or table d'hôte menus from £8.75

Kobe's

10 1C

15a Castle Street
Phone: (031) 225 5869

Kobe's is a bit difficult to find, hidden in the basement under Pizzaland, but it's worth a visit. The decor is relaxing and candlelit which creates an intimate and pleasant atmosphere. The service is cheerful and friendly. There is an extensive menu but the smoked-salmon pâté at £1.40 and the home-made soup both stand out as excellent and good value for money. Steaks are cooked and served on special cast-iron individual grills which give a touch of glamour to an otherwise ordinary but adequate steak. The steak with a mixed bean salad alongside makes a meal in itself. The desserts are imaginative.

Open: Monday to Saturday
Last Orders: 22.00

Credit Cards: Access/Mastercard/ Eurocard/American Express/ Diners Club

Meal for 2, incl. wine, service and VAT—under £16.00

Madogs

10 1C

38a George Street
Phone: (031) 225 3408

Clear, crisp, cool American efficiency with photographs of Hollywood stars on the walls, pop music for background noise and the best American food to eat. At lunchtime there is an interesting and relatively inexpensive menu of snack-type specialities—try the hot turkey sandwich with stuffing, cranberry sauce and gravy. In the evenings the meals are similarly American-based but a recent innovation has been Mexican food which is very hot and full of dangerous chillies. The service is friendly and attentive—iced water, in the true American fashion, is brought to your table. And the exotic cocktails at the bar are certainly worth a try.

Open: Monday to Sunday
Last Orders: 23.30 Sunday: 22.30, snacks only

Credit Cards: Barclaycard/Visa/ Access/Mastercard/Eurocard/ American Express

Meal for 2, incl. drinks, service and VAT—under £15.00

Mermans

4 3C

10 Eyre Place
Phone: (031) 556 1177

Edinburgh's leading fish restaurant is small, intimate and crowded with room for only 20 or 30 people, so booking is essential. You enter the restaurant through the wine bar, where some excellent bar-food is available. The menu is based on four or five set variations although there is a dependence on what is available in season. The oysters, which are Scottish, are excellent, the moules marinière noteworthy; and monkfish in sweet and sour sauce delicious. The house white wine is crisp and dry but inclined to be overpriced for what it is so it is worthwhile exploring the rest of the wine list.

Open: Tuesday to Sunday Lunches: Tuesday to Friday
Last Orders: Tuesday to Saturday 23.00 Lunch: 13.45
Sunday 21.30

Credit Cards: Barclaycard/Visa/ Access/Mastercard/Eurocard/ American Express/Diners Club Discount of 5 percent for cash/ cheque

Meal for 2, incl. wine, service and VAT—under £20.00

Milanos

10 1C   ★

7 Victoria Street
Phone: (031) 226 5260

One of the few Italian restaurants in Edinburgh to have a truly Italian character, this probably has the best trattoria cooking in the city. The service is welcoming and the atmosphere very friendly. Particularly recommended are the pasta dishes—the gnocci, served either with chilli sauce or without; and the tagliatelli de la casa. The veal dishes are a speciality and the meat is exceptionally tender. The carafes are unfortunately not as generous as one might expect from the attitude of the proprietor. But Romeo y Julietta cigars are offered at the end of a meal.

Open: Monday to Saturday
Last Orders: 23.00 Lunch: 14.30

Credit Cards: Barclaycard/Visa/ American Express/Diners Club

Meal for 2, incl. drinks, service and VAT—under £30.00

Phoenix Chinese Restaurant

10 2C

95 Gilmore Place
Phone: (031) 229 4655

A great attraction of this restaurant is that it is very near the King's Theatre and many of the city's main cinemas—and it stays open late. The food is wholesome and well-prepared but the dishes are not over-inspiring. The dim sim (chinese dumpling) menu is limited and includes roast pork dumpling that is tasty, and fried paper prawns, wrapped in a fried flaky-casing. Steamed pork ribs, though not very meaty, are served in a well-flavoured black bean sauce; chicken and chinese mushrooms arrive in a sauce that allows the taste of the mushrooms to the fore. There are a number of set menus but for some inexplicable reason the price per person of the set menus goes up as the number in the party increases.

Open: Monday to Sunday
Last Orders: 01.00

Credit Cards: None

Meal for 2, incl. drinks, service and VAT—under £14.00

The Pompadour Room

10 1C   ★

Caledonian Hotel
Princes Street
Phone: (031) 225 2433

The restaurant's namesake would not have felt out of place in this sumptuous dining room in one of the city's top hotels. The decor is ornate and elegant and the food is of a faultlessly high standard. There is a tempting menu offering the best French haute cuisine using the best quality Scottish ingredients. Served as a starter the salad of the day is simple but perfect and has the splendid addition of warm scallops. Or there is a magnificent cream of lobster soup to savour. For entrees try venison in walnut sauce or, if you can wait for the 40 minutes it takes to prepare, the carre d'agneau (for two) is tender, lightly seasoned and beautifully presented. Vegetables are cooked to perfection and have a few surprises like the unusual 'nuttie tatties'—croquets covered with almonds. There is a fine range of French cheeses and tempting desserts like profiteroles, tiny tart plums, pears in wine and poached peaches with whisky sabayon.

Open: Monday to Saturday
Last Orders: 23.45

Credit Cards: Barclaycard/Visa/Access/Mastercard/Eurocard/American Express/Diners Club

Meal for 2, incl. wine, service and VAT—under £42.00

La Potiniere

20 1C   ★

Main Street
Gullane
Phone (0620) 843214

This is an extremely popular restaurant run by two former Glasgow art students who are very concerned with presentation of each individual dish and the structure of the whole meal. They do only set meals and booking is essential (Saturday evenings are booked for the next two years!) but it is possible to get a table for week-day lunch if you ring a few days in advance. There are no lunches on Wednesdays and Saturdays. The eating house is 40 minutes drive from Edinburgh and holds only 25 people. Soup is always the first course and is excellent—tomato and mint, chestnut or fish served in large tureens and always accompanied by croutons and cream. The next course is light such as a courgette souffle or turkey souffle with stilton sauce and the main course perhaps a bit more ordinary than the rest—steak on a bed of rice with ratatouille; or breast of chicken stuffed with pâté. Salads with chicory and fennel are standard and brie with a slice of apple comes before the desserts. These are small but good—like crème brûlée or chocolate mousse. Altogether it's a place to enjoy the food in a plainly decorated room based on a French country restaurant.

Open: Monday to Saturday Lunches
Monday to Friday
Last Orders 22.00 Lunch 13.00

Credit Cards: None

Meal for 2 incl wine, service and VAT—under £26.00

Prestonfield House

11 3A   ★

Priestfield Road
Phone (031) 667 8000

Put shortly you will find excellent food in superby surroundings here. The house has a 16th century frontage worked by the masons of the Palace of Holyroodhouse, peacocks calling in the gardens, calm and elegant decor and you can eat in the 17th century gallery which has some of the finest plaster-work in Scotland. The food, made from fresh and good ingredients (vegetables from their own market garden) is classic French and European alongside traditional Scottish dishes. The menu and wine list are extensive. Particularly noteworthy dishes are the smoked haddock mousse, avocado salad with stilton dressing served with an unusual pickled aubergine and celery salad and Highland casserole, a venison stew. The dessert trolley is exceptional. Coffee and petits fours are served upstairs in a room hung with tapestries and there is a fire in the winter.

Open: Monday to Sunday Last Orders Monday to Saturday 21.30 Sunday 20.30 Lunch 13.30

Credit cards: All accepted

Meal for 2, incl. wine, service and VAT—under £28.00 Sundays: Table d'hôte menu £11.40 incl. VAT

Shamiana

10 2C

14 Brougham Street
Phone (031) 229 5578

This is a smart but not stuffy restaurant with reliably good, wholesome Indian food. The specialities are tandoori and kashmiri recipes like chicken tikka and lamb shashlik. If some dishes are too hot there is a variety of milder curries to choose from like rogham josh, murgh musallam with accompaniments of fresh nan (indian bread), spinach and curd, chutneys and side-dishes. For dessert try the fresh mango or kulfi (indian ice-cream with pistachios). The decor is cool, but welcoming, with modern furniture, pink tablecloths, elegant cutlery and china and Batik paintings on the walls. The service is attentive but dignified.

Open: Monday to Saturday
Last Orders 23.30

Credit Cards: All accepted

Meal for 2, incl. drinks, service and VAT—under £16.00

Skippers

5 1A

la Dock Place
Leith
Phone: (031) 554 1018

Stuffed shirts are out but it is essential to book at this bistro restaurant that is tucked away in the heart of dockland Leith. It used to be a pub frequented by boat captains (hence the name) and was then derelict for some years. An enterprising art student used it as a studio for a while and then decided to convert it to a bistro adding old Scottish tables and chairs and a traditional bar gantry. The seafood is all fresh from the town's fish market and there is some inventive as well as traditional cooking: sole stuffed with mussels in white wine and pernod sauce, crab salad, fried cod-roes for starters. It is all well-made and good value for money.

Open: Tuesday to Saturday
Lunches: Monday to Saturday
Last Orders: 23.00 Lunch: 14.00

Credit Cards: None

Meal for 2, incl. wine, service and VAT—under £15.00

The Verandah

9 2B

17 Dalry Road
Phone: (031) 337 5828

A high-quality Indian restaurant which could hold its head high in any city. Potted plants, dimmed lights, low-key sitar music and rush matting make it a far cry from the dark plush atmosphere of the average Indian curry-house. There is a range of tandoori specialities and varied curries like methi gust (lamb with fenugreek), or murgi massallam (chicken marinated in spices, mixed with a special sauce and grilled). The accompaniments include the usual Indian breads raita (yogurt with spices and cucumber), and some superb vegetable dishes and two kinds of dahl (lentils)—so the vegetarian could eat comfortably here. There is a wider choice of desserts than usual—an exotic fruit salad, home-made ice-cream and some Indian specialities too. The portions tend to be a bit small but staff are helpful and the menu sets out an interesting guide to those unfamiliar with Indian food.

Open: Monday to Saturday Last Orders: 23.45 Lunch 14.30

Credit Cards: All accepted

Meal for 2 incl. drinks, service and VAT—under £15.00

Vitos

10 1C

55a Frederick Street
Phone: (031) 225 5052

A strong Mediterranean flavour all round: the food served on earthenware; whitewashed walls and shuttered windows and basic wooden furniture but, nevertheless is smart. The largely Italian menu is flexible and interesting. You can start with pasta or pizza and go on to meat; or have a lighter start, like parma ham or stracciatella soup. Fettucine d'Alfredo—egg and spinach noodles served in a cream, ham and garlic sauce—is delectable. An equally good but less filling alternative is linguini with clams, tomato and white wine. The portions are very generous and the choice of desserts, which include profiteroles and extremely tempting gâteaux, is wide.

Open: Monday to Saturday
Last Orders:23.30 Lunch: 14.30

Credit Cards: Barclaycard/ Visa/ Access/Mastercard/Eurocard/ American Express

Meal for 2, incl. wine, service and VAT—under £28.00

Cheap Eats

Nothing is really cheap these days but the eating places recommended in this section will not leave an enormous hole in your pocket. Remember, however, that although a 'snack' will certainly cost you less than a full-scale meal more often than not it can represent bad value for money. In Edinburgh, lunch is mainly the best bet, for as night-time descends on the city, so prices soar correspondingly.

Salads, home-made soups and hot snacks

The Calton Studios

10 1D

Calton Road

Open: morning, afternoon and early evening
Licensed

Clarinda's

10 1D

Canongate

Open: morning and afternoon

Ecbatin

10 1C

Grassmarket

Open; morning and afternoon

The Grassmarket

10 1D

Jeffrey Street

Open: morning and afternoon

Henderson's Salad Table

10 1C

Hanover Street

Open: all day
Licensed

The Laird's Larder

10 1C

Victoria Street

Opening: morning and afternoon

Steaks and hamburgers

Bell's Diner

4 3C

7 St. Stephen Street

Open: all day

Pizza and pasta

Bar Calimero

9 1B

1-3 Grosvenor Street

Open: all day
Licensed

Bar Italia

10 1C

100 Lothian Road

Open: all day
Licensed

Dario's

10 1C

87 Lothian Road

Open: all day
Licensed

Pizzaland

10 1C

15 Castle Street

Open: all day
Licensed

More adventurous

Ossama's Egyptian Cafe

10 2D

53 West Nicholson Street

Open: all day

The Turkish Doner Inn

10 2C

17a Brougham Place

Open: evenings

Pubs

Edinburgh's many and varied pubs are an obvious attraction for both visitors and residents. The former are often surprised by the choice available, as it is often thought that the pub is a peculiarly English institution. There are pubs and bars to suit every taste, ranging from smart cocktail haunts and wine bars to traditional workingman's pubs, in which the authentic Edinburgh atmosphere can be absorbed.

In common with the rest of the Britain, Edinburgh's pubs are governed by licensing laws, though local adaptations can sometimes puzzle the uninitiated. Standard weekday opening times are from 11.00 to 14.30 and from 17.00 to 23.00 (Sundays 12.30 to 14.30 and 18.30 to 23.00), but these can be shortened at the landlord's discretion. Some pubs close an hour earlier in the evening, while, particularly during the summer, a number have all-day or late-night licenses. There are approximately 100 such pubs in the city, particularly in its popular drinking areas. these include Tollcross, the Grassmarket and the High Street, Rose Street, Stockbridge and Leith.

The two traditional Scottish drinks are whisky and beer. As far as the latter is concerned, Edinburgh has a long and honourable tradition of brewing. the reason for this is the existence of an underground lake beneath the Old Town. Stretching from Fountainbridge to Holyrood and out to Craigmillar, the lake's water is rich in gypsum. This magic ingredient is said to give Edinburgh's beer its special flavour. Among the best-known local brews are McEwan's 80/-, Younger's IPA, Maclay, Belhaven, Greenmantle and the rare Traquair House ale. The last is sold only in bottles.

Over 70 Edinburgh pubs now sell real ale, while every worthwhile bar in the city offers a range of whiskies. The pubs in this guide have been selected as a representative sample of the best the city has to offer in terms of atmosphere, good drink and good service.

The Abbotsford

10 1C

3 Rose Street

The Abbotsford is one of a group of three pubs near the east end of Princes Street worth visiting, the other two being the Cafe Royal and the Guildford Arms. As one of Rose Street's few surviving traditional pubs, it is distinguished by a large hand-curved island bar, an intricate plasterwork ceiling and benched seating around some solid wooden tables. Service is good, prices average, and the lunches excellent. A mixed clientele of all ages and occupations drink here; the atmosphere is genuinely convivial.

The Antiquary

4 3C

72 St. Stephen Street

The Antiquary's clientele is almost exclusively young and the latest fashions in clothes, make-up and hairstyles crowd the bar. A colourful bar, spacious and comfortable, it has a separate games room which contains a formidable array of pinball machines against which the youth of Stockbridge pit their wits. A wide selection of beers is sold, the juke box is excellent and, although the prices are fairly high, the service has recently improved.

Open : all day

Athletic Arms

9 2B

1 Angle Park Terrace

Devotees call this pub 'the Diggers', a reference to the grave-diggers who traditionally drank here after labouring at funerals across the road. What sets this bar apart from others is the superb quality of its cask-conditioned McEwan's 80/- ale which some drinkers believe is the best beer in Scotland. Another feature of this pub is the speed with which you are served, even at the busiest periods. Despite its determinedly working-class appearance, it is generally peopled with a wide variety of drinkers who create, with the help of the 80/- ale, a likeable and gregarious atmosphere.

The Bailie

4 3C

2 St. Stephen Street

For several years the Bailie has been one of this area's most consistently popular pubs. Located around the large island bar are drinkers of all descriptions, with a sprinkling of antique dealers, teachers, students, and fashionably dressed women. Service is good, the general standard of cleanliness is high and a wide range of spirits and beers is sold. The lunches are excellent and, since the pub has an all-day licence, you can savour a quiet afternoon drink there after your meal. No games or music.

Open: all day

Bannerman's

10 1D

53 Niddrie Street, Cowgate

A comparatively recent addition to the Edinburgh pub-scene, the decor of Bannerman's is distinguished by an almost genuine feeling of antiquity. Stone-flagged floors, bare stone walls, some tasteful hanging baskets of ferns, a coal fire in winter, and a cool spot for a summer evening's drink combine to make this cellar-type bar a popular, if slightly exclusive, haunt. There is Burton's real ale on tap, and live folk music on occasions.

The Bay Horse

5 2A

63 Henderson Street

Bars in Leith can be eccentric and the Bay Horse has its share of eccentricity. Basically, however, it is an ordinary workingman's pub. It is clean, the service is excellent and the clientele is always ready to chat with strangers. By custom, the bar is divided into two—one section for couples and ladies, the other for 'others'.

Bennet's Bar

10 2C

8 Leven Street

Bennet's is a must for lovers of the traditional trappings of the Scottish pub. Famed for its spectacular interior, featuring mirrors, tiles, and stained glass, the generally high quality of service and beer, and its wide range of malt whiskies, Bennet's is frequented by students, businessmen, residents, and tourists. It is very crowded at times, so it is worth visiting early or at lunchtimes, when real Scottish pub lunches are served.

The Black Bull

10 1C

12 Grassmarket

Though this is a modern bar, the decor tries hard to capture tradition, with plush red velour, imitation brass lamps, multi-level seating, juke box, salad bar, and a frontage of plate glass emblazoned with bulls' heads. The clientele is mainly young and it is one of the most popular Grassmarket pubs. The food (available all day) is recommended, there is live jazz on a Tuesday night, and Maclay's real ale is sold. Good service, but the pub can become extremely busy.

The Burke & Hare

10 2C

2 High Riggs

Known mainly in recent years as a 'go-go' (i.e. 'topless') pub, the Burke & Hare is in the process of changing its image by introducing live music every night of the week. Dancers still perform at lunchtimes and afternoons, drawing labourers, office-workers, and inquisitive visitors from far-flung parts of Scotland into this small but efficiently run pub. The range of drinks is standard, but the Guinness is treated with care.

The Cafe Royal

10 1C

17 West Register Place

This enormous and spectacular Victorian bar is one of the city's most famous pubs. Despite such drawbacks as slow service and less than perfect toilet facilities, it continues to rank high for its character and charm. A note-worthy feature is the tiled mural around the walls, this was made originally for the Great Exhibition of 1851, and is extremely valuable.

The Calton Studios

10 1D

24-26 Calton Road

Calton Studios is a privately run multi-arts centre with a bar, a cinema, a function room, a restaurant, regular live music, and exhibition facilities. It provides a pleasant oasis in drab Calton Road, and although slightly out of the way, it is well patronized and certainly worth visiting. The bar/restaurant is spacious and decorated in Habitat style, service is good, and, as an added bonus, you can take your drinks into the cinema with you.

Canny Man's (Volunteer Arms)

10 3C

237 Morningside Road

The Canny Man's had the distinction of being the first pub to introduce 'go-go' dancers to Edinburgh. However, the days of the dancers are over and the pub's main claim to interest now lies in the extraordinary interior, which is crammed with more junk and bric-a-brac than you would find in half a dozen attics. Consisting of several rooms, two bars, about a dozen gaming machines, space invaders, and an old Wurlitzer juke box, it is popular with local youths and bikers. Service is quite good, but the beer is unremarkable.

Captain's Bar

10 1D

4 South College Street

A genuine Edinburgh local in the old tradition, this bar's name is the inspiration for its nautical decoration. Stained-glass windows showing old sailing ships, original gas-fittings, a very old bar and gantry, and a devoted group of hearty revellers lend this bar a charm which is sadly lacking in so many others in the area. Late-night singing rattles the windows as closing time approaches.

Central Bar

4 2D

7 Leith Walk

At the very bottom of Leith Walk stands the Central Bar. Originally this was part of the old Leith railway station, but, despite its cavernous interior, it is nevertheless a pub of character the owners having made an effort to preserve much of its Victorian identity. A popular workingman's bar, it sells a good pint, offers live music, and various games'such as pool, darts, dominoes, plus 'go-go' dancing.

Charlie Parker's

10 1C

37a George Street

Bar, restaurant, disco, cocktails, expensive pints of lager, marble table-tops, smoked-glass windows, models standing here and there among the palm-fronds, barmaids with pencil skirts, barmen with pencil moustaches, Charlie Parker's is pleasant for lunch and a suitable place to attract wealthy partners, lascivious glances, and to run up an overdraft. Popular, fashionable, but nevertheless likeable.

Clancy's

9 2B

174 Dundee Street

Dundee Street is not everyone's idea of heaven and apart from the Athletic Arms along the road there are few pubs around here where you can feel at home. Clancy's was obviously created in response to this need and responds with an Irish mock-Tudor aplomb. The only complaint is that the bar is at least 50 percent overfurnished, with assorted horse-brasses and items of copperware but it is comfortable with friendly service.

The Claret Jug

4 3C

34 Great King Street

This bar, situated in the basement beneath the Howard Hotel in one of Edinburgh's most spectacular Georgian streets, is popular with rugby players, lawyers, students and landed gentry. Frequently busy, it tends to be rather bland, but the staff work hard to make it run smoothly and the lunches (when the bar is generally quiet) are to be recommended. No music, pinball machines, or other gimmicks.

Clark's Bar

4 3C

142 Dundas Street

Famed for the excellence of its Edinburgh-brewed cask-conditioned Younger's IPA, Clark's is clean, brightly lit, and very much set in its ways. Apart from the core of regulars, a remarkably wide range of customers gathers here, drawn as much by the traditional feel of this fine pub as by the beer. Excellent service and a good atmosphere.

The Cramond Inn

1 2B

Cramond

This inn is worth visiting for the picturesque beauty of its location at the mouth of the River Almond. It is popular with sightseers, tourists, members of the local yachting club, and couples returning from a romantic walk up the river. A perfect spot for a pint outside on a summer evening.

Deacon Brodie's

10 1C

435 Lawnmarket

Despite hot competition from innumerable other pubs in the High Street, Deacon Brodie's continues to attract tourists in the summer and the younger Edinburgh set during the winter. There are two bars—a public one on street level and a low-ceilinged lounge above. The public bar has kept its traditional look, as well as a core of Lawnmarket regulars, while the lounge is modern but quite pleasant.

Drones

10 1C

18–20 Grassmarket

The most attractive feature of Drones' somewhat brassy decor is the beautifully painted sign which hangs outside the pub. Yet this bar (allied to the expensive Beehive restaurant) continues to pull in the customers, many of whom obviously appreciate the wide range of real ales on tap here which include Samuel Smith Bellhaven, and Theakston's Old Peculiar. The atmosphere, helped along by the potency of the beer, is good and seems to appeal to people of all ages. Good service, while the bar itself is spacious and comfortable.

The Edinburgh Wine Bar

10 1C

110 Hanover Street

The exclusive atmosphere of the Edinburgh Wine Bar is typified perhaps by the well-thumbed copy of *Burke's Peerage* on a shelf in the back room, but drinkers in search of a quiet place for a bottle or two of reasonable wine need have no qualms about coming here. Service is pleasant, the food at lunch and evenings is unusual and varied, and the selection of wine is first rate. Given the price of a round of drinks in most city bars, this one is not particularly expensive.

The Golf Tavern

10 2C

Leven Street

Despite having one of the oldest licences in the city, the Golf Tavern is essentially a modern pub. It is situated beside the nine-hole Bruntsfield golf course in an attractive old building, with a restaurant upstairs. The bar is very large, plainly decorated with the odd golfing memento around the walls, but, particularly at weekends, it can be very crowded. It is really a student-orientated pub, although it does a good line in business lunches. Belhaven real ale is sold. Generally a lively and cheerful atmosphere.

The Green Tree

10 1D

184 Cowgate

On your right the bar and colour television, on your left an array of gnarled regulars gazing inquisitively at you. Between the two an assortment of college lecturers, bar-billiard fanatics and sundry other drinkers. Prior to the boom in real ale drinking, the Green Tree was one of the few pubs selling a selection of genuine casked beers. The strong ales are still to be found here (McEwan, Samuel Smith, Theakston, Bateman), as are the discerning beer drinkers. Although less popular than it has been, the pub is worth investigating.

Greyfriars Bobby

10 1C

34 Candlemaker Row

This is really a pub for a casual drink. The service and general atmosphere in the tartan-clad bar and lounge are more or less irreproachable, though the pub as a whole is somewhat subdued and the best that can be said of the Lorimer's beer is that it is passable. The regular clientele consists of groups of nurses from the Royal Infirmary, technicians from the university, shop-owners from the nearby shops, and tourists battling gamely to understand the convoluted tale of Greyfriars Bobby.

The Guildford Arms

10 1D

1 West Register Place

Like its near neighbour, the Cafe Royal, this pub has retained many Victorian features and is run extremely efficiently by a dedicated management. Mainly a workingman's pub and a gathering place for Highlanders in Edinburgh (along with the Oxford Bar and the West End Hotel), it nevertheless attracts a good deal of passing trade as well. The main bar, entered via revolving doors, can be observed from a small gallery bar upstairs and what you will see is a good-natured pub with a bunch of happy regulars glued to the colour television set. Competitive prices too.

The Haymarket Lounge

9 1B

Haymarket
(opposite Haymarket Station)

Casual visitors might be excused for thinking they had stumbled into a multi-storey leisure complex, but there is no doubt that the new Haymarket Lounge is a vast improvement on its anonymous predecessor. A huge island bar stands in a sea of deep pile carpet, a song springs from the throat of the resident folksinger, and a variety of locals play the pinball machines with inextinguishable enthusiasm. Up a precipitous flight of stairs office workers relax over gins-and-tonic and pints of Burton's ale. All in all a large efficiently run, modern lounge with all the trimmings, and capable of appealing to a wide variety of customers.

Jinglin' Geordie

10 1D

Fleshmarket Close
(off Cockburn St. and Market St.)

Though small, this bar tucked away in Fleshmarket Close, has a pleasant and homely feel to it. Jinglin' Geordie was the nickname given to the 17th-century silversmith and money lender George Heriot, and it is he who stands rattling his keys on the sign outside. Inside there is plenty of comfortable seating and a subdued atmosphere appropriate for filling in crosswords or reading

newspapers while the staff quietly go about their business. Journalists and businessmen make up much of the clientele.

Kay's Bar (Kay John & Co)

10 1C

39 Jamaica Street

Reconstructed with the fittings from an old wine merchant's, this bar looks to be older than it actually is. It does a constant and brisk business and is to be recommended for the quality and variety of its beer (about ten kinds, half of which are cask-conditioned), but also for its relaxed atmosphere. Business lunchers, mostly from nearby New Town offices, feature at midday, but later in the evenings a younger crowd moves in and raises the temperature by several degrees.

Open: all day

The Kenilworth

10 1C

152–154 Rose Street

Renowned as a gay bar and as a fine example of what pubs in Rose Street used to look like, the Kenilworth is one of those pubs that never seem to die. Nowadays the gay element is less obvious and a broader section of society frequents this elegant pub. It stays open all day and the service, if slightly brusque at times, is reasonable. A good selection of whiskies is sold but the beer, Double Diamond, is insipid stuff. Do not miss the fine original mirrors and moulded ceiling.

Open: all day

La Grenouille

4 3C

20 Abercromby Place

Imagine a dimly lit cellar, smoke-filled, crammed with late-night drinkers swaying unsteadily to the sound of an eight piece ragtime jazz-band, and you have a fair impression of La Grenouille at midnight on a Friday. The drinks are extremely expensive and considering that when the bar is busy they are sold in plastic glasses and can be difficult to get hold of, you may well decide that this is not your idea of fun. Still, the live music is some compensation and the customers,

mainly young but not exclusively so, are a likeable lot. The bar staff all speak French.

The Laughing Duck

10 1C

24 Howe Street

The Laughing Duck likes to be known as an ordinary pub which just happens to have a largely homosexual clientele, but the ambiance of the small disco-bar downstairs (Bananas) seems to suggest more than a passing interest in the lucrative gay trade. However, it is an extremely well managed and sociable bar—comfortable, spacious, selling a wide selection of liqueurs and real home-cooked lunches.

Open: all day

Madogs

9 1C

38 George Street

Madogs is an extremely small cocktail bar (attached to a larger restaurant) in a George Street basement. Expect some loudish music, subdued lighting, expertly mixed cocktails of all descriptions, cans of cheap American beer at inflated prices, a selection of fashionable clients, and a heavily scented atmosphere. Around the walls are blown-up portraits of Hollywood stars, emphasizing the American approach which Madogs pioneered a few years ago. Expensive, but if you can afford it you can have a good time here.

Marr's Bar

10 1C

39 Thistle Street

This small but cheerful pseudo-cocktail bar claims to have the best-stocked juke box in town, emphasizing its appeal to the young. The 'Marr's Bar' cocktail is guaranteed to send a tremble through the knees, while a constant stock of pizzas and hamburgers are at hand to sustain those wearied by endless pints of kegged beer. Gregarious, good service, a pleasant, middle-of-the-road pub.

Mather's Bar

4 3D

25 Broughton Street

Populated by those who enjoy a good pint of Younger's IPA in a relaxed, if slightly worn, environment. It is a pub for people of all ages and has a distinct character of its own. The staff are as witty as they are efficient and the only problem seems to be a disinclination to wash glasses properly. The main bar affords a glimpse of typical Edinburgh pub-life, while the small upstairs lounge is an ideal venue for more intimate meetings.

Noble's

5 2A

44a Constitution Street

A spectacular Leith pub, from its brightly painted façade to its large antique interior, with stained glass, a large horseshoe bar, and various momentoes from the days of sail around the walls. Indeed, a visit to Noble's can be sometimes like stepping aboard a ship; when the 'go-go' dancers mount the stage at the far end and the audience pushes forwards. You might almost be excused for casting a surreptitious glance behind you in search of the press gang.

The Oxford Bar

10 1C

8 Young Street

Bourgeois prejudices should be left behind when entering this small and dingy temple of Scottish nationalism. Of all Edinburgh's pubs, the Oxford is undoubtedly the most eccentric—a reputation derived exclusively from its owner, Willie Ross. Willie, a Gael of strong persuasions opens and closes his pub at will, frequently refuses to serve Englishmen or women, sells only heavy beer and whisky and absolutely refuses to wash glasses. However, if you are accepted, you can expect some lively, if not bizarre experiences. Gaelic speakers preferred.

Paddy's

10 1C

21 Lothian Road

As the name suggests, Paddy's has an Irish flavour to its decor. Garish and perhaps more Scottish than Irish, it is a spacious and comfortable bar which finds favour with the young West-End drinkers. Part of the Edinburgh chain known

as Antiquarian Inns, it has profited by the recent rise in popularity of real ale, in this case Belhaven. It also has a juke box and a number of Irish decorative fixtures, including a full-size jaunting cart.

Piershill Tavern

6 3C

7 Piershill Place

Although away from the city centre, the Piershill Tavern is well worth visiting if you are in search of the definitive Scottish pub. The beer (real ales included) is first rate, the service equally good, and a wide range of whiskies is available. Basically a workingman's pub, it has one of the friendliest atmospheres in the city, plus many well preserved traditional features. An ideal stopping-off point en route to Portobello and Musselburgh. Don't miss it.

Refreshers

10 1C

112 Hanover Street

Refreshers—the pastel-coloured lozenges that fizz in the mouth—are obviously the inspiration behind this new two-tier, sherbert style cocktail bar. To look your best here, wear the latest in pastel-coloured clothes and drink green or pink drinks. Brightly lit and decorated in a strikingly modern style, it can be oppressive when busy, but the prices are reasonable. Trendy, clean, efficient, fizzy, open until midnight, with good background music. Draught beer available.

Sandy Bells (The Forrest Hill Bar)

10 1C

25 Forrest Road

Sandy Bells has long been a gathering place for folk-musicians, left-wing radicals, and the odd university lecturer. The look of the bar, despite renovation, is still rather rough and ready and the service can at times be very slow indeed. However, the music is usually good value and the atmosphere can be rewarding for those who enjoy a stimulating political debate over half-a-dozen pints. Not perhaps to everyone's taste but a fine pub of its sort.

Open: all day

The Sheep's Heid

11 2B

*The Causeway
Duddingston Village*

Historically, this village pub can claim to have the oldest existing licence in or around Edinburgh and it is worth making the effort to get here on summer evenings, when you can drink outside. Popular with Duddingston locals, students, visitors to the nearby loch and nature reserve, and all others in search of simple but convivial surroundings. The embellished 'sheep's head' in question was given to the pub by an ex-patron James VI and I.

The Southsider

10 2D

3-5 West Richmond Street

The new-look Southsider lacks the character of its hot and sweaty predecessor, but with an all-day licence and a consistently high standard of beer (Maclay's, cask-conditioned) plus an interesting range of clientele (from local workingmen to students and university lecturers), it is one of the bars on the Southside, well worth a visit. A fair range of whiskies is sold and the general standard of service is excellent. Difficult to tell which is the lounge and which is the public bar and if you can avoid looking at the wallpaper so much the better.

Open: all day.

Stewarts

10 1D

14 Drummond Street

Another solid Scottish pub with a long history and a determination to retain its own identity, Stewarts is above all a friendly small bar. The staff are always pleasant and ready to chat, the beer is well kept and sold at what may seem to be yesterday's prices. There is a back room, which can be booked for private drinking sessions, as well as a television lounge. Whisky is sold in quarter gill measures.

St. Vincent Bar

4 3C

9 St. Vincent Street

The Vincent's reputation as a

bohemian bar stretches back to the 1960s and the heady days of hippie culture. Nowadays it continues to play host to a variety of folksingers, actors, students, and local antique dealers. It is a smallish pub, plainly decorated throughout with a carpeted section at the far end where you can peruse the latest works from the Edinburgh Photographic Society. On Tuesday nights various folk-musicians gather here to entertain the other drinkers and at such time the Vincent really comes into its own. Service and the quality of the beer tend to vary.

Open: all day on Saturdays

Tap O'Lauriston

10 2C

80 Lauriston Place

The Tap (also known by its former name 'Clarkes') looks like a glorified bus-shelter from the outside but inside the atmosphere is cheerful and warm. The lounge is inhabited mainly by students from the nearby art college, while a variety of locals gather for darts and pints of heavy in the public bar. Unremarkable in many ways, but by no means unpleasant, with some interesting characters. Cask-conditioned McEwan's 80/- is sold. There is a juke box with an avant-garde selection of records.

The Titled Wig

4 3C

3 Cumberland Street

The Titled Wig goes about its task with obvious determination. The barmen are clad in special green suits, everything from the chequered floor to the plum-blossom ceiling is kept spotlessly clean, there is a wide range of drinks, and the lunches (home-cooked) are a cut above the average. As the name suggests, it is an extremely popular bar with lawyers but it also attracts a variety of other customers of all ages.

The Waverley

10 1D

5 St. Mary's Street

This bar just off the High Street has for years been a folk venue. Music is performed in the upstairs lounge, which is small but cosy, and not infrequently lively. The main bar downstairs is bedecked with old Fringe Festival posters. Pleasant service, a reasonably lively clientele and a peculiar tendency to sell sherry in tumblers. The prices in the upstairs bar are significantly higher.

The Yellow Carvel

10 1D

9 Hunter Square

The Yellow Carvel is a large, double-basement bar situated just behind the Tron Kirk on the High Street. It is distinguished less by the decor (nautically oriented, with the main bar resembling the deck of a sailing ship) than by the throngs of young tourists who crowd in here during the summer, creating a lively and cosmopolitan atmosphere. There is live music here every Thursday night—traditional fiddle music and song—which draws a crowd of regulars during the winter season. Efficiently managed, with good service, and a selection of pub food.

Afternoon Tea

The typical Scot is renowned for his sweet tooth and determined interest in cakes and scones, so it is not surprising that afternoon tea is an Edinburgh institution. The city is packed with shops and cafes where the visitor can sample traditionally-baked buttery shortbread, sticky teabread, fresh scones, pancakes and crumbly oatcakes—all washed down with a pot of superior tea or freshly-ground coffee.

Listed below is a selection of shops at which you can enjoy a well-prepared and served Scottish afternoon tea. Where our reviewers were particularly impressed by the teashop's baking, service and atmosphere, a star (★) has been awarded. Generally, you should expect to pay around £2.50 for afternoon tea for two

Beanie G's

10 3C

173 Morningside Road

Monday to Saturday 09.00-17.00

The Buttery

10 1D

John Lewis
St. James Centre

Tuesday, Wednesday, Friday 09.00-17.15, Thursday 09.30-19.15, Saturday 09.30-18.00, Monday—closed

Clarinda's

10 1D

69 Canongate

Monday to Saturday 08.30-16.45
Sunday 09.30-16.45

The Coffee Cup

10 3C

210 Morningside Road

Monday to Saturday 09.30-17.15, Wednesday 09.30-13.15

Duncan's Land

4 3C

8 Gloucester Place

Monday to Saturday 12.00-16.45, Sunday 10.30-17.30

Ecbatan

10 1C

87 Grassmarket

Monday to Saturday 09.30-18.30

The Fruitmarket Gallery

10 1C

29 Market Street

Monday to Saturday 10.00-16.30

The Garden Room

10 1C	★

Forsyths
30 Princes Street

Monday to Saturday 09.00–16.30

The Glassmarket

10 1D	★

27 Jeffrey Street

Monday to Saturday 10.00–17.30

Habitat

10 1C

32 Shandwick Place

Tuesday to Sunday 10.30–16.30,
Monday—closed

The Laigh Kitchen

10 1C	★

121 Hanover Street

Monday to Saturday 09.00–14.00,
Tuesday to Friday 09.00–17.00

The Lairds Larder

10 1C

36 Victoria Street

Monday to Friday 10.00–17.00,
Saturday 10.00–16.00

The Luckpenny

10 1C

30 Grassmarket

Monday to Friday 09.00–18.00,
Saturday 09.00–17.30

The Netherbow

10 1D

43 Canongate

Monday to Saturday 10.00–16.00,
Wednesday 10.00–14.00

The Rose Street Restaurant

10 1C

Jenners
48 Princes Street

Monday to Saturday 09.30–17.00

The Shelter Shop

10 1C

4 Castle Street

Monday to Saturday 10.00–16.30

The Triangle

10 1C

11 Randolph Place

Monday to Friday 09.30–17.00,
Saturday 09.30–14.00

Useful Information

Baby-sitter

Bruntsfield Helping Hands Agency

10 2C

45 Barclay Place
Bruntsfield Place
Phone: (031) 228 1382

Open: Monday to Friday,
09.00-16.30
Baby-sitters, nurses, help with the
old; there is a 24-hour answering
service for emergency nursing
help

Banks

Opening Hours
Banks are open at the following
times:
Monday to Wednesday, 09.30–
12.30; 13.30–15.30
Thursday, 09.30–12.30; 13.30–
15.30; 16.30–18.00
Friday, 09.30–15.30
In addition a number of banks·
throughout the city remain
open at lunchtimes. These are
listed in main and branch
offices. The following central
banks remain open every
weekday lunch hour.

Bank of Scotland

10 1C

38 St Andrew Square

10 1C

141 Princes Street

Royal Bank of Scotland

10 1C

42 St. Andrew Square

142 Princes Street

Clydesdale Bank

10 1C

29 George Street

National Westminster Bank

10 1C

80 George Street

Most major banks in the city
have 24-hour cash-dispensing
machines which can be used
with the appropriate card.

Currency
Three main Scottish banks —
The Bank of Scotland, The
Royal Bank of Scotland, and The
Clydesdale Bank—issue their
own bank notes (from £1.00 upwards). Although different in
design from English notes they
are worth exactly the same, and
are legal currency throughout
Great Britain. Scotland has the
same coinage as the rest of
Great Britain.

Bureau de Change

Money can be changed during banking hours at the main banks, most of which have specific currency-exchange facilities. There are two Bureau de Change offices, both near Waverley Station at the east end of Princes Street.

Head Post Office

10 1D

2 Waterloo Place

Bureau de Change open: Monday to Friday 08.30–18.00, Saturday 08.30–12.30

Tourist Information Office

10 1C

5 Waverley Bridge

Bureau de Change open: Monday to Saturday 08.30–19.30. Sunday 11.00–15.00

GUIDES

A list of 84 approved guides can be obtained from:

The Tourist Information Office

10 1C

5 Waverley Bridge
Phone: (031) 226 6591
or

The Scottish Tourist Board

10 1C

Tourist Enquiries
5 Waverley Bridge
Phone: (031) 332 2433
or

9 1B

Administrative Offices
23 Ravelston Terrace
Phone: (031) 332 2433

Charges:
½-day city tour £12.00
½-day country, £15.00
foreign languages, £3.00 extra
day tour, up to eight hours,
£20.00.

Guides speaking foreign languages can also be obtained through:

The Scottish Tourist Guides Association

10 3C

9 Jordan Lane
Phone: (031) 447 7190, overseas
and general enquiries
(031) 229 3032, UK enquiries
and bookings

Also

Euroguides Scotland

9 2B

10 Douglas Crescent
Phone: (031) 337 5268

Health

Medical Emergencies
In an emergency—find the nearest telephone, dial 999 (no money is required) and ask for an ambulance

In the event of an accident or acute illness go directly to the nearest hospital with a Casualty Department. The following hospitals have 24-hour casualty services.

The Royal Infirmary of Edinburgh

10 2C

Lauriston Place
Phone: (031) 229 2477

Casualty—first gate East Drive

Western General Hospital

3 2A

Crewe Road South
Phone: (031) 332 2525

In the middle of Crewe Road—for casualty follow the arrows

Leith Hospital

4 2D

Mill Lane
Leith
Phone: (031) 554 3211

Casualty—in main door, turn right

All patients receive emergency treatment free of charge.

Visiting a Doctor
For less serious problems make an appointment to see a doctor at his surgery. Local police stations have lists of doctors and Health Centres; information can also be obtained from:
The Health Board
'Primary Care Section'
Phone: (031) 225 1341

In addition, most hotels will have addresses of doctors.

Visitors intending to stay in the country for three months or longer should register with the National Health Service at the beginning of their stay. They will receive a NHS number and be entitled to free treatment while in the country. There are strict checks to ensure that visitors with serious illnesses have not come to Britain specifically to obtain free treatment. A reciprocal arrangement exists between Britain and some other countries, such as members of the Commonwealth and the European Economic Community, which entitles nationals of these countries to free treatment.

Visitors from abroad who are in Britain, for a limited period can complete form EC19 at the doctor's surgery which will enable them to have free treatment. This is at the discretion of the doctor, who may ask for payment.

If you are a British visitor in Edinburgh and do not have your NHS card with you the doctor will either ask you to pay, (you can claim a refund from your own doctor), or he will ask you to fill out an EC19 form which will register you as a temporary resident—in which case treatment is free.

Prescriptions

Prescriptions issued by doctors should be taken to a chemist, who will issue the prescribed drugs at a cost of £1.00 per item. There are a number of exemptions from this charge, detailed on the back of the prescription form, but these are only applicable to British citizens. Foreign visitors are always required to pay the fee.

Most chemists keep normal shop opening hours (usually 09.00–17.00) but doctors and police stations have lists of chemists who will issue prescriptions outside normal hours, in an emergency. In addition there are chemists on weekend and night duty throughout the city. These can be located from a number of sources—the *Evening News*, notices in local post offices, public libraries, and chemist shop-windows. The Lothian Regional Health Board will also supply this information, phone: (031) 225 1341, 08.30–17.00 Monday to Friday. One chemist (Boots 10 1C) at 48 Shandwick Place—near the west end of Princes Street—has extended opening hours—Monday to Saturday, 08.45–21.00, Sunday, 11.00–16.30.

Lost Property

If you lose a personal possession while in Edinburgh, try ringing one of the city's Lost Property Offices—who may well be able to help.

Police Lost Property Office

3 3B

Fettes Avenue
Phone: (031) 311 3131

Open: Monday to Friday, 09.00–17.00 also Monday, 18.00–20.00

Railway Lost Property

10 1D

Waverley Station
Phone: (031) 556 2477

Open: Monday to Sunday, 06.30–22.45

Lothian Regional Transport Lost Property (Buses)

10 1C

14 Queen Street
Phone: (031) 554 4494

Open: Monday to Friday, 09.00–17.00

Scottish Omnibuses Lost Property (Eastern Scottish Buses)

10 1C

Bus Station
St. Andrew Square
Phone: (031) 556 8126

Open: Monday to Friday, 08.30–12.30, 13.30–17.30

Police

In an emergency—find the nearest telephone, dial 999 (no money is required) and ask for the police

In Scotland, policemen wear black uniforms and flat black caps with a black and white chequered-band around the brim. They are based at the following principal Police Stations.

Lothian & Borders Police Headquarters

3 3B

(opposite Inverleith Park)
Fettes Avenue
Phone: (031) 311 3131

South Edinburgh

10 2D

South Side Police Station
98 Causewayside
Phone: (031) 667 3361

North Edinburgh

4 3D

Gayfield Square Police Station
near top of Leith Walk
Gayfield Square
Phone: (031) 556 2011

West Edinburgh

9 1B

West End Police Station
near Haymarket
Torphichen Place
Phone: (031) 229 2323

East Edinburgh

5 2A

31 Queen Charlotte Street
Phone: (031) 554 1212

The police have the power to tow away a car if a serious parking offence has been committed. It can be retrieved after payment of a maximum fine of £22.00, phone: (031) 311 3131 and ask for 'Traffic Link'.

Post Offices

Head Post Office

10 1D

2 Waterloo Place
Phone: (031) 550 8232

Edinburgh's main post office with Bureau de Change, Passport Service, Philatelic Sales Service for stamp collectors, and a 24-hour service area—telephones, British telephone directories, stamp machines, and lists of postal collection times.

Open: Monday to Friday, 08.30–18.00; Saturday 8.30–12.30

Branch Offices

Branch Post Offices can be found throughout the city. Most have passport and foreign currency services. Normal opening times are 09.00–17.30, although some close for lunch between 12.30 and 13.30.

Useful Addresses

Alcoholics Anonymous

10 1D

38 Cockburn Street
Phone: (031) 225 6090

Automobile Association (AA)

9 1B

18–22 Melville Street
Phone: (031) 225 8468

Open: Monday to Friday,
0900–12.30; Saturday, 09.00–12.30
(24-hour breakdown service)

Citizen's Advice Bureau

4 3C

58 Dundas Street
Phone: (031) 557 1500

Open Monday to Friday,
09.30–16.30, Wednesday and
Thursday, by appointment only
18.30-20.00

Advice and information on a wide
range of subjects.

City of Edinburgh Tourist Information and Accommodation Centre

10 1C

5 Waverley Bridge
Phone: (031) 226 6591
(031) 225 2424 for
accommodation

Open: Monday to Saturday,
08.30-21.00; Sunday, 11.00–21.00 in
summer
Monday to Friday, 09.00–18.00;
Saturday, 09.00-13.00 in winter

Consumer Advice Centre

10 1C

32 Frederick Street
Phone: (031) 225 8706

Open: Monday to Friday,
08.30–16.30; Saturday 09.00–13.00

Advice and information on
consumer problems

Edinburgh Film Festival

10 1C

The Filmhouse
88 Lothian Road
Phone: (031) 228 6382

Festival August 14 to August 23:
programmes available mid July

Edinburgh Festival Society

10 1C

21 Market Street
Phone: (031) 226 4001

Open: Monday to Friday
10.00–18.30; Saturday, 10.00–18.00;
Sunday, 13.00–18.00; during the
Festival, Monday to Sunday,
08.45–17.00
Information and booking

Edinburgh Fringe Festival Society

10 1D

170 High Street
Phone: (031) 226 5257/5259

Edinburgh Military Tattoo Office

10 1D

1 Cockburn Street
Phone: (031) 225 1188

Open: Monday to Friday,
10.00–16.30 in summer; Monday to
Thursday, 10.00–21.00; Friday and
Saturday, 10.00–22.30, during the
Tattoo

Edinburgh Women's Aid

10 2D

141 Buccleuch Street
Phone: (031) 668 2949

Legal Aid

9 1B

40–44 Drumsheugh Gardens
Phone: (031) 226 7061

Meteorological Office

9 2A

231 Corstorphine Road
Phone: (031) 334 9721

For weather reports: Phone: (031)
246 8091

Motoring Information Service

Recorded message
Phone: (031) 246 8021

Royal Automobile Club (RAC)

10 1C

17 Rutland Square
Phone: (031) 229 3555

Open Monday to Friday,
09.00–27.00; Saturday, 09.00–12.30
(24-hr breakdown service)

Royal Highland Show

19 2B

Royal Highland Show Ground
Ingliston (7 miles/11km from
city centre on main road to
Glasgow)

Held June 22 to June 25

Samaritans

Phone: (031) 225 3333

Scottish Experience

10 1C

2 Rutland Place
Phone: (031) 228 2828

Open Monday to Saturday,
10.00–19.00; Sunday, 14.00–18.00
Visitors centre—including Craft
Shop, information service, 15
minute audio-visual show, 40-foot
(12m) illuminated relief map of
Scotland.

Speaking Clock

Dial 123

Teletourist Information

Phone: (031) 332 0471
Information on daily events
between May and end
September

Scottish Tourist Board

9 1B

23 Ravelston Terrace
Phone: (031) 332 2433

10 1C

5 Waverley Bridge
Phone: (031) 332 2433

Section II –
Art galleries, Museums, Stately Homes and Town Houses

This section of the directory gives details of various places of interest in Edinburgh and the surrounding area. The lists are not intended to be complete, but to point out the major sights and to cater for all tastes.

Art Galleries

The following is a selective list of art galleries ranging from the huge National Gallery of Scotland to those of the smaller dealers, and including some interesting showrooms run by the artists themselves. It is advisable to telephone before visiting as times of opening tend to fluctuate.

Abacus

10 1C

1 Victoria Street
Phone: (031) 226 5640

Abacus comprises two small galleries set within a craft shop. One houses a selection of contemporary paintings by Scottish artists such as George Birrell and Duncan Macleod. The gallery upstairs houses works by living British artists. Exhibitions are held for three-week periods throughout the year—these include textiles, woodcarvings, pottery as well as oil and watercolour paintings.

Open: Monday to Saturday, 09.30–17.30

Aitken Dott & Son

10 1C

The Scottish Gallery
26 Castle Street
Phone: (031) 225 5955

Aitken Dott & Son specializes in the work of Scottish artists—oil paintings and watercolours as well as a range of ceramics and sculpture. Exhibitions are held monthly and in the summer there is a special exhibition of the decorative arts with limited edition prints from artists such as John Houston, David Evans and Francis Walker. There is also an antiquarian print department.

Monday to Friday, 09.00–17.30; Saturday, 09.00–12.30

Bourne Fine Art Ltd

4 3C

4 Dundas Street
Phone: Not available at time of publication

A small commercial gallery specializing in 19th- and 20th-century British paintings. It holds about five one-man shows a year with an emphasis on Scottish artists of the past. Also houses a collection of art nouveau furniture and objets d'art.

Open: Monday to Friday, 10.00–17.30; Saturday, 10.00–13.00

The Calton Gallery

4 3D

10 Royal Terrace
Phone: (031) 556 1010

A new gallery, the Calton is part of a Georgian town house with views of the Firth of Forth. The spacious area houses works by known British and European artists—both oils and watercolours and prices range from £20–£2000.

Open: Monday to Friday, 10.00–18.00; Saturday, 10.00–13.00. Appointments can be made

City Art Centre

10 1C

1–4 Market Street
Phone: (031) 225 2424

The City Art Centre presents changing displays of works from the city collection. This includes Scottish paintings dating from the mid-19th century, as well as prints, drawings and sculpture. It also provides facilities for films and lectures and holds a limited number of selling exhibitions.

Open: June to September: Monday to Saturday, 10.00–18.00
October to May: Monday to Saturday, 10.00–17.00
During the Festival: Sunday, 14.00–17.00

Daniel Shackelton

4 3C

23 Dundas Street
Phone: (031) 557 1115

This fine-art dealer offers a wide range of original oil and watercolour paintings, prints, etchings and engravings. The main emphasis is on Scottish historical studies, though works by contemporary local artists such as Jeffrey Roper can be seen. Also for sale are unframed etchings, prints, watercolours and a selection of frames.

Open: Monday to Friday, 10.00–16.00; Saturday, 10.00–13.00

Edinburgh College of Art

10 2C

Lauriston Place
Phone: (031) 229 9311

The college devotes a large exhibition space to the work of its students and other young Scottish artists. During the summer term outside groups hire the area to exhibit their work.

Open: Monday to Friday, 10.00–17.00; Saturday, 10.00–12.00

The Edwards Gallery

4 3C

20 Dundas Street
Phone: (031) 557 1903

A limited collection of 19th-century British paintings, particularly those of the Glasgow and Edinburgh schools 1860–1910. The paintings are hung in rooms housing the principal attraction which is the antique furniture, porcelain and glass.

Open: Monday to Saturday, 10.00–17.00

The Fine Art Society

4 3C

12 Great King Street
Phone: (031) 556 0305

The Edinburgh branch of the Fine
Art Society (established in London
in 1876) was opened here in 1973.
The original character of this New
Town house, built around 1815, is
preserved by the well-appointed
furniture and decoration. There is a
regular exhibition programme of
works by both international and
Scottish artists, though the main
emphasis is on the latter.

Open: Monday to Friday,
10.00–18.00; Saturday, 10.00–13.00

The Fruit Market Gallery

10 1C

29 Market Street
Phone: (031) 226 5781

A large gallery with a varied
exhibition programme, including
both Scottish and international
artists. The gallery also stages
exhibitions which have been
proposed to the Scottish Arts
Council by members of the public.

Open: Monday to Saturday,
10.00–17.30

Graeme Murray Gallery

4 3C

2 Eyre Crescent
Phone: (031) 556 8689

This small gallery exhibits
sculptures and paintings
representing contemporary
international art from as far afield as
the Netherlands, USA and Peru. A
good selection of books and
publications on international art is
also for sale.

Open: Tuesday to Saturday,
14.00–20.00
Appointments can be made

The Henderson Gallery

10 1C

98 Hanover Street
Phone: (031) 225 7464

Exhibitions of traditional and
avant-garde art continue
throughout the year featuring the
works of both established and
known artists. The gallery also
deals in 19th- and early
20th-century paintings and houses

a permanent collection of Ian
Hamilton Finlay tiles, some modern
ceramics, and a wide range of
prints and postcards.

Open: Monday to Saturday,
10.30–17.30

The Malcolm Innes Gallery

10 1C

67 George Street
Phone: (031) 226 4151

This gallery specializes in 19th- and
20th-century Scottish sporting and
natural history paintings. It also
represents the interest of 13 living
Scottish artists, including Elisabeth
Cameron, Brian Rawling and
Louise Wood.

Open: Monday to Friday,
09.30–18.00
During exhibitions open Saturdays

The Mill House Gallery

12 2C

Duddingston Loan
Phone: (031) 669 5690

A tiny gallery run on a part-time
basis with a permanent collection
of 18th- and 19th-century
engravings, etchings and prints. In
addition the gallery holds about six
temporary exhibitions a year.
Prices range from £10–£200.

Open: Sunday, 12.00–19.00

National Gallery of Modern Art

4 3C

Inverleith House
Inverleith Terrace
Phone: (031) 332 3754

The national collection of
20th-century art has been housed
here since 1960 and will be moved
in 1984 to the former John Watson's
School. Most of the major modern
artists like Picasso, Hepworth,
Matisse and Moore are
represented in this exhibition of
painting, sculpture and graphic art.
There is a programme of changing
exhibitions and a very good
collection of modern Scottish
artists. There are also some
sculptures in the nearby garden,
which is the highest point in the
Royal Botanic Garden and
overlooks the city skyline. (For
further details see the Art Galleries
article in the main body of this
book.)

Open: April to September: Monday
to Saturday, 10.00–17.00; Sunday,
14.00–17.00
October to March: Monday to
Saturday, 10.00 to dusk; Sunday,
13.00 to dusk

The National Gallery of Scotland

10 1C

2 The Mound
Phone: (031) 556 8921

This is one of the best of the smaller
galleries in Europe. Opened in
1859, it houses a fine collection of
works by Continental and English
masters from the 14th century to
Cezanne. The National Gallery also
features a section devoted to
Scottish artists. (For further details,
see the Art Galleries article in the
main body of this book.)

Open: Monday to Saturday,
10.00–17.00; Sunday, 14.00–17.00

National Portrait Gallery

10 1C

2 Queen Street
Phone: (031) 556 8921

In the same building as the National
Museum of Antiquities, the gallery
was opened in 1882 to 'illustrate
Scottish history by likenesses of the
chief actors in it'. The Scottish
characters portrayed date from the
mid-16th century to the present day
in all media including 29 calotypes
by the pioneering photographers
David Octavius Hill and Robert
Adamson. There is an annual
exhibition which illustrates a
different aspect of Scottish social or
art history.

Open: Monday to Saturday,
10.00–17.00 Sunday, 14.00–17.00

Netherbow Arts Centre

10 1D

High Street
Phone: (031) 556 9579

The Netherbow is the Arts and
Communication Centre for the
Church of Scotland. There are 12
exhibitions a year in each
gallery—a small number of
paintings on display in the
restaurant, and craftwork,
paintings, sculpture, weaving,
macrame and photography in the
Solstice. Centre policy tends
towards exhibiting works by
lesser-known living Scottish artists.

Open: Monday to Saturday,
10.00–16.00, plus evening theatre
performances
During the Festival: late opening
18.30–22.30

The New 57 Gallery

10 1C

29 Market Street
Phone: (031) 225 2383

Exhibits include a wide range of
contemporary art with a strong
emphasis on feminist works.
Occasionally presents exhibitions
on architecture and design,
sculpture, textiles and
photography. Most of the work
dates from the 1970s and 1980s.

Open: Monday to Saturday,
10.30–17.30
Closed late September after the
Festival

The Printmakers Workshop

10 1C

The Old Fruit Market
29 Market Street
Phone: (031) 225 1098

The only gallery with continuous
exhibitions of contemporary
original prints. The work of modern
Scottish printmakers is shown
alongside those of printmakers
from around the world. Prints from
the workshop are also on sale.

Open: Gallery: Monday to
Saturday, 10.00–17.30. Studio:
Monday to Thursday, 10.00–21.00;
Friday and Saturday, 10.00–18.00;
Sunday, 14.00–17.00

Richard Demarco Gallery Ltd

10 1D

32 High Street
Phone: (031) 557 0707

A small gallery with a policy of
presenting new and experimental
international art. In the past it has
mounted some controversial
exhibitions from countries such as
Canada, Poland and Romania.

Open: Tuesday to Saturday,
10.00–17.30

The Royal Scottish Academy

10 1C

The Mound
Phone: (031) 225 6671

From March to July the galleries of
the Academy house the Academy's
own Annual Exhibition for which
500 works are selected from those
submitted by members and
non-members of the Academy.
During the Festival exhibitions of
well-known foreign artists are held.
The Academy also presents its
Diploma collection once a year,
which includes the diploma works
of aspirant members of the
Academy. During the rest of the
year they show the work of three
societies of practising Scottish
artists: the Royal Society of Scottish
painters and watercolourists in
January and February; the Society
of Scottish Artists in October and
November; and the Society of
Women Artists in November and
December. An annual student's
competition is organized during
February and March and the work
of the successful students can be
seen on display.

Open: Monday to Saturday,
10.00–21.00 during Annual
Exhibitions. Sunday, 14.00–17.00
For other exhibitions check local
press

The Shore Gallery

5 3A

59 Bernard Street
Phone: (031) 225 6753

This small gallery is housed in a
listed 17th-century building,
recently restored by the National
Trust. The exhibitions are run on a
three-weekly programme and
comprise mainly one-man shows of
contemporary Scottish artists.

Open: Monday to Saturday,
11.00–16.00
Changeable half-day Wednesday
or Saturday

Stills

10 1D

The Scottish Photography
Group Gallery
58 High Street
Phone: (031) 557 1140

This gallery holds between eight
and ten exhibitions by national and
international photographers every
year. Their exhibitions in the past
have ranged from the work of Bill
Brandt to examples of the
photographer as printmaker.

Open: Tuesday to Saturday,
12.30–18.00
During the Festival: Tuesday to
Sunday, 10.00–18.00

Talbot Rice Art Centre

10 1D

Old College
South Bridge
Phone: (031) 667 1011 ext. 4308

The Centre has two main exhibition
spaces: one houses the university's
permanent collection, the other
being given over to temporary
exhibitions, of which there are
approximately ten a year. The
permanent collection includes
examples of 17th-century Dutch
painting (Meindert Hobbema, Jan
Both and Hercules Seghers), and a
number of 16th- and 17th-century
bronzes. The major exhibitions are
based on an interesting three-point
policy of promoting Scottish artists
in one-man shows, housing major
touring exhibitions from abroad,
and presenting historical
exhibitions (again with a Scottish
emphasis).

Open: Monday to Saturday,
10.00–17.00

The 369 Gallery

10 1D

369 High Street
Phone: (031) 225 3013

This is the only gallery in
Edinburgh concerned exclusively
with promoting the work of young
Scottish artists. It holds 12
exhibitions a year comprising both
one-man and group shows.

Open: Tuesday to Saturday,
11.00–17.30

The Torrance Gallery

4 3C

29b Dundas Street
Phone: (031) 556 6366

The main emphasis here is on
original oils and watercolours by
contemporary Scottish artists.
Fortnightly exhibitions are held
throughout the year.

Open: Monday to Friday,
11.00–18.00; Saturday, 10.30–13.00

Museums

The ancient City of Edinburgh is rich in historical and especially literary associations. The following is a selection of museums which should cater for most tastes, from the fire-engine fanatic to the bibliophile. Opening times tend to change according to the season, so telephone before making your visit.

Agricultural Museum

19 2B

Showroom Ground
Ingliston
Phone: (031) 333 2674

A branch of the National Museum of Antiquities of Scotland which holds an annual exhibition on an agrarian theme.

Open: 10.00–17.00 during Royal Highland Show in June
Other times: by appointment for special parties

Braidwood and Rushbrook Fire Museum

4 2D

McDonald Road Fire Station
Phone: (031) 229 7222 ext. 53

This museum contains fire-fighting equipment and fire engines ancient and modern, from hand pump to high speed apparatus. There is also a collection of curious artefacts such as a German fireman's helmet which glows in the dark.

Open: Appointments only

Canongate Tolbooth

10 1D

Phone: (031) 225 1131

The Canongate Tolbooth, built in 1591, was a burgh court house and prison for 300 years. Today it serves as a museum with a collection of Highland dress and tartan. Downstairs is a brass-rubbing centre containing a brass commemorating Robert the Bruce.

Open: June to September: Monday to Saturday, 10.00–18.00
October to May: Monday to Saturday, 10.00–17.00
During the Festival: Sunday, 14.00–17.00

Museum of Childhood

10 1D

38 High Street
Phone: (031) 225 1131

A storehouse of memories of childhood—games, dolls, Hornby trains, clockwork mice, costumes and books. A treat for children and a nostalgic experience for their parents. The most spectacular exhibit is the doll's house *circa* 1897, with its running water, electric lighting, full complement of tiny furniture and even a minute orange tree in the guest room. There is also a range of educational toys on display.

Open: June to September: Monday to Saturday, 10.00–18.00
October to May: Monday to Saturday, 10.00–17.00
During the Festival: Sunday, 14.00–17.00

Museum of Flight

20 1C

East Fortune Airfield
North Berwick
Phone: (062) 088 308

Twenty miles (32 km) east of the city, the Royal Scottish Museum's collection of aircraft includes aero-engines and rockets.

For details of special excursions and open days, phone: (031) 225 7534

Open: July and August: Monday to Sunday, 10.00–16.00

Museum of Lighting

4 3C

59 St. Stephen Street
Phone: (031) 556 4503

Part of a lighting emporium is dedicated to the exhibition of the proprietor's collection of early domestic, transport and marine lamps from the past.

Open: Saturday, 10.00–18.00

National Library of Scotland

10 1C

George IV Bridge
Phone: (031) 226 4531

This was formerly the Advocates' Library, founded in the late 17th century. It obtained the right of copyright deposit in 1710, and as a consequence obtained the best works of continental scholarship. In 1925 the Faculty of Advocates presented their library to the nation. The library has about 4½ million printed items, and its collection of Scottish books and manuscripts is unrivalled. There is a map collection, a music collection dating from the early 19th century, the Haxton collection of Bibles, and material relating to the Celtic language, ships and shipping and labour history as well.

Reading rooms: Monday to Friday, 09.30–20.30; Open: Saturday, 09.30–13.00
Exhibition room: Monday to Friday, 09.30–17.00; Sunday, 14.00–17.00

National Museum of Antiquities of Scotland

10 1C

Queen Street
Phone: (031) 556 8921

This museum has collections which show the history of Scotland from earliest times to the present day. There are relics from the Stone Age, Roman times and the Viking invasions. There is also a fine collection of Scottish weapons and tartans. (For further details see the Museum's article in the main body of this book.)

Open: Monday to Saturday, 10.00–17.00; Sunday, 14.00–17.00

New Town Conservation Centre

4 3C

13a Dundas Street
Phone: (031) 556 7054

The centre holds a permanent display of the conservation work in progress on the Georgian New Town. There is a conservation reference library and usually an exhibition on some aspect of architecture. Walks and guided tours are also organized from here.

Open: Monday to Friday, 09.00–13.00, 14.00–17.00

North Berwick Museum

20 1C

School Road
North Berwick
Phone: (0620) 3470

A small local museum concerned with archaeology and natural history. Nearby is the 600-foot (183 m) high volcanic rock known as North Berwick Law.

Open: June to October: Monday to Saturday, 10.00–13.00, 14.00–17.00 Sunday, 14.00–17.00
Easter weekend and only weekends Easter to June. 14.00–17.00.
Closed October to Easter

Reid Hall

10 2D

*Teviot Row, off Teviot Place
Faculty of Music
Edinburgh University
Phone: (031) 667 1011 ext. 2573*

The Edinburgh University Collection of historic musical instruments is housed in glass cases in an ante-room off the Reid concert hall. Instruments include serpents, crúmhorns, sackbuts, early recorders and tambours.

Open: Only during the Festival: 14.00–17.00 and in intervals of concerts on Thursday evenings during term

Museum of the Royal College of Surgeons of Edinburgh

10 2D

*18 Nicholson Street
Phone: (031) 556 6206*

A specialist museum with exhibits of surgical, dental, pathological and historical material.

Open: Appointments only

The Royal Scottish Museum

10 1D

*Chambers Street
Phone: (031) 225 7534*

Scotland's national museum is housed in an imposing mid-Victorian building and displays range from primitive art to space material. There are also mammal and bird collections but the main emphasis is on science and technology. There is a programme of talks, lectures and films throughout the year. (For further details see the Museums article in the main body of this book.)

Open: Monday to Saturday, 10.00–17.00; Sunday, 14.00–17.00

St. Cecilia's Hall

10 1D

*Cowgate
Phone: (031) 667 1011 ext. 4415*

The University's Russell collection of harpsichords and clavichords is on display in this elegant Georgian hall built by Robert Milne in 1762 as the concert hall for the Edinburgh Music Society. There are 36 keyboard instruments including virginals, regals and spinets. The room also contains period tapestries and textiles, and paintings by Giovanni Pannini and Jacob van Ruysdael.

Open: Saturday, 14.00–17.00
During the Festival: Monday to Saturday, 10.00–12.30

St. Cuthbert's Co-operative Association Ltd Transport Collection

9 2B

*Grove Street
Phone: (031) 229 2424 ext. 363*

One of the last commercial firms to use horse-drawn transport for milk deliveries. At their stables they have a wonderful collection of coaches of every description; hearses, gigs, carts as well as harness and livery. They are responsible for the refurbishment of the state carriages which are used in royal cavalcades.

Open: Appointments only

The Scottish Experience

10 1C

*St. Thomas Church
Shandwick Place
Phone: (031) 228 2828*

This comprises two multi-media presentations. 'Spectacular Scotland' is a relief map which helps to locate places of interest at the press of a button; 'The Edinburgh Show' uses back-projection techniques, music and commentary to outline the city's history.

Open: Monday to Saturday, 10.00–19.00; Sunday, 14.00–19.00

Scottish United Services Museum

10 1C

*Crown Square
Edinburgh Castle
Phone: (031) 226 6907*

A military museum illustrating the history of the armed forces of Scotland. There are displays of uniforms, arms and equipment, decorations, portraits and a library. There is also a comprehensive collection of prints depicting the uniforms on display.

Open: April to October: Monday to Saturday, 09.30–17.00; Sunday, 11.00–17.00
November to March: Monday to Saturday, 09.30–16.00; Sunday, 12.00–16.00

Edinburgh Wax Museum

10 1D

*142 High Street
Phone: (031) 226 4444*

The wax museum is housed in a Georgian building which was originally the New Assemblies Hall. The wax figures depict royalty, historical and media personalities, and fictional characters such as Peter Pan, Alice in Wonderland and Pooh Bear. Tableaux illustrate historical events and the waxworks are surrounded by period furnishing and realistic sound effects.

Open: April to September: Monday to Sunday, 10.00–19.00
October to March: Monday to Sunday, 10.00–17.00

Stately Homes and Town Houses

Edinburgh's status as the capital city of Scotland and seat of the Scottish monarch and court accounts for the numerous grand mansions and stately homes in the surrounding area. This section lists those which are well worth a visit, along with a selection of town houses which are of architectural or historical interest. Map references are included for houses which can be found within the area mapped at the end of this book. It is wise to telephone before setting out as opening times are variable.

Abbotsford

Melrose
Phone: (0896) 2043

Once a small farmhouse on the banks of the Tweed, Sir Walter Scott's home is now a museum to one of Scotland's favourite writers. The interior has been kept much as it was, and features as well as paintings by Raeburn and Landseer, Scott's writing materials, his books and relics of Scottish history. (For further details see the Stately Homes article in the main body of this book.)

Open: Third Sunday in March to the end of October: Monday to Saturday, 10.00–17.00; Sunday, 14.00–17.00

Bowhill

Selkirk
Phone: (0750) 20732

Bowhill is the border home of the Duke of Buccleuch and Queensberry. The house contains the Duke's famous art collection, which includes some Elizabethan miniature paintings. There are also Nature trails, pony trekking, a gift shop and tea room.

Open: Weekdays, 12.30–17.00 Sunday, 14.00–18.00

Open Easter weekend: May, June, September open only Mondays, Wednesday, Saturdays, Sundays

July, August open daily except Friday

Dalmeny House

19 1B

South Queensferry
Phone: (031) 331 1888

Only seven miles (11 km) from Edinburgh, Dalmeny House is situated on the shores of the Firth of Forth, with walks through parks and woodland. It contains two fine collections: the Rosebery art collection gathered by the 3rd, 4th and 5th Earls, and the Mentmore collection of fabulous 18th-century furniture, tapestries, porcelain and paintings. (For further details see the Stately Homes article in the main body of this book.)

Open: mid April to end of September, Wednesdays and Sundays, 14.30–17.30

Also open Easter Monday and local Monday holidays

Edinburgh Castle

10 1C

Castle Hill
Phone: (031) 225 9846

There has been a fortress on this site since about the 7th century. The oldest part of the present castle is the chapel built by David I and dedicated to Malcolm's queen, Margaret, in the 12th century. The Scottish crown, sceptre and sword are also kept here. (For further details see the Edinburgh Castle article in the main body of this book.)

Open: April to October: Monday to Saturday, 09.30–17.00; Sunday, 11.00–17.00
November to March: Monday to Saturday, 09.30–16.00; Sunday, 12.00–16.00

Floors Castle

Kelso
Phone: (05732) 3333

Home of the Duke of Roxburghe, and the site of the murder of James II of Scotland in 1460. William Adam helped to build this fine example of 18th-century architecture. The castle contains some porcelain, superb French and English furniture and paintings, tapestries, and even some Gobelin. The collection of Battersea enamelled boxes is particularly worth seeing. There is also a walled garden, garden centre, gift shop and tea room.

Open: Easter weekend, then May to September: Monday to Friday, 11.00–17.30
Garden centre: Daily throughout the year, 09.30–17.00

The Georgian House

10 1C

7 Charlotte Square
Phone: (031) 225 2160

The National Trust of Scotland has restored this magnificent piece of Georgian architecture in amazingly authentic detail. There are furnishings in the style of Chippendale, Sheraton and Hepplewhite, porcelain by Derby and Wedgwood, and paintings and engravings by Morland, Ramsay and Nasmyth. (For further details see the New Town article in the main body of this book.)

Open: April to October: Monday to Saturday, 10.00–17.00; Sunday, 14.00–17.00
November to December: Saturday, 10.00–16.00 Sunday, 14.00–16.30
Closed mid-December to April
Last admissions 30 minutes before closing time

Gladstone's Lane

10 1C

Lawnmarket
Phone: (031) 226 5856

Situated on the Royal Mile, this 17th-century house provides a contrast with the Georgian House, 7 Charlotte Square, in the New Town. Built by Thomas Gledstanes in 1620, the house was originally intended as a tenement with a separate flat on each floor. As it is now, it gives a valuable glimpse of living conditions in a medieval city.

Open: Monday to Saturday, 10.00–17.00; Sunday, 14.00–17.00

Palace of Holyroodhouse

10 1D

Royal Mile
Phone: (031) 556 7371

Once a guest house, Holyroodhouse was turned into a royal palace by James IV in 1488. It is now the official residence of the Queen in the city. (For further details see the Palace of Holyroodhouse article in the main body of this book.)

Open: March to October: Monday to Saturday, 09.30–17.15; Sunday, 11.00–16.30
November to February: Monday to Saturday, 09.30–15.45

Hopetoun House

19 1B

South Queensferry
Phone: (031) 331 2451

The magnificent home of the Marquis of Linlithgow, originally designed by Sir William Bruce, but completed by William Adam and his sons, Robert and John, the latter two being principally responsible for the interior decoration. The surrounding 100 acres (40.4 ha) contain deer, peacocks, St. Kilda sheep, a nature trail and picnic areas. (For further details see the Stately Homes article in the main body of this book.)

Open: From Easter to third Monday in September: Sunday, 11.00–17.30

Huntly House

10 1D

142 Canongate
Phone: (031) 225 1131

Huntly House is a good example of a restored 16th-century town house. A number of the rooms have been decorated to show the changing life-style at various periods in the history of the house. The 17th-century room, for example, shows the elegance of a fairly well-off merchant, and the late 19th-century is recreated with a 'working class kitchen'. There is a collection of Edinburgh silver and glass dating from the 17th-century onwards, Scottish pottery excavated from the Roman fort at Cramond and two rooms displaying relics of the World War I Field Marshal Earl Haig.

Open: Monday to Saturday, 10.00–18.00

John Knox's House

10 1D

45 High Street
Phone: (031) 556 6961

John Knox, the leader of the Protestant Reformation in Scotland, lived here in one of the most ancient dwelling houses in the city. On display are a number of pictures and lithographs of Knox, usually in the act of pulpit-thumping. There are also letters, documents and early editions of his tracts and sermons, including the famous pamphlet *The First Blast of the Trumpet against the Monstrous Regiment of Women.*

Open: April to October: Monday to Saturday, 10.00–17.00
Closed November to March

Lady Stair's House

10 1C

Lady Stair's Close
Lawnmarket
Phone: (031) 225 1131

This solid 17th-century town house contains relics of Robert Burns, Sir Walter Scott and Robert Louis Stevenson. These include the original manuscript of Burns's *Scots Wha ha'e*, locks of hair, knives, quill pens, snuff boxes and umbrellas. The most interesting exhibits are the portraits, including one of Stevenson by Girolamo Nerli.

Open: Monday to Saturday, 10.00–18.00

Lauriston Castle

1 2B

Cramond Road South
Phone: (031) 336 2060

A fine mansion with beautiful grounds overlooking the Firth of Forth, this was once the home of William Robert Reid, a cabinet-maker and collector of objets d'art. A late 16th-century tower house has been incorporated in a Jacobean-style house built in the early 19th-century. Decorated by Reid in the early years of this century, it presents a prosperous Edwardian interior with mostly 18th-century English and European furniture, including a set of Chippendale dining chairs. Among the objets d'art are Reid's collection of ornaments in Derbyshire fluorspar, wool mosaic pictures, and tapestries.

Open: Monday to Sunday, 11.00–13.00, 14.00–17.00
April to October: closed Fridays
November to March: Saturday and Sunday, 14.00–16.00

Manderston

Duns
Berwickshire
Phone: (03612) 3450

A fine Edwardian country house surrounded by formal gardens and woodland park. As well as period furnishings in luxurious surroundings there is a marble dairy, stables and a lake. Gift shop and cream teas available.

Open: Any day by appointment for parties of 20 or more
Mid-May to mid-September: Thursday and Sunday, 14.00–17.30

Mellerstain House

Gordon
Berwickshire
Phone: (057381) 225

One of the most beautiful Georgian houses in Scotland, designed and built by William and Robert Adam. The interior is decorated with their fine plasterwork and pastel colours. There are paintings by the Old Masters (Gainsborough, van Dyck, Ramsay and Raeburn), an outstanding collection of 18th-century furniture, and a library still with its original decoration. Other attractions

include the terraced gardens, lake, gift shop and tea rooms.

Open: Monday to Sunday, 13.30–17.30
Closed Saturday, May to October

Stirling Castle

Stirling
Phone: (0786) 62421

A thousand-year-old castle where great battles of the Wars of Independence were fought by such Scottish heroes as William Wallace and Robert the Bruce. A multi-vision show with narration gives historic facts and details of the people associated with the castle—among them Mary, Queen of Scots and her son James VI and I, who was crowned here. The walled old town also has many historic buildings.

Open: May to September: Monday to Friday, 09.30–18.00; Saturday and Sunday, 11.00–18.00
October to April: Monday to Friday, 09.30–17.05; Saturday and Sunday, 12.30–16.20

Traquair House

Innerleithen
Peeblesshire
Phone: (0896) 830323

Twenty-eight miles (45 km) south of the city, Traquair is the oldest inhabited house in Scotland, dating back to *circa* AD 950. The Stuart family has lived there since 1491 and entertained many tragic figures including Mary, Queen of Scots and Bonnie Prince Charlie. There is a working brewery, craft workshops, a nature trail and a chapel. (For further details see the Stately Homes article in the main body of this book.)

Open: Easter to mid-October: Monday to Sunday, 13.30–17.30
July to end of August: Monday to Sunday, 10.30–17.30

Other Places of Interest

The Camera Obscura and Outlook Tower

10 1C

Castle Hill
Phone: (031) 226 3709

Installed in the 1850s in the Outlook Tower on Castle Hill, the camera obscura throws a clear image of Edinburgh onto a white, concave table top.

Open: Camera Obscura: May to September: Monday to Sunday, 10.00–17.00
October to April: Sunday, 11.00–16.30
Outlook Tower: May to September: Monday to Saturday, 09.30–17.45
Sunday, 10.00–19.00
October to April: Monday to Saturday, 09.30–17.00

Edinburgh Zoological Park

9 2A

134 Corstorphine Road
Phone: (031) 334 9171

Dogs are not admitted. You will need at least half a day to see around the 80 acres (32 ha) of woodland and parkland at the Scottish National Zoological Park, Edinburgh. The animals are displayed sympathically and the zoo's policy is to emphasize the educational aspects of a zoological garden but not at the expense of entertainment value. Don't miss the splendid collection of penguins. Facilities for the elderly, invalids, and the handicapped are available. (For further details see the Edinburgh Zoological Park article in the main body of this book.)

Open: April to October: Monday to Saturday, 09.00–18.00 Sunday, 09.30–18.00
November to March: Monday to Saturday, 09.00–16.30 Sunday, 09.30–16.30

Royal Botanic Garden

4 2C

Inverleith Row
Phone: (031) 552 7171

Established as a Physic Garden in 1670, this is the second largest botanic garden in Britain. A scientific establishment, it is also famous for its collection of rhododendrons. The gardens and plant houses cover 70 acres (28 ha) and are only ten minutes from the city centre.
Invalid chairs are available. Dogs not admitted. (For further details see the Royal Botanic Garden article in the main body of this book.)

Open: Garden: Monday to Saturday, 09.00–sunset Sunday, 10.00–sunset
During the Festival: 10.00–sunset

Closing time 1 hour before sunset during British Summer Time:
March 22 to October 25
Closed 1 January
Plant houses and Exhibition hall:
Monday to Saturday, 10.00–17.00
Sunday 11.00–17.00

The Herbarium and Library are not open to the public. Researchers should apply in writing to the Regius Keeper

Section III – Culture, Entertainment and Recreation

In this section of the directory, the visitor will find information about the city's music, night life, theatre, sport and open spaces. For detailed information about three of Edinburgh's most famous events contact the offices listed below.

The Edinburgh Festival
The Festival is always held in the last two weeks of August and the first week of September.
Details are available from April onwards and throughout the Festival from:
The Festival Society
21 Market Street
Phone: (031) 226 4001

Concert Halls and Theatres

The visitor to Edinburgh can normally rely on finding an opera, concert, ballet or play that is to his taste. During the hectic August and September weeks of the Edinburgh Festival the range of choices is overwhelming, but throughout the year there is an ever-changing cultural programme on offer at the concert halls and theatres listed below. Ring the Edinburgh Bookshop (031) 225 4296, which acts as booking agency for many halls; contact individual box offices at the venues; check the advertisements in *The Scotsman* and *Evening News* or ask at your hotel for details of the current programme.

The box office at the Usher Hall (10 1C) Lothian Road, phone: (031) 228 1155, will provide details of the special lunchtime and evening concerts that groups such as the Edinburgh Quartet and the Scottish Baroque Ensemble put on at country houses and churches in and around Edinburgh.

Standards of performance obviously vary with each company and are outside the scope of these reviews. However, visitors can use these reviews to identify the best seats, and get an impression of the acoustics and ambience of each hall.

Churchill Theatre

10 3C

33a Morningside Road

A municipally owned theatre that presents amateur productions for most of the year, but is used by professional companies during the Festival.

Events: Amateur production of plays and operas by companies of variable ability.

Tickets: Box office at the theatre, phone: (031) 447 7597
Edinburgh Bookshop, 57 George Street, phone: (031) 225 4296.
During the Festival, 21 Market Street, phone: (031) 226 4001.
J. & A. Cruikshank, 62 Morningside Road, (opposite theatre)

Acoustics: Nondescript
Atmosphere: Mundane
Comforts: Minimal

Freemasons Hall

10 1C

96 George Street

At one time Edinburgh's main recital hall, with 600 seats, the Freemasons Hall has become less popular in recent years.

Events: Recitals and chamber concerts, mainly during the Festival

Tickets: Box office only at the Edinburgh Bookshop, 57 George Street, phone: (031) 225 4296. During the Festival, 21 Market Street, phone: (031) 226 4001

Acoustics: Warm and resonant—excellent for string quartets and solo voices, but rather boomy for a piano.

Seats: Best, centre and front stalls; worst, back stalls

Atmosphere: A pillared, marble auditorium complete with an ornate (but musically inadequate) organ console

French Institute

9 1B

13 Randolph Crescent

France's cultural headquarters in Scotland with seating for around 100 people and breathtaking views across the Dean Valley.

Events: Concerts, plays, film shows and exhibitions are presented in the first-floor salon; teaching facilities and a library are also available

Tickets: Box office at the Institute, phone: (031) 225 5366

Acoustics: Acceptable

Atmosphere: An attractive concert room which in recent years has been allowed to go to seed slightly—the Gaveau piano, for example, has seen happier days

George Square Theatre

10 1C

south side of George Square

A modern auditorium with 334 seats, owned by Edinburgh University.

Events: Plays, university opera productions and occasional concerts

Tickets: Box office at the door before the performance Edinburgh

Bookshop, 57 George Street, phone: (031) 225 4296

Acoustics: Geared for speech but adequate for opera—though instrumental tone is dry and the lack of an orchestra pit creates problems in operatic performances

Seats: Best, the sight-lines are good in the centre, less good at the sides

Atmosphere: The raked auditorium with black leather seats is relatively intimate

Comforts: There is a coffee bar in the basement

King's Theatre

10 2C

*Tollcross
Leven Street*

Edinburgh's 'Festspielhaus' was formerly owned by Howard & Wyndham, but is now the property of the city. A handsome, decorative Victorian theatre, which formerly had 1650 seats—the number has been reduced by the brutal insertion of an ugly lighting switchboard at the back of the stalls and a crudely-extended orchestra pit. King's Theatre is used for international opera during the Festival, but is otherwise over-dependent on second rate repertory companies.

Events: Ballet, drama, light opera, opera, pantomime, touring productions, variety

Tickets: Box office in the theatre, phone: (031) 229 1201
During the Festival, 21 Market Street, phone: (031) 226 4001

Acoustics: Basically good, clear and warm, but can be overloaded by operas requiring large orchestras

Seats: Best, in the grand circle, beyond the overhang; worst, at the back of the grand circle

Atmosphere: Potentially a delightful and intimate Mozart house, which can be satisfactory also for 19th-century and modern operas if the productions have been properly geared for the stage. Foreign productions at the Festival often look cramped, and sometimes fail to function effectively. Nevertheless the King's has been the scene of many memorable performances.

Comforts: Unfortunately, the bars are often under-staffed and no food is served, but there are several good restaurants nearby

Leith Theatre

2 3B

28 Ferry Road

Once Leith Town Hall, this cavernous 1442-seat theatre presents amateur opera.

Events: Amateur opera, the odd pantomime

Tickets: Box office at the door before the performance, phone: (031) 554 1408
Edinburgh Bookshop, 57 George Street, phone: (031) 225 4296

Acoustics: Woolly and unexciting, with no impact

Seats: Best, front stalls; worst, back stalls

Atmosphere: A traditional hall—a long rectangle with a shallow balcony that extends round three sides of the auditorium—that does not have the acoustical advantages normally associated with this design

Comforts: Minimal

McEwan Hall

10 2D

*Teviot Row, off
Teviot Place*

A familiar circular landmark in Bristol Street, McEwan Hall is the ceremonial hall of Edinburgh University.

Events: Apart from university ceremonies the hall is used for choral concerts, carol concerts, and organ recitals

Tickets: Box office at the door before the performance, phone: (031) 667 1011 ext. 4343
Edinburgh Bookshop, 57 George Street, phone: (031) 225 4296

Acoustics: So resonant that much music turns instantly to mud, but John Cage's 'Hpschd', with its array of harpsichords, has been performed successfully, and it suits other works which call for something different from normal concert-hall conditions. It would be admirable for Berlioz's 'Grande Messe des Morts' which has never been performed in these appropriately reverberant surroundings.

Atmosphere: Grandly-pillared and palatial

Music Hall

10 1C

54 George Street

Linked to the Assembly Rooms in George Street, the Music Hall has 1178 seats and is municipally owned

Events: Occasional recitals and chamber concerts. The hall is also used by amateur symphony orchestras, such as the Scottish Sinfonia, and by drama groups during the Edinburgh Festival

Tickets: Box office at the door before the performance, phone: (031) 225 3614
Edinburgh Bookshop, 57 George Street, phone: (031) 225 4296

Acoustics: Inadequate and unflattering to all forms of music

Atmosphere: Dull; the hall has been redecorated, but with little success

Nelson Hall

4 2D

2–8 McDonald Road

An annexe of the McDonald Road Public Library, that holds between one and two hundred people.

Events: Concerts at the Nelson Hall are, by a long established Edinburgh tradition, free. Joan and Hester Dickson, the cellist and pianist, organize monthly chamber concerts and recitals by various performers during the winter season.

Tickets: Box office at the door before the performance, phone: (031) 556 5630
From any public library

Acoustics: Adequate

Seats: Best, middle to rear

Atmosphere: Institutional

Comforts: Nil

Playhouse Theatre

4 3D

20 Greenside Place

A multi-purpose auditorium with 3500 seats that was famed in its day as the city's largest cinema—a stage and dressing rooms prove that it once has theatrical aspirations. In 1980 the building was renovated by the Playhouse Society for the Scottish Opera, the Scottish Ballet and anyone else who cares to use it, including rock

groups. Between live shows the auditorium is still used as a cinema, and upstairs a small night-club provides a platform for jazz groups and other more specialized performers.

Events: The Scottish Opera hold short seasons several times a year, and concerts are presented by groups as large as the Scottish National Orchestra (SNO) and as small as the Scottish Baroque Ensemble

Tickets: Box office, 20 Greenside Place (4 3D), adjoining the theatre, phone: (031) 557 2590

Acoustics: Adequate, though in operatic performances the orchestra is favoured at the expense of the singers

Atmosphere: Controversial. The Scottish Opera like the Playhouse because of the size of the audience, but the nature of the auditorium, with its very open orchestra pit and broad but shallow stage means that performances are lacking in balance and finesse. Seats in the grand circle are too far from the stage, causing a serious lack of contact between audience and singers. The decor is crude and makeshift, and the auditorium lights have a dim cinema air.

Comforts: The bars are large, but service is often slow. The audience are often badly supervised—at a performance of the 'Messiah' in 1980 smoking was permitted.

Queen's Hall

10 2D

89 Clerk Street

Edinburgh's best, most active and inviting concert hall, with a maximum of 800 seats (if restricted-view seats are used). Set in a renovated Georgian church, it is the home of the Scottish Chamber Orchestra (SCO) and Scottish Baroque Ensemble (SBE)

Events: Regular concerts are given by the SCO and SBE throughout the winter season. The SCO play mid-week and Saturday evening programmes, with conductors including Roderick Brydon (artistic director) and Raymond Leppard (principal guest conductor), with star soloists in concertos, and a repertoire ranging from Bach to modern music. The SBE, directed by the violinist Leonard Friedman, perform a wide repertoire of music for strings, usually mid-week. There are regular Wednesday lunchtime recitals with guest soloists, organised by the SBE. Lunch can be eaten in the

auditorium itself, or in the adjoining bar. The hall is also hired to other groups such as the Edinburgh Bach Choir, the Meadows Chamber Orchestra and the New Music Group of Scotland, who appear there from time to time. Jazz concerts, lectures and workshop sessions are also given. The Hall has already become a major asset to the Festival, and the long bar is sometimes used for specialised small-scale concerts.

Tickets: Box office in the Hall, phone (031) 668 2117
Edinburgh Bookshop, 57 George Street, phone (031) 225 4296
During the Festival, 21 Market Street, phone (031) 226 4001

Acoustics: Bright and immediate. The audience sit within the reverberation area of the sound instead of outside it, as in many larger halls.

Seats: Best, the centre stalls, particularly towards the rear, but the ground-floor pews though hard, are almost equally good; the upstairs pews are also more than adequate, in spite of poor sight-lines at the side.

Atmosphere: Good, with an involved relationship between audience and performers. The square auditorium, with its restful decor, strikes a nice balance between church and concert hall.

Comforts: A large bar and buffet, with tables and exhibition space, where lunch and pre-concert and post-concert meals are served. There is also a small coffee bar at the other side of the auditorium, which doubles as reception room. The whole place, in its style, flair and friendliness, sets an example to Edinburgh's other halls and auditoriums.

Reid Concert Hall

10 2D

McEwan Hall,
Teviot Row, off Teviot Place

A lofty university hall with 310 seats, that was formerly known as the Reid School of Music.

Events: Much used for chamber music, recitals, programmes of choral music, student concerts and fringe events during the Festival. Though some performers have moved away to the Queen's Hall, the Reid remains a thriving, busy place, with university concerts on most Thursday evenings between autumn and early summer; the hall is also let out to independent concert promoters

Tickets: Box office at the door, phone: (031) 667 1011 ext. 4577 The Edinburgh Bookshop, 57 George Street, phone: (031) 225 4296 for some events

Acoustic: Unflattering and unpredictable. The unusual scale of the auditorium causes some unhappy sound effects, with orchestral works tending to seem rough and congested and chamber music, by contrast, dim-toned and disembodied

Seats: No best seats though chamber music sounds more immediate in the front stalls

Atmosphere: The raked auditorium with no balconies gives the hall a relatively intimate air which is somewhat offset by its height, but an institutional feeling persists.

Comforts: Knee-room in the hall is limited and the foyer is small. No refreshments are available.

Royal Lyceum Theatre

10 1C

middle of Lothian Road next to Usher Hall Grindley Street

Edinburgh's main playhouse the 1200-seat Royal Lyceum is the home of the Lyceum Theatre Company. Apart from plays, there are occasional opera performances — Thea Musgrave's 'Voice of Ariadne' can be heard in a production by the Cologne Opera Studio at the 1981 Edinburgh Festival

Events: Drama performed by the resident repertory company; varied performances during the Festival

Tickets: Box office in the theatre, phone: (031) 229 9697 During the Festival, 21 Market Street, phone: (031) 226 4001

Acoustics: Like most theatres somewhat dry, but acceptable for music. To facilitate opera productions, a pit big enough to hold a medium-sized orchestra was sunk in the early 1970s.

Seats: Best, grand circle

Atmosphere: Warm and traditional, the auditorium is an attractive and intimate example of Victoriana

Comforts: Bar facilities and a restaurant

St. Cecilia's Hall

10 1D

Cowgate

Edinburgh's original Georgian concert hall is now owned by the university, and has been renovated both as a concert hall and a home for the world-famous Russell Collection of harpsichords. But it is more than a museum: it is a 250-seat concert hall where these instruments are put to practical use, forming an ideal setting for the university's annual summer festival, 'Bach at St. Cecilia's Hall'.

Events: Chamber concerts and recitals, including a winter season by the Georgian Concert Society.

Tickets: Seats bookable at the door before the performance, phone; (031) 667 1011 ext. 4415 Edinburgh Bookshop, 57 George Street, phone: (031) 225 4296 During the Festival, 21 Market Street, phone: (031) 226 4001

Acoustics: Ideal for harpsichord and other keyboard instruments from the period before the modern concert grand, but the beautiful oval auditorium has proved less happy for string-tones and tends to reject (quite rightly, some would say) the sound of a modern piano

Seats: Best, those at the side, towards the rear

Atmosphere: The shape of the auditorium gives the hall a special intimacy, portraits, tapestries and chandeliers add to the charm, but sight-lines are poor

Comforts: The 'Laigh' room beneath the auditorium has facilities for coffee and buffet suppers, but is not always open

St. Mary's Episcopal Church

9 1B

Palmerston Place

This lofty Anglican church was completed in 1917; it towers over Palmerston Place

Events: The cathedral choir gives concerts throughout the year, as do visiting choirs. In addition, there are organ recitals and occasional operatic performances e.g. Britten's three church parables, and Peter Maxwell Davies' 'Jongleur de Nôtre Dame', all staged during the Festival

Tickets: Box office at the door before the performance, phone: (031) 225 6293 Edinburgh Bookshop, 57 George Street, phone: (031) 225 4296

Acoustics: Foggy, as is usual in a big cathedral

Seats: All are inadequate

Atmosphere: The imposing gothic architecture is offset by poor sight-lines for opera and concerts and arctic temperatures

Usher Hall

10 1C

Lothian Road

Edinburgh's principal large-scale concert hall, with 2780 seats, is owned by the city and hired out to those who wish to use it—mainly the Scottish National Orchestra during the winter season and a variety of artistes during the Festival

Events: Weekly concerts by the Scottish National Orchestra on Friday evenings between October and April—principal conductor Sir Alexander Gibson; principal guest conductor Paavo Berglund

Tickets: Box office inside the hall, phone (031) 228 1155 Edinburgh Bookshop, 57 George Street, phone: (031) 225 4296 During the Festival, 21 Market Street, phone: (031) 226 4001

Acoustics: Generally admired but patchy. When packed, the sound in the auditorium lacks resonance —though not distressingly so, as in many post-war halls. More disturbing is the lack of real clarity—bass lines, for instance can be hard to hear, and there can be a disturbing lack of impact.

Seats: Best, the upper tier, if you do not suffer from vertigo. These are also the cheapest seats, though undeniably hard to sit on. The worst seats are the back stalls and back rows of the grand tier, where the sound in each case is damped by the overhang.

Atmosphere: A handsome curved hall, but often over-hot and poorly lit

Comforts: Minimal; the new seating is arguably an improvement, but there are still no bar or buffet facilities. The only response to protests has been the provision of plastic cups of coffee, soft drinks and ice-cream.

Discotheques, Night Clubs and Casinos

Edinburgh's residents have never felt the need for sophisticated night clubs, with dinner, a cabaret and dinner jackets—a meal shared by friends in a convivial atmosphere, or an evening in the pub are more to their taste. But younger people do have a reasonable choice of discotheques and night spots, and a selection of these are listed below. Some may become a little noisy, others cater for the youth culture of the moment, and all have, at the least, an over-18 rule. For those who prefer the more chancy delights of roulette and blackjack, Edinburgh has three casinos.

Annabels Discotheque Night Club

10 2C

3 Semple Street
Phone: (031) 229 7733

A long established discotheque that is popular with foreign students, Annabels main dance floor is in a low hot room that is more than half-filled with sofas and small candlelit tables. It looks curiously like an enlarged guest-house lounge—an impression that is reinforced by the chintzy Tretchikoff-style decoration, the tinted mirrors and the bunches of fake flowers.

Open: Monday to Sunday, 21.30–03.00. Entrance £2.00 (men), £1.00 (women)

Bobby McGee's Discotheque

10 1C

96a Rose Street
Phone: (031) 226 6458/225 7795

Noisy, smokey and cavernous, Bobby McGee's is a down-market but popular discotheque in the old tradition. Some of the furnishings have seen better days, and the capable bouncers are occasionally needed, but particularly at weekends the dance floors and bars are packed with groups of Edinburgh's young people.

Open: Monday to Sunday, 21.00–03.00. Entrance £1.00 Monday to Friday; £2.50 for two on Friday, £2.50 per head Saturday

Bungy's

10 1D

5-7 Fishmarket Close
off the High Street
Phone: (031) 225 5428

Bungy's is a relatively new Edinburgh nightspot. It is a place to spend the whole evening, with a coffee-lounge, bistro, and formal dining room. On the first floor there is a cocktail bar and a small dance floor, and on yet another level a wine bar and function suite. An attractively decorated, well-thought-out complex with warm and intimate rooms, Bungy's is popular with all age-groups.

Open: Monday to Sunday, 11.00–02.00. Entrance free

Buster Browns

10 1C

25–27 Market Street
Phone: (031) 226 4224

Buster Browns was the first discotheque of its type to open in Edinburgh. Now the sunken dance floor, small, elegant tables and the pervasive pink lighting seem a little dated and the extensive use of red neon can be oppressive. Nevertheless Buster Browns has style, the best music in Edinburgh and an interesting and smartly dressed clientele.

Open: Sunday, Tuesday, Wednesday, Thursday, 21.30–02.30; Friday and Saturday, 21.30–03.00. Entrance £2.00, Tuesday to Thursday and Sunday; £3.00 Friday and Saturday

Cagney's

10 1D

King James Hotel
St. James Centre
Phone: (031) 556 0111

Attached to the King James Hotel, Cagney's is open to residents and non-residents. The discotheque is small, but makes good use of mirrors and a sophisticated lighting system, while the decor is a mixture of geometric patterns, tiger-strips and photographs from America's Prohibition years. The quality of sound is good, and the music varied, cocktails, hamburgers and pizzas are served.

Open: Monday to Sunday, 21.00–03.00. Entrance £1.00, £2.00 at weekends

Millionaires

10 1C

57 Frederick Street
Phone: (031) 225 3379

Design and presentation are definitely up-market in this new Edinburgh nightspot, and a genial doorman ensures that standards are maintained. Dishes are served from a reasonably priced and wide-ranging lunch and a dinner menu at tables round an underlit dance floor. On Saturday and Sunday the licensing laws oblige the management to provide a free supper after 23.00, with dishes such as scampi and chicken, and bar snacks are available at all times. Drinks and wine are slightly expensive, but cocktails surprisingly cheap. 'Millionaires' is elegant and comfortable and appeals to most age-groups.

Open: Monday to Friday, 12.00–02.30, Saturday and Sunday, 12.00–01.00. Entrance £1.00 weekdays, £2.00 Friday and Saturday

The Nite Club

4 3D

Playhouse Theatre
20 Greenside Place
Phone: (031) 557 2692

The Nite Club is the haunt of those who follow new fashions and trends—until recently anarchy ruled, hair was spiked and T-shirts ripped. Bands would spit and crowds pogo on Fridays and Saturdays; now the ruffles, velvet, lace and relative docility of the 'new romantic' movement are more in evidence.
On Fridays, Saturdays and Sundays the Ital Reggae club holds a discotheque in either the Nite Club itself, or the rooms below. On Friday and Sunday the music is exclusively reggae, on Saturday soul is played as well.

Open: Friday, Saturday, Sunday, 21.00–02.00. Entrance £2.00, members £1.50

Pipers

10 1C

23–25 Lothian Road
Phone: (031) 229 8291

Pipers was once a venue for 'Scottish Nights' and the decor reflects this—scarlet plush wallpaper, formica tables and tartan shields. Now it is a discotheque and young people crowd a long, low room, which has two dance floors and three bars. Drinks are slightly more expensive than in pubs, and notices warn ladies to keep an eye on their handbags, but Pipers is popular and informal, with familiar music and adequate facilities.

Open: Monday to Sunday, 20.00–03.00. Entrance £1.00, weekends £2.00. Over-20s only

Tiffanys

4 3C

99 St. Stephen Street
Phone: (031) 556 6292

A large and versatile nightspot, decorated in a rather synthetic tropical style. The bars are expensive and the staff friendly if obeyed, but Tiffanys is always popular, with a well chosen range of events that varies each evening. Private functions are held on Monday and Tuesday night, but on Wednesday there is a roller-disco for the over-18s—open 20.00–01.00, entrance £1.00, skate hire £1.00. Thursday is 'over-25s' night, when a resident band plays 'golden oldies'—open: 21.00–02.00; entrance £1.80.
Friday and Saturday a discotheque and resident band play for the over-18s—open: 20.00–2.00, entrance £1.80, after 21.00, £2.30

Top O'

10 1C

40–42 Grindlay Street
Phone: (031) 229 6697

A recent addition to the Bella Napoli Italian restaurant, Top O' describes itself as 'Edinburgh's Exclusive Night Spot'. Drinks and coffee are served in a cocktail bar and lounge just past the entrance, and an enticingly-lit corridor leads to the main 'Starlight Room'. Here gracious hostesses preside over a sophisticated and discreetly lit room, with an underlit dance floor and small cocktail bar. Each table has a telephone, which can be used, amongst other things, to contact the disc jockey.

Open: Monday to Sunday, 17.00–01.00; Saturday and Sunday, 17.00–03.00. Entrance £2.00, Saturday and Sunday, otherwise free

Valentino's

10 2C

3a East Fountainbridge
Phone: (031) 229 5151

One of Edinburgh's first discotheques, Valentino's has survived many changes of fashion and fortune. Closed from Monday to Wednesday, and with private functions held on Thursday, the weekend starts at Valentino's on Friday. But it is on Saturday and Sunday that the main dance floor and J.J.'s, the art deco bar upstairs, are packed with the pirates, pageboys and Titanias of the 'New Romantic' movement. In six months, fashions might have changed, but Valentino's will probably still reflect the latest in life-styles.

Open: Monday 21.00–03.00 local groups; Wednesday, 21.00–03.00 'funk'; Thursday, 21.00–03.00 electronic music; Friday and Saturday, 22.00–03.00; Sunday, 20.00–03.00 live groups/disco alternate weeks

Casinos

There are three casinos in Edinburgh, all of which welcome new members. However, to comply with Britain's gaming laws membership is not effective until 48 hours after signing-in. If you go as a guest of a member there are no such restrictions. Men must wear trousers (not jeans) and a collar and tie. There are few frills to Edinburgh casinos, and the atmosphere tends to be low-lit and plush in the manner of Chinese restaurants—which may go some way to explaining the presence in these establishments of large numbers of the city's Chinese community. Minimum stakes are low, especially during the day.

Regency Casino

4 3C

20 Great King Street
Phone: (031) 556 2828

Apart from being decorated with a greater degree of taste than the others, the Regency seems to have a more professional attitude all-round. A complimentary buffet

is available at all times and there is a licensed bar, open from 19.30. American Roulette and Blackjack are played.

Open: Monday to Friday, 14.00–04.00; Saturday, 14.00–02.00; Sunday, 19.30–04.00. Over-18s only

Royal Chimes Casino Club

4 3D

3 Royal Terrace
Phone: (031) 556 1055

Decorated in a rather chintzy style, with red velour and clock wallpaper this privately-owned casino has an easy-going and friendly atmosphere. Meals are served in the restaurant, while coffee and light snacks are available free of charge, and there is a small cocktail bar. American Roulette, Blackjack and Punto Banco are played.

Open: Monday to Friday, 14.00–04.00; Saturday, 19.00–02.00; Sunday, 21.00–04.00. Over-18s only

Casino Martell

10 2D

7 Newington Road
Phone: (031) 667 7763

This is the most 'down-market' of the casinos but it is nevertheless popular. the atmosphere is noticeably more relaxed, with less concern over dress than elsewhere. Coffee and tea are provided free, and there is a restaurant, with waitress service and a bar. American Roulette and Blackjack are played.

Open: Monday to Friday and Sunday, 22.00–04.00; Saturday, 22.00–02.00. Over-18s only

Folk, Dance and Traditional Music

Traditional Scottish music and folk music is very much alive in Edinburgh. Sandy Bell's, as the Forrest Hill Bar, is internationally known and *Sandy Bell's Broadsheet* has a worldwide distribution. But the focus of the year for the city's traditional music enthusiasts is the Edinburgh Folk Festival. During this ten-day Festival (in 1982 March

26 to April 4) there are concerts of every size, workshops, folk-drama events, piping and fiddle courses and jam sessions that are open to all. For further information, write to:

John Barrow
The Director
Edinburgh Folk Festival
170 High Street
Edinburgh
Phone: (031) 226 3645

In the Fringe section of the main Edinburgh Festival (August 16 to September 5, 1981) there is also a sizeable programme of traditional Scottish music. The Fringe programme is available from June, and can be obtained from:

The Festival Fringe Society Office
10 1D
170 High Street
Edinburgh
Phone: (031) 226 5257

Folk, dance and traditional music can also be enjoyed throughout the year at a number of hotels, bars and halls in Edinburgh; a selection of these are listed below.

Edinburgh Folk Club

10 1D

Carlton Hotel
North Bridge
Phone: (031) 229 6583; hotel
(031) 556 7277

Wednesday, 20.00–23.00. Entrance around £1.20

Edinburgh University Folk Song Society

10 1D

Lady Glenorchy's Parish Hall
corner of Roxburgh Place
Drummond Street
and on alternate Fridays
The Tolbooth Tavern

10 1D

167 Canongate
Phone: (031) 339 3946

Fridays during the University term, 20.00–23.00

Fiddlers Arms

10 1C

9–11 Grassmarket
Phone: (031) 229 2665

Monday, 20.00–23.00 Entrance free
Glenelg Hotel

10 2C

12–14 Leamington Terrace
Phone: (031) 229 6481

Wednesday, 20.00–23.00

The Eagle Pipers Society

4 3D

King James Hotel
St James Centre
Phone: (031) 556 0111
Alastair Graham in the Queen's Lounge: Sunday, 20.00–22.30
Entrance free

Menzies Hotel

4 3D

24 Royal Terrace
Phone: (031) 556 6055

Friday and Sunday, 20.00–22.30. Entrance free

St. Vincent Bar

4 3C

9 St. Vincent Street
Phone: (031) 225 7447

Tuesday, 20.00–23.00. Entrance free

Sandy Bell's (Forrest Hill Bar)

10 1C

25 Forrest Road
Phone: (031) 225 1156

Some event is held nearly every night—phone for information, or ask at a hotel or tourist office for *Sandy Bell's Broadsheet*, which gives information on all folk activity in and around Edinburgh.

A number of societies hold meetings and recitals throughout the year. For more information, ring the numbers listed below or watch for advertisements in the local paper:

An Comunn Gaidhealach (Gaelic poetry, singing, ceilidhs or clarodh)
Iain Wright, phone: (031) 334 5130

Edinburgh Highland Reel and Strathspey Society

Iain Cameron, phone: (031) 669 5927

The Clarsach Society
Polly Thomas, phone: (031) 667 6465

Princes Street Gardens
(10 1C)

Between June 20 and September 6, Princes Street Gardens are used as the venue for Scottish Country Dancing evenings. They are held on every Tuesday at 17.30; on alternate Saturdays at 20.00 and on alternate Mondays at 19.30. Visitors can watch the dances for a fee of 15p. and are allowed to join in the jigs, reels and Strathspeys.

A Highland Gathering is held in Princes Street Gardens on the last Sunday in August, with a Highland dancing and pipe band competition. The fee for spectators is 15p.

The Scottish Pipe Band Championships are held in Princes Street Gardens on the last Saturday in June. Spectators are charged 15p.

Jazz

Edinburgh has a thriving jazz scene. On most nights of the week a wide range of jazz styles can be enjoyed in the city's bars and hotels, but the climax of the year for local enthusiasts is the few days in the summer when the Edinburgh Jazz Festival is held (in 1981 August 23–27). On the first day local musicians and internationally known stars parade down Princes Street to hold a 'Mardi Gras' at the Grassmarket; the last event is 'The Final Jazz Band Ball' at Tiffany's. For more information about the Jazz Festival contact—'Platform', the jazz society that promotes concerts throughout Scotland, at 45 Queen Street (10 1C)
Phone : (031) 226 4179

Traditional jazz tends to be the most popular style, but mainstream and modern jazz can be found. Some of the names to look out for are 'The Festival City Jazz Band' (traditional and Dixieland), The Louisiana Ragtime Band' (New Orleans), the 'Scottish Jazz Advocates', 'Swing 1981' and the 'Gordon Cruikshank Sextet' (all modern).

Some of the pubs and hotels at which jazz can be heard are listed below.

Afton Hotel

9 1B

6 Grosvenor Crescent
Phone (031) 225 7033

Thursday and Sunday, 21.00–23.00; Dougie Campbell and Ron Dunn—traditional and modern. Drinks at normal prices no food

Barnton Hotel

9 1A

at Queensferry Roundabout
Queensferry Road
Phone: (031) 339 1144

Sunday, 12.30–15.30; Festival City Jazz Band in the Function Suite. Family atmosphere. Drinks above normal prices, foods available

Black Bull

10 1C

12 Grassmarket
Phone (031) 225 6636

Tuesday, 20.30–23.00; Climax Jazz Band. Drinks at normal prices, food available

Caledonian Hotel

10 1C

west end of Prince Street
Phone: (031) 225 2433

Thursday and Sunday, 20.00–23.45; Scottish Jazz Advocates. Drinks at normal prices, no food

Glenelg Hotel

10 2C

12–14 Leamington Terrace
Phone: (031) 229 6481

Thursday, 20.30–23.00; Gleneig All Stars. Drinks at normal prices, food available

Goblet

10 1C

110–114 Rose Street
Phone: (031) 225 8088

Wednesday, 20.30–23.30; Charlie McNair's Hokum—traditional. Drinks at normal prices, pizzas available. Over-21 only

Grange Hotel

10 3C

8 Whitehouse Terrace
Phone: (031) 667 5681

Tuesday, 20.00–22.30; West End Jazz Band—traditional. Drinks at normal prices, no food

Hopetoun Bar

10 2C

18 Morrison Street
Phone: (031) 229 6683

Wednesday, 20.30–22.45; Bill Salmond's Louisiana Ragtime Band—traditional. Drinks at normal prices, food available

La Grenouille

4 3C

20 Abercromby Place
Phone: (031) 556 2270

Modern to Saturday, 20.30–23.30; varying bands—traditional to modern. Drinks at normal prices, food available.

Menzies Hotel

4 3D

24 Royal Terrace
Phone: (031) 556 1022

Thursday, 20.30–23.00; West End Jazz Band. Drinks at normal prices, no food

Scottish Evenings

These entertainments, which usually include dinner and a 'Scots Cabaret', are designed for those visitors to Edinburgh who do not have friends or relations in the city to show them a more authentic Scottish night out. They represent the popular image of a Scottish evening rather than the actuality — nevertheless, many find them thoroughly enjoyable, and the emphasis on the ghosts of Harry Lauder and Robert Burns and the steaming haggis make it necessary to book well ahead. Several of the venues at which a 'Scottish Evening' can be experienced are listed below.

Jamie's Scottish Night Out

4 3D

King James Hotel
St. James Centre
Phone: (031) 556 0111

A slick, well-run show hosted by Larry Marshall, a veteran of the live audience. Dinner takes up the first hour, with a versatile Scottish dance-band in attendance, and the cabaret, with audience-participation, follows. Halfway through the evening there is a compulsory taste of haggis, and Burn's famous toast.

Scottish cabaret; five-course banquet; haggis supper.

May to October: Monday to Saturday, 19.15–22.15. Price £12.00 per head without wine, £6.00 without dinner

An Evening with Scott Paul Young

5 2A

Kingsway Hotel
14 Hermitage Place
Phone: (031) 554 6206

The Kingsway offers a similar, but rather less sophisticated show to that at Jamie's. After dinner, the evening proper begins with the appearance of Scott Paul Young, a kilted crooner, and an entourage of dancers, a piper and an excellent accordionist. The haggis is toasted and then tasted; comedy antics follow, with the usual audience participation.

Scottish cabaret; dinner.

April to November: Monday to Sunday, 19.30–23.30.
Price: £12.00 per head without wine, £4.50 without dinner

Dalhousie Jacobean Banquet

20 2C

Dalhousie Courte
Bonnyrigg (8 miles/13 km
southwest of Edinburgh)
Phone: (031) 663 5155

The Jacobean Banquet at Dalhousie is markedly different from the other Scottish evenings. The setting is the year 1623—guests sit at long trestle tables, and the entire five-course meal is eaten with the fingers and small knife. Wine and mead flow freely and is served by 'court ladies', splendidly attired in the dress of the period. During and after the meal, these ladies sing from a well-chosen repertoire of contemporary music.

Jacobean banquet, with entertainment.

Monday to Saturday, 19.30–23.30. Price: £12.30 per head; free transport available from and to city centre (bus leaves Edinburgh 18.45)—details on booking.

Recreation

In the following pages the sporting and recreational facilities that can be enjoyed by visitors to Edinburgh are listed.

Fishing

The lochs, rivers and reservoirs around Edinburgh teem with rainbow trout, brown trout and other freshwater fish, and can be fished during the game-fishing season (April 1 to September 30). Below is a guide to some of the many facilities available to the fisherman —but it should be noted that only fly-fishing is allowed in reservoirs.

No map references have been included here for the actual fishing areas. Direction enquiries can be made when obtaining the necessary permits.

Reservoirs administered by Lothian Regional Council

Day-permits for these reservoirs can be obtained from:

The Department of Water Supply services,
Lothian Regional Council
Comiston Springs
55 Buckstone Terrace
Phone: (031) 445 4141

Boat-hire costs £2.35, and up to two rods can be hired for £1.15, except in the case of Gladhouse Reservoir, where permits are for half-a-day. Bank-fishing is only permitted at Harperrig, Roseberry, Talla and Frind Reservoirs, and at Whiteadder Reservoir after June 1. Boats may be used from 08.00 until one hour after sunset. Fishing is allowed from Monday to Sunday during the season, except on those reservoirs listed under 'No Sunday Fishing'.

Monday to Sunday Fishing

Clubbiedean, south of Colinton—15 minutes southwest of Edinburgh
Donolly, Gifford—60 minutes east of Edinburgh
Fruid, Tweedsmuir, Borders—45 minutes south of Edinburgh
Harlaw, Balerno—10 minutes southwest of Edinburgh
Hopes, south of Gifford—60 minutes east of Edinburgh
Roseberry, Temple, Midlothian—30 minutes south of Edinburgh
Talla, Tweedsmuir, Borders—45 minutes south of Edinburgh
Whiteadder, east of Gifford —60 minutes east of Edinburgh

No Sunday Fishing

Crosswood, West Calder, Midlothian—40 minutes southwest of Edinburgh
Gladhouse, Temple, Midlothian—30 minutes south of Edinburgh
Glencorse, Penicuik, Midlothian—15 minutes south of Edinburgh
Harperrig, Mid Calder, Midlothian—30 minutes southwest of Edinburgh

Other Fresh-water Fishing

The waters listed below are administered individually, and a permit is required:

Duddingston Loch and Dunsapie Loch

Coarse fish. No charge but a permit must be obtained from:
Scottish Development Department

9 1B

17 Atholl Crescent
Phone:(031) 229 9321

Bonaly Reservoir

south of Colinton—15 minutes
southwest of Edinburgh

Brown trout. No permit required.
Fly-fishing only.

Union Canal

10 minutes west of Edinburgh.

Coarse fish. No charge but a permit must be obtained from:
Lothian Regional Council

9 1B

Department of Leisure Services
40 Torphichen Street
Phone: (031) 229 9292

Esk River

from Estuary to Buccleuch
Estate

Brown trout. A permit must be obtained from:
T Mealyou Sports Shop

20 2C

11 Newbiggin Musselburgh
Phone: (031) 665 2671

North Esk River

between Dalkeith and
Penicuik

Brown trout. A permit must be obtained from:
G.R. Scott

20 2C

9 Sherwood View
Bonnyrigg
Phone: (031) 663 4919

North Esk Reservoir

14 miles (22.5km) southwest of Edinburgh

Brown and river trout. Fly-Fishing only. A permit must be obtained from:
Mr Jones

20 1D

Fairlie Hope Farm
West Linton
Phone: West Linton 425

Threipmuir Reservoir and Harlaw Reservoir

Balerno, 25 minutes southwest of Edinburgh.

Brown trout and rainbow trout. Fly-fishing from the banks only. Season and weekly permits from:
The Factor

19 1B

The Leuchold
South Queensferry
Phone: (031) 331 1749

Daily permits from:
Alexander Fleming,
Newsagent

19 2B

42 Main Street
Balerno
Phone: (031) 449 3833

Water of Leith

from Balerno to Redbraes.

Brown trout, No charge but a permit must be obtained from:
Lothian Regional Council

9 1B

Department of Leisure Services
40 Torphichen Street
Phone: (031) 229 9292

Beecraigs Loch

30 minutes west of Edinburgh.

Brown and rainbow trout. Permit from:
West Lothian District Council

19 1A

Department of Leisure and Recreation
Old County Buildings
Linlithgow
Phone: Linlithgow 3121

Equipment

Fishing Equipment may be hired from:

Golf and Fishing Centre

9 2B

58 Dalry Road
Phone: (031) 337 5888

Open: Monday to Saturday, 09.30–17.30

Shooting Line

8 1D

23 Roseburn Terrace
Phone: (031) 337 8616

Open: Monday to Saturday, 09.00–17.30; closed Wednesday in winter

Sea Angling

Sea angling is not particularly popular in Edinburgh, even though the potential of the neighbouring waters is considerable. To hire a boat between May and September, and sometimes on weekends through until November, contact:

Alan Spence
70 Haymans Cove
Eyemouth Borders (49 miles/78.8km) west of Edinburgh)
Phone: (0390) 50566

The 'Gill Too' costs £60.00 for a party of 12, or £5.00 per head. The boat leaves between 09.00 and 10.00 and returns around 18.00.

Private Golf Courses

The following golf clubs, all with 18-hole clubs, all with 18-hole courses, allow non-members to play when the course is not too busy.

Dalmahoy Country Club

19 2B

Kirknewton
7 miles (11km) west of city centre on the main A71 road to Kilmarnock
Phone: (031) 333 2055

Open: Seven days a week 09.00–22.00. Green fees: east course £5.50 weekdays, west course £3.50 weekdays, both courses £6.50 weekdays. On weekends the fee is higher, but non-members can rarely play, because the course is crowded.

Craigmiller Park Golf Club

16 1D

1 Observatory Road
Phone: (031) 667 0047

Open; Monday to Sunday, from dawn until dusk. Green fees: £4.00 Monday to Friday. £6.00 Saturday and Sunday. Equipment is available for hire from the professional. Non-members may not book.

Mortonhall Golf Club

15 2B

231 Braid Road
Fairmilehead
Phone: (031) 447 2411

Open: Seven days a week 08.00–dusk; non-members Monday to Friday only. Green fees £5.00 a round, £6.00 a day. Equipment is available for hire from the professional.

Public Golf Courses

There are seven public golf courses around Edinburgh. Five of them have 18-hole courses with green fees for adults of £1.80, Monday to Saturday, and the greens open from 07.00–21.30. Children and Senior Citizens playing between 09.00 and 17.00 are charged 30p for a round, but before or after these times pay the full green fees. A set of clubs can be hired for £6.80 of which £5.00 is a refundable deposit. Three of the courses are also open on Sundays when all green fees are £1.85

Braid Hills

16 2C

about 3 miles (5km)
south of the city centre
Phone: (031) 447 6666

Braid hills has two 18-hole courses, one course is open Monday to Saturday all the year round; the other is open Monday to Saturday in the summer only

Carrick Knowe Golf Course

8 2D

Balgreen Road
Phone: (031) 337 1096

18 holes, open seven days a week

Craigentinny Golf Course

6 3C

Craigentinny Avenue
Phone: (031) 554 7501

18 holes, open seven days a week

Silverknowes Golf Course

2 2C

Silverknowes Parkway
Phone: (031) 336 3843

18 holes, open seven days a week

Portobello Golf Course

12 1D

Stanley Street
Phone: (031) 669 4361

9 holes, open and Monday to Saturday, 30p per round for adults; 15p per round for Senior Citizens and under-16s.

There is also a short-hole course at Inverleith Park, East Fettes Avenue behind the Royal Botanic Garden. The charges for 18 holes are 25p for adults, and 20p for Senior Citizens and under-16s, with hired clubs these charges increase to 40p for adults and 30p for Senior Citizens and under-16s. The opening hours are Monday to Friday, 12.00–17.00, 18.00–21.00 and Saturday, 10.00–13.00, 14.00–19.00. Inverleith Park is closed on Sunday.

Golf Range

Port Royal Golf Range

19 2B

Eastfield Road
Ingliston (next to Edinburgh Airport)
Phone: (031) 335 4377

Open: Seven days a week, 10.00–23.00 (except for Royal Highland Show week in June)

Facilities include: 24 all-weather floodlit golf bays, 9 targets, 36-hole putting green, practice sand-bunkers, snack bar and lounge. Professional tuition is available at £4.50 per half hour which includes a bucket of approximately 55 golf balls. Without tuition a bucket of golf balls costs £1.00; golf clubs can be hired at a cost of 50p each

Putting Greens

There are several municipal putting greens in the city, all 18-hole courses. Adults are charged 25p for a round, which includes the hire of a club. Under-16s can play for 20p and Senior Citizens for 5p.
Open: Monday to Friday, 12.00–17.00, 18.00–21.00 and Saturday, 10.00–13.00, 14.00–19.00 All greens are closed on Sundays.

Bruntsfield Links

10 2C

Melville Drive

East Pilton

3 2B

Pilton Drive

Harrison Park

9 3B

Harrison Gardens

Inverleith Park

3 3B

between East Fettes Avenue and the Royal Botanic Garden

Leith Links

5 2A

Links Place
Leith

Princes Street Gardens

10 1C

Princes Street

St Margaret's Park

7 2B

off Corstorphine High Street
Corstorphine

Saughton Park

8 2D

Balgreen Road

Victoria Park

4 2C

Ferry Road at junction with Craighall Road

Horse Riding

The following stables, all within 30 minutes drive of Edinburgh's city centre, have horses for hire. They generally offer tuition—either for individuals or as part of a group. Hard hats may be hired, usually for a small charge.

Drum Mohr House

20 2C

Levenhall
Musselburgh, (20 minutes drive east of city centre)
Phone: (031) 665 8333

Open: Monday to Thursday, 09.00–21.30; Saturday and Sunday, 09.00–17.30; closed Friday. Group instruction is £4.30 per hour (adult), £3.80 per hour (child), individual instruction at £9.00 per hour (adult), £4.00 per half hour (child). Rides without instruction cost £4.30 per hour (adult), £2.50

per half hour (child)
Nine ponies and 10 horses; hard hats may be hired for 20p. British Horse Society (BHS) approved.

Edinburgh and Lasswade Riding Centre

20 2C

*Kevock Road
Lasswade, (6½ miles/10.5km south of city centre)
Phone: (031) 663 7676*

Open: Tuesday to Friday, 09.15–21.30; Saturday and Sunday, 09.15–17.30; closed Monday. The largest indoor riding school in Scotland it has three outside schooling-rings and a lunging arena.
Group Riding tuition costs £4.00 per hour, individual tuition costs £7.50. Group jumping tuition costs £5.50 for one and a half hours, private jumping instruction costs £10.00 per hour. Over 60 horses; hard hats may be hired for 20p; there is a tack shop.

Fulmer School of Equitation

2 2C

*Muirhouse Parkway
Silverknowes
Phone: (031) 332 7777*

Open: Tuesday to Sunday, 10.00–17.00; closed Monday. Group instruction £4.80 per hour (adult), £3.80 per hour (child). Individual instruction £7.50 per half hour (adult), £5.50 per half hour (child). Jumping lessons are also offered at the stable and the prices are the same as for individual instruction. Twelve ponies and 6 horses; hard hats may be hired for 5p. School only offers tuition. BHS approved.

Tower Farm Riding Stables

17 2A

*85 Liberton Drive
Phone: (031) 664 3375*

Open: Monday to Wednesday, 10.00–13.00, 14.00–17.00, 18.30–20.30; Thursday, Saturday and Sunday, 10.00–13.00, 14.00–17.00; closed Friday. Group lessons are £4.00 per hour, private lessons £6.50 per hour; rides are £4.00 an hour. Children under-12 are charged 50p less.

Twelve ponies and 10 horses. There is a tack shop. Association of British Riding Schools (ABRS) and BHS approved.

West Acres Hunting and Livery Stables

13 3A

*581 Lanark Road West
Balerno (9 miles/14.5km drive from city centre)
Phone: (031) 449 4142*

Open: Monday to Sunday, 10.00–1400, 19.00–20.00. All rides cost £6.00 for two hours, tuition is provided where needed. All day cross-country rides are offered for £15.00 with a pub lunch included. Seven horses; hard hats provided free.
Hunting at around £15.00 is offered on Saturdays between October and February.

Ice-skating

Murrayfield Ice Rink

9 2A

*Riversdale Crescent
Murrayfield
Phone: (031) 337 6933*

Open: Monday to Sunday. Opening times vary daily. Entrance 35-55p, skate hire 5-10p

Roller-skating

Coasters

10 2C

*3 West Tollcross
Phone: (031) 229 3252*

Roller Disco: Monday to Sunday, 19.00–22.00, until 22.30 on Friday and Saturday; Saturday and Sunday, 10.30-13.00 and 14.00-17.00. Entrance £1.00, skate hire 50p.

Skiing (dry slope)

Hillend Ski Centre

19 2B

*Biggar Road (4 miles/6.4km south of city centre)
Phone: (031) 445 4433*

The largest artificial ski-slope in Europe, with three artificial and three grass slopes. Instruction, equipment hire, cafeteria.

Open: September to April: Monday to Sunday, 09.30–21.00. May to August: Monday, Wednesday, Friday, 09.30–21.00

Shooting

It is extremely difficult for the visitor to Edinburgh to find any shooting at short notice—parties are normally made up several months in advance. But deer stalking, driven partridge and pheasant, mixed shooting and wild fowling on the Island of Islay are all available on application in advance to:

The Sporting Department

10 1C

*10 Rutland Square
Phone: (031) 229 7366*

Snooker

Snooker and Squash Club

9 3A

*146 Slateford Road
Phone: (031) 443 2211/2*

Open: Monday to Sunday, 09.00–23.30. Day membership: £1.00, tables £1.20
Fully licensed.

Sports Centres

Visitors who are not members of these centres are allowed to use some of the facilities—usually for a small entrance fee and an additional charge for the specific sport. Equipment can often be hired, and all the centres have changing rooms and showers. Every centre listed has facilities for the disabled, who in most cases are admitted without charge. Tuition is generally available and in some cases compulsory.

Each sports centre is listed below with the activities that it offers. In the first paragraph below each entry are the general sports that may be enjoyed by non-members; in the second are specialist activities for which a certain level of proficiency, or team-membership, is required.

Craiglockhart Sports Centre

9 3B

*177 Colinton Road
Phone: (031) 443 0101*

Open: Monday to Friday, 09.00–23.00; Saturday and Sunday, 09.00–22.30. Entrance Non-member adults 50p, under-18 25p

General: Badminton, squash, table tennis, indoor and outdoor tennis courts (some floodlit), fitness training, boating and canoeing

Specialist: Archery, fencing, weight training, keep fit, netball, karate, yoga

Jack Kane Centre

12 3C

*Sports Wing
208 Niddrie Mains Road
Phone: (031) 669 0404*

Open: Monday to Sunday, 09.00–23.00. Entrance Non-member adults 50p, under-16 25p

General: Badminton, table tennis, indoor tennis

Specialist: 'Trim course', basketball, boxing, fencing, football, gymnastics, jogging, judo, karate, keep fit, rugby, volleyball

Meadowbank Sports Centre

11 1B

*139 London Road
Phone: (031) 661 5351*

Open: Monday to Sunday, 09.00–22.30. No entrance fee charged for those using and paying for the facilities, but 25p charged if just using the cafeteria or spectating. Crêche available Monday to Friday, 09.30–12.00, 14.00-16.00

General: Athletics, badminton, cricket practice, cycling (with own bike), golf practice, fitness training,

squash, table tennis, tennis

Specialist: Archery, basketball, boxing, cycling (only members may hire bikes) fencing, football, gymnastics, handball, hockey, judo, karate, music and movement, pistol and rifle shooting, rock climbing, trampolining, volleyball, weight-lifting and training, wrestling and yoga

Westerhailes Education Centre

7 2B

*5 Murrayburn Drive
Phone: (031) 1442 2201*

Open: Monday to Friday, 09.30–22.30; Saturday and Sunday, 09.30-18.00
Swimming pool open: Monday to Friday, 09.30–21.30; Saturday and Sunday, 09.30–1630. Indefinite membership for adults is 54p

General: Badminton, Keep fit, squash, swimming, table tennis

Specialist: Basketball, fencing, gymnastics, karate, volleyball

Squash

Several squash courts in Edinburgh are available for the use of those who do not belong to private clubs. These are in great demand, and it is essential to book a court as far in advance as possible.

Craiglockhart Sports Centre

9 3B

*177 Colinton Road
Phone: (031) 443 0101*

6 courts, open: Monday to Friday, 09.00–23.00, Saturday and Sunday, 09.00–22.30. Non-members entrance fee is 50p, hire of court is £1.70 for 30 minutes. Non-members cannot hire equipment. Changing rooms and showers.

Dalmahoy Country Club

19 2B

*Kirknewton (7 miles/11km west of city centre on A71 to Kilmarnock)
Phone:(031) 333 2055*

3 courts in the hotel, open: Monday

to Sunday, 09.00–22.00. Hire of court is £1.60 for 40 minutes. Racquets and balls can be hired, but booking must be made in advance. Changing rooms, showers, restaurant and bar.

Meadowbank Sports Centre

11 1A

*139 London Road
Phone: (031) 661 5351*

6 courts, open: Monday to Sunday, 09.00–22.30. Hire of court is £1.70 for 30 minutes. Non-members cannot hire equipment but purchases may be made at the shop. Changing rooms, showers and cafeteria.

Westerhailes Education Centre

7 2B

*5 Murrayburn Drive
Phone: (031) 442 2201*

2 courts, open: Monday to Friday, 09.30–22.30; Saturday and Sunday, 09.30–18.00. Indefinite membership for adults is 54p. Hire of courts is at £1.07 for 40 minutes. Advance booking is essential. Equipment is available for hire. Changing rooms, showers and cafeteria.

Swimming

A number of swimming pools in Edinburgh are open to the public. Generally the fee is around 50p for adults and 25p for children under-16. All have showers and provide costumes and towels for a small charge. Other facilities that the pools offer are listed below.

Dalry Swimming Pool

9 2B

*middle of Caledonian Crescent
Phone: (031) 337 3915*

Open: Monday to Friday, 12.00–13.30; Tuesday, Thursday and Friday, 17.30–19.00; Saturday, 12.00–15.30

Glenogle Swimming Pool

4 3C

West end of Glenogle Road
Phone: (031) 332 5508

Open: Monday to Friday,
09.00–19.00, Saturday, 09.00–14.00

Infirmary Street Pool

10 1D

Infirmary Street
Phone: (031) 556 5006

Open: Monday to Friday,
09.00–19.00; Saturday, 09.00–16.00

Leith Swimming Pool

4 2D

Junction Place
Phone: (031) 554 1953

Open : Monday to Friday,
15.00–1900; Saturday, 09.00–16.00

Royal Commonwealth Swimming Pool

10 2D

21 Dalkeith Road
Phone: (031) 667 7211

Diving pool, teaching pool, sauna
with solarium, plunge pool,
cafeteria, lavatories and entry
ramp for disabled.

Open: Monday to Friday,
09.00–21.00; Saturday and Sunday,
08.00–19.15.
Sauna open: Monday to Friday,
10.00–20.00 (£2.00 + 60p for
solarium); Saturday to Sunday,
10.00–15.00 (£2.50 + 60p for
solarium)

Warrender Swimming Baths

10 2C

Thirlestane Road
Phone: (031) 447 2780

Open: Monday to Friday,
12.00–19.00; Saturday, 09.00–16.00

Turkish baths and steam room
open: Monday to Friday,
14.00–19.45 (£1.75); Saturday,
09.00–12.00 (£2.00)

Tennis Courts

Courts cannot be booked in
advance, but all are manned by
an attendant who hires out both
the courts and equipment, if required. The charge for 40 minutes for all of the courts listed
below is 25p (adult) and 15p
(under-16) All courts are closed
on Sundays, and most on one
other day. Open: Monday to
Friday, 12.00–17.00, 18.00–
21.00; Saturday, 10.00–13.00,
14.00–19.00.

Racquets and balls may be
hired at reasonable rates. The
courts are open from the beginning of April until the end of
September.

North

East Pilton

3 2B

Pilton Drive

2 courts, no attendant, no charge

Inverleith Park

3 3B

*between East Fettes Avenue
and the Royal Botanic Garden*

8 courts; closed Monday

Victoria Park

4 2C

*at the junction of Ferry Road
and Craighall Road*

7 courts, closed Thursday

South

Canaan Lane

10 3C

Morningside

3 courts; closed Friday

East Meadows

10 2C

Melville Drive

16 courts

Harrison Park

9 3B

Harrison Gardens

8 courts; closed Monday

Priestfield

11 3A

Prestonfield Avenue

5 courts, closed Wednesday

East

Leith Links

5 2A

*Links Place
Leith*

6 courts

Rosefield Park

12 1D

Brighton Place

6 courts, closed Tuesday

West

Paties Road

14 2D

*Colinton Road, opposite
Redford Barracks*

3 courts

St Margaret's Park

7 2B

*off Corstorphine High Street
Corstorphine*

4 courts; closed Monday

Watersports

Edinburgh, bounded by the
Firth of Forth, with numerous
reservoirs, lochs and rivers
within 30 minutes drive, is a
natural base for watersports.
Some of the facilities available
are listed below.

Mach Enterprise

20 2C

*Post Road at Jet Garage
Tranent
Phone: (4) 61021*

Windsurfing boards may be hired for £2.50 per hour; £8.00 per day; or £20.00 for the whole weekend. (A refundable deposit of £50.00 must be paid for long hire.) Instruction is available at a cost of £6.00 per hour. Open throughout the year. Wet suits can be rented.

Portobello Water Sports Club

12 1D

*61–63 The Promenade
Portobello
Phone: (031) 661 3885*

Non-members may use the club, but must take out a day's membership which costs £2.00. Hardly any instruction is offered, making this a club for those who have achieved a reasonable level of competence. The sports available are water-skiing at £2.00 a run; windsurfing at £2.00 an hour; coastal rowing at 50p an hour; canoeing at £2.00 an hour. Wet suits can be hired.

Open: Monday to Friday, 18.30–21.00; Saturday and Sunday, 10.00–18.00

Sailing Centre

19 1 1B

*Port Edgar
South Queensferry (9 miles /14.5km west of city centre)
Phone: (031) 331 3330*

Run by Lothian Regional Council, this centre offers a wide variety of watersports. Instruction is given in dinghy-sailing, canoeing, windsurfing, and power-boating, while special courses are also available for the disabled. Sailboats and windsurfers can be hired for two hours; the charge for sailboats varies between £2.70 and £7.10 (adult) and between £1.35 and £3.55 (child)—depending on the size of boat. Windsurfing-boards cost £2.70 for two hours, or £3.70 with instruction; children are charged half-price.

Open: Easter to October; three sessions daily, 10.00–12.00, 14.00–16.00, 19.00–21.00

Section IV – Shopping in Edinburgh

Edinburgh is famous for the quality and variety of its shops. This section tells the visitor where traditional Scottish products can be bought, and describes the arts and crafts shops, the antiquarian bookshops, markets, auctions and fairs that are a feature of the city's life.

As a general rule, shops in the city centre are open from Monday to Saturday, between 09.00 and 17.30. Outside this area, shops tend to close for lunch and may have half-day closing on either Tuesday, Wednesday or Saturday; a few, such as John Lewis, are closed all day Monday. Very few shops open on Sunday, or on the numerous Edinburgh bank holidays.

In the main body of this book there are articles on the history and manufacture of many traditional Scottish products. Below are listed some of the shops in Edinburgh at which these can be bought.

Bagpipes

Discount Highland Supply

10 2C

*122 Lauriston Place
Phone: (031) 229 6127*

Open: Monday to Saturday, 09.30–17.30.

Gillanders & McLeod

10 2C

*2 Whitehouse Loan
Phone: (031) 447 8863*

Open: Mondays to Friday, 09.00–13.00, 14.30–17.00; closed Saturday.

J. & R. Glen

10 1C

*497 Lawnmarket
Phone: (031) 225 8065*

Open: Monday to Saturday, 09.00–18.30; Sunday, 11.00–18.00.

Inveran House

4 3B

*10 Dean Street
Phone: (031) 332 8115*

Open: Monday to Friday, 08.00–16.30; closed Saturday.

Hugh Macpherson

9 1B

*17 West Maitland Street
Phone: (031) 225 4008*

Open: Monday to Friday, 09.00–17.30; Saturday, 09.00–13.00.

William Sinclair & Son

4 1D

*1 Maderia Street
Phone: (031) 554 3489*

Open: Monday to Friday, 08.30–12.00, 14.00–17.00; closed Saturday.

Haggis and Scotch Beef

Campbell Brothers

10 1C

*60 Queen Street
Phone: (031) 225 5471*

Open: Monday to Friday, 08.30–17.30; Wednesday and Saturday, 08.30–13.00.

Charles Macsween & Son

10 2C

130 Bruntsfield Place
Phone: (031) 229 1216

Open Monday to Friday,
09.00–17.30; Tuesday and Saturday,
09.00–13.00.

A. Lurie

10 2D

30 Buccleuch Street
Phone: (031) 667 2421

Open: Monday to Friday,
09.00–17.30; Saturday, 09.00–13.00.

Ian Proudfoot

3 3B

6 Learmouth Avenue
Phone: (031) 332 5785

Open: Monday to Saturday,
09.00–17.30; Wednesday,
09.00–13.00.

T. J. W. Struth

4 3C

39 Deanhaugh Street
Phone: (031) 332 2325

Open: Monday to Saturday,
09.00–17.30; Wednesday and
Saturday, 09.00–13.00.

T. G. Willis & Co

10 1C

135 George Street
Phone: (031) 225 2102

Open: Monday to Friday,
09.00–17.30; Saturday, 09.00–13.00.

Kilts, Tartans and Highland Dress

R. W. Forsyth

10 1C

30 Princes Street
Phone: (031) 556 3333

Open: Monday to Saturday,
09.00–17.30.

John Morrison

10 1C

461 Lawnmarket
Phone: (031) 225 8149

Open: Monday to Saturday,
09.00–17.30; Sunday, 11.00–17.00.

Kiltmaker

10 1C

45 Princes Street
Phone: (031) 556 6330

Open: Monday to Saturday,
09.00–18.00.

Kinloch Anderson

10 1D

John Knox House
45 High Street
Phone: (031) 556 6961

Open: Monday to Friday,
09.00–17.30; Saturday, 09.00–17.00.

Scotch House

10 1C

60 Princes Street
Phone: (031) 226 5271

Open: Monday to Saturday,
09.00–17.30; Thursday, 09.00–18.00.

Tartan Gift Shop

10 1C

98 Princes Street
Phone: (031) 225 5551

Open: May to October: Monday to
Friday, 09.00–19.30; Saturday,
09.10–18.00.
October to May: Monday to
Saturday, 09.00–17.30.

Salmon, Smoked Salmon and Kippers

G. Campbell & Sons

9 1B

18 Stafford Street
Phone: (031) 225 7507

Open: Tuesday to Friday,
07.00–17.30; Monday and Saturday,
07.00–13.00.

Croan & Bee & Co

10 1D

56 High Street
Phone: (031) 556 2607

Open: Tuesday to Friday,
09.30–17.30; Saturday, 09.30–16.00,
closed Monday.

George Armstrong

3 3B

80 Raeburn Place
Phone: (031) 332 3609

Open: Tuesday to Saturday,
08.00–13.00, 14.30–17.00; closed
Monday.

George Hughes & Sons

10 2C

197 Bruntsfield Place
Phone: (031) 447 1183

Tuesday to Saturday, 08.30–18.00;
closed Monday

J. Hogg

4 2D

267b Leith Walk
Phone: (031) 554 3203

Tuesday to Friday, 07.40–18.00;
Saturday, 08.30–17.00; closed
Monday.

A. Thomson & Sons

7 2B

104 St. Johns Road
Phone: (031) 334 4969

Open: Tuesday to Saturday,
08.30–17.30; closed Monday.

Scottish Cheddar, Orkney and Arran Cheeses

Choosa Cheese

10 2C

178 Bruntsfield Place
Phone: (031) 229 8482

Open: Monday to Friday,
09.00–17.25; Saturday, 09.00–18.00.

3 3B

43 Raeburn Place
Phone: *(031) 343 1748*

Open: Monday to Saturday,
09.00–17.30.

10 2D

19 South Clerk Street
Phone: *(031) 667 0737*

Open: Monday to Saturday,
09.00–17.30.

4 2D

60 Great Junction Street
Phone: *(031) 554 5444*

Open: Monday to Saturday,
09.00–17.30.

10 2D

6 Montague Street
Phone: *(031) 552 3720*

Open: Monday to Saturday,
09.00–17.30.

Forsyths Food Hall

10 1C

30 Princes Street
Phone: *(031) 556 3333*

Open: Monday to Saturday,
09.00–17.30

T.G. Willis

10 1C

135 George Street
Phone: *(031) 225 2102*

Open: Monday to Friday,
09.00–17.30; Saturday, 09.00–13.00

Young & Saunders

9 1B

5 Queensferry Street
Phone: *(031) 225 6075*

Open: Monday to Saturday,
09.15–17.30; Saturday, 09.15–13.00

Shortbread, Oatcakes Porridge, Marmalade and Mustard

Country Taste

10 1D

193 Canongate
Phone: *(031) 557 2051*

Open: Monday to Saturday,
10.30–17.30; closed Wednesday.

Crawford's

9 1B

Hostess Shop
42 Queensferry Street
Phone: *(031) 225 7388*

Open: Monday to Saturday,
09.00–17.30.

Farmer Jacks

4 3D

65–67 East London Street
Phone: *(031) 556 2043*

Open: Monday to Saturday,
09.30–17.30; Sunday, 10.00–16.00.

Forsyths Food Hall

10 1C

30 Princes Street
Phone: *(031) 556 3333*

Open: Monday to Saturday,
09.00–17.30.

J. W. A. Ireland

4 3C

52 Dundas Street
Phone: *(031) 556 6816*

Open: Monday to Friday,
08.00–17.30; Saturday, 08.00–13.00.

Lairds Larder

10 1C

36 Victoria Street
Phone: *(031) 226 5519*

Open: Monday to Saturday,
10.00–17.30.

T. G. Willis

10 1C

135 George Street
Phone: *(031) 225 2102*

Open: Monday to Friday,
09.00–17.30; Saturday, 09.00–13.00.

Young & Saunders

9 1B

5 Queensferry Street
Phone: *(031) 225 6075*

Monday to Friday, 09.15–17.30;
Saturday, 09.15–13.00.

Tweed, Harris Tweed and Cashmere

Edinburgh Woollen Mill

10 1C

139 Princes Street
Phone: *(031) 226 3840*

Open: Monday to Saturday,
09.00–17.30; Thursday, 09.00–19.00.

10 1D

51 High Street
Phone: *(031) 556 9786*

Open: Monday to Saturday,
09.00–17.30.

10 1C

453–455 Lawnmarket
Phone: *(031) 225 1525*

Open: Monday to
Saturday, 09.00–17.30.

(10 1C)

Seconds Shop
9 Randolph Place
Phone: *(031) 226 3593*

Open: Monday to Saturday,
09.00–17.30.

Henry Ballantyne of Scotland

10 1C

449 Lawnmarket
Phone: *(031) 226 5366*

Open: Monday to Saturday,
09.00–17.30; May to September:
Sundays, 12.00–16.00.

Kinloch Anderson

10 1D

45 High Street
Phone: *(031) 556 6961*

Open: Monday to Friday,
09.00–17.30; Saturday, 09.00–17.00.

Scotch House

10 1C

60 Princes Street
Phone: (031) 226 5271

Open: Monday to Saturday,
09.00–17.30; Thursday, 09.00–18.00.

Whisky, Drambuie and Glayva

Wm. Cadenhead

10 1D

172 Canongate
Phone: (031) 556 5864

Open: Monday to Saturday,
10.00–18.00; Tuesday, 10.00–13.00.

Cockburn & Campbell

10 1C

101 Hanover Street
Phone: (031) 225 3832

Open: Monday to Friday,
09.15–17.30; closed Saturday.

Howgate Wines

4 3C

7 Cumberland Street
Phone: (031) 556 7362

Open: Monday to Thursday, closed
Monday morning, 10.00–12.30,
13.30–18.00; Friday and Saturday,
10.00–12.30, 13.30–20.00.

Justerini & Brooks

10 1C

39 George Street
Phone: (031) 226 4202

Open: Monday to Friday,
09.00–18.00; closed Saturday.

Lambert Bros

10 1C

9 Frederick Street
Phone: (031) 225 4642

Open: Monday to Friday,
09.00–18.00; Saturday, 09.00–15.00.

Section V – Touring and Travel

Edinburgh, the focal point for the political, cultural and sporting life of Scotland, is easily accessible by road, air and rail. This section of the directory tells the visitor how to get to Edinburgh, how to travel around the city, how to use it as a base for touring the Lothian area and the borders, and how to return home after his stay.

Gateways to Edinburgh

Air Travel

The quickest and easiest way of getting to Edinburgh is by air. As one would expect of a busy tourist centre, Edinburgh is well served by a variety of airlines. Although it may not always be possible to fly direct from outside Britain, British Airways run a regular shuttle service from Heathrow Airport, London. British Caledonian also offers a variety of special fares on its scheduled flights from Gatwick, London.

Edinburgh Airport

Situated six miles (10 km) west of Edinburgh, the airport has a restaurant, buffet, two bars, tourist information desk, bank, duty-free and gift shop. There are facilities for the disabled and a qualified nurse is always in attendance. Three car-hire companies operate from the airport and there is reasonably priced short and long-term car parking. For information about arrivals and departures, phone: (031) 333 1000 and ask for the Airport Information Desk.

Getting to and from the Airport

There is an Airlink Coach Service which travels regularly between the Air Terminal at Waverley Bridge (10 1C) in the centre of Edinburgh, and the airport. The journey takes about 25 minutes and costs £1.00 single, luggage included.

For timetable details contact: Lothian Regional Transport, Airport Terminal, Waverley Bridge, Phone: (031) 556 5656.

The alternative to this service is to travel in by taxi, which should cost approximately £4.00.

Coach

If you are travelling on a limited budget you may well find Cotters Coachline service useful. This offers coach travel to and from London twice daily, departing at 09.45 and 22.30. The journey lasts eight hours and costs £10.50 single, £19.50 return—there is a toilet on the coach and also a kitchen; films are shown en route.

Contact

Cotters Coachline, 59 Lothian Road (10 1C), phone (031) 228 6045 or Cotters Coachline, 279 Lillie Road, London SW6, phone: (01) 381 5368.

More frequent, but rather slower services to London are offered by Scottish Omnibuses and British Coachways (associated with Ellerman Travel). Both companies offer inexpensive services to a wide variety of destinations in Britain.

Contact

Scottish Omnibuses Ltd (10 1C)

St. Andrew Square, phone (031)
556 8191.
British Coachways, (10 1C) 34
Frederick Street, phone (031)
226 6911.

Rail Travel

One of the most convenient
ways of getting in and out of
Edinburgh is by train. The British Rail network extends
throughout the country and provides a relatively fast and
trouble-free service. There is
an excellent high-speed '125'
service to and from London running every hour during the day
from Monday to Saturday, taking around five hours. All '125s'
have a buffet, and often a restaurant as well, and there are
sleeper carriages on the less
frequent night trains. Several
different return fares are
offered according to length of
stay, and there are a number of
special offers—so ask for details at the ticket office before
buying your ticket.

Edinburgh's Stations

Waverley Station *(10 1D)*
The main station of Edinburgh
is open from 02.30 to 24.00. The
information desk is open seven
days a week during the daytime
and there are information displays in the main hall. There is a
cafe, a left luggage office and
24-hour car parking. Many of
the trains to and from Waverley
Station also stop at the much
smaller Haymarket Station,
which is open from 06.00 to
23.45.

For information about rail
travel to and from Edinburgh
contact: The Ticket Office,
Waverley Station, (031) 556
2451 (24 hours), or any British
Rail Passenger Information
Service in other areas of Britain.

Rail Tours

British Rail offers several
special tickets for people
wishing to tour by train.
'Day Tour' Tickets—available
daily from Waverley Station,

May to August. These offer day
tours to selected areas such as
Loch Lomond or the Trossachs,
and can include bus and /or
boat trips.
'Runabout' Season Tickets —
allow up to seven-day trips
within defined areas of Scotland. They are available from
March to October and are valid
for seven consecutive days.
'Freedom of Scotland', 'Gold'
and 'Silver' Tickets—valid for
one or two weeks, these tickets
permit unlimited rail travel in
Scotland.

Air Taxis

Edinburgh Air Taxi Company
has a fleet of aeroplanes of all
sizes available for long and
short-haul sightseeing or
travel. It also offers a 15-minute
aerial tour of Edinburgh for
three passengers at approximately £20.00.
Contact
Edinburgh Air Taxi Company,
Edinburgh Airport, phone:
(031) 333 1075.

Bicycle Hire

Edinburgh is not ideal for
cycling, having more than its
share of hills and many cobbled
streets. However, hiring a bicycle is a cheap and effective
means of broadening your hori-
zons without the worry of parking or timetables.

Edinburgh Cycle Hire

10 2C

8 Alvanley Terrace
Whitehouse Loan
Phone: (031) 667 6363 between
09.00 and 18.00 Monday to
Sunday.

Cycle Shop

10 2D

12 West Preston Street
Phone: (031) 667 6239 between
09.00 and 17.00, closed
Wednesday and Sunday.

Boat trips

John Watson Marine Services

19 1B

Priory Bank
South Queensferry
Phone: (031) 331 1454

One of the signs of the Edinburgh area is undoubtedly
Inchcolm Island in the Firth of
Forth—with a 12th-century Augustinian Abbey, bird sanctuary and grey seal colony. Two-
hour boat trips leave from
Hawes Pier, South Queensferry
(nine miles/15 km) northwest of
Edinburgh) on every day except Monday throughout the
summer. Shorter cruises under
the Forth Road and Rail Bridges
are also offered.

Fred Marr

20 1C

24 Victoria Road
North Berwick
Phone: (0620) 2838

The Bass Rock, at the mouth of
the Firth of Forth, is world-
famous among ornithologists
for its nesting gannets, of which
up to 30,000 gather annually.
One-hour trips around the Bass
Rock leave from North Berwick
(23 miles/37 km) east of Edinburgh) daily throughout the
summer, weather permitting.

R. E. Rusack

19 2B

Bridge Inn
Ratho
Phone: (031) 333 1320

A rather more sedate trip can
be taken on the 'Pride of the
Union' canalboat restaurant
which operates from Ratho
(seven miles/11 km) west of
Edinburgh) all year round from
Monday to Saturday. This offers
a dinner-dance, with an à la

carte menu, and a full selection of wines and spirits, at a cost of approximately £14.00 per person. This 3½ hour cruise is extremely popular, so it is essential to book well ahead.

Useful Information

Bus lanes

On the main roads into Edinburgh, the left traffic lane is marked by a solid white line. These lanes are reserved for buses from 08.30 to 09.15 and from 16.40 to 18.00 and it is an offence for a private vehicle to enter them at these times.

24-hour Breakdown Services

Automobile Association, phone; (031) 225 8464. Royal Automobile Club phone: (031) 229 3555. Members only, but non-members can join the spot

Rosebank Auto Services

13 3A

*57 Lanark Road West
Currie
Phone: (031) 449 4420; 449 4892, or 449 6226 outside working hours*

Restalrig Service Station

5 2B

*126 Restalrig Road
Phone: (031) 554 3175*

Spare Parts on Saturday Morning

Alexanders

10 2C

*Semple Street
Phone: (031) 229 3331*

Rosebank Auto Services

13 3A

*57 Lanark Road West
Currie
Phone: (031) 449 4420; or 449 4892; 449 6226 outside working hours*

Smith & Saunders

19 2B

*46 Bavelaw Road
Balerno
Phone: (031) 449 3802*

Weekend Breakdown Services

Firrhill Service Station

15 2A

*Colinton Mains Drive
Phone: (031) 441 1225*

Scott Vehicles

12 2D

*Eastfield Garage
Milton Road East
Phone: (031) 669 2693, 669 9354 or 669 2883.*

24-hour Petrol Stations

Ross Motors

10 3D

*28 Ratcliffe Terrace
Phone: (031) 667 6926*

Edinburgh Service Station

4 3D

*69a East London Street
Phone: (031) 556 5284*

Meadowbank Autopoint (Belmont Garages)

4 3D

*63–67 London Road
Phone: (031) 661 7966*

Restalrig Service Station

5 2B

*126 Restalrig Road
Phone: (031) 554 3175*

Station Supreme Ltd

9 2B

*West Coates
Roseburn
Phone: (031) 337 3762*

Self-drive car hire

Do not hire a car without first comparing the rates of several firms. This can, however, prove difficult as no two firms present their data in the same way, and brochures vary in terms of detail and clarity. Some firms have an unlimited mileage allowance, others have a limited allowance (100, 130, 200 or 250 miles); some have a flat basic rate and charge extra for each mile travelled. It is obviously best to have some idea of how far the car is to be driven in order to get the best bargain. Other factors involved in calculating the cost are the type of insurance offered (third-party or comprehensive), and whether VAT is included.

Insurance

Alexanders, Ross, SMT and Western include comprehensive cover in their prices, and personal accident insurance is available as an extra from Godfrey Davis, Hertz, Kenning, Avis and Budget. The driver is usually liable for the first part of any damage to the car (this varies from £45 to £200). In most cases this liability can be waived by payment of an extra premium called Collision Damage Waiver (CDW).

Driving Experience

Normally at least one-years driving on a full licence is required, but some companies will accept six months on a provisional and six months on a full licence. Carnies require two-years experience.

Age Restrictions

If you are under-25 or over-65, you may be able to hire only under certain conditions. Examples of these restrictions are: must purchase CDW; must pay higher CDW; may not purchase CDW but must leave higher deposit; can only drive certain cars. Kenning will accept drivers under-21 and Hertz drivers between 70 and 79 under special conditions, while Bradbury and Avis have no upper age limits.

Licence Endorsements
Companies vary in their attitude to endorsements. Some will ignore these if they are for minor offences. Avis is alone in accepting a driver endorsed within the last five years for drunken driving.

Minimum Hire Period
Usually one day. Budget will hire for as little as three hours; Croft stipulate two days and SMT three days.

Major Self-drive Car Hire Companies
(this is not intended as a complete list)

Alexanders
10 2C
Semple Street
Phone: (031) 229 3331

Avis (local)
9 2B
100 Dalry Road
Phone: (031) 337 6363

Avis (UK)
19 2B
Edinburgh Airport
Phone: (031) 333 1866

Bradbury
4 2D
37 Haddington Place
Phone: (031) 556 1406

Budget
3 3B
Comely Bank
Phone: (031) 332 5054

Carnies
4 1C
Craighall Road
Phone: (031) 552 5521

Cascade
5 2A
17 Poplar Lane
Leith
Phone: (031) 554 0461

Christie
10 1C
80 Lothian Road
Phone: (031) 229 2339

Croft
5 2A
118 Duke Street
Phone: (031) 661 3866

European
9 1B
3 Sunnybank Place
Phone: (031) 661 7304

Godfrey Davis (Costcutter)
4 3D
24 East London Street
Phone: (031) 661 1252

Godfrey Davis Europcar
19 2B
Edinburgh Airport
Phone: (031) 333 2588

Forth
4 3C
9 St. Bernards Row
Phone: (031) 343 1001

Hertz (local)
4 3D
10 Picardy Place
Phone: (031) 556 8311

Hertz (UK)
19 2B
Edinburgh Airport
Phone: (031) 344 3260

Kenning
9 2B
40–44 Duff Street
Phone: (031) 337 8145

Mitchells
9 1B
32 Torphichen Street
Phone: (031) 229 5384

Reasonable
10 3D
3 Fountainhall Road
Phone: (031) 668 2979

Ross
10 3D
2-40 Ratcliffe Terrace
Phone: (031) 667 6984

SMT
10 2B
89–91 Haymarket Terrace
Phone: (031) 229 2488 (day), 229 7270 (night)

Swan National (local)

72A

19 Glasgow Road
Corstorphine
Phone: (031) 334 6464

Swan National (UK)

101C

St. Andrew Bus Station
Phone: (031) 556 5515

Ward's

43D

Annandale Street
Phone: (031) 556 3548

Western

151A

62 Colinton Road
Phone: (031) 443 5596

Wheels

103C

36 Canaan Lane
Phone: (031) 447 6184

**Major Self-drive Minibus
Hire Companies**
(this is not intended as a complete list)

Budget

33B

Comely Bank
Phone: (031) 332 5054

Cascade

52A

17 Poplar Lane
Leith
Phone: (031) 554 0461

SMT

92B

89–91 Haymarket Terrace
Phone: (031) 229 2488 (day),
229 7270 (night)

Ward's

43D

Annandale Street
Phone: (031) 556 3548

Taxis

There are taxi ranks at the west end of Princes Street, at Waverley Station, Haymarket Station, St. Andrew Square Bus Station, in most of the side streets off Princes Street and elsewhere. There is an initial charge of 75p for a taxi and thereafter it costs about 50p per mile. There is a 5p surcharge for each passenger after the first two, up to a maximum of five passengers. There is also a night surcharge of 20p between 22.00 and 06.00. Central Radio Taxis, phone: (031) 229 5221.
City Cabs, phone: (031) 228 1211.
Radio Cabs, phone: (031) 225 6736.

Further information on travel and touring in and around Edinburgh can be obtained from:

The Tourist Information Centre

101C

5 Waverley Bridge
Phone: (031) 226 6591 ext. 49 or
50

Monday to Saturday, 08.30–20.00;
Sunday, 11.00–21.00

A selection of other travel agents is listed below. This is not intended as a complete list.

Bennetts Travel

43C

15 Dublin Street
Phone: (031) 557 3144

Ellerman Travel

101C

34 Frederick Street
Phone: (031) 226 6911

Globespan

101C

59 George Street
Phone: (031) 226 3771

Mackay Brothers

101C

19 South St. David Street
Phone: (031) 557 2010

Nairn Travel

101C

1 Queen Street
Phone: (031) 557 2491

P & O Travel

101C

30 George Street
Phone: (031) 225 5373

Pimtrad Travel Service

72B

St. Johns Road
Corstorphine
Phone: (031) 334 9181

Sibbald Travel

91B

10 Queensferry Street
Phone: (031) 225 1402

Thomas Cook

101C

9 Castle Street
Phone: (031) 225 7125

Region and City Maps

The following pages contain detailed, complete maps of the city, plus a regional map locating features outside the city boundaries. The grid on each map is keyed to the entries in the directory of Essential Information, while the master grid (above) indicates which area of Edinburgh each map covers.

1

A   B

1

RIVER ALMOND

Esplanade

C R A M O N D

Cramond Road

Cramond Glebe Gardens
Cramond Glebe Terrace

Caddell's Row

School Brae

Fair-a-Far

Fair-a-Far Cottages

Cramond Green

Cram Pl

Cramond Crescent

Cramond Terrace

Cramond Park Gro

Cram Gro

Cramond Gdns

Cramond Road

Cramond Road North

Cramond Road

Avenue

Inveralmond Grove

Cramond Vale

Invera Gdns

Road

Cramond Cres

Cramond Bank

Inveralmond Drive

Peggy's Mill Road

Gamekeeper's

BRUNTSFIELD
GOLF COURSE

Northlawn Terr

Barnton

2

Road

Avon

Avon

Avon Grove

Place

Essex Brae

Essex Road

Cramond Regis

Regis Ct

Upper Cra Ct

Dun'n

Barnton Brae

Barnton Avenue

West

Garden Terr

Easter Park Drive

Essex Park

Essex

Whitehouse

Barnton

Barnton Loan

Barnton Avenue

East

Bar

Barnton

Brae Park Road

Brae

Park

Road

ROYAL BURGESS

Barnton Park

Queensferry Road

Almond Court

Braehead Ave

Brae Park

Drive

Braehead Loan

Braehead Ave

Braehead

Grove Bank

GOLF COURSE

Barnton

Park

P B Pk

BARNTON

Barnton View

Barnton Pk. Dr.

Barnton Park Pl

Grand Dell

DAVIDSONS MAIN PARK

Strath Ct

Strath Green

Strathalmond Pk

Brae View Road

Brae View

Barnton Ct

Barnton Grove

Barnton Park

Barnton Park Gdns

B Pk Wd

Barnton Park Crescent

Barnton Pk Grove

Barnton Park Grove

QUEENSFERRY ROAD

Clermiston Avenue

Clermiston Hill

3

Cammo Road

Cammo Grove

Cammo Pkway

Cammo Brae

Cammo Hill

Cammo Pl

Gardens Bk

Cammo Gro

MAYBURY ROAD

Blackthorn Court

Barntongate

Birch Ct

Barntongate Terr

Barntongate Dr

Blac Gdns

Braeside Dr

DRUM BRAE NORTH

Avenue

Parkgrove Ave

Parkgrove Drive

Parkgrove St

Pk Pl

Parkgrove Terrace

Parkgrove Gardens

Parkgrove Ne

Parkgrove Loan

Parkgrove Row

Pk Grove

Pke

Pke Bk

Parkgrove Road

Pkgrove Pl

Clermiston Loan

Clerm Green

Clermiston Drive

Clermiston Place

Clermiston Grove

Clermiston Crescent

C L E R M I S T O N

Clermiston Road

Cammo

Cammo Walk

Craigmount

N Ct

Craig Bk

Craig Pl

Drum Brae Walk

Craigmount Hill

Bughtlin Neuk

N Bughtlin Brae

N Bughtlin

Craig'mount Hill

Drum Brae Walk

Drum Bend Walk

Drum Brae Terrace

Drum Brae Drive

Dochart Drive

Brae Gro Ct

Glenure Loan

Rannoch Ter

Rannoch Pl

Rannoch Grove

Fox Pl

Covert Ave

Oak La

F C

CLERMISTON PARK

CLERMISTON GARDENS

Clermiston Gardens

Clerm Ter

Clermiston Pl

Clerm Grove

Clerm View

Clerm Mway

Clermiston Road

A   B

C   D   **6**

1

FIRTH OF FORTH

2

ny Ave.

Fillyside Rd.

SEAFIELD

Nantwich

Drive

Avenue

Fillyside Terr.

TINN

Fillyside Ave.

ROAD

Drive

Stapeley Avenue

Promanade

Road

EAST

Wakefield

Crescent

Craigentinny

Christiemiller

Vandeleur

Kekewich

Bryce

Avenue

Goff. Av.

Avenue

Craigentinny

Cr.

Syd.
Pl.

Sydney
Pl.

Syd.
Pk.

Terr.

Van.
Pl.

Avenue

Avenue

Bry.
Gr.

King's
Terr.

King's Pl.

3

Chris.
Pl.

Chris.
Gr.

Van.
Av.

Craig.
Grove

Avenue

Van.
Gr.

Inchview Terr.

King's
Terr.

Craig.
Pl.

Craig
Pl.

Terr.

King's Road

Moira

ROAD

Rosebank
Lane

PORTOBELLO

BELLO

Parker
Ave.

Parker Rd.

Parker
Terrace

Baileyfield

STREET

Bridge St.

Pipe

Street

P O R T O B E L L O

PIERSHILL
CEMETERY

Farrer

Rd.

12

HIGH

Beach Pl.

13

A   **7**   B

SIGHTHILL PARK

Brhous Path

Bankhead Broadway
Bankhead Crossway
North

Bankhead
Drive

Bankhead Broadway

Bankhead Medway
Terrace

Bankhead Avenue

BROOMHOUSE RD

Brhe

Sighthill Bank

S. Wynd

1

Bankhead Crossway
South

Bankhead Street

Bankhead Place

Bankhead Way

Loan

Sighthill Cr.

Sighthill
Green

SIGHTHILL

Loa

Bankhead Drive

Sighthill

Neuk

Sighthill
Road

Sighthill
Place

Sighthill Gardens

Sighthill Terrace

Sighthill

D

CALDER   ROAD

Calder View

Gardens

WESTER

Court

Calder
Gardens

Sighthill View

Sighthill Rise

Street

Cres.

Sighthill

Murrayburn

Murra.

Calder

Calder Park

Place

Calder
Gardens

Calder Cres.

Calder Drive

HAILES

Mburn
App.

Mburn
Drive

Murrayburn Place

Hailesl.

Calder Grove

Murrayburn

ROAD

Murrayburn
Gate

P.

Union Canal

Westburn Gdns.

Westburn Ave.

Park

We

Grove

2

Riccarton Mains Road

WESTE

Gardens

B.M.

Brae
Way

Rise
Baberton Mains

Lea

Hill

Drill

Baberton

Mains

B.M.
Terrace

WESTER

Wester Hailes I

Way

B.M. Wood

Grove

B.M.
Park

Drive

Place

B.

Baberton
Cres

BABERTON

Baberton Cres

Row

Mains

Drive

Ct.

BABERTON

Bank

Wynd

Green

Baberte
Cres

GOLF COURSE

Foulis

Juniper
Pk Road

Woodhall Terr.

Woodhall Ave.

Juniper
Gro

Belmont
Grove

Baberton
Road

Woodhall
Drive

Juniper
Pk. Road

Baberton
Pk.

**JUNIPER
GREEN**

Juniper Terr.

Juniper Av.

Baberton
Ave.

LANARK

Baberton
Loan

Nether Currie Crescent

Muirwood
Road

Muirwood
Road

3

Knowe Crescent

Riccarton Dr.

Corslet Rd.

Muirwood
Pl.

Road

Nether
Currie Cres.

Nether
Muirwood
Gro

Crescent

Pl.

Drive

Water of Leith

CURRIE

F View Cres

Forth

Palmer
Pl.

Palmer
Pl.

Currichill Road

Riccarton Avenue

Mains

Riccarton

Grove

Bryce Co Pl.

Thomson

Corslet Cres.

Bryce
Cres.

Bryce
Pl.

Road

E. Currie
Cres.

E. Currie
Terr.

Thomson
Crescent

Thomson Road

Thomson Drive

LANARK   ROAD   WEST

Pentl
Pl.

View
Cres

Riccarton

Cres

A

Blinkbonny Road

B

MORNINGSIDE

Rd.
West
's Place
Wood Pl.
Canaan Lane
an Lane
Woodburn
Terr.
South Oswald Road
St. Albans

Nile
Grove
Cluny
Terr.
Clung
Pl.

Cluny
Ave.

Cluny

Cluny

Gardens

Corrennie
Drive

Corrennie
Gardens

Braid

Midmar Gardens

Drive

Hermitage

Drive

Hermitage
Gardens

HERMITAGE OF BRAID

Oswald Road
Mortonhall Road
Glensla
Gdns
Chaterhall Gro.

Chaterhall
Rd

Midmar
Ave.

Midmar

Drive

**Blackford
Pond**

BLACKFORD

HILL

The Royal
Observatory

Blackford
Hill Grove
Blackford
Hill View

Observatory

Maurice

Ladysmith
Rd.

Black
Hill Rise

Observatory Road

St. Albans
Avenue
Relugas Rd. Relugas
Blackford
Bank
Relugas Pl.

West
Savile Terrace
MacDowall
Road
W Savile Rd.
Gilmour Road

Blackford
Bank

West

Waterloo
Rd.

Blackford
Ave.

Rankin Rd.
Dr.

Langton Rd
Ross Gardens

Lussielaw Rd

Suffolk
Rd.

Granby

Wilton
Road

Rankin Rd.

Rankin

Drive

Rankin

Av.

Lygon

Mayfield

Road

Esslemont
Road

Hailhead

WEST MAINS ROAD

CRAIGMILLAR PARK

GOLF COURSE

1

Braid Burn

Braid Burn

Blackford
Glen
Road

Road
Braid
Hills
Drive

Hills Road

Hills Approach
Braid
View

Bram Gro.

Bram Rise

Bram

BRAID HILLS

GOLF COURSE

BRAID HILLS

Leaderyvale Road
Clackmae Rd
Ola
Lead Terr

Kedslie

Kedslie
Rd Pl.

Liberton

Dr.

2

17

MORTONHALL

GOLF COURSE

Elf
Loch

Buckstone
Grove

Buckstone
Bank

Crescent

Bucks.

Buckstone
Way

Bucks
Row

Bucks. Hill

**Bucks
Neuk**

Bell

Drive

Road
Bucks
Rise

Buckstone

Buckstone
Court

Buckstone
Grn

Buckstone
Place

Bucks.
Wynd

Loan

Buckstone
Lea

Bucks.
Loan

E.
Loan
S.

Bucks.
Close

Buckstone

ROAD

Terrace

Avenue

FAIRMILEHEAD

GANGS
RD.

anston Terr.

stonGro

Swanston
Av.

ston Drive

BIGGAR

ROAD

Frogston Av

Frogstone Av

Frogs.
Gro.

Frogstone Terr.

Frogstone
Gdns

FROGSTON

Winton
Gro.

Winton
Terr.

Winton Terr.

Winton Loan

Winton
Pl.

en Drive
W

Alnwickhill
Terr.

Alnwickhill
Court

Howden Hall
Court

Alnwickhill
Gdns

Drive

Alnwickhill
Loan

Alnwick
Grove

H Hall
Loan

Alnwick
Park

Howden

View

Drive Cres.

H.H.
Park

Alnwick

H.Hall Cres

H.Hall

Hall

Dr.

MORTONHALL

CEMETERY

3

Mortonhall Pk
Avenue
Mortonhall
Pk.View

M Pk.
Gro

M.Pk.
Ln.

M.Pk.
Grn.

Mortonhall Pk
Way

M'hall Park

M'hall Park
Gdns

ROAD

WEST

FROGSTON

ROAD

D

C